International Handbook of Play Therapy

International Handbook of Play Therapy

Advances in Assessment, Theory, Research, and Practice

Edited by
Charles Schaefer
Judy McCormick
Akiko Ohnogi

JASON ARONSON
Lanham • *Boulder* • *New York* • *Toronto* • *Oxford*

Published in the United States of America
by Jason Aronson
An imprint of Rowman & Littlefield Publishers, Inc.

A wholly owned subsidiary of
The Rowman & Littlefield Publishing Group, Inc.
4501 Forbes Boulevard, Suite 200, Lanham, Maryland 20706
www.rowmanlittlefield.com

PO Box 317
Oxford
OX2 9RU, UK

British Library Cataloguing in Publication Information Available

Library of Congress Cataloging-in-Publication Data

Schaefer, Charles E.
   International handbook of play therapy : advances in assessment, theory,
research, and practice / edited by Charles Schaefer, Judy McCormick, and
Akiko Ohnogi.
     p. cm.
   Includes bibliographical references and index.
   ISBN 0-7657-0122-7 (cloth : alk. paper)
   1. Play therapy. I. McCormick, Judy. II. Ohnogi, Akiko. III. Title.

RJ505.P6S295 2005
615.8'5153—dc22   2004025006

Printed in the United States of America

♾™ The paper used in this publication meets the minimum requirements of
American National Standard for Information Sciences—Permanence of Paper
for Printed Library Materials, ANSI/NISO Z39.48-1992.

Contents

Preface

In the past twenty-five years, the practice of play therapy has increased exponentially in America and throughout the world. In the past decade the number of national play therapy associations and international play therapy conferences/congresses has risen sharply. Nevertheless, the vast majority of play therapists are still unaware of the exciting advances in the field that are being accomplished by play therapists in other countries.

This handbook brings together an international group of scholars and therapists to address a wide variety of topics relevant to the rapidly expanding field of play therapy. The primary goal of the handbook is to provide play therapists across the globe with practical information they can put to immediate use in their clinical work with children and adolescents. Thus the focus is on advances in assessment, theory, research, and practice that have universal appeal, rather than on adaptations of play therapy to specific cultures.

Play therapists and students from diverse cultures, professional disciplines, and theoretical orientations will find this book to be a comprehensive resource for keeping abreast of innovations in the field. This handbook is designed as a window to the world for play therapists seeking more information and contact with colleagues in other countries. The infusion of knowledge from around the globe offers us a unique opportunity not only for intellectual growth, but for overcoming the insulation and isolation that tend to exist among play therapists in different countries.

I

PLAY THERAPY MODELS

1

Family Play Therapy

Shlomo Ariel

Below is a short scene from a family play therapy session conducted in the Israeli Play Therapy Institute some months ago. The participants were thirty-nine-year-old Miriam Oren, her nine-year-old daughter, Vered, and the therapist, Shlomo Ariel.

The relationship between Miriam and her husband, Dan, has always been—which word should I choose?—hellish. As in many strife-torn families, the children took sides. Vered, the eldest, was her father's daughter, at odds with her mother, Miriam. The other children, eight-year-old Rama (a girl) and six-year-old Tomer (a boy), sided with their mother. A week before this session Miriam had a road accident. She suffered pains in her neck and back and could not turn her head sideways.

The same day, in the afternoon, the following typical scene took place: Miriam told Vered to put her room in order. Vered refused. Miriam told her that she would not let her go to the swimming pool with her dad unless she put her room in order first. Dan responded by undermining Miriam's authority. He said to Miriam, "You shouldn't be so harsh with her" and told Vered to get ready for the swimming pool. Miriam reacted by shouting and cursing him. He returned in kind. Then Miriam phoned her mother, who lived next door, and asked her to come and intervene. Dan yelled that if her mother came, he would break her legs and Miriam's teeth. He began throwing objects at Miriam, which barely missed her. Then he grabbed her arm and shook it violently. Miriam shouted, "Stop! I am in pain, I had an accident!" And only then did he let her go. Miriam ran out and met her mother at the entrance, and then they called the police. They came and took Dan to the station. An injunction forbidding him to come near home for ten days was issued. He left and stayed at his sister's home, determined to start divorce proceedings. Vered blamed

Miriam and insisted on staying with her father. She said, "If you don't let me, I'll live in the street!" Both Miriam and Dan yielded. Vered stayed with Dan for a few days, until his sister began complaining that it was too difficult for her to keep both him and his daughter. Dan realized that he would not be able to take care of Vered, since his electrical engineering business was very busy. He wanted her to go home, but Vered yelled, "I can't be at home with this monster of a mother and a sister and brother I hate! I can't sleep at night if you don't kiss me good night!"

The session from which the following scene was taken was one of a series of family play therapy sessions conducted with the Orens for six months. The immediate purpose of the session was to clear the air between Miriam and Vered and prepare the ground for the latter's returning home.

Miriam, plump, unkempt, still in pain, depressed, and confused, sits on a low armchair in the corner of the play therapy room. Vered, her back to Miriam and Shlomo, is choosing dolls from a shelf. She is arranging the dolls she has chosen in a row at the wall, her back still to Miriam and Shlomo.

Shlomo [addressing Miriam]: Let's join her.

[Miriam and Shlomo sit next to Vered. She is ignoring them.]

[Shlomo picks up a monkey doll.]

Shlomo [monkey voice, addressing Vered's dolls]: I am Koko. Can I join you guys?

Vered: No, but you can watch us playing.

Shlomo [to Miriam, offering her a selection of dolls]: Who are you?

Miriam [listlessly]: I am . . . I don't know. [Hesitantly she picks a tattered, nondescript doll representing a squirrel.]

Shlomo: Hello I-Don't-Know. How do you feel today?

Miriam: Not very good.

Shlomo: I can see. You don't look so well. Why, what happened?

Miriam: I don't know.

Shlomo: Of course you don't know. After all, that's your name: I-Don't-Know. But I don't know what you know and what you don't know. For instance, do you know these animals over here? [Points at Vered's doll.]

Miriam: No.

Shlomo: I don't know them either. [Shlomo brings his monkey doll near Vered's dolls.] I am Koko. Who are you? Can you introduce yourselves?

Vered [without looking at Shlomo]: This [pointing at a cat doll] is Sister, and this [pointing at a bird doll] is Mother-Bird, and this [pointing at a dog doll] is Bad-Daddy-Wolf.

Shlomo: They all live here?

Vered: Yes. They all live in this house.

Shlomo: But aren't Sister and Mother-Bird afraid to live in the same house with Bad-Daddy-Wolf?

Vered [putting the dog doll in front]: No, he guards the house.

Shlomo: But I thought he was bad?

Vered: He is bad to those who want to come to the house and do bad things to Sister and Mother-Bird.

Shlomo: I-Don't-Know, do you want to visit Sister and Mother-Bird?

Miriam: No. I am afraid of Bad-Daddy-Wolf.

Shlomo: But he is only bad to those who want to do bad things.

Miriam: I don't know; I don't trust him.

Shlomo [addressing Vered's dolls]: Mother-Bird and Sister, will you come out and meet I-Don't-Know? She is afraid of Bad-Daddy-Wolf.

Vered [as Sister]: No, I'm busy. I have to take care of Mother-Bird.

Shlomo: You are not like us monkeys. Mother monkeys take care of sisters, not the other way round!

Vered: No, I'm not a sister sister, I'm a nurse sister. Mother-Bird fell off a tree and broke her wing. I have to cure her.

Shlomo: Now I understand. Vered, let's pretend Mummy is Mother-Bird and I am both Koko and I-Don't-Know. [Shlomo is taking the I-Don't-Know doll from Miriam's hand. He is placing a pillow between Vered·and Miriam.] Mother-Bird can't fly. She has to lie in this bed. [Vered is putting the Mother-Bird doll on the pillow.]

Shlomo: Mother-Bird, does your wing hurt?

Miriam: Yes, it does.

Shlomo [as Koko]: I-Don't-Know, do you think Sister can cure Mother-Bird? [As I-Don't-Know]: I don't know. [As Koko]: I think she can, but she has to be careful, not to hurt her even more. [Addressing Miriam]: Do you want Sister to take care of you, Mother-Bird?

Miriam: Very much.

[Shlomo makes the I-Don't-Know doll hop up and down vigorously.]

Shlomo [as Koko]: I-Don't-Know, what happened to you? Are you crazy? [As I-Don't Know]: I am not I-Don't-Know anymore. My name now is I-Do-Know! [As Koko]: What do you know then? [As I-Do-Know]: I do know that Mother-Bird will recover soon, and then she will be healthy enough to say to Sister nurse: You don't have to be Sister nurse anymore, you can be just Sister, and I'll take care of you!

This vignette illustrates some of the main features of the method of family play therapy introduced in this chapter.

First, the major change agent is play. The course of the play is openly or subtly directed by the therapist, so that well-defined curative properties of play—bug busters—are activated. These "bug busters" are expected to remove or weaken "bugs" in the family's communication. Such bugs interfere with the family's information processing, reduce its level and quality of functioning, and cause stress in its members. The main dysfunctional pattern to which the therapeutic intervention in the above scene was aimed was the unavailability, to all the family members, of crucial information concerning the relationship between Vered and her father and mother. On the face of it, Vered loved her father, hated her mother, and had always taken her father's side. Miriam was not the affectionate mother for Vered, only the harsh disciplinarian. Dan was the affectionate father, who had been protecting Vered of her mother's excesses. Under the surface, however, the relationships were more complex and ambivalent. The above play intervention exposed some of these covert feelings and thoughts. One of the bug busters used by the therapist in this vignette was the *basic duality* of play, the fact that the player is both herself and an imaginary play figure. When the therapist suggested, "Let's pretend Mummy is Mother-Bird," he emphasized this play property. He conveyed to both Vered and Miriam the information: "Mother-Bird is Miriam and Sister is Vered." Another bug buster activated at the same time was *symbolic coding*. The scene in which Sister (a "nurse") was curing Mother-Bird's broken wing was a symbolically coded message, exposing covert aspects of the mother–daughter relationship: Vered's concern about Miriam's having been injured in a road accident and brutalized by her husband, and Miriam's wish to be taken care of by Vered. Once these hidden aspects had been unveiled, a better interpretation of Vered's motives for opting for her father suggested itself: she preferred the parent who seemed to her stronger. Another bug buster set in motion in this scene was *possible worlds*. When the therapist turned I-Don't-Know, the doll Miriam had previously chosen to represent her weak self, into I-Do-Know, a vigorous creature predicting Mother-Bird's recovery and resumption of a caretaker role with respect to Sister, he created, in make-believe, a possible, better world for both Miriam and Vered.

Why playing? Why not talking? Play serves as a kind of projective technique exposing covert, subconscious feelings and thought which would not be surfaced in the course of an ordinary conversation. Furthermore, for children it is more natural to explore their emotions and thoughts in play than in a rational, orderly conversation. Play provides an opportunity to *experience* what has been denied or ignored, in the safe, benign, fun world of pretend. The play experience lives in the twilight zone between cognition and emotion, where the defenses are not on the alert.

Second, play is used not just as a change agent but also as the vehicle of therapeutic communication. Therapists and family members converse in the metaphorical language of verbal and nonverbal make-believe play. Instead of saying "Now you feel weak, confused, and helpless, but in the near future you will regain strength and self-confidence," the therapist made "I-Don't-Know" hop vigorously and changed its name to "I-Do-Know."

Third, the play metaphors are not initiated by the therapists but by the family members. The image of Mother-Bird with the broken wing was created by Vered. The I-Don't-Know image was the therapist's reflection of Miriam's choice and behavior.

Fourth, family play therapy is a total therapy, in the sense that anything can be used in it and anything can happen in it. Play is a singularly rich and flexible medium of expression and communication. It speaks through words, sounds, actions, objects, and materials. A pillow can become a hospital bed. A doll hopping vigorously can stand for recovery. The players, therapist included, can be themselves and something or somebody else at one and the same time. Roles and modes of behavior can be flexibly changed at will and a limitless number of events and situations can be made up freely. The therapist can be one moment himself or herself, another moment the director of a show and immediately afterwards an actor in the show.

This model of family therapy has been practiced by the writer and his trainees in Israel and abroad with children presenting a wide range of difficulties: conduct disorders, ADHD, psycho-physiological disorders, social maladaptation, fears and phobias, depression, and so forth. The children's families have come from a wide variety of cultural, religious and socioeconomic backgrounds. In many cases this form of intervention has proved to be both brief and effective. Apparently, this can be attributed primarily to the use of play as a precision instrument, the activation of "bug busters" that bypass the defenses and are aimed at well-defined errors of information-processing in the family's communication.

This chapter presents a brief introduction to the main components of this model of family play therapy.

THEORETICAL FOUNDATIONS

The Integrative, Multisystemic Approach

Family play therapy is a part of an integrative, multisystemic therapeutic framework that often includes individual therapy, consultation with the school's educational team, and peer group play therapy. Usually these forms of intervention are not conducted simultaneously. Their order is dictated by the requirements of the case in hand. In some cases the child is so stormy and regressive that he or she needs the therapist all for herself for a while. Only after he has settled into a more or less stable state he can function in a family framework. Group therapy usually follows individual and family therapy, after the child has gained the strengths and ego skills needed to profit from group work.

The integrative theoretical model informing all these forms of therapy embraces the family and wider ecological systems, culture, psychodynamics, and the individual's cognitive and socioemotional development. All these have been synthesized, systematized, and formalized by the writer in the language of cognitive science, which borrows its concepts and terms from information-processing theory (see Johnson-Laird 1989), cybernetics (the science of feedback systems; see Maltz 1987), and semiotics (the science of signs and symbols; see Cobley, Jansz, and Appignanesi 1997; Deely 1982). (Various aspects of this integrative, multisystemic model are introduced and discussed in Ariel 2002, 1999, 1997, 1996, 1994, 1992, 1987, and 1984; and Ariel, Carel, and Tyano 1985.)

The Information-Processing Jargon

In this model all the above-mentioned systems are represented as sets of information-processing programs stored in individual minds. A human information-processing program is a rule regulating the kinds and amounts of information received and perceived (input), the ways this information is interpreted, the manners by which it is organized in one's mind and the kinds of outward behavioral responses it leads to (output).

One of the systems conceived of in this manner is the family. The Oren family, for instance, may be viewed as a group of five intercommunicating "living computers." The relationship between Miriam and Vered can be explicated as the manifestation of particular information-processing programs stored in their respective minds. One such program, residing in Miriam's mind, leads Miriam to ignore all input attesting to Vered's attitude toward her, except Vered's insubordination, rejection of Miriam, and wanting only Dan. The output of this program is denying affection from Vered and disciplining her in an aggressive but ineffective manner. A program stored in Vered's mind causes her to see Miriam not only as cold and aggressive but also as weak and helpless. The output is avoiding and rejecting Miriam, disobeying her and looking for support, protection, and warmth from her father. Both programs are "bugged." They contain information-processing errors leading to a dysfunctional relationship.

Types of Information-Processing Bugs

As noted above, the main targets of family play therapy are information-processing bugs, snags that have somehow settled themselves in programs. Such bugs cause various kinds of errors and distortions in the processing of information. The therapeutic properties of play, nicknamed bug busters, have the power to remove or weaken such bugs.

Bugs in human information-processing programs belong to various types. Here are some of these types:

Flooding versus Turning Off the Tap

The relevant programs fail to regulate the amount of information necessary for efficient communication. It takes in too much input or produces a superfluous amount of output (flooding), or, conversely, an insufficient amount of input/output (turning off the tap). *Examples:* Miriam disapproved of Dan's habit of staying in his office late and coming home after 10: 00 P.M. She used to flood him with complaints and biting remarks, over and over again, never letting up. This only reinforced his unwillingness to come home earlier (flooding). Dan used to do things related to the household without informing Miriam. For instance, he would take Miriam's car to the garage without letting her know. She would go out to find that her car had disappeared. Such surprises would throw her to a state of panic (turning off the tap).

Horse Blinders

The relevant programs leave out input or output crucial for efficient communication and therefore restricts the communicants' vista. This bug, unlike turning off the tap, has to do with the relevance of information received rather than with its amount. *Example:* The programs in charge of Miriam's relationship with Vered left out input attesting to Vered's view of Miriam as a weak and helpless person. These programs were also blind to disapproval of Dan's behavior (Bad-Daddy-Wolf) on the side of Vered.

Baron von Munchhausen

The relevant programs distort the person's judgment of reality and tell the person false, fantastic tales. *Example:* Miriam, being absent-minded, confused, and disorganized, was often committing errors of omission such as forgetting to carry out Dan's request to withdraw cash from the bank. Dan would attribute such errors to a malicious scheme, deliberately designed by Miriam and her mother to upset him and make things difficult for him.

Topsy-Turvy

The relevant programs reduce the person's ability to process input or produce output in an orderly, consistent manner. *Example:* Rama, the Orens' eight-year-old daughter, often alternated, for no apparent reason, between age-appropriate behavior and regressive conduct of a babbling baby clinging to her mother's breast (literally).

Such bugs do not necessarily attest to cognitive limitations. The misunderstandings, errors of judgment, and irrational responses characterizing them issue mainly from emotional sources. They belong to the same broad category as psychological defenses such as repression, denial, and rationalization.

Where Do Bugs Come From? Dysfunctional Attempts to Preserve or Restore Simplicity

The emergence of bugged family programs is explained in this model as the outcome of dysfunctional responses to stress. When members of a family are faced with information they cannot understand or cope with, their previous programs lose their simplicity. In this context, the notion of simplicity subsumes three subnotions: comprehensiveness (the ability to process all the information needed for proper functioning), plausibility (the ability to read the information correctly and reach the right decisions), and consistency (the ability to settle apparent contradictions in the information and respond consistently). A dysfunctional family system is characterized by attempts to restore the lost simplicity only partly, for example, in preserving consistency but sacrificing comprehensiveness and plausibility, forgoing plausibility to maintain comprehensiveness, and so on. Abandoning comprehensiveness breeds bugs such as turning off the tap and horse blinders. Sacrificing plausibility gives rise to bugs such as Baron von Munchhausen and flooding. Forsaking consistency creates the topsy-turvy bug. (For fuller discussions of the etiology of dysfunction, see Ariel 1999, chapters 2 and 8, 1997, 1996, 1994, chapter 1, and 1987.)

Bug Busters

The main change agent in this model of family play therapy are the therapeutic properties of symbolic, make-believe play, the so-called bug busters. In the course of a family play therapy session, the therapist steers the play in a way that set in motion bug busters that have the power to fix or weaken bugs.

Where does the curative power of make-believe play come from? Where can the sources of bug busters be found in the realm of play? There are three such sources. Some bug busters are derived from the very definition of make-believe play. Other bug busters are deduced from the function of make-believe play as an homeostatic mechanism, a machinery for balancing the level of the players' emotional arousal. The remaining bug busters are drawn from the function of make-believe play as a social homeostatic mechanism, a communication medium whose role is to regulate the level of tension and conflict around issues of interpersonal distance and control.

A formal definition of make-believe play is proposed in Ariel 1984 and Ariel 2002, chapter 1. According to this definition, make-believe play is primarily a mental activity with verbal or nonverbal manifestations, or both. This mental activity includes three mental operations performed simultaneously inside the player's mind. (1) Evoking a mental image (e.g., a nurse, a bird with a broken wing) and animating it by implicitly or explicitly declaring it to be actually present in the immediate environment, not as mental images but as concrete entities in external, perceptible reality. (2) Verbalizing the mental operation of animating (e.g., saying that the bird has a broken wing) or identifying some perceptible entity in the immediate play environment (e.g., a bird puppet, the player's mother, a piece of paper, a hand gesture, anything) with it. Identifying in this context means claiming silently that the entity in question is no longer what it usually is, but has actually been transformed into the animated mental image. (3) Disclaiming the seriousness and validity of the above-mentioned mental operations (i.e., the operations animating verbally and animating by identifying).

Animated images are the signified contents of make-believe play. Expressions verbalizing the animation and tangible entities identified with these signified contents are the make-believe play signifiers.

The bug busters described in the following are derived from this definition.

Play Framing

Nonplay behavior is reframed as play, so the player is likely to make the mental claims of animation, identification, and disclaiming seriousness about it. *Therapeutic applications*: Reducing one's commitment to the validity of certain data. This can take the edge off bugs such as Baron von Munchhausen. *Example*: When Rama tried to force Miriam to breast-feed her, the therapist said, "Rama is playing at being a nursing baby."

Owning-Alienation

Since the player performs the mental operations of animation and identifying, he or she owns the signified contents of his or her play—committed to its being real. Since, however, the player also performs the mental operation of disclaiming seriousness, he or she is also alienated from this content, not committed to its being real. *Therapeutic applications:* This property can be used to shake deep convictions about oneself or others (from owning to disowning), or to make one accept previously rejected truths about oneself or others (from disowning to owning). Both applications can weaken Baron von Munchhausen, turning off the tap, and horse blinders.

Examples: When Vered played Sister-Nurse curing Mother-Bird's broken wing, she automatically alienated herself from her conviction that she hated Miriam. But since this scene was produced in the frame of make-believe play, she could continue owning this conviction. She also owned her concern about Miriam's accident and vulnerability to her husband's violence and at the same time alienated herself from her own emotional involvement. The bug buster owning-alienation had induced a cognitive-emotional experience in her that enabled her to get in touch with the complexity of her ambivalent thoughts and emotions with respect to her mother.

Basic Duality

Owing to disclaiming seriousness, the player is both inside the play and outside it, a self-observer. *Therapeutic applications:* Increasing self-awareness regarding bugs; creating or exposing contradictions between various levels of communication. These applications have the power to dilute turning off the tap, horse blinders, Baron von Munchhausen, and topsy-turvy. *Examples:* When Miriam declared that she wanted Sister-Nurse to take care of Mother-Bird, she was aware that she was really talking about the relationship between herself and her daughter. In the twilight zone between cognition and emotion, she could experience the complexity of this relationship and become aware of her problematic wish to be her daughter's daughter.

In another session Rama tried to force Miriam to let her suckle her breasts. The therapist arranged a make-believe game in which Rama could be "a baby playing as if she's a big girl" and, afterward, "a big girl playing as if she's a baby." The mother's breasts were represented by a rubber ball. The purpose of this intervention was to weaken Rama's topsy-turvy bug by placing the two sides of Rama's inconsistent behavior, the age-appropriate side and the regressed side, in two levels of make-believe play—the level of the real player and the level of the role she plays. This had the effect of turning inconsistency into consistency (the two levels do not contradict each other) and also of posing the question, Who is the real Rama? more explicitly.

Arbitrariness of Signifier

Thanks to the claims of animation and identification there should not necessarily be any similarity between the signifier and its signified content. *Therapeutic applications:* (1) softening the impact of emotionally laden information to lower defenses blocking this information. This application can weaken bugs such as turning off the tap, horse blinders, and Baron von Munchhausen. *Example:* After Miriam's car accident Tomer, the youngest, asked her why she could not turn her head sideways. Miriam said, "Don't you know? I told you why!" Tomer said, "You didn't." Then the therapist invited Miriam and Tomer to a game of collisions, using soft pillows as signifiers for the colliding objects. (2) Exaggerating contradictions to increase one's awareness of inconsistencies. This application has the power to enfeeble bugs such as topsy-turvy and Baron von Munchhausen. *Example:* Rama was good at playing the recorder. When she played "a nursing baby in the crib," the therapist handed her a recorder as a signifier for mother's breast. This was designed to emphasize the contradiction between her age-appropriate and regressive selves and at the same time separate the two selves.

Possible Worlds

Thanks to the claims of animation and identification, any potential or imaginary situation can come alive in make-believe play. *Therapeutic applications:* Information left out or distorted by bugs such as turning off the tap, horse blinders, and Baron von Munchhausen can be accessed and experienced by the family. *Example:* Prior to Dan and Miriam's separation, the children had often played a game of buying and selling in stores. In a session following the separation Dan and Miriam were led by the therapist to set up two different stores in different parts of the playroom. Goodies—sweets, toys, and other things children like—were sold in both stores.

Other bug busters are derived from the emotional–homeostatic functions of make-believe play: Many investigators of make-believe play and its therapeutic applications have argued that one of its functions is to let the child express her emotional concerns without becoming overstressed. An integrative theory accounting for this emotional balancing function of make-believe play has been proposed in Ariel 1994, 40–45; Ariel 2002, chapter 5. The following bug busters are derived from this theory.

Repetition

If themes related to the child's central emotional concerns are introduced into his play over and over again, this has a habituating effect, which reduces their emotional impact. The therapist can prompt and facilitate such repetition. *Therapeutic applications:* This and the other emotional–homeostatic bug busters function by diluting the emotional fuel that energizes bugs. *Example:* Following the police incident, the therapist arranged some sessions in which the children could express their fear and anger concerning what the family has gone through in various symbolic disguises.

Distancing

In their make-believe play children evoke signified contents belonging to the core of their emotional concerns (e.g., themes of violent death, loss of parental figures, etc.). Sometimes this heightens the level of their emotional arousal to a barely tolerable level, and then, to soothe themselves, they distance their play from this hard core by bringing in more benign, less arousing themes, such as resting, having fun, and so on. When they have calmed down, they go back to hard core themes, and so on and so forth (Ariel 2002, chapter 5). When children are exposed to extreme pressures, this homeostatic mechanism can stop functioning. In such a case the child is liable to work herself up, even within the make-believe play frame, into a state of extreme mental agitation without being able to distance herself from the disturbing content. If this happens, the therapist is advised to help the family activate the distancing mechanism deliberately. *Therapeutic applications:* Facilitating the expression of emotionally difficult contents, softening the impact of such contents and working them through. *Example:* In the first family session after the police incident Rama and Tomer were extremely wrought up. They played make-believe games with destructive content such as stores exploding from bomb attacks, car crashes, and so on, and were not able to stop. They called themselves crazy animals. Then the therapist put out the lights, brought blankets, and said, "Night time. The crazy animals went to sleep. They wanted to rest, to have strength to do other crazy things in the morning." After the children calmed down under the blankets, the therapist "went to sleep" too. He whispered, "You know what I'm dreaming about? I'm dreaming about a fairy who made all the things destroyed by the crazy animals being put together again by magic."

Introducing Protective Devices

Another technique by which children balance the level of emotional arousal in their make-believe play is introducing signifiers and signified whose function is to protect them against the impact of troubling themes that previously entered into the play. When necessary, this technique can be deliberately employed by the therapist. *Example:* When Rama and Tomer played "crashing cars" with big toy cars, the therapist fastened soft pillows to the toy cars and said, "These are like the crashing cars in an amusement park."

Symbolic Coding

Another emotionally balancing technique in natural make-believe play is representing a disturbing theme by less upsetting signifiers and signified. The latter are used as symbolic codes for the former. This technique can also be used therapeutically. *Example:* In previous sessions the children used to "bake cakes." Following Dan and Miriam's separation, the therapist "baked a cake" for the family and then said, "I am going to cut this cake into two equal parts. Daddy will get half and mummy will get the other half. The children can get slices from daddy's cake and slices from mummy's cake."

Covert Communication

This bug buster is derived from the social-communicational functions of make-believe play. Children often disguise and tone down their mutual conflicts and tensions around issues of interpersonal distance and control by transferring them to the world of make-believe play. (For a detailed discussion, see Ariel 2002, chapter 3.) *Therapeutic applications:* Softening the emotional impact of interpersonal messages to open up information channels blocked by bugs such as turning off the tap, horse blinders and Baron von Munchhausen. *Example:* Consider the following dialogue, cited from the play session referred to above.

> *Shlomo* [addressing Vered's dolls]: Mother-Bird and Sister, will you come out and meet I-Don't-Know? She is afraid of Bad-Daddy-Wolf.

> *Vered* [as Sister]: No, I'm busy. I have to take care of Mother-Bird.

Translated into plain language, this covert-communicational make-believe play dialogue might look as follows:

> *Shlomo* [addressing Vered]: Vered, can you get closer to your mother, who is weak and confused? She can't get closer to you because she is afraid of your father's influence over you.

> *Vered*: No, I'm not ready to get closer to her as a daughter to mother, but I am worried about her and am willing to show it.

THE FAMILY PLAY THERAPEUTIC PROCESS

Conducting a Diagnostic Evaluation

Family play therapeutic interventions should take into account diagnostic data collected before the therapy and continuously throughout the therapeutic process. Beyond the standard psychological and family therapeutic assessment tools, the following diagnostic instruments have been designed in the framework of Ariel's integrative, multisystemic model: a semiotic technique for transcribing and analyzing play behavior (see Ariel 2002, chapters

2–6 and appendix; Ariel 1999, 122–26; Ariel 1994, 75–126); the presenting problem interview (see Ariel 1999, 125–26); and the case history interview (see Ariel 1999, 127–30).

The most important output of a family play therapeutic diagnostic evaluation is a formulation of the main dysfunctional, bugged family programs and a list of the bugs subsumed under them. Informal descriptions of some of the Orens' dysfunctional family programs and bugs have been presented above. Writing full, explicit formulations of such programs requires special training. (For relevant concepts, terms, instructions, and examples, see Ariel 1999, chapter 10; and Ariel 1994, 115–26.)

Types of Family Play Therapeutic Moves

The term "moves" refers to the verbal and nonverbal play therapeutic acts performed by the therapist. There are three types of moves: main moves, preparatory moves, and auxiliary moves. Main moves are designed to weaken, however slightly, specific bugs in particular dysfunctional family programs. Preparatory moves prepare the ground for the activation of main moves. A family play therapist cannot just jump on the family with his main moves. He or she should perform a series of preparatory moves to get the family members ready to cooperate with him, be receptive to his main moves. Auxiliary moves accompany main or preparatory moves. They serve various purposes, such as directing attention to family members who are not in the focus of the therapist's attention, reflecting people's feelings, reducing anxiety provoked by the tactic governed moves, overcoming resistance, keeping an atmosphere of interest and excitement, and so on.

The therapist can make her moves from various positions, alternatively or simultaneously. The major positions are those of an audience, a director, and an actor. From the position of an audience she can make a great variety of verbal and nonverbal comments on the family's make-believe play. She can interpret it by explicating what is implicit and reinforce various aspects of it by cheering, clapping, or booing. From the position of a director (which includes also the positions of playwright, producer, dresser, makeup person, prop-person, sound man, prompter, and so on) she can tell the participants what their behavior should be. She can disqualify certain ways of doing things and recommend other ways. As an actor she can influence the family members by communicating her own feelings and ideas.

The choice of moves is subject to the therapist's creative imagination and playfulness. However, cumulative experience in family play therapy has compiled a large repertory of moves, which can be standardized, classified, and more or less formally defined. I describe the major move types in the following.

Mimicking

Mimicking is imitating family members' play behavior. *Therapeutic functions:* Joining, reflecting, commenting. *Example:* Tomer wore "a shopkeeper's hat." The therapist wore a similar hat to join the game. Then Tomer exclaimed, addressing Miriam, "Hey, buyer! Do you want to buy a cake?" Miriam lay prostrate on the armchair. She was too tired and depressed to respond. Tomer made some gestures and sounds of frustration. The therapist imitated these gestures and sounds to reflect Tomer's feelings and comment about Miriam's lack of cooperation.

Pacing

Pacing refers to mimicking and then gradually changing one's own play behavior. *Therapeutic functions:* Leading a player's play to a desired direction. Miriam "built a palace" on a pile of pillows in a corner of the room, away from the other family members, and declared, "The princess lives alone in this palace on this mountain!" She lay on the pillows, assuming a fetal posture.

The therapist "built a palace" on another pile of pillows, lay down in a similar posture, and declared, "The prince lives alone in this palace on this mountain." After a while he rose to a sitting position, looked through an imaginary window, and called out, "What a beautiful view!" Miriam followed suit.

Focusing

Focusing involves stressing aspects of play behavior by sound and lighting effect or verbal and nonverbal comments. *Therapeutic functions:* Turning attention, interpreting. Vered threw pillows at Miriam, laughing. When a pillow hit Miriam, the therapist produced a loud pounding noise with a big drum to emphasize Vered's anger and aggression.

Explicating

Explicating involves making hidden entities explicit by verbalizing them or acting them out nonverbally. *Therapeutic functions:* Emphasizing, interpreting. Rama clung to Miriam's chest, like a nursing baby. The therapist made a crying baby voice and said, "I'm hungry! I'm hungry! I didn't have enough milk from mummy!"

The Double

The therapist represents a family member's play directly or through a doll. *Therapeutic functions:* Serves as a mouth for a family member who refuses or can't play. In the session described above Vered rejected Miriam's attempts to involve her in play. She hid under the therapist's desk and barked like a dog. The therapist took a toy dog, barked, and then played the dog role for Vered.

Providing Stimuli

The therapist provides behavioral or material stimuli for play. *Therapeutic functions:* Encouraging certain kinds of play activities. When Rama clung to her mother's chest the therapist took hold of a big woman's doll and said: "This mummy has lots and lots of milk in her breasts."

Illusion of Alternatives

The therapist suggests two alternatives for play, hoping that a family member will choose the more attractive one. *Therapeutic functions:* Influencing the course of the play. *Example:* Following the latter move, the therapist took a doll representing a slim male figure and said to Rama, "Do you want the mummy or the acrobat?"

Obedient Actor

The therapist asks for permission to join the play in any role. *Therapeutic functions:* Becoming a member of the club. Vered was angry at the therapist because he directed her parents to get her back to her mother's home. She refused to let him into her play. The therapist asked, "What can I be, then?" Vered said, "You can be the bad snake." The therapist said okay and began hissing like a snake.

Willy-nilly

The therapist performs a play act that engages a family member in a complementary act. *Therapeutic functions:* Influencing the course of the play. During the session described above the therapist said to Vered, "I used to be the bad wolf but I lost my teeth. Dentist, please fix my teeth!"

Some of the types of moves described above are illustrated in the following transcription from a session with the Orens. This session took place two weeks after the session narrated at the beginning of this chapter. A few days after the latter session both parents told Vered that her father would not come back home and that she should return to her mother's home. Vered reacted by intensifying her private war against these decisions. When her mother picked her up at school, she screamed like a wounded animal and ran off. She showed up in her father's sister home later that evening. The therapist, realizing that her main attachment figure was her father, advised her parents not to force her to go back home for the time being and continue with some play therapy sessions designed to lessen her resistance.

Although only Miriam and Vered were invited to this session, the whole family showed up. Dan sat in a corner of the room quietly. Tomer began "constructing a musical instruments store" in another corner of the room. He wore "a shopkeeper's hat." Rama brought a physiotherapy ball the size of her body from the other room and began rolling on it. Vered tried to roll on it too, but Rama pushed her and she fell. She was not really hurt but began screaming and crying, "Daddy! Daddy!" Miriam approached her and said, "Sister-Bird fell off a tree and Mummy-Nurse will cure her!" She attempted to hold Vered. This was an excellent move, evoking the previous session, but too early for Vered. She pushed Miriam away, ran to Dan, and screamed, "Daddy! Daddy!"

Rama continued rolling on the ball. Shlomo, the therapist, put on a "shop-keeper's hat" (mimicking Tomer) and said to Dan, "Hey, buyer, [willy-nilly] the seller [Tomer] and I opened a beautiful musical instruments store. Would you like to buy a recorder for your daughter [Rama], the musical acrobat?" This intervention included an auxiliary move designed to give play attention to Tomer and Miriam, although the session was designed to focus on the relationship between Miriam and Vered. The same intervention included a preparatory move aiming to involve Dan in play with his other two children and clear the ground for Vered and Miriam to sort out things between themselves.

In a way, the same intervention contained also a main move, using the bug busters' covert communication and possible worlds, leading Dan to engage in positive interactions with his other two children, not just Vered. The latter, however, would not allow any of these. She physically held her father's shirt, attempting to pull him away from his other children. Then Shlomo realized that Vered, in her present emotional state, was powerful enough to prevent the family play therapy session to go on profitably. He said, "The bird's broken wing is now completely cured. In fact I have never seen a bird with such strong wings. This bird can carry a whole grown man on her wings" [focusing; using the bug buster covert communication to remove, from Dan's, Miriam's, and Vered's eyes, the horse blinders that prevented them from seeing not just Vered's weak and helpless side but also her powerful, manipulative side]. Then the therapist asked Dan to leave the clinic with Rama and Tomer and come back by the end of the hour. When Vered realized that she would not be able to prevent this by physical force and screaming, she hid under Shlomo's desk and began howling, barking, and threatening Miriam and Shlomo with her "claws." Miriam and Shlomo sat by the desk. Shlomo brought a variety of dolls and toys. Shlomo took a toy dog, directed it at Vered, and began barking and growling [mimicking; play framing as a preparatory move]. Vered, realizing that continued barking and growling would mean playing with Shlomo, fell silent.

Miriam [knocking on the side of the desk]: Hey, doggie, my wing has been cured. I am strong now. Can I come in?

Vered did not respond. Nor did Shlomo, who was enchanted by the way Miriam has learned the lesson of the previous session, without any explicit working through or verbal analysis.

[Miriam picks up a plastic tube and looks at Vered through it.]

Miriam: If I can't come in, I'll see what's going on through the window.

[Shlomo places a toy dog near Vered underneath the table (providing stimuli). Vered ignores it.]

Miriam: How do you feel in this kennel, little doggie? Are you hungry? Shall I get you some food?

[Vered doesn't respond.]

Shlomo [takes hold of the toy dog he previously put near Vered; he holds it in the direction of Miriam and says in a little doggie's voice]: I'm not hungry. I'm angry [the double].

Miriam: I know. Do you know that I miss you?

Vered: Go away!

Miriam: It's not me, it's the dog.

[Miriam is placing her toy dog in a shoe.]

Miriam: The dog is in this boat. There was a big storm in the ocean. The captain fell into the ocean, the little doggie fell into the ocean. The dog is now alone in the boat. He is afraid, he misses the little doggie.

Shlomo [as little doggie]: Help! Help! I am drowning! Who's going to save me? [The double, covert communication, owning and alienation, basic duality; a main move designed to weaken the horse blinders preventing Vered from realizing that she needs and can get help from Miriam.]

Miriam [navigating the "shoe ship" toward the doggie]: My little doggie! I found you! Don't worry! I'll help you!. Miriam is taking the little doggie and is putting it inside the ship.

Shlomo [as doggie]: I'm cold, who'll warm me up? [providing stimuli]

Miriam is "warming up the little doggie" on the palm of her hand. Vered is stretching her arm toward the top of the desk, fumbling with her finger, groping for something. Shlomo hands her a pencil and a bunch of paper slips. His guess was correct. Vered is ready for written negotiations. Shlomo attributes this to effects of the previous play dialogue. He hypothesizes that images of "the big dog left alone in the ship and then saving the drowning doggie" managed to partly break Vered's horse blinders and Baron von Munchhausen bugs, which had prevented her from empathizing with her mother's plight and recognizing her mother's positive side.

At this point Vered and Miriam began a long series of exchanges through stick figures drawn on slips of paper. Vered drew a house with four figures in it. She wrote the names of the figures: her name, her father's name, her aunt's name, and the name of her cousin, her aunt's daughter. In response, Miriam drew two houses, one with herself, Vered, Rama, and Tomer and the other with Dan. She drew lines between the children and Dan. Vered took the note and drew a cross over Miriam's figure, and then added a smile to both homes. Then she drew a home with her father, Rama, Tomer, and herself, without Miriam, and drew a smile on it. This was a progress in the negotiations because previously she would not hear of sharing her father with her brother and sister. Miriam sent her a note with a smiley drawn on it. Vered added sharp teeth to the smiley.

Although in these exchanges Vered stubbornly resisted Miriam's approaches, I saw positive development in her very willingness to conduct this sort of dialogue. She used the bug buster repetition to work through and melt down her anger at Miriam and suspicion of her motives.

This exchange was cut short by Dan, Rama, and Tomer, who came back from their stroll outdoors. While these lines are being written, the Oren family drama is still rolling on, and so is the therapy.

Training in Family Play Therapy

This has been a bird's-eye view of the main features of this family play therapy model. Conducting therapy in accordance with this model can be exciting, challenging, and rewarding—but is not easy. This genre of family play therapy is an art requiring complete, active mastery of the theory behind the diagnostic evaluation and interventions, an excellent command of the language of play, a combination of many skills, and a great deal of practice and experience. Various parts and aspects of the model can be acquired through reading and brief training workshops, but becoming an expert practitioner takes years of theoretical and technical training, as well as supervised practice.

REFERENCES

Ariel, S. 1984. "Locutions and Illocutions in Make-Believe Play." *Journal of Pragmatics* 8: 221–40.

———. 1987. "An Information-Processing Theory of Family Dysfunction." *Psychotherapy* 24: 477–94.

———. 1992. "Semiotic Analysis of Children's Play: A Method For Investigating Social Development." *Merrill-Palmer Quarterly* 38: 119–38.

———. 1994. *Strategic Family Play Therapy*. 2nd paperback ed. Chichester: Wiley.

———. 1996. "Re-storying Family Therapy." *Contemporary Family Therapy* 18: 3–17.

———. 1997. "Strategic Family Play Therapy." In K. J. O'Connor and L. M. Braverman, eds., *Play Therapy, Theory, and Practice,* 368–95. New York: Wiley.

———. 1999. *Culturally Competent Family Therapy: A General Model*. Westport, Conn.: Praeger.

———. 2002. *Children's Imaginative Play: A Visit to Wonderland*. Westport, Conn.: Praeger.

Ariel, S., C. Carel, and S. Tyano. 1985. "Make-Believe Play Techniques in Family Therapy." *Journal of Marital and Family Therapy* 11: 47–60.

Cobley, P., L. Jansz, and R. Appignanesi. 1997. *Introducing Semiotics*. New York: Totem.

Deely, J. N. 1982. *Introducing Semiotics: Its History and Doctrine*. Bloomington: Indiana University Press.

Johnson-Laird, Ph. N. 1989. *The Computer and the Mind: An Introduction to Cognitive Science*. Cambridge: Harvard University Press.

Maltz, M. D. 1987. *Psycho-Cybernetics*. New York: Pocket Books.

2

Narrative Play Therapy: A Collaborative Approach

Ann Cattanach

Narrative play therapy is a way of playing with children using stories and narratives to share and make sense of life events. It is a collaborative experience where the therapist helps the child order his or her experiences through the use of imaginative play processes. In true narrative style, I begin with a story.

"THE GIRL WHO EMPTIED THE INEXHAUSTIBLE MEAL CHEST OF THE FAIRIES"

Once upon a time there was a young girl who went to drive her father's cattle on the hill. A Fairy Hill lay in her path, and as she came in sight of it she met a band of Fairies with a leader much taller than the rest. This one took hold of her and with the help of the others took her away to the Fairy Hill.

As soon as she was within the Hill the leader put her under an obligation to bake into bread all the meal in the meal chest before she would receive her wages and permission to go home.

The chest was very small so the girl thought it would be easy to empty it but as soon as she emptied it was filled again. She realized that her task would never end and so she was captive forever.

In the Fairy Hill was an old woman who had been carried off by the Fairies in her youth and who had been there so long she had lost all hope of getting out. The woman saw the plight of the girl and she remembered her own misery when the same thing had happened to her. She took pity on the girl so told her how to empty the chest.

"Every time you stop baking, you are making bread of the remaining sprinkling of meal but you should put the remaining sprinkling of meal

23

back in the chest and it will be emptied of all the meal it contains in a short time."

The girl did as the old woman had said and the meal soon came to an end.

When the girl saw the empty chest she went to the leader of the Fairies and asked him to let her go because she had finished the task he had set.

But he did not believe her until he looked into the chest and saw that it was empty.

Then he gave the girl her wages and let her go. And as she was going out he said, "My blessings on thee, but my curse on thy teaching mouth."

Stories often contain nuggets of understanding that connect to our lived experiences and it can be a helpful way to think more clearly about our own lives safe in the structure of an imaginary story. Arab storytellers begin their stories with the phrase *kan ma kan*, "It was it was not." We are free to engage or disengage with the elements of the story; we can connect with our lived experience or we can discard the connection because it is just a story. This is often what children say when they make up a story in therapy, which connects very strongly with a lived experience. "It's only a story, Ann," they say, looking for reassurance that the narrative will be held and absorbed in the therapeutic space.

The story about the inexhaustible meal chest of the fairies contains themes that connect to my life as a play therapist. There are descriptions about being trapped and controlled by others, being given work by adults which is really hard and can't be ended, the longing for home and the need to do anything to get back there. These kinds of descriptions are constant themes in stories of children who have experienced difficult life circumstances. What is powerful for me in this story is the older woman helping the young girl escape. The older woman can remember what it felt like when she was young and so helps the girl. I can connect to the trapped feelings experienced by both child and older woman and the pleasure of seeing the child move away from despair. I am also reminded at the end of the story of the blame experienced by therapists working with children. Adults find the harm done to children very painful and frequently blame the messenger as a way to tolerate the despair they feel. "My blessings on thee, but my curse on thy teaching mouth."

The story is from the Highlands of Scotland, very local for me. Fairies here are not sweet creatures but rather malevolent. They live in a parallel world but intervene in the lives of humans around them and must be appeased. Those who understand this special world and the creatures who inhabit it are considered to have the gift of "second sight" and are sometimes called walkers between worlds. I think the sensitive play therapist spends much time walking between the worlds of the child's imagination and the lived world of the child as a life is revealed to us.

The play therapy intervention itself is also a special world in physical space and time where play rules as the child's means of expression. The play therapist must respect the creativity and fluidity involved in watching a child play and beware of using this process simply to define the child in a medical model of disorder. Children play out their experiences through imaginative stories, but we must always remember that the child plays "it was not" just as much as "it was." Play is also the place where the child can take on roles he or she does not wish to bring to the lived life. I sometimes feel concerned about the way children's stories are used in assessment on the assumption that they only reveal the child's internal model of their world. Children do explore stories that contain experiences and ways of being, which are not part of the child's lived world and are discarded once the play is ended.

So we tell and play imaginary stories, which contain aspects of ourselves and what happens in our lives as a way to make sense of the world and our place in it. Sometimes an imaginary story or a metaphor in a story contains more powerful expressions of our own circumstances and play is a safer place to think about our own lives than the endless repetition in talk of our own lived stories of grief and loss. Children "looked after" in the care system often trade their life story to each worker they meet and as a result devalue their lives through the endless re-telling of their story without transformation, just repetition of pain because it gets attention and a reward from the adult. This then becomes the core identity and dominant story for the children and can prevent the more positive aspects of the development of identity.

THE FUNCTION OF NARRATIVES AND STORIES IN PLAY THERAPY

If the play therapist uses a narrative approach, then the following functions can underpin and support the intervention.

1. Telling stories and playing stories can be a way of controlling our world and what happens to us in that world. For a child who lacks power, it can be an enriching experience. For once the child can say, I'm the king of the castle and you're the dirty rascal, and not live the consequences in their reality world.
2. The use of narratives and stories in play therapy can help children make sense of their own lives and also learn empathy through imagining how other characters in their stories might feel.

3. Working with stories and narrative play means that there is collaboration between child and therapist where what happens in the sessions is coconstructed between the two.

4. This model is based on social construction theory and narrative therapy, which describe the development of identity as based on the stories we tell about ourselves and the stories others in our environment tell about us.

5. Some dominant stories we have about ourselves are not helpful and can lead to victimization. In play therapy we can explore ways to shift and expand aspects of identity through exploring roles and ways of being in play knowing that we do not have to take all these experiments into our lived lives.

6. This approach also recognizes the fact that the developing child is part of an ecological system, not an isolated individual. We live in a time and a culture, and this influences our way of seeing.

7. In this kind of collaboration, the child plays with small toys and objects, or draws a picture or just makes marks on clay or slime, while telling a story about what he is doing. My role as therapist is to listen, perhaps ask questions about the story if required and record the story by writing it down if requested by the child. I might also share a story, which might be congruent with the play of the child or as a way to deepen the relationship by the shared experience of telling and listening.

SOCIAL CONSTRUCTION THEORY

If we are to use narratives in a collaborative approach between child and therapist, we need to understand aspects of social construction theory, which defines narrative as the way we construct our identity.

This theory (Burr 1995) states that all ways of understanding are historically and culturally relative, specific to particular cultures and periods of history. Products of that culture and history are dependent on particular social and economic arrangements prevailing in that culture at that time. Knowledge is sustained by social processes, and shared versions of knowledge are constructed in the course of our daily lives together. We make use of words in conversations to perform actions in a moral universe. What we define as truth is a product not of objective observation of the world but of the social processes and interactions in which people are constantly engaged with each other.

So child and therapist construct a space and a relationship together where the child can develop a personal and social identity by finding stories to tell about the self and the lived world of that self. The partnership agreement between child and therapist gives meaning to the play as it happens. The stories children tell in therapy are imaginative expressions of what it feels like to live in their real and imagined worlds. The world of stories presented can be mediated by the therapist, who can help sort out cognitive confusion present in the play and stories. Sometimes there is a process of restorying, when the child can try out new aspects of self by taking on a role and exploring a world in that role. A major aspect of this kind of play is the constant affirmation between child and therapist that it is only a story and does not necessarily have to be lived in the real world.

NARRATIVE THERAPY

These processes of storying experiences are also explored in narrative therapy. LeVay (2002) describes the expression of narrative identity as one of the fundamental processes in play therapy because this process enables the child and therapist to explore relationships via the symbolic and metaphoric imagery that is cocreated during the course of the play.

Humans have a natural inclination to story personal experience. The richness of symbolism and metaphor in this process becomes embedded in the relationship between child and therapist. So narrative frameworks are constructed that allow children to begin to sequence, order, predict, and make sense of complex feelings that can exist as a result of trauma and abuse.

LeVay (1998) considers that we realize ourselves through the stories and narratives that we tell both ourselves and others. The words we say, the sentences we construct, and the events we choose to include or omit all contribute to the generation of narrative identity through which we aim to make sense and order out of experience.

Lax (1992) states that the interaction itself is where the text exists and where the new narrative of one's life emerges. This unfolding text occurs between people, and in therapy clients unfold their stories in conjunction with a specific therapist so the therapist is always coauthor of the unfolding story, with the client as the other coauthor. The resulting text is neither the client's nor the therapist's story but a coconstruction of the two.

Lax (1999) defines a narrative therapist as someone who assists persons to resolve problems by enabling them to deconstruct the meaning of the reality of their lives and relationships and to show the difference between the reality and the internalized stories of self. The narrative therapist encourages the client to reauthor their own lives according to alternative and preferred stories of self-identity. Narrative therapy has links with therapies that have a common respect for the client and an acknowledgment of the importance of context, interaction, bonding, and the social construction of meaning.

THE CHILD AS PART OF AN ECOLOGICAL SYSTEM

Children need adults to care for them if they are to survive in the world. When you are working with children in play therapy, it is important to consider the ecological system in which the children live if the intervention is to make sense or help keep the children safe. Sometimes the desire to rescue overcomes the therapist, who does not consider the consequences of intervention for the children in their environment; then children feel betrayed. The therapist becomes just another person in the adult world who has let them down.

One of the problems for children in the care system is the number of professionals they meet during their time in care, and this can distort their ability to attach to adults who are parenting them.

For abused children the confidentiality of the sessions, if there is no communication with the adults who care for the children, can seem like abuse. Confidentiality becomes keeping secrets, and the therapeutic relationship becomes distorted. Rules and boundaries are always important in the relationship so that both children and therapist are clear about the meaning of the intervention and the importance of being kept safe. If children are learning to attach into a new family, the therapist must take care not to distort that attachment. Supporting the children within their family is crucial. It is sometimes better to support the work of the new parents than to work directly with the children. These are professional decisions for the therapist about how best to develop family attachments.

Bateson (1972) describes the person and the symbolic world of culture in a system of interdependent relations. He defines the unit of survival as a flexible organism in its environment. He views the individual as part of a larger aggregate of interactional elements. These interactions involve information exchanges, and the totality of these exchanges make up the mental process of the system in which the individual is only a part.

Bronfenbrenner (1979) defined the ecology of human development as progressive mutual accommodation between the growing human being and the changing properties of the immediate settings in which the developing person lives. This development is affected by relations between these settings and by the larger contexts in which the settings are embedded.

He defined three systems: the micro (small) systems, the meso (middle) systems, and the exo (large) systems. All these systems are contained in a macro (large) system.

> The microsystem is the child's life in the family with the daily routines, roles, and interpersonal relations experienced by the developing person in the immediate setting of home and school.
> The mesosystem is the interrelations among two or more settings in which the developing child actively participates, for example, relations b

tween home and school and the local peer group. A looked-after child may have a constantly changing system as he or she moves from foster home to foster home that might also result in changes of school and peer group.

The exosystem refers to one or more systems that do not involve the developing person as an active participant, but events occur in these systems that influence what happens in the setting containing the developing person. So what happens in the parent's workplace for example could profoundly affect the environment of the child.

The macrosystem is the culture and the society into which the individual is born. In this system are the cultural beliefs of the society, for example, what it is like to be a child and how children should be reared.

Bronfenbrenner defines human development as a process through which the developing person acquires a more extended, differentiated, and valid conception of the ecological environment, and becomes motivated and able to engage in activities that reveal the properties of, sustain, or restructure that environment at levels of similar or greater complexity in form and content.

I have stated elsewhere (1994) that these ideas of ecological systems are important for the therapist who is considering whether a therapeutic intervention is appropriate and safe for the child, who can be very powerless in his or her ecological environment. When the therapeutic hour is over, the child returns to that system and there must be some form of containment there for the child.

It is sometimes important for the therapist to explore aspects of the environment with the child and perhaps place some issues into a social context so the child has more understanding of her situation. So a child who is sometimes troubled by the behavior of a parent who has bouts of mental illness might use dramatic play to describe their life together to make sense of the relationship. I might suggest that some information about the parent's illness would be helpful and that information sharing may also be part of the meetings because the child wants to understand and knowledge is power. That information sharing might also be part of a dramatic enactment or just straight talk. The child will decide.

STRUCTURING THE SESSIONS WITH THE CHILD

It is important to negotiate the way the sessions are to be conducted with the child so that the reasons for the intervention are clear. The first meeting is usually with the referrer, the child's caregivers, and the child so that everyone is clear about what happens in play therapy.

If it is decided at that meeting that play therapy is appropriate, then I talk to the child to explain what we might do together and ask if the child wants to participate. I usually say something like, "I am coming to play with you so we can sort out what has happened to you." We might have a discussion about the issues that led to the referral, for example, talk about changes in the family for a child in foster care. Then I would talk about the sessions and what we might do together. "I've got lots of toys and stuff and we are going play and make up stories together but not about you, just pretend stories. But I bet that some of the same things that happened to you will have happened to people in your stories."

I then talk about the structure and rules of the sessions. How long each session lasts, and this can be an hour or less, depends on the concentration span of the child. I say, "I will tell you ten minutes before we have to stop playing, which means time for just one more story or finish what you are doing now. No hitting or hurting, My responsibilities are to bring the toys and keep them safe, to keep you safe, to ask questions if I don't understand what you are playing, help you with your stories if asked, and your responsibilities are to play and to keep the rules. So we share the tasks and responsibilities."

SOME NARRATIVES FROM PLAY THERAPY

All the children whose stories follow are using toys, Play-Doh, slime, and sometimes a sand tray to tell their stories. They move the toys or materials about as they explain what is happening and I write down what they say. Sometimes I ask questions to clarify meaning.

This is a story from a seven-year-old boy, T, who was sexually abused by several family members. This story was told at the beginning of our meetings and as a statement of T's sense of helplessness, anger, and desire for revenge. He said he couldn't change anything in the story; it was sad and that was that.

"The Spider"

There was once a big spider that always was naughty. I asked how he was naughty. Not kind to people. I asked what he did.

When his friends came, he nicked sweets off his friends. He did rude stuff with his willy and the children got upset.

At first the children didn't tell anybody because they were too scared but then they did and the spider got higher here to do it.

They had loads of naughty friends who were caught the children and the end the children and the mums and dads lived e

e sad about their children but they didn't to help t

The spider had loads more friends to help him. They beated up the mums and dads and they ate them all so in the end there were only spiders in the world doing bad things. All the children were dead and all the parents.

This is a sad story. The End

When he finished, he said, "We can't write it any other way because that's just how it is." The themes in the story are congruent with some of T's life circumstances, and we were subsequently able to develop his stories and explore ways of being which would keep him and other children safe from abuse.

J is four. She has just been removed from a family that intended to adopt her but couldn't manage her behavior. She is angry, confused, blaming herself, missing her birth mum, missing and not missing her adoptive family, lost in the world.

"THE VERY, VERY CROSS SPIDER"

The spider called Mr. Bum Bum is very cross indeed.

Lisa, who is a very, very naughty girl, is teasing Bum Bum. That is not his real name but Lisa called him Bum Bum because she is horrible. His real name is Victoria Ruth.

When she is angry the spider pulls her hair off and she can't find any of her clothes.

She is angry because she misses her home. She wants her old home again and she is sad and angry. The spider will get less angry tomorrow.

Some of the themes here were about what her adoptive family defined as behavior that led to their rejection of J, so in subsequent sessions we explored stories about what it means to be called a "very naughty girl."

P is 8. He is in foster care because he was neglected by his birth mother. He uses the pens in my bag to create his story. He wants to believe that his birth mother can look after him and this story expresses that longing. He also expresses the anxiety he feels about playing with me, stuck in the pen bag with rats in the bottom.

"THE GREEN PEN"

Once upon a time there was a green pen called Harry and he lived in a pen bag with a lot of other pens. It was nasty there because there were rats down in the bag.

He had a mum and dad but he was fostered. He missed his mum one hundred times very much.

He remembered his dad but didn't miss him as much as mum.

The rats moved toward him and made him stink and he didn't like it. His mum and dad couldn't keep him clean and tidy. Then he went out with his new foster mum and he got new clean clothes.

One day he heard that he was coming home to see his mum and he had a very nice time and he lived happily ever after. When he went home this time his mum kept him clean. The End

P knew that his mother was not able to look after him, but it was a consolation to think that she might learn to care and he needed the space in play to share his longing and be heard.

V is thirteen. She has learning difficulties and is fostered with her older sister and two brothers. It is hard for her to assert herself with her siblings and make sense of her family history.

"The Slime Pie"

The dough for the slime pie is green. It is healthy for monsters. It is a pie for Ann and she is a monster.

The dough is flattened on a tray. The pie is round. The pie became a pancake and farted and was rude. So it had to be made again.

All the teddies are going to try a piece of pie when it is ready.

The ingredients are slime, purple colorings, and hard yellow sugar cane. It is 25p per cake because you have to pay for everything in human life.

Now the cake is ready. You don't have to cook this.

Vicky cut it. All the teddies had a piece.

It is best just to have a little piece each day. If you have a lot you are sick.

Vicky has the biggest piece but in the end the teddies have it all and Ann and there was none left for Vicky.

But never mind because Vicky can make the cake and then she can have it all. Vicky made ice cream for herself then went out to the shops.

Yummy! The End

V was learning to share and she played this out many times through her stories and play about giving and receiving food and finding a balance between eating too much or getting no food at all. The same with love: you can get none or too much of the wrong sort.

T is thirteen and in foster care. She was sexually abused as a young child. We have known each other for five years. This story expresses her exploration of her identity and her anxiety about sex as she enters adolescence.

"THE WORLD OF KATHERINE ARABELLA PLOP"

This girl called Katherine Arabella Plop has lots of things going on in her head. She is piggish, sheepish, moody, hairy, strong-headed, and happy. She is plob-a-lob full of happiness, sadness, joy, and anxiety. All these things in the head stay separate and clear. She is content. She is rich and she eats mince pies all day.

The world outside is full of fighting soldiers. There is nothing else but fighting with the odd spark of joy in between.

There is no sex in this world. It is not allowed. You have to have a license. The soldiers are trying to control the population. You can have optional sex on Christmas Day but no other days because Christmas Day is a time of joy.

Everybody has microchips to check up on them and make sure they have no sex. A family can have one girl and one boy.

Divorce is not allowed. Parents must look after their children. There are no churches. No healthy food, only junk food. This is a strange world.

T often felt out of control and wanted others to make rules so she could feel safe. Sometimes in her stories, the rules were punitive because T often felt worthless and to be punished and victimized was all she deserved. We explored alternatives to this narrative about how to become a hero in your own eyes.

All the stories show how children explore their lived life through the imaginative stories they create with a therapist. There is no literal translation from one world to the other, just strands of meaning and feeling expressed in the containment of the imagination. The world of the imagination is as real as the lived life. Like those with second sight, we are all walkers between worlds in our own lives and through the relationships we have with children who tell us their stories.

REFERENCES

Bateson, G. 1972. *Steps to an Ecology of Mind*. New York: Chandler.

Bronfenbrenner, U. 1979. *The Ecology of Human Development*. Cambridge: Harvard University Press.

Burr, V. 1995. *An Introduction to Social Constructionism*. London: Routledge.

Cattanach, A. 1992. *Play Therapy with Abused Children*. London: Jessica Kingsley.

———. 1994. *Play Therapy Where the Sky Meets the Underworld*. London: Jessica Kingsley.

———. 1997. *Children's Stories in Play Therapy*. London: Jessica Kingsley.

——— 1999. "Coconstruction in Play Therapy." In *Process in the Arts Therapies*. London: Jessica Kingsley.

Lax, W. 1992. "Post-Modern Thinking in a Clinical Practice." In K. Gergen and S. Mc-
namee, eds., *Therapy as Social Construction*. London: Sage.

———. 1999. "Definitions of Narrative Therapy." Dulwich Centre Conference on Narrative, Adelaide.

LeVay, D. 1998. "The Self Is a Telling." Thesis, University of Surrey, Roehampton.

———. 2002. "'The Self Is a Telling' in the Story So Far." In A. Cattanach, ed., *Play
Therapy Narratives*. London: Jessica Kingsley.

3

Theraplay for Children with Self-Regulation Problems

Susan Bundy-Myrow

Consider this scene: It is a beautiful day. Two five-year-old children are playing cooperatively on the shore, making sand structures. Their parents chat on the beach. Billy fills a pail with water but stumbles as he returns to his friend, dumping the contents on his play partner. Reactions are surprise and mild protest from Michael, the "receiver." Billy is concerned about his friend and says, "I didn't mean it!" Michael, dripping, says, "Be careful!" and "Put the water here!" indicating the sand trench. They continue playing.

Consider this different scene: Two five-year-olds are playing on the shore as their parents watch from the beach. One child, Marcus, is attempting to avoid sitting in the sand and is squatting over his sand creation as he guards his pail and shovel. Each time the waves approach his feet, he is distracted and has to repeatedly restart his building. The second child, Adam, is covered with sand. He has completed his own structure and wants to "help" Marcus. He sees the pail, takes it despite protest from his friend, and is unresponsive to his parent's voice to stop. Adam twirls, filling the pail with water. Attempting to run, he trips, splashing Marcus and knocking him into the sand. Marcus screams and kicks. Adam hits him with the pail saying, "You, stupid!"

While there are many ways to conceptualize the differences between the children in these scenarios, self-regulation is presented as a basic, unifying concept. The chapter will discuss self-regulation, its development, and the influence of parenting to support its growth. Theraplay is subsequently presented as an attachment-based, family play therapy to assist children with self-regulation problems to modulate arousal and emotional responses, and to increase adaptive control of behavior.

35

SELF-REGULATION

Definition

An often used yet elusive term, *self-regulation* has no single definition, and there is no consensus on how it develops. Self-regulation denotes automatic functioning as well as freedom from external control. All living things have self-regulatory functions to maintain the mechanisms of life. Self-regulation in humans, however, connotes the very qualities that differentiate humans from other animals—consciousness and a subjective self who can plan, make choices, and think about thinking. A working definition follows with discussion of several aspects of self-regulation pertinent to the child's journey to experience a calm, focused state, emotional attunement, and behavioral flexibility. *Self-regulation is the evolving ability by which one integrates personal, interpersonal, and environmental experiences to maximize adaptive functioning.*

The term *evolving ability* indicates an innate potential that unfolds in the process of development. Self-regulation for the one-year-old, as she diligently directs small and large muscle movements, is different from that of the four-year-old who springs forth with delight in "leaping" her turn with "frog" friends. The seven-year-old seems so sophisticated now as she thinks to herself, discusses with mom, and plans an alternate play date for a friend who can't come to her birthday party. How does self-regulation unfold? *Integration of various experiences* implies a dynamic building process over time in which the various elements influence and in fact change each other. The powerful concepts of coconstruction and shaping are further discussed by Siegel (1999) regarding the interaction of nature and nurture.

As defined here, the various experiences include those classified as *personal, interpersonal,* and *environmental. Personal* experiences are biologically based tendencies that may or may not be further expressed. Expression of these tendencies depends on experience. Included are one's temperament, sensory capacities, capacity to process auditory and visual information, motor control and planning, and cognitive aptitudes to attend, focus, remember, and interpret verbal and perceptual information. Typically conceived as nature, these personal endowments are labeled "experience" to emphasize both developmental potentiality and the uniquely human ability to be aware of one's endowments; and thus they function as an active agent in one's own development. *Interpersonal* experiences include the central role of emotions, patterns of interaction, and attachment experiences that interface with *personal* tendencies, leading to one's perception and conceptualization of the world (Bowlby 1969).

Environmental experiences are external, nonpersonal factors that may also shape one's perception of self and the world. In his ecosystemic play therapy model, O'Connor maintains that a child is influenced by every system with which he has contact; ranging from family size and living situation to sociocultural factors operating in his section of the country (O'Connor and Ammen 1997; O'Connor 2000). He addresses the total child within the context of his ecosystem. For example, the effect of parental job loss on a child's perception of security may differ whether he resides in a single-parent household or a multigenerational household. The importance of including environmental factors in assessing mental health is underscored by the historical inclusion of psychosocial stressors as Axis IV in the American Psychiatric Association's *Diagnostic and Statistical Manual of Mental Disorders* (1994). The National Center for Clinical Infant Program (NCCIP) diagnostic manual also assesses this domain via the Adequacy of the Environment Scale. In keeping with an interactional focus, ratings are made with regard to the appropriateness of environment factors *to the individual child* (Emde, Bingham, and Harmon 1993).

Finally, the term *adaptive functioning* refers to ongoing self-management across several areas; age-appropriate care of self, attainment of positive, healthy relationships, and continuous growth and need fulfillment in socially acceptable ways. *Adaptive* connotes change and flexibility. Siegel (2003) notes that as our human system develops, both increased complexity as well as integration are necessary to achieve stable, flexible, and adaptive states of mind. Self-regulation, then, entails the seeming paradox of maintaining the basic working model of self and others, while at the same time changing and being changed by outside experiences.

Related Theories

Psychologists have used various terms to discuss self-regulation such as impulse control, self-direction, and independence. The emphasis for behavioral and social learning theorists is the control of external behavior as this is an important indicator of adjustment at home and school. In contrast, developmental psychologists and information theorists focus more on the control of cognitive systems such as directing attention, thinking, and problem solving (Bronson 2000). For this discussion, a self-regulated child is one who can modulate arousal and emotional responses, and who demonstrates adaptive control of behavior. In order to exhibit these aspects of self-regulation, the assumption is made that the child *has experienced* a calm, focused state, emotional attunement from his caregivers, and behavioral flexibility in his ecosystem. The research on attachment theory and Stanley Greenspan's work on regulation speak to the importance of the caregiving experience in the development of biologically based potential.

Attachment Theory

Attachment theory has become a cornerstone for understanding and promoting healthy growth and development. Bowlby's (1969) ethological attachment theory has stimulated significant research on the nature of attachment, classification of attachment, qualitative assessment of attachment relationships, predictive validity of infant classifications, and the reliability of attachment classifications in adults (Zeanah 2000). The more than fifty years of research in this area has resulted in important observations, pertinent to investigations today. Harlow and Zimmerman's (1959) primate research provided evidence that attachment was an innate, independent process, different from meeting physical needs. Bowlby subsequently concluded that attachment to a mothering figure is necessary for normal development (Zeanah, Mammen, and Lieberman 1993).

Mary Ainsworth and her colleagues established an attachment classification system for infants based on the activation of both the desire to explore and the need to be reassured by their mothers (Ainsworth, Blehar, Waters, and Wall 1978). Securely attached infants may or may not cry on separation from their parents but either directly approach their parents at reunion or reestablish positive interactions quickly, and subsequently resume play and exploration. Avoidantly attached infants do not cry at separation, and ignore their caregivers at reunion, focusing instead on their surroundings. Attachment classified as resistant refers to infants who actively protested separation, approach their caregivers upon reunion, yet ambivalently resist comforting and take a prolonged time to settle down to play with the toys.

Main and Solomon (1990) have described a fourth attachment classification, the "disorganized/disoriented" type. Characterized by interrupted, confused, or incomplete strategies for obtaining comfort from their parent, this type of attachment is more common in high-risk situations, for example, parents with unresolved grief and trauma, who are maltreating their children, or have bipolar disorder or alcoholism (Zeanah et al. 1993).

Children with trauma histories and concomitant disorganized attachment patterns may also exhibit differences in neuronal development and size of brain structures. Higher reactive stress hormones, such as cortisol levels are also evident, and when sustained, can lead to neuron cell death (Siegel 2003).

The stability of attachment as a predictive construct is observed in six-year-olds (Main and Cassidy 1988), although greater variability is noted in high-risk, low-income samples. Securely attached infants are more likely to become securely attached children characterized at age 6 by warm, engaging exchanges with their parents, and comfort with physical touch. The child forms close friendships and can sustain them in larger peer groups during middle childhood. In contrast, the avoidantly attached child demonstrates unenthusiastic exchanges with an absence of physical contact. Friendships in middle childhood may be marked by exclusivity and isolation from the group. Ambivalence continues to characterize the resistantly attached child, mixing intimacy seeking with hostility toward her parents. This child has later difficulty sustaining friendships (Karen 1994). Recent studies provide an optimistic view of the attachment relationship; children often have a different pattern of attachment to mother and father, and attachment patterns can have the potential for change (Karen 1994; Solomon and Siegel 2003).

The Relationship between Attachment and Self-Regulation

The drive for relationship is necessary for survival. Parents and infants are biologically motivated to become attached to each other. For the vast majority of infants, the attachment process unfolds according to a predictable sequence (Zeanah et al. 1993). The attachment system has an external goal of stimulating the infant to seek physical closeness to the caregiver and an internal goal of stimulating the infant toward stress reduction and "felt" security. Attachment is a regulatory function (Sroufe 1995). According to Bowlby (1969), actual interactive experiences with caregivers lead to the infant's organization of attachment. Described as one's "internal working model," the individual develops expectations of others that guide behavior, and further influence the way future interactions are evaluated. When an individual has experienced sensitive and emotionally available caregiving, attachment may also provide a protective function, insulating the individual from psychological risks. The quality of attachment and care affects the child's capacity for emotional self-regulation and behavior control (Shore 1997). In addition, children with suboptimal attachment histories are more at risk for the negative effects of trauma than children with secure attachments (Siegel 2003).

What are the important components that promote attachment and concomitantly self-regulation? Through the process of attunement, the infant and parent engage in a mutual "dance," a synchrony and mirroring process in which the carer holds, gazes at the infant, rouses, matches, and calms. At first the newborn shows a preference for his mother's voice over others, as well as her scent. Later the infant uses his eye contact to look or look away, thereby regulating the amount of stimuli he receives. In the case of secure attachments, the minds of parent and child can function as a single adaptive system, and a balance develops in the patterns of regularity and novelty. Siegel (2003) identifies this balance as attunement and "contingent communication." Most significant is that these states allow the brain the most self-regulation via flexibility and stability.

The other powerful aspect of attachment leading to self-regulation is touch. Skin is our largest sense organ and when activated by relatively firm pressure and stroking, as in massage, increased physiological organization occurs. Stimulation of the vagus nerve through massage is associated with slowed heart rate, decreased stress hormones, increased attention and task performance, and enhanced sleep (Field 1995, 2003).

Myrow (1997) summarizes touch research that delineates the "hardwiring" of touch to assist the infant to take in sensory information. Babies whose mothers carried them from the hospital in a soft front pack were more often securely attached at eleven months of age than babies leaving the hospital in a carry cradle (Anisfeld, Casper, Nozyce, and Cunningham 1990).

Sensory Regulation: Greenspan and Wieder

Stanley Greenspan and Serena Wieder (1993, 1998) discuss regulation as biologically based processing abilities including attention; sensory processing like kinesthetic, auditory, visual-spatial; motor planning; and sequencing. Optimal levels of self-regulation contribute to a calm, focused state (optimal arousal) necessary for learning. Some children tend to be over or under sensitive in different areas. Being overstimulated can contribute to feelings of anxiety. The anxiety can then trigger greater levels of activity. For others, feeling anxious and out of control can lead to shutting down, greater levels of passivity, and tuning out. A regulatory disorder is diagnosed when a child exhibits both a distinct behavioral pattern and difficulty in sensory, sensorimotor, or processing difficulties that affect daily activities and relationships. Consider the infant who is irritable and reactive to everyday experiences. If the child is also overreactive in sensory areas such as touch (tactile defensive) and hearing (e.g., loud sounds), a regulatory disorder may be diagnosed. Without documented over- or underreactivity in sensory, sensorimotor, or processing difficulties such as auditory-verbal or visual-spatial discrimination, another diagnosis may be considered. An anxiety or mood disorder might be considered with regard to the infant who is irritable and overreactive in daily interactions *without* the observed sensory differences (Greenspan and Wieder 1993).

Because their difficulties are not due to primary mental retardation or autism, children with regulatory disorders may have the *innate* capacity to relate warmly, communicate, and think without severe cognitive deficits. However, despite these basic abilities, they may exhibit difficulties in learning and behavioral problems; attention, focusing, and organizational problems; eating and sleeping challenges. Greenspan has described children with five types of regulatory disorders: sensitive/fearful, defiant, self-absorbed, active/aggressive, and inattentive. Ultimately regulatory disorders are evident in how the child negotiates his daily life; whether he shares with others, how he handles frustration, as well as how he learns. Learning is facilitated in the context of positive emotional interactions.

Early emotional interactions form the basis for thinking and sense of self (Greenspan and Wieder 1998). Greenspan's therapeutic response is to assess the child's functional emotional skills, unique strengths and weaknesses, and provide services such as occupational or vision therapy to address sensory challenges. He then *emotionally* connects to the child through play, and involves the parents as therapists. The parents learn new ways to engage and comfort their child. In the context of emotionally rewarding interactions attuned to their child's sensory needs, both the attachment process and optimal self-regulation can proceed.

Attachment, then, is an inborn sensory-based process activated experientially between the infant and his parent as a function of caregiving. Attachment promotes regulation; the quality of which is associated with *attuned* interactions and comforting touch. When an infant is born with a physiologically based sensory difference, it may challenge the attachment process. It may be difficult for the infant to settle into the calm, focused state one associates with a mother gently rocking, cooing, and matching the gaze of her beautiful baby.

DEVELOPMENT OF SELF-REGULATORY FUNCTIONS

Historically, development has been seen as a function of nature—inherited genetic endowment with which one is born, versus nurture—the experiences one has in his/her environment during the formative years. Most clinicians and researchers now acknowledge the importance of both in development. Siegel (1999) maintains that despite the expansion of neuroscientific research emphasizing the biochemical processes of psychiatric disorders, to choose nature over nurture inhibits clear examination of the complex developing human mind. Recent research on the *interaction* of biology and experience indicates that interpersonal experiences shape the development of brain structures and function (Eisenberg 1995). The terms self-regulation, self-control, self-management, and self-direction further imply a subjectively experienced entity that directs the organism and its experiences. Siegel (1999) refers to this unseen entity as the *sense of mind*. The mind emerges from *neural connections* shaped by *human connections*.

Solomon and Siegel (2003) discuss the ways in which the social environment, including relationships in early childhood and beyond, change aspects of the structure of the brain and ultimately the mind. In examining the effects of trauma on brain and behavioral functioning, the contributors better understand the development of neurotypical (Gray 1996) functioning. Two specific observations are made: the central role of emotions in the functioning of healthy minds, brains, and relationships; and that the body also influences the nature of the mind and subjective experience. Experiences with an emotional valence, be it positive or traumatic, have an impact on the development of organized functioning and interpersonal relatedness.

The Brain and Self-Regulatory Systems

At birth the infant has an abundance of genetically programmed neurons that become activated through experience. A primary source of experience in infancy is the parent–infant relationship. Experience activates particular neural pathways via connection and transmission between neurons, known as synaptic development. As the genes are further expressed with continuing experience, proteins are produced that enable neuronal growth and the creation of new synapses. Thus experience is instrumental in maintaining, creating, and strengthening basic neuronal pathways that form the brain circuitry for complex mental processes.

In infancy the connections among the neurons are immature but attain increasing complexity as the right hemisphere plays a dominant role over the first three years of life (Siegel 2003). Processing nonverbal information, developing the ability to self-soothe, and deriving meaning from the nonverbal aspects of language are critical aspects of this sensorimotor period. The child can comprehend tone of voice, gestures, and facial expressions well before he can produce speech. The right hemisphere also predominates in registering and regulating the state of the body and the perception of emotion. Between nine and eighteen months, the child becomes able to share attention with another regarding an object. Baron-Cohen (1997) discusses shared attention as a prerequisite for mind reading. Mind reading, or theory of mind, is the advanced evolutionary process by which the child makes inferences about others, nonverbally interpreting the intent of their behavior.

The left hemisphere increases in complexity as the process of language development unfolds. Information is processed linearly via words and in a logical, sequential fashion. The telling of a story reflects the elements of left hemisphere functioning. It requires the logical use of language presented sequentially via beginning, middle, and end. Siegel (2003) emphasizes the importance of autobiographical narratives as an integrating function in self-regulation. To tell one's story and make sense of one's experiences requires neural integration *across* hemispheres via the corpus callosum.

Although interpersonal experience continues to be important in brain functioning across the lifespan, the basic, deep structures associated with self-regulation and response to stress develop in the earliest years. What brain structures and processes are important for development of the "mind" and self-regulation? Neural linkages between the basal ganglia (lower brain), limbic system (emotional brain), and neocortex (rational brain) are necessary for optimal development of memory, emotion, and self-awareness. The specific regions of the brain include the hippocampus, prefrontal regions, anterior cingulate, corpus callosum, and cerebellum (Rourke 1995; Panksepp 1998).

Bronson (2000) notes that between twelve and twenty-four months, the frontal lobes peak in number of neural connections ushering in a prolonged period of flexibility and readiness to receive personal, interpersonal, and greater environmental stimuli. The executive self-regulatory functions are operating well by school age. Full integration of self-control, however, may not be completed until early adolescence (Barkley 1997). The prefrontal cortex is particularly important in its integrating role. In addition to receiving social, emotional, and bodily experiences, the prefrontal cortex is associated with the ability to "make sense of" one's experience by constructing an autobiographical narrative based on left and right hemisphere coordination.

Developmental Milestones in Self-Regulation

There are many well-developed systems that chronicle infant and childhood milestones across developmental areas such as Piaget, Erikson (1963), Woods, Bronson (2000), and Greenspan (1998) (O'Connor 2000). Included here are the highlights of infancy through primary school stages with an emphasis on the regulatory function a milestone permits. Commonly observed in preschool settings, for example, are teachers encouraging their young negotiators to "Use your words!" rather than hands and feet to express displeasure in losing a toy. The development of speech as a regulatory tool in peer relationships is pivotal for future emotional and social adjustment. Following this overview, self-regulatory milestones are revisited in the next section on the power of parenting to facilitate self-regulation.

Infancy

Infancy is the period of rapid growth from birth to approximately twelve months of age during which the baby absorbs stimuli and makes sense of sensation first in global, whole-body movements, to increasingly specific, coordinated actions. Early self-regulation is largely reactive; external events and internal biological needs and reflexes set the stage for later voluntary control of actions. The infant is born with certain sensory tools that help him "receive" the world and begin to make sense of it as familiar or novel, comfortable, and safe, or not. The world for the infant *is* his primary caregiver and we will identify this person as mother, for simplicity. His eyes can focus best at just the distance it takes to see mother holding him in her arms and he knows her scent and the sound of her voice (Zeanah et al. 1993). Use of these sense modalities help him recognize similarity, predictability, and to experience comfort. Managing states of arousal is a critical milestone for the infant (Bronson 2000). Internal states like hunger or discomfort arouse the infant, as do certain external stimuli from interesting sights, sounds, and motions. Soothing sensations occur with the cessation of negative internal states, and by external interventions of holding and rocking. Heartbeat sounds and mother's voice are soothing as is the infant's own efforts at thumb sucking. By three months of age, the infant can turn away from sources of stimulation. Eye gaze in particular can help maintain, terminate, or avoid social stimuli by looking toward or away.

Between three and twelve months, the baby begins to make voluntary actions as simple as extending his arm to grasp something, to waving goodbye. This older infant can respond to people, objects, and events at will. Kopp (1992) calls this later period sensorimotor modulation. Whereas the younger infant soothes himself by sucking his hand or thumb, clasping his hand, and moving arms and legs, the older infant six to twelve months of age can push an object away, move away himself, or move toward his mother. As he practices goal-directed action, he not only becomes more capable of his own intentional action, but he comes to understand what his mother wants. Given a loving relationship between parent and infant, he is now developmentally ready to motorically respond to such simple directions as "come," "look," or "give to mama."

The "roots of control" (Sroufe 1995) take hold during infancy as a function of sensory, sensorimotor, and sensoriaffective integration. The infant experiences pleasure, fear, and anger as general affective states linked to physiological responses. Early, automatic smiles become specific responses associated with mother and the provision of nurturing care. Fear, based on startle or pain, is expressed by crying and later wariness, active fear, or avoidance. Anger is first expressed as diffuse flailing when the infant's actions are thwarted, and in toddlerhood may be seen as rage. The repeated association between related cues and emotionally connoted interactions leads to varied expectations of the world as caring, predictable, and inviting, or inattentive, uncertain, and discouraging.

Toddlerhood

Spanning the period from twelve months to thirty-six months, toddlerhood transports the infant to an upright explorer of the concrete world. With greater control over his body, the growing ability to think symbolically, and the ability to be a verbal communicator, the toddler has the means and motivation to grow in geometric proportions! While the two-year-old is busy operating on his world, internally his brain is changing too. Toddlerhood marks the beginning of "executive competence and independence" (Kopp 1992), and the period of greatest initial density in the frontal lobes. It is not until after the 7 that this level declines (Thompson 2000). Opportunities for new self-regulatory functions abound. The one-year-old engages in deliberate exploration of novel actions on objects that helps him discover the predictable nature of the physical world. As he nears age 2 however, the physical trial and error is replaced by the internal representations, symbolization, and make-believe play characteristic of Piaget's last stage of sensory-motor intelligence (Jernberg 1983). The child seeks to practice and master his world, cognizant that important figures and objects continue to exist when not seen. Motivation to be autonomous increases at the same time as a sense of vulnerability, because the toddler realizes his parents can really leave. He is still inextricably bound to them; thus the working through of healthy ambivalence regarding being in control becomes the task of both parent and child. Sroufe (1995) notes that as little ones attempt to develop autonomy, they are more likely to imitate their parents when there's a warm, attuned relationship.

Preschoolers

Preschoolers, including three- to five-year-olds, face an expanding personal and interpersonal world. The child is more capable of self-regulation that includes rules, strategies, and plans. He is less dependent on the constant monitoring necessary for the toddler, and more able to comply with directions to both initiate and inhibit actions. This child can talk about how someone's face appears and how he might be feeling. It is an important time to begin to internalize parent's standards of behavior and pro-social rules and values.

A major hallmark at this stage is the emergence and use of "private speech" (Flavell 1964). The term refers to all speech phenomena not obviously meant to communicate with others. However, the strong connotation of *voluntary* use of the meaning of words implicitly excludes any involuntary speech. Zivin (1979) proposed a broader term, *acommunicative speech,* that includes the full set of phenomena linked to self-regulatory speech. Although notable language theorists Luria and Vygotsky, for example, are both concerned with the function of speech, Luria views the purpose of the preschooler's acommunicative speech *to control* behavior. For Vygotsky, the preschooler *happens* to speak aloud because he has not yet learned to inhibit the thought that is newly linked to speech. Both aspects lead to increased competence in coordinating the preschooler's world.

Interpersonally, the quality of relatedness between the child and his parents continues to be particularly important. The loving interest of the parent or other carer influences the child's sense of self, which is then reflected in his interactions with others (Bronfenbrenner 1990). The acquisition of affect-specific emotional organizations such as fear, anger, sadness, harmony may be a factor influencing the way the child engages his world (Malatesta 1990). The preschooler is interested now in expanding his world beyond the centrality of his parents to a greater interest in peers. The developmental task is to increase focus on negotiation and reciprocity, which necessitates a decreased need to have one's own way. Cooperative play develops, and emotional regulation is enhanced with the ability to use fantasy and enact social roles with dramatic play.

Although this youngster does not yet make detailed plans in advance of an activity, the learning process has expanded to include "planning while in action." The child uses strategies, is more organized, makes decisions, and checks progress toward the goal he has selected. The child is still process oriented, however, and the goal can change quickly if necessary. The verbal intention to draw a car, for example, could ultimately result in an image he proudly labels a house.

Primary School

Primary school children, starting at approximately age 5, experience shifts in mental functioning and self-regulation that assist in managing emotions and behavior (Bronson 2000). The frontal lobes of the brain support the development of "executive functions" being a "conscious decision maker" who is increasingly aware of self, actions, and behavior. The child's increasing ability to inhibit and control behavior is in part associated with an increase in working memory that allows the child to "hold events" in mind and consider alternatives (Barkley 1997). There is less need for immediate and frequent external rewards; rather, increased internal satisfaction occurs with the assurance of delayed rewards and goal achievement. Self-speech becomes internalized and assists self-regulation by helping the youngster, for example, (1) identify to herself how she feels about losing the board game and (2) decide whether she will stay and try again or stop playing. Thus the child begins to consider internal and external events in conjunction with planning and directing behavioral responses (Vygotsky 1962). Children at this age can also control attention better, enabling them to focus on something positive or to think about strategies for coping.

The early elementary school child is also moving beyond egocentrism to more clearly understand the feelings and perspectives of others. They then can more consciously adjust their own emotions and behaviors to that of others. An example is the seven-year-old who receives a second play date invitation, and although the latter is preferred, she declines the second invitation thinking that her first friend would be disappointed if she canceled. The child's cumulative attachment experiences with caregivers and others have now been transformed into internalized views of the world affecting how she evaluates and judges behavior. These internalized standards apply to her own behavior and the interpretation of others' behavior. The performance standards serve to self-regulate and provide a guidepost for one's own behavior (Bandura 1997).

A significant variable differentiating high- vs. low-achieving students is the degree to which they become regulators of their own learning (Zimmerman and Schunk 1989). A child's sense of himself as competent or incompetent affects his motivation to engage in numerous activities, such as interpersonal, academic, sports, or creative endeavors. The belief that a child can control his own outcome in school or other tasks makes him more interested in these areas and more persistent in achieving positive outcomes (Harter 1992). Experiences that increase esteem, present opportunities to demonstrate capabilities, and create positive external and internal evaluations are necessary to counter a child's negative expectations. Because early relationships set the stage for internalized beliefs about self and others, it is important to involve parents where possible to modify the child's self-evaluations and maintain and strengthen his fragile sense of competence across areas.

PARENTING AND THE THERAPLAY MODEL

In reviewing healthy emotional and social development in children, parents are the prime teachers, yet too often they feel far less prepared for this highly influential job than for the job they do at the office. The previous sections have emphasized several points:

- Self-regulation, as discussed in this chapter, consists of optimal arousal, emotional attunement, and behavioral flexibility
- Optimal self-regulation is associated with functional stability, flexibility in problem solving, and neuron complexity
- Development of the brain is a function of interpersonal experience that operates on biological potential with primary growth during the earliest years of development
- The quality of interpersonal experience is a function of the attachment relationship
- The attachment process has a regulatory function with secure attachments associated with flexibility and resiliency under stress, positive social skills, close friendships
- Insecure attachments (disorganized attachments) are associated with impaired emotional regulation, aggression, and violence
- Biologically based sensory differences can interfere with the infant's attachment process
- Interventions that facilitate the development of secure caregiver–child attachment are necessary to (1) assist parents in their critical role, (2) assist children in their journey of self-regulation, and (3) assist families in their patterns of interactions that weave their fabric of home life

Theraplay is introduced as an attachment-based, family play therapy model to assist parents and children in many ways, including self-regulation. Developed by Ann Jernberg (1979), Theraplay is built on Bowlby's and successors' views that attachment is instinctual, necessary for survival, thwarted by separations, and reduces stress through physical closeness. It emphasizes the healthy parent–infant relationship by attending exclusively to the child in attuned, emotionally connected ways. The parent is warm, playful, and ensures that the needs of her child are met.

In observing healthy parent–young child interactions, Ann Jernberg (1979, 1983) proposed four components necessary for healthy child development. Following Jernberg's death, Phyllis Booth, her long-term colleague, updated Theraplay and integrated it with emerging developments in attachment theory and child development (Jernberg and Booth 1999; Booth 2003a). Just as the healthy parent–infant relationship grows, the Theraplay components—structure, engagement, nurturance, and challenge (SENC)—provide a parenting model that also *grows* with the child over the developmental periods. A definition of each component follows with examples to promote self-regulation at each stage.

The Theraplay Components

Structure

Structure promotes predictability and rhythm to the child's world by clearly delineating time and space, guiding and defining. It communicates to the child that adults are trustworthy and will keep him safe. They set limits, establish regularity in everyday activities as well as play. "Wait until I count to three, then jump!" is a playful example of structure. Organizing the environment so the child experiences predictable routines supports biologically based regulation. Structured touch helps the child organize and modulate his activity—to keep him safe and provide developmentally appropriate control.

Engagement

Engagement refers to activities that entice and command one's attention, delight, rouse, and stimulate to attain an optimal level of alertness. Fun surprises serve to enhance the child's experience of self as a separate individual who can be aware of others and enjoy playful give and take. Peek-a-boo is a game that appeals to all ages—from the infant who's learning object constancy to the preschooler and schoolchild playing hide-and-seek. Eye contact and joyful discovery capture the spirit of engagement—inviting the child to say, "More!"

Nurture

Nurture constitutes warm, comforting activities; moments of closeness that involve emotions and touch. Quiet, soothing times allow the child to be seen and "felt." Intimacy unfolds in feeding the infant, gazing into each other's eyes, and marveling over the mutual love affair that has developed. Nurturance communicates to the child that he is lovable; that his needs for attention, affection, and care will be met. While the foundation is laid in infancy, the practice continues to grow, change, and enrich the lives of parent and child over the lifespan.

Challenge

Challenge refers to the process that assists the child to go beyond internalized limits. Adults encourage the child to try something new, take a risk, and to increase independence and competence. This is developmental "stretching" that results in mastery because the adult provides support and manageable steps to "climb." Examples are walking over a pillow bridge, and crawling under a "human" bridge fast or slow, and participating a little longer, "one more time" (Booth 2003a).

SENC and Self-Regulation: Birth through Seven Years

SENC in Infancy

SENC in infancy focuses first on the regulatory functions of establishing predictable routines and modulating physiologically based states of arousal such as sleep and wake cycles and degree of sensory stimulation. Structure sets the general framework for cycles and routines whereby parents personally and environmentally support signs of inborn regularity such as wakeful and sleepy times. Engagement and nurturance work hand in hand to increase and decrease arousal to achieve the focused attention associated with emotional attunement. The "devoted dyad" gaze at each other, mirror and imitate each other; practicing opening and closing circles of interactions. Mama smiles and looks at her six-month-old, saying in her lilting voice, "Hello sweet Emmy!" The baby kicks excitedly and returns a winning smile. Mama grasps baby's feet, placing them in front of her face, saying, "Where's Emmy?" Baby's eyes grow big as she quiets. Mama peeks from behind baby's toes, "Peek-a-boo!" she says, using just the right volume for baby to grin and vocalize "Ahh." "Again?" mama interprets. Baby returns mama's eye contact and mama "hides" behind baby's feet again. The sequence begins again—the looking, listening, vocalizing, and touching—perhaps ending as mama kisses baby's toes saying, "You're delicious!" Although peek-a-boo emphasizes engagement and nurturance, it contains structure and the stretching of challenge as well.

SENC in Toddlerhood

SENC in toddlerhood provides continued structure to ensure safety and predictability as the little one ventures from and returns to her caregiver for reassurance and cuddling. Little ones need their parents to celebrate their curiosity, exploration, desire to "help" with busy routines, and practice favorite activities again and again! While it might seem, at times, that days pass more smoothly when toddler "runs the show," she is far too little to know what is best for her. Rather, she needs her parents to tell *and* show her "what's next," to continue to be emotionally available as a secure base, as described by Mary Ainsworth (Karen 1994). Rather than ignoring distress to foster independence, caregivers need to attune to her internal states, and manage her world and arousal by calming, soothing, and helping her transition to the next event. This little one can best develop in the context of warm, predictable relationships with her parents.

SENC for the Preschooler

The ages three to five are a bustling time, indeed! For many children, morning preschool is the first organized peer program without mom or dad. Other children appear to be "veterans" because adults other than their parents have already assisted in their care on a regular basis. It is particularly important at this stage to ensure engaging and comforting time to reconnect with each other to nourish their relationship.

In order for the child to internalize a secure and competent model of himself and others in his world, parents must continue to "get to know" their ever-developing child. They can do this several ways. The parent can relate in emotionally supportive ways: "You kept trying and you did it!" The parent supports competency by appreciating the importance of the child's activities, for example, "Now that the toys are put away, we have room to kneel to play tunnels!" and "Thanks for helping me put the groceries away. You know right where to put the soup." The preschooler makes "plans in action" and the structure of teaching problem-solving strategies can support the child's development; for example, "Hmm, Let's see what you did so far . . . It's heavy, isn't it? Let's try this together. Ready, set, push!"

This is the age when the child's view of the world is becoming more consistent. He too is behaving more consistently with prosocial or antisocial tendencies. Some parents report societal pressure for their little ones to achieve and perform at earlier and earlier ages. Despite the fact that the brain is primed to acquire information, learning is facilitated in the context of positive emotional interactions (Greenspan and Wieder 1998). One loses the joy of curiosity, exploring, and discovery *in relationship*, when the "business of moving *through* life" usurps the quality of attuned, here-and-now interactions.

SENC for the Elementary School Child

Given that the world of this child is expanding beyond the home to the increasing influence of peers, school, and media, one might wonder whether the formative opportunities of parents are over. Absolutely not! In contrast, the parent–child relationship is of primary importance because it provides continuity between past and future self-development. The continuity of the past supports the internalized present self—competencies and evaluations of self and others. Looking forward, the relationship then serves as a present-day anchor from which the child can explore cognitively, emotionally, and behaviorally. The connectedness is not dissolved; rather it is transformed (Sroufe 1995) as parents support the degree of autonomous self-regulated activity with which the child is capable. In addition, children with a history of close and secure relationships *are* better able to assume more autonomous self-regulated activities.

The SENC principles are particularly salient here. Parents typically know their children best and are in the position to observe the effects of "dysregulation" on their functioning. How do they handle new people and situations, being on their own, many transitions, changes in sleep and eating schedules, extended periods sitting or listening? What are the early warning signs that the child is becoming stressed and dysregulated? For some children it is withdrawal; others may cling to the parent, while others become irritable or avoidant. The attuned, engaged parent plans for the needs of her child and makes changes in activities, as the need to counter excessive stimulation arises. Agendas that vary activity with calm periods *according to the child's capability*, rather than perceived pressure to achieve or the parent's busy schedule, provide structure and the kind of stretching to promote growth in self-regulation.

During the early elementary years, children become more consciously aware of themselves in relation to peers and more vulnerable to peer judgments. Bronson (2000) notes the effect of nurturance and positive structure in insulating the child from negative peer influences. In contrast, children judged to be extremely peer-oriented had parents who exhibited less concern and control of their children (Condry and Siman 1974; cited in Bronson 2000). Children need the continuation of routines that include hugging, eye contact, and time to review their day. Mary and her mom enjoyed daily "comfy" time, where they focused, sometimes briefly, only on Mary's news. Her mom became experienced in knowing when to listen, support and celebrate; when to intervene on an adult level.

THE THERAPLAY TREATMENT MODEL

The SENC Theraplay components have been described as necessary variables in all healthy, parent–child relationships. In the following section, the components: Structure, Engagement, Nurturance, and Challenge form the prescription from which the particular individual and family Theraplay *treatment* is designed. The Theraplay treatment model is briefly defined and described, with modifications discussed for self-regulation difficulties. A case example illustrates use of SENC activities as applies to self-regulatory deficits using the Theraplay treatment model.

Theraplay Defined

Developed by Ann Jernberg in 1967, revised by Phyllis Booth (Jernberg, and Booth 1999), and maintained by Sandra Lindaman and the Theraplay Institute (Chicago), Theraplay is a trademarked method, with clinical certification in group, individual, and family Theraplay. Practiced in ten countries and instructed by national and international trainers, the interested reader is referred to www.theraplay.org, www.theraplace.com, and references by Jernberg (1979, 1983, 1993), Jernberg and Booth (1999), and Munns (2000).

Booth (2003a, 4) defined the method: "Theraplay is a structured play therapy for children and their parents. Its goal is to enhance attachment, self-esteem, trust in others and joyful engagement. The method is fun, physical, personal and interactive and replicates the natural, healthy interaction between parents and young children." Children have been referred for presentation with overactive-aggressive behavior, withdrawn or depressed behavior, phobias, tantrums, and difficulty socializing. Children with learning and developmental disabilities may also exhibit various behavioral and interpersonal difficulties. Given that Theraplay is an attachment-based therapy, families with foster and adoptive children find it to be a logical choice for their needs. Theraplay also serves as a preventive program to strengthen parent–child relationships when faced with family or environmental stressors.

Myrow (2000) noted that Theraplay's focus on the *emotional* age of the child, coupled with an emphasis on physical closeness and warmth, expedites the building of a therapeutic alliance whether or not the attachment bond is the focus of treatment. Unlike traditional child-centered approaches, the Theraplay therapist is the primary playroom object and actively facilitates building trust to establish the calm, focused, attuned state so many children need. Theraplay is tailored to give corrective experiences that organize the sensory system in an experiential-dependent way, foster emotional coregulation through attunement of low-intensity and high-intensity states, and support the turbulence of positive change. The result of Theraplay is multisystem change in the child and parent's experience of self, other, and world (Makela 2003).

The Family Theraplay Treatment Plan

Consisting of approximately nineteen sessions (4 assessment, 11 treatment, and 4 follow-up), Family Theraplay is presented as follows (Jernberg and Booth 1999).

Session 1. Initial interview with parent(s), gathering history, presenting problem, family dynamics to ultimately assess the parent–child relationship.

Session 2. One parent and child participate in the Marschak Interaction Method (MIM) (Lindaman, Booth, and Chambers 2000). The Theraplay therapist observes and videotapes this interaction.

Session 3. MIM 2. In two-parent families the MIM is administered to the other parent.

Session 4. Feedback session with the parent(s) in which the MIM observations are viewed and discussed, followed by a plan for treatment.

Sessions 5–8. Theraplay Parent and Child apart. The therapist interacts with the child for a thirty-minute session followed by consultation with the parent(s) as they view the videotaped session together. When two therapists are present, the "interpreting" therapist observes the session with the parents as it is occurring. They discuss the rationale for the SENC activities, link history and dynamics to present-day behavior, and discuss how parents can begin to apply these components to home.

Sessions 9–15 (or more if appropriate). Theraplay Parent and Child together. Sessions continue as before, except that parent(s) now join the child and therapist in the playroom for the last fifteen minutes of the session. Parents receive guidance from the therapist(s), frequently in the form of coaching and role play. The final session ends with favorite activities and a good-bye party.

Sessions 16–19. Additional sessions and/or quarterly follow-up sessions occur with parents and child over the next year.

Distinctive Characteristics of the Child with Self-Regulation Difficulties

Children with self-regulation problems, as discussed earlier in this chapter, are those experiencing one or more of the following: sensory-based arousal difficulties, trouble modulating emotions, and/or demonstrating behavioral flexibility according to normative expectations. These characteristics may also be seen in children meeting the descriptive criteria for other diagnostic classifications such as the American Psychiatric Association *Diagnostic and*

Statistical Manual, 4th edition (DSM-IV) and Zero to Three National Center for Clinical Infant Programs; *Diagnostic Classification Manual* (Greenspan and Wieder 1993). Other labels may include sensory integration (SI) problems, attention deficit disorder (ADD), attention deficit hyperactivity disorder (ADHD), learning disability (LD), nonverbal learning disability (NLD), pervasive developmental disorder (PDD), obsessive compulsive disorder (OCD), oppositional defiant disorder (ODD), behavioral disturbance, and subclinical presentations of these disorders (Greenspan and Wieder 1998; Zeanah 2000).

Theraplay for children with self-regulation problems has to address the fact that sensory differences may have made these children less able to feel comfortable, perceive the world as safe, achieve routines and develop warm reciprocity with parents in typical activities as holding, or rocking. Therefore, the child is likely to have unmet needs and appear emotionally as a much younger child. In contrast, the "neurotypical" preschooler *has* experienced the multisensory messages of his parents and greater environment as generally positive, consistent, and reassuring. He is now better able to internalize, remember, and apply those models more independently to new situations. The child with self-regulation difficulties, however, is "out of whack," as if in need of an automobile major tune-up. Despite his chronological age, he needs more external support from adults to negotiate tasks because it was difficult for him to experience the calm, focused state of optimal arousal necessary for learning. As a function of his difficulty "connecting" to his parents, this child also has unmet attachment needs that are necessary to soothe him. Finally, secondary adjustment problems are common because adults in the greater environment expect more from this child than he is capable of performing.

MODIFICATIONS FOR CHILDREN WITH
SELF-REGULATION PROBLEMS

When children exhibit difficulties managing their emotions and behavior, it is often helpful to investigate possible difficulties associated with the sensory aspects of self-regulation. Does the child appear to be oversensitive or undersensitive to various sensory experiences? In addition to assessing the child's attachment history during the intake interview, include questions regarding preferences for or sensitivities to light, noise, temperature, smell, movement, or touch. Registered occupational therapists may specialize in the assessment of sensory integration disorders. Greenspan and Wieder (1998) are recommended for an in-depth discussion of biologically based processing abilities and the means to strengthen them.

Activities to Address Self-Regulation Difficulties

Theraplay treatment can specifically include activities to address body awareness and response to the sensory aspects of self-regulation. The Theraplay therapist must learn what level of stimulation leads to an optimal state of arousal and which activities help the child organize his sensory functioning. The therapist must then provide the degree of structure needed to help the child successfully regulate his excitement and activity level (Jernberg and Booth 1999). Intricate to Theraplay is the *emotional and interpersonal connection* with any activity.

Underarousal versus Overarousal

Greenspan and Wieder (1998) note that if a child is undersensitive or underaroused, it's necessary to generate a great deal of affect through different sensory modalities to assist the child to interact, focus, and attend. For the child who is oversensitive or overaroused, combining soothing activities with a gradual introduction to a greater range of sensory input is necessary. Some children may appear quiet and withdrawn in response to their oversensitivity to stimuli. In contrast, an overactive child may have a high activity level because he is *craving* stimulation due to underarousal concerns.

Mastering Body Movements

Children increase their sense of competence when they can direct their bodies to move, as well as relax their bodies in the safety of trustworthy arms. Activities that include jumping, running, and changing directions, deep tactile pressure as in massage, swinging and spinning, looking and reaching, or listening and reaching are examples to master movement. When different movements are combined, the child practices motor planning and sequencing abilities. Activities that can be modified to address the child's ability to direct her body include Simon Says, wiggling left or right arm/leg, Statue (Catch me moving), hand/body tracing (keep body still!), popping bubbles with left elbow, right toe, and so on, catching a bean bag that falls from therapist's head, blanket ride with eye controls, jumping on "pillow islands" to reach therapist's hug, and surprise spin! During the course of a Theraplay session, high activity is followed by quiet, calming activity.

Modulating Activity and Experience

Many activities can involve speed variation–fast, medium, slow as in jumping, running, or spinning. Degree of pressure can vary as well, for example, high-five game (therapist's and child's hands slap hard, medium, soft). Stack hands slowly up, quickly down, slowly up and hug! Play "giant walk": child stands on top of therapist's feet, facing each other as therapist walks slow to fast, and back to slow. Can you stick together? Child jumps on pillows as therapist faces child, holds child's arms and directs the jumping fast or slow, high or low. The motor boat game involves song and regulated movement as therapist and child sit opposite each other, holding hands as they move their bodies in a circle. "Motor boat, motor boat, go so slow. Motor boat, motor boat, go a little faster. Motor boat, motor boat, step on the gass-er. Until we stop . . . And run out of gas." The child calms in a quiet hug as they bend forward, touching the floor (Bundy-Myrow 2000).

For the Oversensitive Child

This child needs a combination of nurturing activities and gradual exposure to increasing sensory stimuli. The child needs a soothing, comfort state, a symbolic safe place, and activities to concretely experience that. Speak slowly in low tones and include rocking (nestle the child in a big bean bag like peas in a pod), deep tactile pressure (e.g., wrapped in a blanket). Slowly and gradually expose the child to greater auditory, visual, or tactile input. With each input, check the child and return to the safe state (e.g., self-hug) before introducing a greater challenge. In the context of a dyadic game, the therapist first monitors the degree of input. Later the child can give the commands: Loud, soft, or medium; fast or slow; hard or gentle; big, medium, small. Practicing positive coping, for example, self-hug (cross arms and squeeze), deep breath can simulate the safe state for generalization. As the child moves his body through different activity levels, he learns to be in charge of his own sensory and motor experiences, and thereby learns self-regulation (Greenspan and Wieder 1998). Additional activities are referenced in Jernberg and Booth (1999), Rubin and Tregay (1989), and Munns (2000).

Theraplay Components for Children with Self-Regulation Difficulties

All of the Theraplay components, over the course of treatment, are likely to be salient for this child to accomplish the goals of (1) developing a comfortable physiological state in interpersonal context, (2) receiving nurturance to address unmet emotional and attachment needs, (3) specifically applying Theraplay strategies to regulate self across situations. The components structure, engagement, and nurture are emphasized first. Structure forms the framework to make the therapeutic experience predictable, comprehensible, and safe, especially for children with regulatory concerns. Engagement for self-regulation has two functions. First is the overarching jective of establishing the particular conditions for attunement with this unique child. Phyllis Booth (2003) noted the complementary roles of engagement and nurture to increase arousal and calm the child when he becomes too excited. Engagement, in this latter instance, refers to the stimulating and exciting aspects of this Theraplay component. As Booth emphasizes, nurturance is needed to help the child experience calm, and to learn ways to self-soothe; necessary for self-modulation. Additional nurturing may be necessary when the child has not been able to experience the world as caring and if he sees himself as unlovable (Jernberg and Booth 1999). Unmet nurturing needs further make it difficult to modulate emotional expression and control behavior.

Finally, challenge, particularly the "stretching" aspect, is used in two ways. As the child begins to experience brief, integrated moments of comfortable, interpersonal contact, the therapist will want to practice extending those moments. Second, challenge becomes operative in the generalization process beyond the Theraplay room. While coaching parents for in-session and home practice is typical in Family Theraplay and promotes generalization, specific additional practice for the child with self-regulation difficulties may be useful. The developmentally young child enjoys repeated practice to increase his sense of mastery. Practicing body movements and different levels of activity (e.g., fast versus slow, hard versus soft) promotes self-regulation. Further, strategies learned in a positive emotional context are more likely to have meaning and be retained (Greenspan and Wieder 1998). This latter statement bodes well for Theraplay; however, the developmentally younger child cannot yet *independently* recognize physiological and social cues, and implement strategies learned in a different context. She will need the external support of her caregivers to practice strategies that have been "packaged" and "transported" from her Theraplay experience.

For example, consider eight-year-old Kathy, who responded to her auditory sensitivities with fearfulness followed by prolonged withdrawal. Her visual skills were intact and she giggled and relaxed when visual (not auditory) surprises were presented. In the context of Theraplay, she learned to stay involved when various sounds were heard as she "beeped" Dr. S's and her mom's nose, ear, chin. It was especially funny to Kathy when she peeked to discover Dr. S's surprise purple cotton ball "nose." The purple nose story, and simply touching one's nose, soon became a reminder of fun and relaxation. Dr. S. and mom devised a plan to use the nose signal to remind Kathy to relax in noisier environments and use her auditory strategies (join family members, cotton ear plugs, use her own headphones). Kathy no longer withdraws, initiates her own strategies more often, and has been known to "do the purple nose signal" just to make mom smile.

Case Illustration

Following is a description of a Theraplay case as it might unfold for this sample five-year-old exhibiting externalizing behaviors, overactivity, physiologically based sensory differences, and related difficulties in mother–child attachment. At a time when one would expect the child to better manage emotions and behavior via use of private speech and pretend play, be able to start *and* stop actions when directed, and be focused on reciprocity and negotiation with peers, "Gannen" resembles a much younger child. His parents are worried he'll have difficulty in school following directions and "knowing when to stop." Gannen has received occupational therapy in school, which has been helpful. At home Gannen is a mover and shaker; in motion and touching everything he sees. While he's drawn to many things, he doesn't spend much time focusing on each activity. Eye contact is fleeting. He is verbal and likes to direct conversations. When given a direction, he may initially ignore the adult; when "cornered," he argues until he escalates to tantrum proportions. It's difficult for Gannen to complete tasks. Either something is grabbing his attention like a magnet, or he's chasing around, frequently bumping into things. Gannen has many bumps and bruises. His parents are frequently telling him to slow down. Often he surprises his parents and older sister by "slowing down" as he bumps into them. Gannen is a little whirlwind who sweeps up everyone in his path.

Theraplay Session 1

As they walk down the hallway to the "green rug room" Dr. S says, "Mom says you've been playing soccer, I'll have to check your strong leg muscles." Taking his hand, "Let's see if we can hop over to that bean bag chair." They hop holding hands, and as Dr. S. stops, he leaps ahead of her into the bean bag and smiles. "Wow, you're a big jumper," she says as she sits facing him, grasping his leg to admire his "soccer" muscle. "Yeah, I can do more stuff," attempting to twist away. "You sure can, with *these* muscles! *Look* at these soccer muscles. She continues checking his leg muscles, admiring how he can make his muscle "grow" as he moves his foot. She notices all his bruises, and introduces two kinds of lotion to fix his "hurts." Gannen likes the "smelly" peach lotion. Cradled in her arms now, he loves the nurture but pulls away when her touch is too soft or tickly. "Your arm moved real fast. I'm going to try that a different way so it feels better," she said. Dr. S. verbalizes what she has learned about what feels good to Gannen. He becomes distracted, begins talking, no eye contact. The session ends with a pillow balance on his head which, while difficult, is fun. They then share the big pillow, like an umbrella, as Dr. S. sings a special ending song.

Process. In his seeking firm touch (e.g., leaping hard into the bean bag), Gannen exhibits underreactivity to touch. His excessive running, jumping, and fidgeting are likewise consistent with an underreactivity, for which he would continue to amplify his movements in his solitary manner, if permitted. Nurturing him with a firm grasp, and long lotion strokes engaged and calmed him. He also needs to know how strong and competent he is. This initial "settling in," while positive, will likely be temporary.

Theraplay Session 3

Gannen greets Dr. S. happily but as they approach the playroom door, he starts to pull away. "I'm glad you brought your pulling muscles today!" she said as she grasps his other hand, spins him so he is positioned over the bean bag, and they both sit down. Still holding his hands, Dr. S. slowly moves them in a circle, while seated, singing, "Motor boat, motor boat goes so slow." Gannen looks at Dr. S. with interest, as they "Go a little faster!" and then, "Step on the gass-er!" Gannen is gleeful with eyes bright. Dr. S. decelerates, "Until we stop . . . and run out of gas." "Do it again!" he shouts, as Dr. S. helps him bend forward to calm him with a big hug. It's important for Gannen to experience a calm, focused state before he accelerates again. Dr. S. checks each arm and leg to be sure they are ready. They repeat the "Motor boat" game. Gannen takes great pride in showing Dr. S. that his "hurts" are healing. He is able to attend and participate without "pulling away" emotionally and physically for twenty minutes, after which he begins to argue, demand, yell, kick, and cry, "I want a different snack now! I want to do it myself!" Dr. S. identifies his feelings, "You're mad! You're mad because I won't let you play by yourself. I'll help you calm down. I won't let you hurt me or yourself." She holds him close and rocks him as he gradually settles down.

Process. Gannen has entered the "working through" stage of therapy. While we have found ways to provide a level of sensory input that is comfortable for Gannen, and he less frequently zooms through the house banging into walls, his underlying nurturing needs remain. As a result of overactivity (actually craving contact), and early avoidance patterns that developed, Gannen has been unable to experience a calm *physiological* state within an *emotionally* calm context. His parents have not felt confident to structure and nurture; often interactions have resulted in tantrums. His attempts to secure his own structure and calming has, of course, been overwhelming and he does not yet know if he can trust this different way. Gannen needs to experience coherence between body and emotions before he can be *stretched* developmentally to internalize this "working model" and competently apply it himself, behaviorally.

Theraplay Session 4

Dr. S sees Gannen is genuinely responsive until he "catches himself," at which point he begins directing, avoiding contact, and becomes squirmy. Dr. S checks his arms and legs for quiet readiness, then "rows the boat" with long, firm rubs on his arms. "Ready, set go!" also helps his body get ready. Gannen especially likes "bumping" one, two, or even three pillows off his tummy without use of his hands. Dr. S. marvels about her discovery that three big, heavy pillows help Gannen be calm, and also strong! Next Dr. S. introduces a drink in a traditional baby bottle with straw secured by rubber band. She lets him choose the straw versus the nipple. He bites the straw, then rejects it and settles into the bean bag with the nipple-topped baby bottle. Dr. S. cradles Gannen *and* the bean bag as she holds the bottle, and they listen to the bubbles he makes.

Process. Gannen's accepting the bottle and choosing the nipple indicates that it is "in tune" with his unmet needs. When children do not need this level of intervention, they simply are not interested. Gannen persists for several sessions in asking if Dr. S "brought the bottle drink." Gannen has entered the "growing and trusting" phase of Theraplay, and his mom will soon join them for the latter part of each session.

Theraplay Session 7

Gannen is calmer; Dr. S. doesn't need to keep such close proximity to him. With his advanced verbal skills, Gannen enjoys picking the magic word of the week to indicate, "Go!" Dr. S. instructs Gannen to stand against the big door. "Here's the starting place to get your body ready. See that big pillow on the floor? When I say your magic word to start, you run, stop, jump on the pillow, and make your body FREEZE, like this" (extending arms out to the side). Dr. S. surprises Gannen at the end with a spin and hug. To get ready for mom joining the session, he hides excitedly in the playroom so she can discover him. Mom joyfully hugs him, admires how his hurts are almost gone, and nurses him with the bottle. She explains that he was always such a "busy guy" that it was hard for him to enjoy being calm. Now he and she can have this special time together.

Theraplay Sessions 8–14

Theraplay continues to involve mom and later dad with attention to the kind of activities that help Gannen calm and ?, le? ? the ?la?e ?lls physical and emotional responses, and enjoy ? ?ew ? an? ?d ?h- gagem?nt ?'s found with his parents. Gannen ?? ?res? ? ?ll? ? ?

- He creatively puts the straw inside the nipple of the bottle in order to have both, as he gradually weans himself from the bottle. Gannen retains the calm, secure position of "cuddling" with mom.
- Mom learns the Theraplay activities of the week via presession roleplay and coaching from Dr. S. Rocking in the blanket becomes a favorite Theraplay activity that helps Gannen at home, with his craving for movement.
- Mom and dad also enjoy calm cuddle time with Gannen wrapped in a blanket roll. They are thrilled that he is "going with the flow"; they feel more comfortable and successful "being in charge." They realize he needs preparation to end an activity and ready himself for another.
- Gannen seeks new challenges as he gains better control of his body. Obstacle courses with zigzag turns are his favorite. At home, parents note that he is beginning to monitor himself better, saying "Oops, no hurts. That's the rule!" and responding well to mom's "Get your body ready, so we can. . . ." He is beginning to initiate in more planned than impulsive ways.
- In addition to his verbal skills, Gannen begins to enjoy visual signals such as eye-winks. A visual okay signal used in Theraplay to indicate the start of a relaxation game (tense and relax certain muscles) becomes his secret code to generalize his optimal arousal experience of Theraplay. Dr. S. and Gannen's mom "package and transport" the strategy.
- When Gannen has to wait now, he has several options to help his body be calm. He can do a "chair pull" (while sitting in a chair, he grasps the seat of the chair with his hands, pulls upward as if he were lifting himself and the seat into the air) or cross his arms in a self-hug. If his body becomes too wiggly, mom reminds him with their secret okay signal (squeeze thumb and forefinger together making the letter *o* while remaining fingers resemble a letter *k*). Making the okay signal with both hands is the beginning of the "tense and relax" activity he enjoyed in Theraplay.

Theraplay Sessions 15–16

Dr. S and the family prepare for their final sessions. They make a list of favorite activities, and Gannen selects a special snack. He is the guest of honor who celebrates with his family and Dr. S. Thereafter, he will have quarterly checkups over the next year.

CONCLUSION

Self-regulation is defined as the evolving ability by which one integrates personal, interpersonal, and environmental experiences to maximize adaptive functioning. Historically, focus on self-regulation has included internal cognitive factors and external behavior. Research in infant development investigating the role of somatosensory differences on young children's early relationships (Greenspan and Wieder 1998) extends the realm of self-regulation to include biologically based sensory differences in addition to emotions and behavior. The importance of early relationships in specifically shaping brain structures and function (Siegel 2003) further supports the proposal for attachment-based interventions to assist difficulties in self-regulation. The chapter discussed the genetic-environmental relationship to self-regulation and developmental self-regulation milestones in children from birth to school age. Theraplay is introduced as an attachment-based, family play therapy model emphasizing structure, engagement, nurture, and challenge (SENC) to assist parents and children in many ways, including self-regulation. The SENC components are applied to each developmental age, followed by an illustration of the Theraplay treatment process as it might unfold to assist a child modulate arousal, emotional reactivity, and externalizing behavior.

REFERENCES

Ainsworth, M. D. S., M. Blehar, W. Waters, and S. Wall. 1978. *Patterns of Attachment: A Psychological Study of the Strange Situation*. Hillsdale, N.J.: Erlbaum.

American Psychiatric Association. 1994. *Diagnostic and Statistical Manual of Mental Disorders*. 4th ed. Washington, D.C.: APA.

Anisfeld, E., V. Casper, M. Nozyce, and N. Cunningham. 1990. "Does Infant Carrying Promote Attachment? An Experimental Study of the Effects of Increased Physical Contact on the Development of Attachment." *Child Development* 615: 1617–27.

Bandura, A. 1997. *Self-efficacy: The Exercise of Control*. New York: Freeman.

Barkley, R. A. 1997. *ADHD and the Nature of Self-Control*. New York: Guilford.

Baron-Cohen, S. 1997. *Mindblindness: An Essay on Autism and Theory of Mind*. Cambridge: MIT Press.

Booth, P. B. 2003a. Personal communication with author. June 7, 2003.

———. 2003b. "The Role of Touch in Theraplay." Presentation at the First International Theraplay Conference, Chicago, June 27, 2003.

Bowlby, J. 1969. *Attachment and Loss*. Vol. 1, *Attachment*. New York: Basic.

Bronfenbrenner, U. 1990. "Who Cares for Children?" *Research and Clinical Center for Child Development* 12: 27–40.

Bronson, M. B. 2000. *Self-Regulation in Early Childhood: Nature and Nurture*. New York: Guilford.

Bundy-Myrow, S. 2000. "Group Theraplay for Children with Autism and Pervasive Developmental Disorder." In *Theraplay: Innovations in Attachment-Enhancing Play Therapy*, edited by E. Munns, 301–20. Northvale, N.J.: Jason Aronson.

Eisenberg, L. 1995. "The Social Construction of the Human Brain." *American Journal of Psychiatry* 152: 1563–

Eisenberg, N., and R. A. Fabes, eds. 1992. *Emotion and Its Regulation in Early Development: New Directions for Child Development*. San Francisco: Jossey-Bass.

Emde, R. N., R. D. Bingham, and R. J. Harmon,. 1993. "Classification and the Diagnostic Process in Infancy." In *Handbook of Infant Mental Health*, edited by C. H. Zeanah Jr., 225–35. New York: Guilford.

Erikson, E. H. 1963. *Childhood and Society*. New York: Norton.

Field, T. 2003. "Touch and Touch Therapy." Presentation at the First International Theraplay Conference, Chicago, June 27, 2003.

Field, T., ed. 1995. *Touch in Early Development*. Mahwah, N.J.: Erlbaum.

Flavell, J. 1964. "Private Speech." Paper presented at the annual meeting of the American Speech and Hearing Association, San Francisco.

Gray, C. 1996. "Gray's Guide to Neurotypical Behavior: Appreciating the Challenge We Present to People with Autistic Spectrum Disorders." *Morning News*, 9–13.

Greenspan, S. I., and S. Wieder. 1993. "Regulation Disorders." In *Handbook of Infant Mental Health,* edited by C. H. Zeanah Jr., 280–90. New York: Guilford.

———. 1998. *The Child with Special Needs: Encouraging Intellectual and Emotional Growth*. Massachusetts: Perseus.

Harlow, H. F., and R. R. Zimmerman. 1959. "Affectional Responses in the Infant Monkey." *Science* 130: 421–32.

Harter, S. 1992. "The Relationship between Perceived Competence, Affect, and Motivational Orientation within the Classroom: Process and Patterns of Change." In *Achievement and Motivation: A Social-developmental Perspective,* edited by A. Boggiano and T. Pittman. New York: Cambridge University Press.

Jernberg, A. M. 1979. *Theraplay: A New Treatment Using Structured Play for Problem Children and Their Families*. San Francisco: Jossey-Bass Publishers.

———. 1983. "Therapeutic Use of Sensory-Motor Play." In *Handbook of Play Therapy*, edited by C. E. Schaefer and K. J. O'Connor, 128–47. New York: Wiley.

———. 1993. "Attachment Formation." In *The Therapeutic Powers of Play,* edited by C. E. Schaefer. Northvale, N.J: Jason Aronson.

Jernberg, A. M., and P. B. Booth. 1999. *Theraplay: Helping Parents and Children Build Better Relationships through Attachment-Based Play*. 2nd ed. San Francisco: Jossey-Bass.

Karen, R. 1994. *Becoming Attached: Unfolding the Mystery of the Mother–Infant Bond and Its Impact on Later Life*. New York: Warner Books.

Kopp, C. B. 1992. "Emotional Distress and Control in Young Children." In *Emotion and Its Regulation in Early Development: New Directions for Child Development*, edited by N. Eisenberg and R. A. Fabes. San Francisco: Jossey-Bass.

Lindaman, S. L., P. B. Booth, and C. Chambers. 2000. "Assessing Parent–Child Interactions with the Marschak Interaction Method." In *Play Diagnosis and Assessment,* vol. 2, edited by K. Gitlin-Weiner, C. Schaefer, and A. Sandgrund. New York: Wiley.

Main, M., and J. Cassidy. 1988. "Categories of Response to Reunion with the Parent at Age 6: Predictable from Infant Attachment Classifications and Stable over a 1-Month Period." *Developmental Psychology* 24: 415–26.

Main, M., and J. Solomon. 1990. "Procedures for Identifying Infants as Disorganized/Disoriented during the Ainsworth Strange Situation." In *Attachment in the Preschool Years: Theory, Research, and Intervention,* edited by M. T. Greenberg, D. Cichetti, and E. M. Cummings. Chicago: University of Chicago Press.

Makela, J. 2003. *What Makes Theraplay Effective: Insights from Developmental Sciences.* Presentation at the First International Theraplay Conference, Chicago, June 27, 2003.

Malatesta, C. Z. 1990. "The Role of Emotions in the Development and Organization of Personality." In *Socioemotional Development.* Lincoln: University of Nebraska Press.

Myrow, D. L. 1997. "In Touch with Theraplay." *Theraplay Institute Newsletter,* Fall 1997, 1–4.

———. 2000. "Applications for the Attachment-Fostering Aspects of Theraplay." In *Theraplay: Innovations in Attachment-Enhancing Play Therapy,* edited by E. Munns, 55–77. Northvale, N.J.: Jason Aronson.

O'Connor, K. 2000. *The Play Therapy Primer.* 2nd ed. New York: Wiley.

O'Connor, K., and Ammen, S. 1997. *Play Therapy Treatment Planning and Interventions: The Ecosystemic Model and Workbook.* San Diego: Academic.

Panksepp, Jaak. 1998. *Affective Neuroscience: The Foundations of Human and Animal Emotions.* New York: Oxford University Press.

Rourke, B. P., ed. 1995. *Syndrome of Nonverbal Learning Disabilities: Neurodevelopmental Manifestations.* New York: Guilford.

Rubin, R., and J. Tregay. 1989. *Play with Them: Theraplay Groups in the Classroom.* Springfield, Ill.: Thomas.

Shore, R. 1997. *Rethinking the Brain: New Insights into Early Development.* New York: Families and Work Institute.

Siegel, D. J. 1999. *The Developing Mind: How Relationships and the Brain Interact to Shape Who We Are.* New York: Guilford.

———. 2003. "An Interpersonal Neurobiology of Psychotherapy: The Developing Mind and the Resolution of Trauma." In *Healing Trauma: Attachment, Mind, Body, and Brain,* edited by M. F. Solomon and D. J. Siegel, 1–56. New York: Norton.

Solomon, M. F., and D. J. Siegel, eds. 2003. *Healing Trauma: Attachment, Mind, Body, and Brain.* New York: Norton.

Sroufe, L. A. 1995. *Emotional Development: The Organization of Emotional Life in the Early Years.* Cambridge: Cambridge University Press.

Vygotsky, L. S. 1962. *Thought and Language,* edited and translated by Eugenia Hanfmann and Gertrude Vakar. Cambridge, Mass.: MIT Press.

Zeanah, C. H., ed. 2000. *Handbook of Infant Mental Health.* 2nd ed. New York: Guilford.

Zeanah, C. H., O. K. Mammen, and A. F. Lieberman. 1993. "Disorders of Attachment." In *Handbook of Infant Mental Health,* edited by C. H. Zeanah Jr., 332–49. New York: Guilford.

Zimmerman, B. J., and Schunk, D. H., eds. 1989. *Self-Regulated Learning and Academic Achievement: Theory, Research, and Practice.* New York: Springer-Verlag.

Zivin, G., ed. 1979. *The Development of Self-Regulation through Private Speech.* New York: Wiley.

4

Embodiment-Projection-Role: A Developmental Model for the Play Therapy Method

Sue Jennings

Embodiment-projection-role (EPR) is a developmental paradigm that uniquely charts the progression of dramatic play from birth to seven years. Based on extended observations with babies and young children, as well as pregnant women, it provides a parallel progression alongside other developmental processes such as physical, cognitive, emotional, and social.

EPR is value free: it does not rely on a particular school of psychological theory. Indeed, it can be integrated into any psychological model or therapeutic or educational practice.

EPR charts the dramatic development of children, which is the basis of the child being able to enter the world of imagination and symbol, the world of dramatic play and drama. The early attachment between mother and infant has a strong dramatic component through playfulness and role reversal. Even in pregnancy the mother is forming a dramatic relationship with her unborn child.

Competence in EPR is essential for a child's maturation:

- It creates the core of attachment between mother and infant
- It forms a basis for the growth of identity and independence
- It establishes the "dramatized body": the body that can create
- It strengthens and further develops the imagination
- It contributes to a child's resilience through "ritual and risk"
- It enables a child to move from "everyday reality" to "dramatic reality" and back again, appropriately
- It facilitates problem solving and conflict resolution
- It provides role play and dramatic play, which in turn create flexibility
- It gives a child the experience and skills to be part of the social world

Embodiment-projection-role are the *markers* of life changes, which are ritualized through playing and drama from one stage to the next.

During the E stage we can see how the child's early experiences are physicalized and are mainly expressed through bodily movement and the senses. These physical experiences are essential for the development of the "body self": we cannot have a body image until we have a body self. The child needs to be able to live in his or her body and feel confident about moving in space. The changeover from the E stage to the P stage is a time of transition, which is also a marker where Winnicott (1974) describes the "transitional object." It can be a piece of cloth or soft toy. Both texture and smell are important, being linked to the child's sensory experience. It is usually considered the child's first symbol—usually representing the absent mother figure. The transitional object is both ritualized and creative. It has to stay the same, even though it might become grubby, and it is named; but it also changes and becomes a mask to hide behind, a blanket for a doll or a scarf for a costume.

During the P stage the child is responding to the world beyond the body, to things outside the body. The child's responses may well be physical, for example, when a child plays with finger paint. But the important point is that the paint is a substance outside the body boundaries. As the P stage develops, children not only relate to different objects and substance but place them together in shapes and constellations. We see an increasing use of stories through the objects such as the dollhouse or puppets. Then there is a second stage of transition as the child decreases projecting roles and stories through the puppets and begins to be the characters. The second transition may be marked with different kind of objects, maybe an object of authority. It may be a stick or a sword or a specific costume that allows the child to take control and direct the action as well as being in the action.

Eventually the child starts to take on the roles, sometimes several in a scene, and we can observe the emergence of the R stage. There is a development of "what is right" for a scene or a role ("mummies don't do that" or "monsters walk like this"). Not only are roles acted but scenes are directed and there is an increasing awareness of design.

It is as if the child has fully integrated E, P, and R as they create plays with movement, costumes and props, and various characters. Usually the three stages of E and P and R are completed by age 7. However, it does not stop there. We continue to visit these stages in preteen and teenage development, not always in the EPR sequence. Nevertheless they are experimented with, tried, and tested as identity continues to develop. Finally we make choices as adults based on the stage that we have dominance in, and usually take up jobs and hobbies that have either an E or P or R focus.

Conflict or distress can ensue if we make a life choice that is not based on our own choosing but comes from the pressure and expectations of others.

EMBODIMENT

Most of our early physical and bodily experience comes through our proximity to others: usually our mothers or carers (I shall continue to use the word "mother" in a generic sense of the person who cares for us).

We are cradled and rocked as we cooperate with rhythmic rocking and singing. Babies respond and mothers respond again, as there is a collaborative approach to physical expression. Already the movement takes on some ritual/risk qualities: on the one hand we engage in ritualized rocking movement and on the other bounce up and down with glee.

I learn about my own body by being bodily engaged with another; thus I am mimetically engaged (see Wilshire 1982, chaps. 3–4).

The body is the primary means of learning (Jennings 1990), and all other learning is secondary to that first learned through the body. Therefore children with bodily trauma need extended physical play in order to rebuild a healthy, confident body.

A child's embodiment development can be distorted through the following:

- Being overheld; the child who is overprotected, overdependent; there is a perpetual fused state and a blurring of body boundaries. The child is always physically "with" the mother and has never separated and been "against" her (Sherborne 1990, 2001)
- Being underheld; the child who is left for long periods of time in isolation; develops anxiety rather than autonomy, is mistrustful and often confused about body and spatial boundaries
- Being violated through physical or sexual abuse; the child's bodily boundaries are invaded with resultant trauma and confusion; there is often fear and anxiety and either an avoidance of physical contact or inappropriate physical rage or unboundaried touch

Many therapists find it difficult to consider using embodiment in their work because of traumatic experiences in the child's or therapist's past, or with the ever-present fear of misunderstood touch and possible litigation. There are several solutions: work in groups and do group movement, which is very good for social development—working in pairs then threes and so on or explain clearly and in detail to the child and the parents that touch is involved, with a description of what touch and why, and have it built into the contract. Parents will usually understand that appropriate touch is important for the healing of the child, and indeed it is possible to have embodiment workshops for the whole family.

Having said that, not all movement has to involve touch and there are many healing movement games for the child and therapist to do together. You may also work with various props such as hoops, string, or silk scarves;

the scarf establishes a contact with the child through the scarf. This is especially useful for autistic children.

Embodiment techniques include the following (see Sherborne 1990, 2001;
Jennings 1995, 1998, 1999):

- Gross body movement involving the whole body
- Fine body movement with different body parts
- Sensory movement involving textures, sound, taste, smell, and sight
- Singing games which name body parts as they are touched
- Rhythmic movement and dance
- Sword play and wrestling
- Creative ideas of moving as monsters, aliens, mice
- Stories with sounds and movement

It is important for the therapist and play worker to feel comfortable with
movement and dance and to have additional training in these areas.

Case History

Sarah was referred for play therapy because at age 8 she was an extremely
tense child, neat and orderly, polite to extremes, watchful and wary. She
would greet me as a fellow adult and ask about my weekend and was very
solicitous toward my health. She would be grateful and thank me for materials and for the session. She would always say that she was fine. I knew she
was witness to scenes of extreme domestic violence and was very much the
"little mother" to younger siblings. However, these were not talked about
and only alluded to as people being "unwell."

She told me she loved drawing, and children have the freedom to start with
whatever they want from the choices in my story room. It used to be called
the playroom but I changed it to appeal to all age-groups: I go into more detail about the space and equipment later. I made sure that a range of drawing
materials was available for her. She initially chose charcoal, but then changed
to pencil and created pictures of formal houses and landscapes which she
then painted. She painted in a very controlled way, mixing colors until they
were just right and using a range of brushes to get the desired effect: all very
focused projective work. This lasted for several sessions until we talked about
her having her own box to put her things in and she decided to decorate the
box both inside and out. She started painting with the finger paints but using
a brush and I asked her whether she would like to use them as finger paints.
She looked at me and said, "I haven't done that since nursery school," and
proceeded to paint her hand with the paints. This made her very frustrated so
she scooped some paint and pressed it between her hands. Unexpectedly for
her it made 'farty' noise, at which point she burst into endless giggles—the

first time she had laughed since coming to see me. So now she was quickly finger painting her box in order to have more paint to make rude noises. She was now in the embodiment stage, having been in very controlled projection. She is slowly becoming more relaxed as her play is less controlled, and her sessions are a combination of embodiment and projection combined with a little storytelling; she is not yet ready to take on roles. The next major stage of her play is described in the section on projection.

Transition 1

Around 12–14 months we can observe the time of transition from the body to the world "out there," the world of projection and objects that are separate from my own body. As Winnicott (1974) has suggested, the first attachment to an object—often soft and cuddly such as a blanket or shawl—marks the transition to other objects, just as the attachment to the primary carer will lead to healthy attachments to other people.

However the object itself, as stated above, it not just a ritual symbol, representing the absent mother; it is also a creative object that can turn into many things and be played with. It almost always has a name and it has to stay the same (woe to anyone who puts the transitional object [TO] in the washing machine), but it also becomes personified and is talked to; it can be a hiding place or a mask. The TO is a prime example of flexibility and of ritual and risk (see Jennings 1998 for the ritual/risk balance in play therapy structures and assessment).

PROJECTION

As children develop more and more into the P stage, we notice they move from exploratory play, where things are tasted and tested, to more patterned and organized play with objects, to more dramatized play with stories. Although it has these variations it is still projected play—beyond the body—and objects take on roles and meanings rather than the child.

Without confusing the issue, we could even say that the P stage has EPR stages in it as described below. However it is clear on closer examination that all the activities are projective ones.

- E: when the child is sensorily exploring media such as finger paint and water play
- P: pure projection when bricks are built, patterns are made, pictures are crayoned, collages are created
- R: when stories are told with the dollhouse or puppets or scenes made with animals (sculpting)

Projective techniques include the following (see Oaklander 1978; Jennings and Minde 1993; Cattanach 1994; Jennings 1995, 1999; Astell-Burt 2001):

- Play with substance: sand, water, finger paint, clay, Plasticine
- Play with pictures: crayons, paints, drawing, collage with varied media
- Play with bricks and counters: patterns, constructions, "all fall down"
- Play with toys: sand tray stories, sculpts
- Play with scenes: dollhouse, puppets (making puppets too)
- Play with natural media: pebbles, bark, twigs, leaves

Children can be encouraged to create in different media, and therapists can create at the same time so the child does not feel scrutinised. The child and therapist can cocreate an artistic construction, thus building a shared endeavor. Creating with the child is not the same as either imposing on the child or directing the child.

Case History

Sara, whom we met earlier, made a major shift in her play after her messy play (embodiment and projection) seemed to run its course; she went from finger paints to clay over several weeks. There was a return to formal work that coincided with another outburst of domestic violence. I had at last acquired my large circular sand tray, about which I describe elsewhere (Jennings 2003). This seemed the stimulus for Sara to get into story mode and she created elaborate constructions in the sand while recounting a mythic-style narrative that I wrote down for her. This was typed up for her on the word processor and she had it to read the following week. The following is her first story, told as she was making a fortress and moat in the sand tray with a large number of archetypal people and animals.

Once upon a time there was a wicked old hag. She took the beautiful fairy princess of Avela and took the mighty treasure of King Bartholomew, and also his beautiful twin daughters, Helga and Thelga. She imprisoned them in a fortress with evil dragons, a dinosaur, and two fearsome gorloks and a phoenix.

Many brave men and women tried to rescue them. They tried to cross over the bridge but none could get past the phoenix. Others tried to swim across the moat but the place was heavily guarded with gorloks and fearsome dragons. Others met with the witch herself and were doomed as a toad in the murky marsh.

One day a group of friends—a phoenix, three centaurs and two warriors—went to rescue them. The phoenix destroyed the phoenix and helped destroy the dinosaur and the dragons, not to mention the fearsome gorloks.

They poisoned them—struck them with spears—kicked them—and set fire to them on the bank—and then with their swords went to rescue the princess—they killed the hag—breathed fire on her—stabbed her from behind—slashed her with a sword—and kicked her.

They returned the girls—returned the treasure—and the warriors married the twin princesses—the phoenix finds a mate and the centaurs do the same—the beautiful princess finds a handsome prince in the fair land of Avela—the treasure is returned to King Bartholomew.

It is remarkable how physical this story is with a lot of very intense violence, and anger on behalf of the narrator. However, the ending is neat and tidy, which she longs for in her life, for things to be predictable. Sarah is not yet playing the roles but with the vivid characters she is describing, she is very near. This story, apart from any other thought that we might have about its content, is an example of some integration of E, P, and R.

Transition 2

We can observe toward the end of the P stage that a child's play is becoming more and more dramatized with stories and scenes being enacted from newly created stories or stories that already exist. A child is developing her own narrative structure, stories that have a beginning, a middle, and an end. Children are increasing their capacity for free play, what adults would term improvisation, where you start with a topic or an object and see where it goes. We could also refer to it as stream of consciousness, which may well feed into a later narrative structure, but is a quality and skill that is invaluable as a life skill.

During this transition we can observe children become their own directors and the directors of others as they organize events and create plays in which they both perform and direct. They often acquire symbols of authority such as sticks, swords, magic batons, or special uniforms or costumes. They are able to exist separately with their creativity as well as being part of pair or small group.

ROLE

Role may be summed up as follows: I learn about myself and others through taking the role of the other (see Mead 1934; Smilansky 1968; Wilshire 1982; Jennings 1990, 1998; Berg 1998; Schaefer et al. 2000).

Dramatic play, or the R stage, is the culmination of the primary EPR stages and is usually complete by about age 7. We can see a difference in the "drama" of children at this age from the "dramatic play" of the years before. Dramatic play involves the child taking on roles in stories from texts or through improvisation, and involving the therapist and other things in the role: chairs draped with material, large toys and so on, can all take on roles in the scene. Children may make and wear masks, and masks need to be a part of the play therapist's equipment. It is crucial that the character and the scene and indeed the space are "de-roled" (Jennings 1990) before the session is ended. The child needs to be very clear what belongs to the "dramatic reality of the story or the play, and what belongs to the everyday reality of the child's and therapist's worlds. Anything is possible within the drama, and the dramatic play gives permission to do things that in everyday life would not be permissable or wholesome" (Jennings 2002).

> Mead should have said that we both actually feel some pain by this pretending pain. By yelling as if you were scared you get scared. By weeping you get sad. By dancing with a person you fall in love. By taking the part of a role play you can become the person you are acting. The play of children is full of this wonderful self-generating expressivity. (Berg 1998)

It is important for children to have the opportunity to play distanced roles—those that are in stories and plays—because the paradox is that children are likely to come nearer to their own experience than if they enact their specific, immediate situation. This is the paradox of drama: I come closer by being more distanced (Jennings 1998).

This also is the hardest thing for therapists to handle because we want to know what is going on. We have invented interpretation in order to explain things and probably reduce our own anxiety. At another level we "know" what is going on and certainly the child knows. Maybe we have to learn to bear "not knowing" to stay with the chaos and allow the meaning to emerge.

Role techniques include the following (see Slade 1954, 1997; Chesner 1995; Cattanch 1997; Jennings 1990, 1998, 1999):

- Use simple roles with single feelings: the angry person, the sad person; and maybe draw the faces of the people
- Create animal characters that interact
- Use favourite stories to enact together
- Use the dressing up box to allow a dramatised story to emerge
- Use a mask as a starting point for a story
- Use the idea of writing a TV script together and then enact it
- Use ideas that have been generated through projective play

CASE HISTORY

Tom was referred for low self-esteem and anger management because of the sudden outbursts of temper he has within the family. He is a nonidentical twin, both boys, and is the older by ten minutes. He is almost sixteen, bright and sure of what he wants to do: he wants to go to the local college and work with cars. Although I requested interviews with the whole family, only his mother was prepared to see me. She said she longed for some peace and quiet and Tom was the cause of everything. He was angry, shouted, made unreasonable demands, and was not at all like his popular, intelligent twin. She said that he had been angry all his life; he was born angry. I asked if any other people in the family were angry and she said that her husband had rages and that her mother was angry and strict. I asked her how it was living among so many angry people and her eyes welled up with tears. She said it was terrible and she was exhausted and went to bed very early to get away from it all. She then said that Tom was the one who had to change; she could not expect the others to change, which is why he was seeing me.

The early sessions consisted of discussion led by Tom about how difficult everything was and how things were just unfair. Whatever he did was never good enough and his mother was constantly saying that she was disappointed in him. He was desperate to shine in her eyes and had virtually no communication with his father apart from the huge rows about anything and everything. He did a little drawing, which did not engage him, but he leaped at the chance to do drama. We used masks and cloths on chairs to set various scenes that were difficult at both school and home. He took all the roles and I acted as narrator of the scene. We practiced various strategies to stop the rows emerging or at least modify them once they got under way. Tom had a chance to practice between sessions and report back the next time.

I was clear in my planning that this should be a brief intervention to build confidence in Tom and foster coping strategies, and also the knowledge that he had been heard and believed. Little else could be done unless the main players in the family would come to address the issues of scapegoating and blame. There are complex issues regarding the sexual health of the family, not necessarily at a reality level but definitely at the fantasy level. For example, when Tom and I discussed a social club where he could meet new people and find new interests, his mother's reaction was that the people who went were not nice and would only teach him dirty things. Indeed it was shortly after this occasion that she wanted Tom to stop coming immediately. Tom and I negotiated a number of sessions to practice necessary skills and to work at closure, and in the end his mother agreed. He has finished this work now and is somewhat wistful at leaving. However, he has some solid armory there to try and assist him deal with his situation in the short term, and he has commented that once he can leave home he might well come back to see me.

This example of some role work with an adolescent is very focused and goal oriented. Tom made use of his enthusiasm for playing roles to explore in a very immediate way what is currently taking place at home. A dramatic distance is created through the use of the masks and cloths. It needs to be a brief intervention since the home situation will not change. Tom should know that his is succeeding and is not a disappointment, and that his anger is justified. He now has some strengths to continue with less stress, until he is able to leave home. This example illustrates how EPR stages are revisited during adolescence.

CONCLUSION

We have considered how embodiment-projection-role forms the basis of human dramatic development and therefore can be applied in play therapy both for assessment and application. Horley (1998) has done extensive research using the EPR method in order to identify children who are "non-players." She suggests that dramatic play is a "situation where role playing becomes more complex and includes dressing up, developing dialogue and creating environments within which to play different roles. Scenes and stories are enacted with peers being included although there may be some situations of a child playing in a dramatic way on their own."

EPR can be integrated into all approaches of psychology and play therapy, although it works more efficiently where therapist and child can cocreate the scenes and activities together. The early roots of EPR can be traced to pre-birth experience in the dramatized relationship between mother and unborn child (Jennings 1998, 1999), so we can say that the infant is born already "dramatized."

It is important that therapists using EPR both reexperience these stages for themselves as well as making observations of children in these stages. This research is still being developed and play therapists are encouraged to test it in their own research.

Assessment through EPR is written up in Jennings 1998 and 1999; you also need to be aware of Courtney's developmental checklist in Jennings 1998. Above all, the approach to play and play therapy through embodiment-projection-role focuses on the playful attachments and resilience that develop through playing. This is essential to the child's healthy maturation and forms a basis for future relationships.

The starting room for the play therapy method is a light, airy room with a raised stage taking up a third of it. There are simple costumes, hats, cloths, and masks, a messy area for clay and paint work, and a variety of archetypal figures of varying sizes for work on stories. There is a large circular sand tray with a variety of miniatures as well as stones, shells, bark, and sticks. There is also a sand tray for wet play. Children (and adults) choose which medium they wish to work in and it may be to create stories or to retell their own stories. We can dance and paint, dramatize and make masks as a piece of cocreation or self-direction.

REFERENCES

Sue Jennings's videos and publications are from Rowan Studio, 33 Hill Head, Glastonbury, Somerset, BA6 8AW, UK. Please contact Sue Jennings for information on International Training Courses in EPR and The Playtherapy Method© at drsuejennings@hotmail.com.

Astell-Burt, C. 2001. *I Am the Story: The Art of Puppetry in Education and Therapy*. London: Souvenir.
Berg, L. E. 1998. "Developmental Play Stages in Child Identity Construction: An Interactionist Theoretical Contribution." Draft paper presented to the OMEC Conference, Copenhagen, 1998.
Cattanach, A. 1994. *Play Therapy: Where the Sky Meets the Underworld*. London: Jessica Kingsley.
———. 1997. *Children's Stories in Play Therapy*. London: Jessica Kingsley.
Chesner, A. 1995. *Dramatherapy for People with Learning Disabilities*. London: Jessica Kingsley.
Horley, E. 1998. "Developmental Assessment of Dramatic Play." Paper presented at OMEC Conference, Copenhagen, 1998.
Jennings, S. 1990. *Dramatherapy with Families, Groups, and Individuals*. London: Jessica Kingsley.
———. 1995. "Playing for Real." *International Play Journey* 3: 132–41.
———. 1998. *Introduction to Dramatherapy*. London: Jessica Kingsley.
———. 1999. *Introduction to Developmental Playtherapy*. London: Jessica Kingsley.
———. 2001. *Embodiment-Projection-Role*. Video with Gordon Wiseman. London: Actionwork.
———. 2002. "Play, Drama, and the Brain." Paper presented at the International Symposium Arts and the Brain, Oslo.
———. 2003. *Embodiment-Projection-Role 2*. Video. London: Actionwork.
Jennings, S., and C. Minde. 1993. *Art Therapy and Dramatherapy: Masks of the Soul*. London: Jessica Kingsley.
Mead, G. H. 1934. *Mind, Self, and Society*. Chicago: University of Chicago Press.
Oaklander, V. 1978. *Windows to Our Children*. Utah: Real People Press.
Schaefer, C. E., H. E. Jacobson, and M. Ghahramanlou. 2000. "Play Group Therapy for Social Skills Deficit for Children." In *Short-Term Play Therapy for Children*. Edited by C. E. Schaefer and H. G. Kaduson. New York: Guilford.

Sherborne, V. Movement system from Concord Films, Ipswich.

———. 1990. *Developmental Movement for Children*. Cambridge: Cambridge University Press.

———. 2001. *Developmental Movement for Children: Mainstream, Special Needs and Pre-school*. London: Worth.

Slade, P. 1954. *Child Drama*. London: Hodder & Stoughton.

———. 1997. *Child Play*. London: Jessica Kingsley.

Smilansky, S. 1968. *The Effects of Sociodramatic Play on Disadvantaged Preschool Children*. New York: Wiley.

Wilshire, B. 1982. *Role Playing and Identity*. Bloomington: Indiana University Press.

Winnicott, D. 1974. *Playing and Reality*. London: Penguin.

5

Barriers, Bridges, Breakthroughs: Play Work with Autistic Spectrum Children

Shoshana Levin

The referring information accompanying three-year-old Dave concluded that Dave suffered from autistic spectrum disorder (ASD). The middle child of three, Dave was exhibiting a cluster of worrisome developmental symptoms: a strong tendency to isolate himself in his own world of books and computers; expressive language difficulties, including echolalia and lack of the pronoun *I*; and frequently nearly mute behavior. Dave was in imminent danger of being expelled from his nursery school because of his tendency to scream and then completely undress when frustrated. Other professionals were urging his parents to place him in a special kindergarten setting for communication-impaired children.

The parents of three-year-old Sara wrote in anguished detail of her developmental problems: loss of sparse language at an early age; a largely mute presentation with occasional jargon (gibberish); poor eye contact; selective hearing; toe walking; a restricted repertoire of foods she was willing to eat; and overall significant developmental delay. Seen previously at several clinic settings, Sara had been diagnosed as suffering from pervasive developmental disorder (PDD). Special education had been recommended.

Three-and-a-half-year-old Sam had been diagnosed elsewhere as PDD with autistic features. Referral reports described his lack of eye contact, almost complete lack of expressive language, much jargon, stubborn resistance to being held or cuddled, lack of purposeful play behavior symbolic or otherwise, and frequent intense temper tantrums.

Fast-forward to the writing of this chapter, and we find Dave a precocious, verbal, socially well-adjusted fourth grader who is thriving in a regular school. Sara, nearly six years old, still evidences traces of her earlier developmental delay; but she has begun to use expressive language, meaningfully repeats many of the words and phrases spoken to her, loves to play dolls with her three sisters, increasingly shows warmth and delight in physical and emotional closeness, and benefits from her integrated kindergarten setting. Sam, now seven, possesses a charismatic and alive personality with a fine sense of humor. His eye contact is warm and meaningful. His language is nearly fluent with a well-developed vocabulary. He loves to create elaborate pretend play scenarios and act them out; and he has adjusted well to a small special first grade class where he is ably learning to read and write.

Each of these children at a very young age had exhibited complex clusters of symptoms related to serious communication impairment and developmental delay. All had been diagnosed previously in other settings as suffering from a variation of ASD or PDD. Their encouraging progress, which runs counter to earlier prognoses, is a tribute to the courage and hard work of their parents in adopting a worldview different from many approaches commonly used with PDD and ASD youngsters, and to parental perseverance in seeking like-minded therapists and educational settings to assist these children in the transition from pathology toward more normative functioning.

What paradigms can be employed to meet the type of challenging barriers that Dave, Sara, and Sam presented and to help them grow and change? This chapter discusses three extant theoretical paradigms from varying fields, each of which offers distinctive concepts, ideas, and strategies which have the potential to significantly enhance the progress of autistic spectrum children: child-centered therapy (Axline 1947); Feuerstein's theories of structural cognitive modifiability and mediated learning (Feuerstein, Rand, and Hoffman 1979); and the "floor time" or DIR model of Greenspan and Wieder (1998).

These disparate paradigms, each with its own unique contribution to child development from the fields of child psychotherapy, educational psychology, and child development respectively, can find common ground in the realm of play, acknowledged as a powerful catalyst in the overall process of child development (Garvey 1990). Play can serve as a basis for qualitative functional assessment of the autistic spectrum child (when applying Feuerstein's theories), as media for parent–child interaction (when using the DIR model), and as the route to the initially inaccessible inner world of such children (when working according to the principles of Axline).

This chapter begins with essential background on problematic assumptions prevailing in the field of autism and with a general consideration of the usefulness of play in assessing autistic conditions. The order of the presentation of the three core theoretical paradigms reflects a personal odyssey, as it parallels the authors own chronological exposure to them. Following the presentation of these paradigms as they apply to both autistic children and the realm of play, the discussion returns to the stories of Dave, Sara and Sam in order to better understand how they sometimes overlap in applications of these paradigms, with work grounded in play, can help create bridges of connection with children suffering from severe developmental and communication impairments.

Work with autistic spectrum children can be highly demanding, frustrating, and often very humbling. The children's struggles find a parallel in my own professional odyssey. Exactly one month after completing doctoral studies in play therapy, I was on the plane to Israel to carry out a postdoctoral research project on autism at the center directed by educational psychologist Reuven Feuerstein. I faced not only the transition from generally comfortable North America to stressful and often resource-poor Israel, but also a complete turnabout in clinical focus: I had been trained to prioritize the emotional realm, yet the center specialized in cognitive/developmental profiles. I arrived fairly confident in using longer-term child-centered treatment strategies, yet the center focused on child assessment and consultation to parents. In addition, life and work in Israel required mastering spoken Hebrew. Dave, Sara, and Sam, and many other children like them, were not the only ones growing and changing.

ASSUMPTIONS WORTH QUESTIONING

A pall of pessimism regarding the developmental potential of the autistic spectrum child hovers over much of the related professional literature. This atmosphere of pessimism strongly influences many treatment approaches whereby parents are advised to accept the child's limitations. Often parents are informed that while some skill improvement may occur, they should not expect meaningful, global improvement.

This pessimism evidently derives from several core assumptions that are widely, but not universally, accepted within the field. The primary assumptions resounding in the field are that autism has biological, genetic, and/or neurological causes; that autism may be treatable but is not curable; and that mental retardation, as measured by conventional tools of assessment, is intrinsic to the autistic child (Frith 1989).

Granted, an accruing body of research employing cutting-edge medical research techniques has established some biological, genetic, or neurological correlates to the autistic condition (cf. Frith 1989). Yet even though science has ascertained some physiological correlation (e.g., differentially sized brain chambers; excess or lack of certain neurotransmission chemicals), we must still question, challenge, and wonder whether the concreteness of science has captured fully the nuances and mystery of human development as regards autism. For example, do the results of such studies define *causes*—or have they revealed biological/neurological *effects* of development gone awry? As later discussion summarizes, the entire topic of the diagnosis of autism currently leads to many false positives. Can we be certain that all of the children researched were truly autistic? Perhaps an entire range of developmental abnormality is being studied, not only autism. The fundamental question is whether biological givens, if they indeed exist, must *determine* the functioning of the child. The career-long work of Feuerstein, for example, powerfully illustrates how a corrective environment can override much of the influence of biological givens and create unexpected degrees of positive change in an impaired person (Feuerstein and Rand 1997).

Regarding the assumption of incurability, the field of autism is currently operating largely from the medical model: a "cure" is being sought for autism as if it were a disease, even as many professionals paradoxically maintain that autism is incurable (Frith 1989). When a developmental, rather than a medical, model is employed, a sea change in perspective results. Biological givens are acknowledged but, when placed in a developmental context, are not necessarily interpreted as determinants of autism. From a developmental perspective, the expectations of the child's abilities rise because we refocus on the environmental factors that are within our control and begin to weight these factors more heavily. We are no longer seeking a "cure" for a medical condition but the most effective composite of developmental treatments to bring about the most favorable changes possible.

Concerning a tendency to assume associated mental retardation, even the *Diagnostic and Statistical Manual of Mental Disorders* maintains that "in most cases, there is an associated diagnosis of mental retardation, which can range from mild to profound" (DSM-IV; American Psychiatric Association 1994, 71). However, the assumption that retardation is inherent to the autistic condition can and really must be reframed in a developmental context. Retarded functioning or retarded performance does not necessarily mean retarded potential (Feuerstein and Rand 1997). If the child has not performed in a specific developmental area to date (e.g., language), as documented by a conventional test, can we say with 100 percent certainty that the child lacks the ability to develop language?

Conventional testing generally assesses performance, not latent potential. Most conventional testing requires verbal abilities to score and a basic level of task orientation in order for the child to even begin to function on a test. In the case of the autistic child, both of these areas are usually impaired at the start. The playing field for these children is uneven, so to speak. I often use the following analogy to help parents understand the limitations of conventional assessment and help them consider that their child may be more intelligent than IQ or performance results suggest: "If you put masking tape on my mouth and handcuff me, then ask me questions or have me tasks to perform, I will not be able to respond, not because I cannot or do not know the answers. I am prevented from answering and performing." It is critical to unlock the autistic child's latent communicative potential, to tap the virtual gag and handcuffs, and to release them from their developmental restrictions *before* conventional intelligence testing can be considered meaningful with this population. While some of these children may indeed prove in the end to have limited mental abilities, an automatic presumption of mental retardation is a dangerous one (Feuerstein and Rand 1997).

As stated, not all intervention paradigms for autistic spectrum children take these common assumptions at face value. The paradigms of Feuerstein, Greenspan, and Wieder, and others (e.g., Kaufman 1995; Tinbergen and Tinbergen 1983), may implicitly acknowledge biological, hereditary givens but in practice they then launch proactively into multifaceted treatment programs in order to: raise developmental expectations of the child; treat the child as whole being rather than focus on isolated skills; and avoid the discouraging self-fulfilling prophecies that often derive from application of the assumptions under discussion. While the work is challenging and one cannot presume instant improvement with such children, it is important to unfetter oneself from automatic pessimism regarding the potential of the autistic or autistiform (autistic-like) child and to work energetically and hopefully toward change.

ADVANTAGES OF PLAY-BASED ASSESSMENT

The determination of a diagnosis of ASD or the even more ambiguous term PDD is a theoretical and practical minefield fraught with dangers. The primary danger, of course, is that of false positives of the ASD or PDD diagnoses which, in our estimation, proliferate. A much-warranted in-depth look at the highly problematic issue of conventional methods of diagnosing autism or PDD is beyond the scope of this chapter. However, it is important to highlight some of the thorny issues of conventional diagnosis as a counterpoint to understanding and appreciating the potential contribution of play-based assessment. Play-based assessment, in our view, can help the practitioner arrive at more meaningful, individually accurate, and developmentally relevant information than the rigid and often ill-supported technical diagnosis by conventional means. It was information gleaned from play-based descriptive assessment strategies, as per the theory and practice of Feuerstein, that helped peer beyond the presenting diagnoses of Dave, Sara, and Sam and that revealed insights into their potential strengths, previously masked by conventional diagnostic means.

When Kanner (1943) first summarized his clinical observations of severely emotionally withdrawn and language-impaired children, and applied the term "autism" to that condition, he identified two key diagnostic criteria: an extreme emotional "cut-offness" and an obsessive insistence on sameness. Kanner's criteria, still today the "golden standard" of true autism (Cytryn

1998), are noteworthy in intimating that true autism is an extreme human phenomenon.

Regrettably, the understanding of autism as an extreme developmental condition has gotten lost in the diagnostic shuffle, as conventional means of assessment tend to tally symptoms while failing to take into consideration the impact of the degree of the autistiform symptom or, more importantly, the capacity of the symptom to be modified (Feuerstein and Rand 1997). The early autism behavior checklist (ABC; Krug, Arick, and Almond 1980) lists symptoms to which the practitioner answers yes or no to such items as: spins objects, actively avoids eye contact, seems not to hear. The sum total of symptoms beyond a certain numerical threshold, without an in-depth consideration of symptom gradations, yields a positive diagnosis of autism.

The Childhood Autism Rating Scale (CARS; Schopler, Reichler, and Renner 1988) does consider gradations of symptoms, with a five-point scale related to frequency and intensity of such symptom clusters as relating to people, object use, and adaptation to change. Summing points leads to the determination of whether autism is mild, moderate, or severe. With the CARS, the question arises as to whether such symptoms must be considered monolithic and unchangeable. That is, even if a symptom is intense and frequent, can it not be modified?

The more current Autism Diagnostic Observation Schedule (Lord et al. 1989) is modular: one of a possible four graduated assessment modules is used with the child depending on the child's level of speech development. Practitioners code responses and establish a diagnosis based on cutoff scores. The fact that none of the modules can be used with entirely nonverbal children is problematic.

Even the widely accepted foundational diagnostic criteria in the DSM are of themselves problematic. The DSM criteria for autism center around three primary clusters of developmental difficulties, namely: qualitative impairment in social interaction, qualitative impairment in communication, and a restricted and repetitive repertoire of stereotypical behaviors. Each of the three clusters contains four possible criteria, with a sum of six of the twelve (within a certain array), yielding a positive diagnosis. The degree of "qualitative impairment," ranging from minimal to severe, is not reflected within the twelve possible criteria, creating a situation in which a child with even a mild communication difficulty can potentially be misdiagnosed as autistic.

The DSM description of PDD-NOS (not otherwise specified) is just that: a catchall term with no specific diagnostic criteria cited. It is widely and inaccurately used synonymously for mild autism, while the criteria for autism of itself remain much too elastic and a far cry from the extreme criteria identified by Kanner. It is not surprising, then, that our clinical experience reveals a plethora of misdiagnoses for autism as well as near-epidemic use of the term PDD.

Yet it is indisputable that the children whom we see are experiencing developmental and communication difficulties. If they are not truly autistic, and if the term PDD offers no real diagnostic insight, then how can we identify the children's difficulties and, most importantly, how can we help them? By switching from the quantitative tallying of symptoms to a qualitative understanding of the conditions under which symptoms appear or diminish (Feuerstein, Rand, and Hoffman 1979). By deemphasizing the listing of symptoms and instead actively seeking to engage the child behind the symptoms. And by using play activities as a basis for assessment and intervention.

Play possesses the developmental power to reach into the interstices of the child's innermost world and abilities. For several generations, play theorists and practitioners have researched the catalyzing influence of play in core developmental areas: cognition and learning (Bruner, Jolly, and Sylva 1976); attention span (Ruff and Lawson 1990); fine and gross motor development (Payne and Isaacs 2001); sensory stimulation (Berk 1994); personality development and emotional growth (e.g., Allan 1988); language development and motivation for communication (Mundy et al. 1987). Play when viewed in a developmental context functions as a two-way street. Play activities possess the potential to enhance and strengthen a given developmental realm. Conversely, the child's play serves as a virtual mirror. The child's functional levels within given developmental realms are directly expressed through the child's play activity. This power of play can be harnessed as a tool of enormous functional power in assessing core developmental strengths and difficulties in a child thought to be autistic.

While means of formalized play-based developmental assessment do exist (cf. Schaefer, Gitlin, and Sandgrand 1991), in assessing Dave, Sara, and Sam and many other children like them, a combination of careful observation followed by active engagement with the child in play activities has yielded rich developmental information and has provided concrete direction for a plan of intervention. This method of using play activities as the milieu of assessment, based on the principles of Feuerstein (with parallels in the work of Greenspan and Wieder) has been more fully elucidated elsewhere (Levin 1997). In essence, instead of listing symptoms, the practitioner seeks evidence of the modifiability of the child's autistiform symptoms. In both observation and interaction phases of assessment, the practitioner constantly seeks answers to questions that pertain to the frequency, intensity, appearance of symptoms and, in particular, the dynamic conditions that cause symptoms to diminish.

The silent self-talk of the practitioner working in this way during the observation phase of play-based dynamic/qualitative assessment might unfold something like: "The child has been in the room for twenty minutes and has not yet looked at me. He looked at his parents briefly. When dad takes out a musical toy, the child smiles in recognition. The child is purposeful as he digs through mom's purse for a candy. Mom's humming relaxes the child and yields a little more eye contact." The practitioner observes carefully how and when developmental strengths appear, no matter how faintly, and under what conditions symptoms diminish in intensity or frequency.

During the active play phase of the assessment, the practitioner seeks to understand qualitatively as per Feuerstein's theories and in congruence with the sensory emphasis as developed by Wieder and Greenspan. Which play activities create a sense of contact with the child? Does the child like action or calm? Raucous noises or soft, gentle sounds? Does the child show improved eye contact with such kinesthetic experiences as tickling and rocking? Or does soft humming help the child move closer? Are there any islets of symbolic play understanding? What kind of play activities get babbling or vocalization going? Does gentle or firm massage help this child stop hand flapping? Can boisterous play such as jumping or spinning help this avoidant-looking child to display a sense of pleasure or fun? Which play materials help elicit a sense of contact? Can the child solve play-based problems such as finding a lost ball?

A meaningful play-based assessment of an autistiform child may begin with an activity as simple as blowing bubbles, jumping with the child, or providing the simplest props for symbolic play. Important information can be gleaned. For example, the child's lack of eye contact may not be absolute. The quality of eye contact may change from avoidance or seeming indifference to a look of curiosity and delight at the colors and motion of bubbles. Through the "safety" of a screen of bubbles, the child might even be prepared to risk a little direct eye contact. Similarly, many silent children suddenly burst into excited babbling when lifted repeatedly in front of a mirror. They enjoy the brief sense of weightless freedom. The excitement of being lifted can even surprise a child out of an avoidant repertoire into warmly shared laughter. As well, autistiform children may reveal that they possess an incipient sense of self and understanding of the concept of empathy, when they show an interest in symbolic play (e.g., in an activity as simple as offering the doll a bottle).

It is primarily through play, in our experience, that examples of non-symptomatic or even normative behavior can be found, symptoms can be revealed or coaxed to be modifiable, and a sense of connection, whether verbal, vocal, or nonverbal, can be made with the autistiform child. It is play that enables the practitioner to move beyond misleading presumptions and statistical summation to achieve dynamic contact with the child. While children with ASD and PDD diagnoses are clearly experiencing developmental difficulties, the uniqueness of their individual profiles and, more importantly, their potential to change are more often than not masked or obscured by these very diagnoses.

By applying the type of play-based assessment summarized here, it has been possible to look beyond the presenting diagnoses and to discern more specific explanations and etiologies for their conditions. Play-based assessment modeled on the theories of Feuerstein (following) has yielded such differential diagnoses as: hearing processing difficulties; giftedness with an imbalance between visual and expressive modalities; normal children with oral dyspraxic conditions; specific expressive language difficulties unrelated to autism; sensory hypo- or hyperreactivity affecting the child's overall developmental profile; borderline, pre-, or post-psychotic conditions; undetected hearing loss; and garden variety developmental delays that were essentially not pathological. Though experiencing developmental trouble, the vast majority of those previously diagnosed as ASD or PDD were not suffering from true autism nor were their developmental difficulties necessarily pervasive. Their strengths went unrecognized behind the all-encompassing fit into the superelastic criteria of ASD or PDD.

In all, play materials and activities offer virtually limitless opportunities for making contact, exploring the presence of the child's inner affective world, and exploring the potential modifiability of autistiform symptoms. Play activities may range from active, sensory-motor-based play—such as tickling, swinging, rocking, cuddling, jumping—to quietly drawing the child into connection using interesting toys such as a ball that lights up or a musical jack-in-the-box. We have often found that painstaking observation of the child coupled with active play provides a much clearer picture of a child's developmental strengths, weaknesses, avenues for emotional connection, and evidence of the modifiability of symptoms than instruments which sum symptoms as uniform, unchangeable entities. Yet engaging the autistiform child in play activities is a challenging and not at all simple enterprise. Fortunately, the clinical paradigms of Axline, Feuerstein, and Greenspan and Wieder provide more than theoretical interest. They light the way, and each offers unique conceptual and practical guidelines for this challenging population.

APPLYING CHILD-CENTERED PLAY THERAPY PRINCIPLES

A therapist well-grounded in the principles of child-centered play therapy actually already possesses foundational tools for launching into meaningful work with autistic spectrum children. Several, though not all, of Axline's (1947) eight core tenets of child-centered play therapy underlie the therapeutic attitude helpful in beginning to work with autistic children. Axline identified the following tenets: warm rapport, acceptance of the child, a permissive attitude, recognizing and reflecting feelings, respecting the child's choices, following the child's lead, not pushing the pace, and minimal limit setting.

Warmth can be sensed by autistiform children, even though initially their difficulties may not enable them to respond to warmth directly. A therapist's gentle tone of voice and the therapist's own comfort with silence can help convey a message of underlying belief in the child, that behind the symptoms, the practitioner knows that "someone is home." We have repeatedly observed how the nonverbal communication of warmth and acceptance of themselves can encourage frightened or cut-off autistiform children to dare to make a little more eye contact or to venture into more active, sensory-motor play.

Rather than trying to "train away" or to limit certain symptoms in a disciplinary manner, a stance of acceptance and the corollary permissiveness set the stage for further work. A significant body of research, as exemplified by Prizant (1983) and Yates (1986), supports the notion that there exists an inherent intentionality of communication in the symptoms of the autistic child. They are not nuisances that must be trained away. The autistiform child's typical hand flapping, spinning, or lining up of objects can be considered expressive of emotional states such as tension, excitement, happiness, fear. As such, they may be interpreted as attempts at nonverbal communication. Even though we might not be able to "read" the actual meaning of the symptomatic behavior, we can certainly *respond* to the child's symptoms as meaningful, and thus use the behavioral symptom as a building block to first nonverbal and then verbal communication (Greenspan and Wieder 1998): "You really like to line those cars up all by yourself. You don't want me to have even one!" The practitioner who is operating from a stance of rapport, acceptance, and permissiveness even of the unusual behaviors of autistiform child, and who is sensitive to the latent intentionality and meaning inherent in the child's behaviors, is already laying the groundwork for entering into a sense of contact with the child.

A few of Axline's tenets, in our experience, require modification when applied to the autistic population. Verbal reflection in the early phases of work can often intrude on a sense of connection with the child. Initially, nonverbal contact through gentle baby play, sensory or motor activities, the use of music, or even silence, seems to be a much more powerful communicative tool. In later work, once the child begins to change, the practitioner's verbal reflections of the child's feelings or verbal description of the child's actions can have a powerful developmental valence. Often parents and practitioners stop speaking to the autistiform child as a person, believing that "the child doesn't understand anyway." In our experience, it is essential for parents and practitioners to speak to the autistiform child, who deep inside is hungry for the sound of the parents' voice. Speaking to the child helps lay the child's receptive language groundwork for the scaffolding of later expressive language. The timing, intensity, and frequency of verbal reflections to the autis-tiform child pose challenges to practitioners, as these depend so clearly on the level of permeability of the child's autistiform shell.

Axline's notion of respecting the child's choices and following the child's lead is important in principle in working with autistic-type children. Moving in too quickly and demanding behavioral "performance" can cause the child to withdraw emotionally or to resist. We have found that the most effective play-based strategies to help build a sense of relationship and communica-tion with the ASD child begin with the adult's respect for the child's initial choices of activity and play style. (Greenspan and Wieder's play intervention strategies rest on this very premise.) While it is important to note and respect the child's sensory and activity preferences, the child's own choices more of-ten than not serve as a starting point, with the adult needing to respond much more actively, proactively, and even directively than in classic child-centered therapy.

In general, the practitioner who is imbued with child-centered principles is likely to be comfortable in reading the play language of the child; at ease with nonverbal communication; experienced in using play materials to make contact with children; and committed to operating from a sense of deep em-pathy for the personhood of the child behind the perplexing and challeng-ing symptoms.

In launching into qualitative/functional or dynamic assessment work, as termed by Feuerstein, it therefore felt quite natural when working with autis-tic children to flow with and to support the child's actions, initially accept the child's symptoms, and to try to tune in to the emotional or communicative intent that might be present in the child's nonverbal behavior (e.g., anxious hand flapping, fearful eye contact, excited and happy jumping). Yet I often encountered the feeling that I was moving down a river that was ultimately dammed shut. A sense of empathic understanding was helpful in attuning, and an attitude of permissiveness helped me not to panic in the presence of certain unusual behaviors. Yet there was so often a sense that the child and I were getting stuck in the same place. The sense of movement that play therapists enjoy in child-centered play therapy with higher functioning chil-dren, watching them take charge and blossom before our very eyes, seemed to elude me in my early work with seriously communication-impaired chil-dren. Refraining from pushing the pace with higher functioning typical chil-dren so often leads to spontaneous growth. Yet not pushing, not proactively influencing the pace with the ASD and PDD child seemed to lead to a dead end. The question that took shape, however, was how best to maintain a re-spectful stance for the humanity of the impaired child and belief in the child's potential to grow beyond difficult symptoms without simply getting stuck with the child. Subsequent exposure to other paradigms helped to an-swer that question.

FEUERSTEIN'S TENETS OF MODIFIABILITY AND MEDIATION

Feuerstein's far-reaching theories within the field of educational psychology are not generally familiar to therapeutic play practitioners. However, in their forward-looking philosophical attitude, with concepts and strategies that stress the actualization of the child's potential, the internalization of the essence of Feuerstein's theories, I have found, can strengthen one as a practitioner.

Educational psychologist Reuven Feuerstein, a protégé of Piaget, began his pioneering work in the field of educational psychology more than two generations ago. His lifelong work with special needs populations of virtually all types and ages, such as Down syndrome, learning disabled, gifted underachievers, stroke victims, and many others, rests firmly on the theoretical bedrock of his term "structural cognitive modifiability" (SCM; Feuerstein and Rand 1997). SCM theory states, in essence, that the very propensity of the human being for cognition can be modified. Unique within the field of educational psychology, the term refers to much more than the notion of specific skill acquisition, such as learning to count or to read. SCM theory posits a process of fundamental change in the orientation of the learner toward learning in general. This change is "structural" in the sense that it becomes a permanent part of the individual's functioning. Beyond skill acquisition, there is an all-encompassing change in the ability of the learner to absorb, process, and convey new information. The learner's overall willingness and ability to engage in a learning process are entirely modified.

Embedded within SCM theory is the insight that the basic responsiveness of the human being and the ability to change are not, and should not, be solely or even primarily determined by the dictates of genetic makeup, physiological impairments, environmental constraints, age, or even the assumptions deriving from a given clinical/diagnostic category. While all of these factors unarguably influence development, Feuerstein's SCM theory maintains that the quality of the conscious, purposeful, sensitive, and active input of the adult teacher or mediator possesses the power to override many genetic, diagnostic, prognostic, and similar "givens" to create meaningful change within the individual.

The theory of SCM represents a positive philosophy, an optimistic belief in the ability of the human organism to change. However, this optimistic belief system is not a naive one. Rather, the theory is sensitive to the insight that human beings generally grow according to the expectations imposed on them, and that human beings possess an inherent ability to overcome obstacles to growth—that is, the ability to change. Had these ideas remained only in the world of theory, they might have been wrongly dismissed as simply wishful thinking. However, SCM theory has spawned the development of learning potential assessment instruments (Feuerstein,

Rand, and Hoffman 1979), tools for the development of metacognition (Feuerstein, Rand, Hoffman, and Miller 1980), hundreds of research studies, and groundbreaking clinical work with special needs and typical populations (Feuerstein and Rand 1997). Current research on brain plasticity, which demonstrates the changes in brain cells and brain neurotransmissions as a result of the intensity of external stimuli (cf. Kandel, Schwartz, and Jessel 2001), scientifically substantiates what this forward-looking theory proposed two generations ago.

When the clinician working with autistic spectrum children adopts and internalizes the principles of SCM, the practitioner approaches autism not as a terminal condition from which change can never be possible but rather as a starting point from which change must ensue. We acknowledge that the child before us presents, at times, with an overwhelming sense of impairment and *apparently* intransigent symptoms. However, when we apply SCM, we recall that the human organism, by its very nature, contains within it the propensity for growth and change. The fact that autistic children present an extraordinarily difficult challenge does not mean that they are beyond change. When we conclude so, we may be only acknowledging our own sense of frustration or failure with them, which I have naturally experienced as well. There is no need, however, to project our frustration and discouragement onto the autistic child. If we internalize the notion that the human being is inherently modifiable, we are forced to persevere in our efforts to bring about change, which at first may be so subtle as to be practically microscopic. With SCM in mind, the practitioner will not conclude, as is all too common in the field today, that the child is necessarily doomed to a life of retarded function. While one would never falsely promise change, it is important to attempt to work with the expectation that the propensity for modifiability is part of the human condition, and that autistiform children are worthy of and can surely benefit from this worldview.

The core process of helping the individual to achieve potential is that of effective mediation by the adult toward the child or learner. An in-depth discussion of mediated learning experience (MLE) is beyond the scope of this chapter (cf. Feuerstein, Klein, and Tannenbaum 1991; Feuerstein and Rand 1997). Essentially, mediation is the conscious, focused effort of the adult to translate the outer world in such a way that the child/learner can absorb the information efficiently on the level of input and to assist the child/learner on the level of output to express verbally, effectively, and accurately thoughts and understanding. A mediated learning experience is one that is characterized by active intentionality and reciprocity. The adult works to ensure that the child can apply knowledge learned to other realms (transcendence) and that the units of learning acquired are melded to the overall thinking patterns because they have been relayed to the learner in a meaningful way. While the play practitioner may find these terms unusual

at first, internalizing the essential meaning—that one works with intentionality to convey and help the child express meaning—has clear implications
for work with autistic children.

This discussion of mediation, SCM, brain cells, and cognition appears on
the surface to be so distant from the spontaneous, symbolic richness of the
world of play therapy. Yet, Feuerstein's SCM theory in a sense resonates in
kind with Axline's belief that the troubled child possesses the ability to overcome emotional difficulties. While the focus and means of each theorist dif-
fers, cognition on one hand and emotion on the other, the themes of inherent modifiability (Feuerstein) and the child's latent ability to overcome
emotional difficulties (Axline) are bridgeable. In actual practice, internalization of the SCM purview meant that I would not automatically assume that
the initial presentations of Dave, Sara, Sam, and many others like them represented the limits of their expressive and developmental abilities. Rather,
their initial presentations were just the beginning of their stories.

PRINCIPLES OF DIR OR FLOOR TIME INTERVENTION

The DIR method is also not yet widely known in play therapy circles. The
method possesses both strong commonalities with play therapy practice as
well as some clear differences. As developed by Greenspan and Wieder
(1998), DIR is a form of parent-directed and therapist-coached interactive
play intervention, commonly known as "Floor Time." This graphic term
helps emphasize the focus and realm of activity: down on the floor with the
child and playfully attuned to the child's presenting state. The initials DIR refer to a developmental approach (D), sensitive to individual differences (I),
and relationship-based (R). Greenspan and Wieder have elucidated their
theory and its practical applications in numerous sources (Greenspan 1992;
Greenspan and Wieder 1997; Greenspan and Wieder 1998). This discussion
summarizes the essentials of that approach.

Greenspan and Wieder, who began by researching normative infant development in a relational context, identified six phases of early child development, whose end result should be a communicative, playful, relational
child who can learn from and respond to the environment through rich language, symbolic play, and emotional investment. These clinicians further
identified a functional developmental goal or milestone that is necessary for
the child to achieve in order to successfully negotiate progress to the next
phase. The phases and milestones are not rigidly sequential. There is a dynamic overlap with an overall progressive developmental direction.

In the first phase of self-regulation, the infant must be able to move back
and forth smoothly between states of excitement or stimulation and states
of calm. In this phase, the infant should be able to sustain early interest in

the world without becoming overly stimulated and overwhelmed on one hand or without lapsing into prolonged avoidance or withdrawal on the other.

Drawing heavily from the sensory integration literature in the field of occupational therapy (cf. Ayres 1964), Wieder and Greenspan have particularly weighted their understanding of early childhood development toward attuning to children's patterns of sensory reactivity. Is the child undersensitive or hyporeactive to various sounds, colors, textures; or is the child oversensitive or hyperreactive, to such stimuli? Is the child's sensory profile a complex mix, hyposensitive to some stimuli, hypersensitive to others? The child who screams because of the blender's whirring may be hypersensitive to this particular auditory stimulus. An infant's gazing at the ceiling for hours might reflect an underreactive profile.

In this model, adult attunement to an infant's or child's sensory preferences and degree of reactivity can impact strongly on the process of development. For example, the hyporeactive baby lying passively in a crib for hours needs the input and stimulation of active parental strategies. By this model, the mother who is calm and quiet herself would need to learn strategies to help her baby energize, using sensory and motor play in order to help the infant display more active interest in the world. Similarly, a highly reactive infant, screaming at each new sound, movement, or texture, will require parental strategies that convey soothing.

The infant who is not caught at the extremes of being too overwhelmed or too avoidant is able to progress to the next phase of achieving a sense of intimacy. The infant now responds to parental overtures for contact with signs of pleasure. Or the infant may exhibit displeasure or distress when the adult is unavailable. In this phase, long before language emerges, the infant is learning about the primary emotional reality of warmth in a nonverbal dialogue of emotional reciprocity. Warm eye contact, a tiny smile, pleasure at supportive touch, or distress when warm contact is interrupted—all indicate that the infant is learning the basic language of emotional exchange.

Building on this ability to delight in and share emotional energy, in the next phase the toddler or young child begins to show signs of achieving simple two-way communication. This level of communication is largely preverbal but continues to lay the foundation for speech. An infant engages in two-way communication when s/he returns a parent's cooing sounds or even shares meaningful eye contact in a peek-a-boo game. The young child engages in two-way communication through even the simplest of nonverbal gestures: s/he reaches out to be picked up, or takes mother's hand to open the door. The dialogue of intimacy through amorphous feelings begins to assume a more tangible form in gestures, imitative movements, imitative vocalization (babbling), and nuance-laden eye contact in response to the situation. A parent's ability to respond to and participate in these preverbal exchanges thus strengthens the child and lays the foundation for the next phase, that of achieving complex communication.

In the phase of complex communication, the infant, toddler, or child can respond purposefully with a series of gestures, vocalizations, and/or words to achieve a desired goal. The child remains communicative through words, touch, gestures, play activity, or a combination of these in a relational context. The key in this phase is the chaining of elements of communication, for example, the child whimpers, looks at mother, walks over to her, pulls her hand toward the shopping bag, urges her to take out a bag of chips, and says "Mmm." Here the child has successfully chained several preverbal communicative components to achieve a goal within a relational context.

As complex communication skills evolve, the young child approaches the next developmental stage of expressing emotional ideas. The DIR term "emotional ideas" parallels the common understanding of symbolic play. The child can now begin to develop and initiate symbolic play ideas (e.g., putting dolly to sleep). Fluency with the world of symbols emerges. This may be through play, language, pictures, and/or spoken language—all of which begin to assume meaning and bear expressive value for the child. Beyond the realm of immediate needs, the young child is now able to express feelings and ideas, even if in rudimentary fashion, through a varied repertoire of symbols.

The sixth phase, logical thinking, encompasses higher-level chaining of ideas and affect. The child can respond to or initiate play ideas and, further, can link play ideas together in logical sequences ("First dolly wakes up, then she goes to the park"). Cause and effect connections appear in the child's play and speech: "Bad dolly gets a spanking and no dinner. Next time no spilling." Or, "The doctor put Gramma in the hospital because she was sick." Or even: "Why raining?" More complex language, higher-level thought processes and reasoning, along with the ability to express these through a varied repertoire of symbolic behavior, have emerged via a process of increasingly intricate emotional and communicative reciprocity.

Wieder and Greenspan posited that these six identified phases and milestones of normative child development can be understood and utilized as a developmental blueprint to be achieved by the impaired child. The entire thrust of DIR intervention, then, is to help parents proactively employ specialized play techniques that have the power to move the child up the developmental ladder: from a state of regulated attention to the world, to engagement in a milieu of warmth and intimacy, to two-way communication that is at first nonverbal and then verbal, to coaxing the child into pretend play skills and comfort with the expression of ideas, and, finally, toward helping the child develop notions of problem solving and patterns of more advanced thinking.

DIR intervention views parents as pivotal to their ASD child's development, along with the addition of multidisciplinary therapies. In contrast to the filial therapy model in which parents are trained primarily in verbal reflective techniques (Guerney 1964), in the floor time model parents are coached to use creative play techniques that attune to the child's developmental stage and sensory needs to work toward achievement of the identified milestones. Parents learn nonverbal and preverbal play strategies so that they can playfully build reciprocal communication with children in whom reciprocity at first appears to be entirely lacking. As the ASD or PDD child begins to engage, parents are coached to expand the child's functionally expressive repertoire, and ultimately, to expand the child's rudimentary verbal and symbolic play ideas.

Wieder and Greenspan have coined the term "circles of communication," which is, in a sense, a unit of meaningful interactive communication. The baby smiles (opening a circle of communication) and mother smiles back (closing the circle). Mother then sings to baby (opening another circle), and baby smiles and coos with pleasure (closing another circle) and waving her arms (opening another circle). The ASD child's perseverative door banging, instead of being considered annoying evidence of developmental pathology, becomes reframed in this paradigm as a potential opening for communication by the responsive adult. How to close such a circle? Wieder and Greenspan suggest, for example, that the adult get behind the door and turn the perseverative activity into meaningful interaction, perhaps by making each closure part of a peek-a-boo game. Or, a parent might playfully apply pressure to the door so that the child will even more actively try to close it, creating a nonverbal dialogue of action between parent and child. Even a child's protest can be seen as an expression of meaningful contact with the world, with each response offering another opportunity for an adult's communicative response.

Play activities and a playful attitude are intrinsic to every phase of DIR intervention. In the early developmental levels of this model, the play strategies are particularly attuned to sensory or vestibulatory (movement) needs: holding, rocking, swinging, or tickling the child. The parents of the screaming autistiform child overwhelmed by the sound of the vacuum cleaner may learn to hold or rock him gently while softly humming to achieve calm. There are playful object-focused strategies to help children move toward relationship. For example, if a child routinely lines up small cars in a row without averting his or her gaze from them, parents may be coached to playfully hoard the rest of the cars and tuck them one at a time into pockets. This playful maneuver forces the child into a circle of communication, perhaps digging into dad's pocket or looking into dad's eyes with an expressive whine. In the higher developmental stages, parents are coached to add verbal strategies to their play repertoire, creating little problems for the child to solve, introducing new ideas, challenging the child, and playfully encouraging the child to link ideas in a play context. Mother: "But dolly doesn't want to go to sleep. She's still very hungry and upset. How can we help her?" To achieve maximum benefit, the creators of this paradigm encourage parents to carry out DIR or floor time strategies for several hours daily. When clinical experience is grounded in the reflective child-centered approached of following the child, often the most difficult aspect of mastering the DIR strategies is the need to do the polar opposite: "play dumb" and appear not to understand; be proactive and initiate play ideas; allow dissonance and frustration to prompt reaction and relationship.

UTILIZING UNIQUE PARADIGMS

Child-centered play therapy from the field of child psychotherapy, SCM from the realm of cognitive development, DIR rooted in child development— these three paradigms arise from disparate fields but each offers practical contributions to play-work with autistiform children. For the clinician who may wish to variously apply aspects of these three paradigms, the end result is not a new consolidated paradigm, for each paradigm maintains its own integrity, but a wealth of possibilities.

The belief in modifiability as formulated by Feuerstein provides inspiration and direction needed for the play-work. Like a beacon, a belief in inherent modifiability guides the clinician to continue seeking changes, openings, bridges, and new evidence of connection or breakthroughs. The deeply rooted empathic attitudes of child-centered play therapy provide the clinician with strength of purpose in the face of perplexing behaviors. The DIR model offers a developmental perspective and specific interactive play strategies.

Sometimes the work might demand that the clinician begin in a client-centered stance, of quietly accepting the child and supporting his or her choices. At other times, proactive DIR type strategies are required from the first moments of contact. Invariably, the underlying belief in the child's intrinsic modifiability, coupled with active mediation through play, guides the way to change.

Naturally, there are times when, sensing that no clear strategy is helping to open the door to the child, I discard all preconceptions and try whatever I can—playfully—to reach the child. It is not so much a matter of techniques borrowed, although these are certainly helpful, but of purpose and attitude. For Dave, Sara, and Sam, change resulted when we learned what each child had to teach.

Dave's Story

A relatively brief series of play sessions from a general, child-centered perspective initiated a process of positive developmental change for Dave.

Dave's serious developmental difficulties, previously diagnosed as ASD in another clinic, were blatantly apparent on Dave's first visit: sparse expressive language, frequent echolalia, and avoidant eye contact. As noted earlier, these difficulties were seriously overshadowed by the fact that Dave was about to be expelled from nursery school because of his tendency to strip off his clothes when frustrated.

When he first entered the office, I beheld a spare and vulnerable child, just over three years old, with fear reflected in his dark eyes. His parents looked close to despair. In this new setting Dave was extremely anxious. He clung to his mother in fear. Letting Dave wander about the room to find his own level of comfort, I observed that his eye contact was poor toward me but better toward his parents. He appeared to be repeating in the barest whisper a few words he overheard. This echolalia was interspersed with much unclear jargon. Early in the session Dave did not attempt any symbolic play with the toys laid out on the carpet. In a short time, anxiety flooded him. He began to scream and cry. In one deft move he peeled off his shirt and opened the office door. He continued to scream as he ran through the corridors, undressing as he fled. His mother dashed after him, scooped him up, and brought him back, panicked and overwhelmed.

Despite his level of fear, since his parents were present in the room, I decided to lock the office door. This was done first of all to allow the door to "do the talking," so that I would not have to actively tell him "no" repeatedly. Naturally, this move initially induced further screaming, but ultimately it served to contain his fear. Drawing comfort from his parents' hugs, Dave began to calm. By the last fifteen minutes of the ninety-minute initial assessment session, he had calmed enough to begin to explore some of the toys on the floor.

Dave sat down beside the small dollhouse with its furniture and human figures. He mumbled to himself as he looked through the windows and doors of the dollhouse for several minutes. As he explored, Dave was very quiet, with occasional jargon or a barely decipherable word. Sensing an opening to nonverbal contact with him, I quietly lay on the carpet in such a way that it was possible to make a little eye contact with Dave from the other side of the dollhouse. He peered at me cautiously through the dollhouse window. So as not to overwhelm this highly reactive and fearful child, I decided to keep words to a minimum; my vocal tone remained soft, slow, and gentle in order to keep his anxiety level down. Silently initiating a play idea, I arranged little chairs around the tiny table on the "lawn" of the dollhouse. Dave quietly put some tiny figures in the chairs and in the faintest whisper said, "Birthday party." Dave possessed incipient symbolic understanding! The child figures seated together had triggered a fleeting but emotionally meaningful association and prompted verbal expression.

It was a challenging start. Working in this session primarily from the viewpoint of SCM theory, I was looking for evidence of changeability of his initial symptoms. Even microscopic evidence of change can be meaningful. Dave had shown that he was capable of calming via interaction with his parents and of achieving enough calm to be able to explore play materials in a rudimentary symbolic fashion. Within his jargon and echolalia were embedded appropriate words. Dave's most pressing problem, however, was beyond the bounds of the office: days earlier Dave had finally been expelled from his nursery school. I advised his parents to look for a small home-based nursery school with few children and a warm caregiver, and to avoid putting him in a special nursery for communication-impaired or ASD youngsters. Yet, with such a high degree of reactivity, and his screaming/undressing behavior, how long could Dave last in the new setting without some help?

With his parents' enthusiastic agreement, I decided to launch a series of six client-centered play sessions with Dave. In keeping with basic play therapy practice, the goal of these sessions was to provide Dave with a safe and protected space in which to express the intermingled rage, fear, panic, and sadness which so often flooded him. Hopefully, a short-term intervention would serve to trouble-shoot the intensity of his panic reactions and stabilize him enough to be able to adapt to the new nursery setting. Fortunately, this hypothesis proved correct; and the next six sessions, with child-centered play as their focus, helped move Dave along.

At the first of these sessions, Dave clung to his mother, who sat opposite me. To keep Dave and his fears contained, with his mother's consent I again locked the office door. Clinging to his mother, Dave cried and screamed for twenty-five minutes, during which time I sat calmly and tried to appear non-threatening. When Dave's sobs subsided, I quietly placed a couple of teddy bears on the desk. Dave looked at me and angrily flung one of the bears to the floor. It was an opening! Thinking "nonverbal empathy," I flung the other one in mock anger to the floor after him. Dave smiled—another promising opening. I brought out more stuffed animals. Dave began flinging these, too, as I offered them to him one at a time. Sometimes I also took turns "angrily" throwing the stuffed animals. Dave smiled more frequently and began to calm markedly, clearly enjoying this parallel play activity and "empathy through action" rather than through words. There was a sense of movement in this session.

A week later, Dave again began his session by crying while clinging to his mother. However, this time he cried for only ten minutes. When he calmed, I brought out some stuffed animals. Dave knew what he wanted to do. Soon we were taking turns flinging the animals all over the office. Dave really warmed to this activity. So out came the basket of miniature plastic animals; and these, too, we flung all over the room. Dave calmed further, evidently encouraged by the fact that his rage was not overwhelming the therapist. Nonverbal participation in his play evidently had communicated enough of a sense of emotional safety to enable Dave to become a little more relational.

It seemed safe to add verbal elaboration to our activities. I decided to speak for him, reflecting his feelings in the first person rather than the second person; in a sense, taking on and expressing for him his rage and fear. As I flung some of the animals, I said softly in mock anger, "Yuck! I don't want this crummy bear." Dave brightened. It seemed safe to go a little further. "I'm mad and I don't want this dumb tiger!" Dave continued to calm. The verbal assumption by the therapist of his difficult intermingled feelings served to legitimate those feelings.

Flinging little animals around the office became our play focus for a further four weekly sessions. During the last of these sessions, Dave felt secure enough to climb off his mother's lap and to again explore the dollhouse and furnishings. This time, he did so with more confidence, talking and even singing to himself, with improved eye contact, and more frequent, audible speech.

Dave's parents and the caregiver in his new small nursery setting reported dramatic improvement in Dave's overall presentation and behavior after the first three toy flinging sessions. Dave was calmer, warmer, and more relaxed at home, with far fewer temper tantrums. Though still anxious, as when parting from his parents, Dave was coping better and beginning to follow the other children in his nursery, playing in parallel. Once, he became flooded with fear and peeled off his clothes in the nursery, but the caregiver handled this event calmly and supportively. Dave was able to calm and return to the nursery activities. In parallel with these mood improvements, Dave began to speak more and in a more audible tone. Vocabulary improved and sentence length grew incrementally. His jargon diminished. Dave's parents excitedly reported that he was beginning to show interest in symbolic play with small figures at home.

Following this series of play sessions, nondirective in spirit, Dave and his parents participated in follow-up visits, at first every few weeks, then monthly, and then with decreasing frequency as Dave improved and his progress stabilized. For about a year during follow-up sessions, the focus remained on building Dave's symbolic play skills, his ability to express affect, and cause and effect relationships through play.

As Dave improved in these areas, the focus of the work shifted toward the mandate of the center where I work, that is, to the cognitive realm. A much-improved though still powerful little personality, Dave at ages 4 and 5 was very intelligent—enough to seek to avoid any learning tasks that emphasized his weaker verbal skills rather than his highly developed perceptual skills. Gradually, Dave's cooperation and functioning in challenging cognitive tasks improved. His parents then sought the help of an occupational therapist expert in sensory integration exercises, whose intervention advanced Dave markedly. After one month of daily massages and eye-hand coordination work by the parents as coached by the occupational therapist, Dave's language blossomed further.

Our recommendations to his parents throughout the follow-up period of several years were far-ranging and reflect the broad range of disciplines that must by taken into consideration when helping a developmentally delayed child improve. We provided guidance on how to mediate effectively according to Feuerstein theory; how to speak with Dave slowly and clearly, emphasizing key words; on techniques for supporting his rudimentary symbolic play; on the importance of limiting video, computer, and television hours; on the necessity of ensuring that he had many symbolic play materials on which to scaffold language development; on the potential usefulness of supplementing conventional medical intervention with qualified alternative practitioners for his frequent ear infections; on Dave's need for "play dates" for social skills practice; and on the importance of maintaining Dave in a regular school setting, supplemented by therapies (as needed) in the afternoon.

Often an early diagnosis of ASD or PDD, like a menacing shadow, trails even the child who has emerged from his difficulties. This was certainly the case with Dave, who at age 5 and 6 was speaking in clear sentences, participating in kindergarten activities, reading fluently and learning ably, although still experiencing mild difficulties with peer contact. It was necessary to meet with his kindergarten teacher several times in order to reassure her that Dave should no longer be considered "ASD" and that he was fully capable of further normative growth. Ultimately, his parents transferred him to a more receptive educational setting.

Now nine years old, Dave is a highly competent fourth grader, active in afterschool activities and well liked by his friends. The fearful child who first entered the office at age 3 displayed severe expressive language difficulties, panic-tinged emotional reactivity, and avoidance symptoms. A series of child-centered play therapy sessions initially forced an intensification of Dave's symptoms in the office. The safe and protected space of the playroom, along with the supportive presence of his mother, helped Dave establish a basis of ego strength. Once Dave was stronger emotionally, it was possible to progress to more developmentally complex goals associated with learning.

Sara's Story

The entire family arrived for Sara's first visit. Two of her three sisters lost no time playing with the toys scattered around the office. The baby fidgeted in her stroller, while her parents sat looking depressed and discouraged, speaking openly of their worries about her PDD diagnosis. Sara walked silently in figure-eight circuits around the room. She avoided eye contact, mumbled largely uncipherable jargon, and occasionally repeated the odd word without affect. When she finally sat down on the carpet, she plunked away on a little xylophone or repeatedly worked a simple color-matching puzzle in silence, without glancing up as the noise and activity of her family swirled around her for the entire session.

Working from an SCM viewpoint at first, and thinking in terms of the kind of environment needed to bring about a change in her worrisome symptom presentation, initial guidance to her parents focused on the necessity of talking to (or "at") Sara, even though she was not responding: "Your child needs to hear the sound of your voice. The child's ability for verbal output depends in no small measure on the level of verbal input addressed to her. Speak to your child despite your discouragement. Talk about what's happening and what's going to happen."

As per the largely consultative mandate of the center, Sara's progress was followed once monthly for two years in a consultation mode to her parents. Sessions generally consisted of two components: (1) play work, through which I attempted to get a "reading" of where Sara was holding functionally in a number of core developmental areas (expressive and receptive language, relatedness, task orientation, focus and concentration, and symbolic play): and (2) consultation to her parents based on the knowledge gleaned through the updated hands-on work with her each session. For example, in working with Sara on simple puzzles, it became evident that using a sing-song voice (for example, singing "Who wants the red one?") prompted Sara to respond with brief eye contact, a little smile, and her own sing-song response ("I want red"). This then became the basis of practical input to her parents: "Try using a sing-song voice to get Sara's attention and eye contact at home. You might trying singing to her around routines, such as 'Time for pajamas. Let's get dressed.'"

Each child has something unique to teach us. Sara was a challenging teacher, and I often felt like a slow learner. For nearly a year, I worked with Sara each month from a nonplay stance, using simple game-based learning activities, such as matching shapes, colors, or pictures, and then proceeding to slightly more challenging preschool learning activities. When I sat at the table directly across from Sara in an attempt to enhance frequency and duration of eye contact, she sometimes sang little ditties such as "I want the red triangle. I want the purple one." Yet these responses seemed wooden and rote.

Like many parents of children with complex communication difficulties, Sara's parents were continually fighting waves of discouragement. Somehow, however, they mustered the energy to begin to speak to her more and to respond to her jargon as meaningful (as Feuerstein's principles of mediation and the DIR term of circles of communication encourage). Eye contact began to improve. More isolated words emerged. In her integrated kindergarten setting that also offered individual therapies, Sara began to happily follow the other children around the kindergarten. She even began some parallel play—largely silently. Her crying tantrums of frustration decreased while her ability to adjust to changes in routines improved.

Progress was slow and painstaking. After cognitive work at the table, I usually brought out a few baby dolls and props. Unprompted, Sara showed emotional interest in the play and an ability to portray rudimentary symbolic ideas: She happily combed the dolls' hair, dressed or cuddled them, cooed to them (often in her jargon), and sometimes mincingly uttered single words as she fed them: "ice cream," "banana."

On one hand, her symbolic investment was an encouraging sign. Sara possessed enough of a sense of self to comprehend the existence of the "other." She was able to pretend, a faculty that the literature usually considers impossible for the truly autistic child (Frith 1989). She related to the dolls with affection as she kissed them, but turned a cold shoulder toward me when I awkwardly tried to offer them some play food or to coax Sara by means of doll play into verbal or nonverbal play interaction with me.

On the other hand, Sara's ability to engage in pretend play left me feeling even more frustrated. The vivacious little girl was missing. Where were Sara's own spontaneous utterances and her warm playful energy? Where was her delight in contact? Her emotional repertoire was all so measured and controlled. These questions ultimately prompted a shift to more proactive, relational, and playful strategies.

Within the first few months of working with Sara, as her eye contact, verbal output, task orientation, and symbolic expression slowly improved, it became clear that she was certainly not suffering from autism, as her personality was much too "present" to fit that category. It was equally clear that the broad term PDD only obscured her difficulties, while offering no real insight into her as an individual. Increasingly, Sara's tight-lipped presentation and emotional restraint suggested that, rather than true withdrawal, Sara was suffering from a degree of elective mutism.

This "new and improved" diagnostic term offered little comfort. When my frustration at her lack of exuberant or warm contact reached a peak, I decided to borrow a few specific DIR strategies. Thinking both clinically and developmentally, the reasons unfolded as follows: "There has been some improvement, and Sara even has some symbolic play skills now; but something is clearly missing in her profile. She is very jealous of her baby sister. Has she received enough of the physical closeness, emotional indulgence, and wooing that she needs? There appears to be a need to move into warmly physical baby play. Instead of attempting to create connection through the dolls, an exercise that has repeatedly proven frustrating in achieving emotional interaction, it seems more important to tune in to Sara's own baby needs, to attend to the developmental phase of regulation of behavior, to warm up her energies and to create initial engagement through active physical play." Following his reasoning, I put the cognitive-based activities on hold temporarily and began to employ strategies typical of her floor time paradigm as suited to the early developmental stages, that is, activities replete with sensory stimulation and/or movement: tickling, rocking, jumping, gentle holding, and simple peek-a-boo games.

With the application of active, sensory-based play, Sara began to unfold. In our monthly sessions, I lifted her high repeatedly as we both faced the mirror. Sara loved the exciting sense of momentary weightlessness and physical support. She maintained eye contact through the reflection in the mirror and delightedly began to count along with me as she jumped. Using the gentlest of touches, I tickled her tummy and toes. Sara looked away but purred with delight. Covering her with a little blanket, I tickled her inside the blanket and combined the game with repeated peek-a-boo. Catching her feet, I playfully held them until the slight frustration prompted her to vocalize in protest.

Such playful interventions helped ignite Sara's natural energies. These baby playtime techniques were easily demonstrated and taught to her parents, one of whom was present in the room in all sessions. They could see for themselves how indulging Sara's infant sensory and emotional needs playfully helped her to come alive and connect. Movement and baby playtime on the most basic level of touch and holding—rocking, catching, and cuddling her—began to unlock a different Sara, whose own energy at last began to emerge.

The monthly consultation sessions took a new turn from the previous somewhat frustrating table work. Sara's mother and I took turns holding Sara in front of the mirror, singing nursery songs to her or with her, and playfully imitating her sounds and hand/body movements as we shared improved eye contact with her via the mirror. Sara loved this warmly indulgent toddler type of play. Sara's mother had often found other types of play with Sara difficult to carry out. These interactive play activities on a largely preverbal level were of clear and immediate benefit to Sara, and her mother felt more confident that she could do them at home with Sara satisfactorily. Sara's mother began playing tickle games, rocking Sara in front of the mirror, or playing peek-a-boo behind a blanket at home. The pace of Sara's progress began to accelerate.

From the perspective of Feuerstein's theories, Sara was benefiting from more effective mediation attuned to the aspect of reciprocity. Viewed through the lens of the DIR paradigm, Sara's parents could be said to be employing play strategies typical of earlier developmental stages. For the play therapist, it is interesting to note that in unadulterated form, floor time practitioners actively coach and train parents in its principles and strategies, who in sessions are encouraged to have much more "hands-on" work with the child than the therapist. With very challenging children, I often find it necessary to try various strategies myself, drawing from a range of options, before I coach the parent, to ensure that the new strategies actually help build the communication flow. In contrast to the common play therapy practice of an hourly session per week, for maximum success in the DIR paradigm, Wieder and Greenspan encourage parents to spend hours daily with the child, employing these unique play strategies. In Israel, where both parents are often working long hours, or mother may be overwhelmed with the care of many more children than the North American norm, it has proven necessary to modify the directives to parents. Sara's parents were encouraged to play with her daily as above, even if only for ten or fifteen minutes, whatever they could manage in a busy household with four children. While hours of warm interactive play would clearly have been even more helpful to Sara, it seemed preferable that she experience brief and frequent play interventions daily rather than longer sessions seldom, or perhaps not at all.

Two years have passed since Sara's first office visit. Though residual evidence of her earlier difficulties exists, significant growth has occurred. Sara is happier and much more confident. She repeats words meaningfully: a welcome echolalia. She is now spontaneously using words, phrases, and three- to four-word sentences with affect. Her eye contact is generally sustained and reflects a range of emotions. Although a tendency toward mutism can still be detected, Sara more frequently presents as alive, alert, engaged, and reciprocal, especially when play intervention focuses on latent infant needs. Each infant or toddler type of play interaction energizes her a little more and provides her with pleasant sensory and emotional stimulation, propelling her to take another developmental step.

Sam's Story

On his initial visit, Sam entered the office with his parents like a whirlwind. He plowed through the toys on the low shelf without engaging meaningfully with any, cried angrily when limited in any way, avoided eye contact, and resisted being held by his parents. He was in constant motion but without evident meaningful focus. In the early half of the session, no words were heard, in part because, at three and a half, Sam refused to part with his bottle, which remained firmly in his mouth. He spoke jargon, engaging in animated gibberish "conversations" with his image in the mirror, and accompanied his jargon with animated hand gestures and prosodic (inflected) vocal tones. While his eye contact with his own reflection bore warmth, this quickly evaporated when he turned toward other people. Any attempts to slow him down or engage him with a play material were met with clear and intense avoidance behaviors: his turning, walking away, or screaming and crying in protest.

Suddenly during this first largely observational session, Sam initiated his own purposeful activity. He moved a small table against my desk, then two little chairs next to the table, creating the means to climb onto the desk. Standing on the desk, Sam yelled, "One, two, three, jump!" and he did. Landing on the carpet, he was clearly delighted with himself. His eyes were bright as he looked directly at his parents and then me with enthusiastic pride in his accomplishment. He applauded himself, expressing by meaningful eye contact that we should applaud and yell "Hurray!" along with him. Encouraged by repeated applause at each landing, Sam continued many repetitions of climbing, counting, jumping, looking at us, and happily applauding with us. In Feuerstein's terms, Sam was responding to the adults' encouragement of reciprocity. In floor time parlance, by counting, jumping, looking, and applauding, Sam was opening and closing many circles of communication.

Against the backdrop of Sam's serious developmental difficulties—overall lack of expressive language, general lack of meaningful play material usage, emotional reactivity, and active avoidance of interpersonal contact—his jumping sequence contained encouraging developmental information. Sam was able at times to organize himself toward meaningful play activity that involved motor planning (arranging the chairs) and vestibulatory stimulation (jumping and landing); he possessed latent language, which included knowledge of counting and a sense of anticipation ("one, two, three, jump"); he was not as entirely avoidant as he had initially appeared, since his eyes lit up with warmth and delight in response to activity and praise. Even his prosodic jargon suggested that Sam was listening to the music intrinsic to language. Yet in this first session, the balance lay in favor of his symptoms. Sam needed help. We advised his parents to find a safe place at home to let Sam jump while they were to provide active, enthusiastic responses to help encourage reciprocity, to chain many circles of communication. It was an unusual beginning.

Many more jumping sessions followed that initial session. During that first school year of work with him, jumping remained a strong focus of activity and relationship. Meanwhile, a speech therapist worked effectively with him that year, helping Sam begin to engage in table work activities such as animal picture lotto. Despite our strong recommendation that Sam be integrated among typical children, his parents decided to enroll him in a small special preschool for autistic spectrum children. The dedicated staff was helpful to him. Sam's attention span during learning tasks improved, as did his confidence. Single words and two-word strings emerged, as eye contact and task orientation improved. Yet Sam still had tantrums and remained largely avoidant. At four and a half, his language and play skills remained seriously delayed and rudimentary.

The next school year, in order to help push his developmental pace, we began play sessions with a strong emphasis on building interactive symbolic play. Through these, Sam moved from avoidant, isolated, object-focused play to parallel, then associative, and ultimately more interactive, cooperative pretend play. In the initial phase of the work, the question that drove our play interventions reflected an underlying premise also characteristic of floor time: how to intervene playfully in Sam's activities in such a way as to transform his solo play into nonverbal, verbal, or symbolic interaction?

Not surprisingly, Sam began the first of two more years of work together with his jumping-off-the-table activity. His father was present at all weekly sessions, and was encouraged to maintain reciprocity, to respond to and reopen circles of communication (by applause, cheers, etc.) in an attempt to capitalize on the unique interpersonal openings embedded in his active play. In the weeks following, Sam became interested in arranging the office tables and chairs so he could crawl under or jump off them. I often attempted to create connection by gently interrupting his play (e.g., to playfully hold a chair to invite protest or to entice him into a peek-a-boo game under the chairs or table). Sam usually responded to these attempts at interaction with a grunt or whine of dismissal. It was difficult to reopen the communication flow as Sam contentedly went about arranging the office furniture.

About a month into our work, noting that Sam liked crawling and hiding, I put out a fabric tunnel. Sam collected a few play materials from the cupboard and disappeared with them into the tunnel. From within the tunnel, we heard a distinct roar—a glimmer of hope! From the hidden safety of the tunnel, Sam revealed that he could assume a rudimentary play role. He was also expressing aggression. I responded that we heard a big lion. Sam could not develop this idea further but it was an encouraging sign.

Sam remained a master of avoidance, still avoiding eye contact when I tried to play peek-a-boo with him at the tunnel opening. Yet he would accept objects passed to him inside, such as plastic food. After several weeks with Sam usually hidden in the tunnel, I decided to store the tunnel in a colleague's room, as my strategies for turning avoidance into interaction using it seemed to be unproductive.

Lacking the safety of the tunnel, Sam was forced back into the reality of the office. Sitting at the little table, an act which of itself reflected progress, two months into the year, Sam suddenly showed interest in the Power Ranger figures and a little dollhouse. His symbolic interest was a small breakthrough in itself, evidence of the higher cognitive/developmental level of symbolic expression and a hint of the Emotional Ideas stage of DIR. Sam repeatedly stuffed the Power Rangers into the dollhouse and slammed the door shut, in a play sequence reflecting purpose and affect. His father or I spoke for the trapped Rangers, as Sam displayed delight in the Rangers' evident punishment. Sam seemed more open to verbal rather than primarily nonverbal responses to his play: "Help! Let us out of here." Sam responded with a smile. Father deftly took a little car and put the Rangers inside. Associating, Sam said, "Tunnel." As his father had been filling elsewhere in principles of floor time, in order to chain circles of communication, father took a piece of cardboard and quickly created a tunnel for the Rangers' car. Sam sustained this simple symbolic play for a while, driving the Rangers from the car to dollhouse and back again, driving them through the cardboard tunnel, with one-word utterances describing the action: "Tunnel. Power Rangers. Car. Going. House."

This rudimentary pretend play sequence accompanied by a simple play soliloquy was another encouraging sign. Another small breakthrough occurred a month later when Sam pretended to cry like a baby, grabbed a small bottle, and wrapped himself in a blanket. A floor time dictum of "expand, expand, expand" came to mind as I gently pulled Sam toward me and cuddled him in my lap, trying to milk this emotionally loaded pretend play segment for all of its interactive, interpersonal content. For several weeks following, interspersed between largely avoidant behaviors or isolated play, Sam would suddenly make forays into my lap, completely covering himself with a blanket.

In those moments, I switched paradigm channels and, rather than be proactive, became quietly receptive. The play therapist voice within cautioned, "This is a very sensitive moment. He is reenacting deep infant needs. Don't do anything that might threaten him or cause him to bolt from his blanket womb." Sam could stay contentedly under the blanket for five to ten minutes.

By December, Sam was uttering some three-word strings. He was more confident, and the frequency of temper tantrums was decreasing. His first cooperative pretend sequence evolved most likely from his earlier baby-in-the-blanket play. Pretending to cry like a baby, Sam lay down on the carpet, covered himself with a blanket and motioned for me to lie next to him. We both pretended to sleep. He maintained his calm "sleep" for several minutes, pretended to wake up and then repeated the sequence. Sam's assuming a role along with another player was significant.

The pivotal session for that school year occurred in February when Sam suddenly swept all the toys off the desk. This in itself was not unusual for Sam, who often did this when frustrated. Humming little songs to himself, Sam astounded us when he flung the blanket over the table like a tablecloth and proceeded to set the table with play cutlery and all the plastic food. He took two large markers and stood them upright. Suddenly we understood. Sam was setting the table as if for a Friday night Sabbath dinner, and these were the Sabbath candles. Sam switched from humming to singing special Sabbath songs. His father, delighted at the complexity of the evolving play and knowledgeable in principles of interactive play, involved Sam in pouring wine, serving us dinner and singing songs together. In this pretend play segment Sam uttered many three- or four-word strings; he also added songs with words and responded to our verbal overtures ("more chicken, please") with appropriate words or pretend play actions. Beyond new play skills evident here, Sam's sense of delight in representing a complete and complex scene was palpable. When for two weeks in a row, Sam set the table, served dinner, and happily sang songs with most of the words intact, we knew he had crossed a threshold.

Over the remainder of that school year, Sam grew in his abilities of symbolic representation, as his language improved in parallel. He began to draw. While the execution was simple, the objects were identifiable. Most exciting, Sam told us "stories" about his drawings: "This bathtub. Much water. Take a bath." Or: "This mud. Yucky mud! Little duck, big duck. Swim in mud. Bad duck, dirty." Similarly, toward spring Sam purposely slammed the cupboard door on a small plastic duck and then assumed the role of comforter: "Poor little duck. I help you. Go sleep. Better now."

Toward the end of that year, a conflict with Sam over limits resulted in another encouraging breakthrough. As Sam improved in language, presence, and confidence, it was only natural that this strong little personality would begin to test limits. One day, Sam banged the toy cupboard door repeatedly and would not stop when limits were set in play therapy style ("I understand you are angry but children cannot . . ."). Sam needed to be contained. I gently held him as I explained he could not bang the cupboard door any more. Sam was furious, but I continued to hold him very gently yet firmly in my lap as I verbally recognized his anger. He began to struggle. Not wanting to see this contact turn into a physical fight and yet sensing an opening, I attempted to turn his (by now) kicking into playfully catching his feet and tickling them, and then tickling his tummy. The intent was to turn the gentle holding for the purpose of setting limits into a warm, silly baby playtime for positive contact. Could Sam make the transition, let go of his anger, and accept playful, intimate baby nurturance? Fortunately, he did. When he calmed, it was a much deeper and more related calm than ever before.

Sam then took a pile of stickers and plastered them all over the doctor kit, delighting in his creativity and looking directly at me as, reciprocally and floor time style, I handed him stickers one at a time, pulling for more frequent eye contact. More importantly, as he did this, he talked about what he was doing. Further, he alternated his sticker activity with looking at a picture book, a new activity for him. When he found a picture of four gingerbread cookies, he smiled, pointed, and named each one for a member of his family. Content, he returned to decorating the doctor kit. His ability to transfer between two significant activities and sustain appropriate attention in each constituted another first.

After an extended summer break, Sam began his second year of weekly sessions in a completely different developmental phase than the preceding September, and a far cry from the impaired little boy of two years ago, whose only contact could be made when jumping off the table. Sam entered the office tanned, confident animatedly interactive and talking nonstop in largely correct four- to seven word sentences.

During that school year Sam engaged in ri   )   le pretend play sequence. Plot, character, logical sequences,   dynamics, and symbolic expression replete with emotional   ged. Sam was no longer stuck. He could spontaneously chain many circles of rich language, while maintaining the symbolic expression of emotional ideas, without prompting. He was at long last self-propelled by his own ideas to communicate through play. The work with him was no longer as painstakingly challenging in seeking out openings for reciprocal communication. Sam could reciprocally open and close such circles fluently now. However, he did require help sometimes to sustain play movement, to solve emotional and logistical problems that arose in the play, and to contemplate and explore the emotional implications of his play. From a Feuerstein perspective, Sam's improved language and vocabulary were enabling him to master concepts and make playful associations. In floor time terminology, Sam was functioning well at the stage of emotional ideas. Related strategies to support linkage of cause and effect were used, yet most often Sam's sessions assumed the atmosphere of a child-centered play therapy session, with Sam initiating the play scenarios, and enjoying the verbal or nonverbal support of a receptive adult.

In the beginning of that year, Sam spent the first few sessions playing doctor. He set up his office by moving the furniture around, scribbled on a piece of cardboard for the office sign, tended to a sick doll using the doctor kit, wrote prescriptions, and even drove the ambulance (kiddy car). The play segments flowed seamlessly, with plausible associations and sequencing. Sam's play soliloquy was rich, with much improved vocabulary and syntax: "Poor dolly, you've got a tummy ache. Doctor Sam will help you. This hurt a little. Go home. Take medicine. Drug store. I will put you in the ambulance." His father and I often described what was unfolding, or asked open-ended questions, such as "How does dolly feel?" or "What happens next?" to help him build on his strengths in the stage of emotional ideas and become more proficient at the stage of logical thinking. We could virtually see his cognitive abilities stretch with each new imaginative link in his symbolic play.

Around midyear, Sam spent several sessions repeatedly creating a coffee house scene. Once again rearranging the office furniture with a clear symbolic purpose, Sam created a coffee house that served food and drinks. On the (blanket) ceiling of his coffee house, he affixed a small plastic box: the coffee house radio. Sam, who loved music, then sat inside the structure and "broadcast" the songs coming from the radio, in English and in Hebrew, complete with the sounds of static. When he informed us that the radio "broke," we offered to fix it or handed him imaginary tools to fix it himself. Sometimes we ordered food from him or sat near the outer edge of his blanket and chair creation, and pretended to groove to the music Sam provided.

Complex drawings evolved during the final phase of symbolic play work toward that last year of play intervention. By that time, Sam was able to sit for an entire hour session and draw plausible stories, to which we responded with prompts and questions that encouraged Sam to make connections and to consider cause and effect. One story, which he wove into his drawings and which he repeated over several sessions, concerned a "silly monkey" who tried to break the fire alarm but got burned. Later the mischievous monkey went to a restaurant, and had pizza and fries, but was terribly disappointed that the video player in the restaurant did not work. That meant he could not see the movie *Snow White.*

Rich in projective content—Sam's fear of fire alarms, his aggressive impulses, his love of food and videos—Sam's stories were full of appropriate affect and a sense of drama. Sam talked nonstop as the drawn images unfolded. These picture stories and Sam's verbal elaboration of them reflected a long road traveled by a previously seriously impaired child. Although a special educational setting contradicted our strong recommendation of inclusion in a regular classroom for this charismatic and creative child, his parents feared that the large class size would work against his progress. When last contacted, Sam's parents were pleased to report his successful adaptation to a small special first grade classroom where Sam was continuing to improve and was keeping apace with a modified first grade curriculum.

Aspects of all three paradigms were employed with Sam to help bring about change. First, in accordance with SCM principles, even during the difficult first sessions, his jumping sequence had revealed several encouraging signs of a capable, modifiable child, behind the complex symptoms. Proactive attempts using various floor time strategies helped create and link circles of communication, and later helped him grow in symbolic fluency and logical thinking. Underlying the need to continually seek and create evidence of modifiability and the focus of creating and chaining circles of communication was the play therapy attitude of supporting Sam's every attempt at communication, even when not fully understanding where he was going with his jumping, hiding in the tunnel, or playing baby. As Sam's expressive language, symbolic play skills, and confidence improved, the work with him gradually utilized child-centered play therapy tenets of acceptance and reflection, in order to help Sam understand and deal with emotional material that he had at last begun to express through more elaborate symbolic play.

CONCLUSION

The challenge in working with autistic spectrum children is to look beyond the diagnosis, to see and to seek the child behind the symptoms. As Dave, Sara, and Sam have illustrated, the delight in working with these children occurs when a child begins to improve and even flourish beyond initial expectations. Professionals working with autistic spectrum children need to fortify themselves by embracing theoretical models that stress and enhance the child's latent potential and that are not contaminated by pessimism. A playful attitude combined with playful interaction strategies can energize the interaction process with autistic spectrum children and help propel them past developmental barriers toward the childhood they deserve.

REFERENCES

Allan, J. 1988. *Inscapes of the Child's World*. Dallas: Spring.

American Psychiatric Association. 1994. *Diagnostic and Statistical Manual of Mental Disorders*. 4th ed. rev. Washington, D.C.: APA.

Axline, V. 1947. *Play Therapy*. New York: Ballantine.

Ayres, A. J. 1964. "Tactile Functions: Their Relation to Hyperactive and Perceptual Motor Behavior." *American Journal of Occupational Therapy* 18: 6–11.

Berk, L. E. 1994. *Child Development*. 3rd ed. Newton, Mass.: Allyn & Bacon.

Bruner, J. S., A. Jolly, and K. Sylva, eds. 1976. *Play: Its Role in Development and Evolution*. New York: Penguin.

Cytryn, L. 1998. "Classification of Childhood Disorders." Lecture to Feuerstein center staff. Jerusalem, Israel.

Feuerstein, R., M. Hoffman, and R. Miller. 1980. *Instrumental Enrichment: An Intervention Program for Cognitive Modifiability*. Baltimore: University Park Press.

Feuerstein, R., P. S. Klein, and A. J. Tannenbaum. 1991. *Mediated Learning Experience MLE: Theoretical, Psychosocial, and Learning Implications*. London: Freund.

Feuerstein, R., and Y. Rand. 1997. *Don't Accept Me As I Am: Helping Retarded Performers Excel*. Arlington Heights, Ill.: Skylight.

Feuerstein, R., Y. Rand, and M. Hoffman. 1979. *The Dynamic Assessment of Retarded Performers: The Learning Potential Assessment Device, Theory, Instruments, and Technique*. Baltimore: University Park Press.

Frith, U. 1989. *Autism: Explaining the Enigma*. Oxford: Basil Blackwell.

Garvey, C. 1990. *Play*. Cambridge: Harvard University Press.

Greenspan, S. I. 1992. *Infancy and Early Childhood*. Madison, Conn.: International Universities Press.

Greenspan, S. I., and S. Wieder. 1997. "Developmental Patterns and Outcomes in Infants and Children with Disorders in Relating and Communicating." *Journal of Developmental and Learning Disorders* 1: 87–141.

———. 1998. *The Child with Special Needs*. Reading, Mass.: Addison-Wesley.

Guerney, B. 1964. "Filial Therapy: Description and Rationale." *Journal of Consulting Psychology* 28: 303–10.

Kandel, E. R., J. H. Schwartz, and T. M. Jessel. 2001. *Principles of Neural Science*. 4th ed. New York: McGraw-Hill.

Kanner, L. 1943. "Autistic Disturbances of Affective Contact." *Nervous Child* 2: 217–50.

Kaufman, B. N. 1995. *Son-Rise: The Miracle Continues*. Tiburon, Calif.: Kramer.

Krug, D. A., J. R. Arick, and P. J. Almond. 1980. *Autism Screening Instrument for Educational Planning*. Portland, Ore.: ASIEP.

Levin, S. 1997. "The Dynamic Assessment of Autistic Children." In A. Kozulin, ed., *The Ontogeny of Cognitive Modifiability*, 181–94. Jerusalem: ICELP.

Lord, C., M. Rutter, S. Goode, J. Heemsberger, H. Jordan, L. Mawhood, and E. Schopler. 1989. "Autism Diagnostic Observation Schedule: A Standardized Observation of Communication and Social Behavior." *Journal of Autism and Developmental Disorders* 19: 185–212.

Mundy, P., M. Sigman, J. A. Ungerer, and T. Sherman. 1987. "Nonverbal Communication and Play Correlates of Language Development in Autistic Children." *Journal of Autism and Developmental Disorders* 17: 349–64.

Payne, G., and L. D. Isaacs. 2001. *Human Motor Development: A Lifespan Approach*. New York: McGraw-Hill.

Prizant, B. M. 1983. "Language Acquisition and Communicative Behavior in Autism: Toward an Understanding of the 'Whole' of It." *Journal of Speech and Hearing Disorders* 48: 296–307.

Ruff, H. A., and K. P. Lawson. 1990. "Development of Sustained Focused Attention in Young Children during Free Play." *Developmental Psychology* 26: 85–93.

Schaefer, C. E., K. Gitlin, and A. Sandgrund, eds. 1991. *Play Diagnosis and Assessment*. New York: Wiley.

Schopler, E., R. J. Reichler, and B. R. Renner. 1988. *Childhood Autism Rating Scale*. Los Angeles: Western Psychological Services.

Tinbergen, N., and E. A. Tinbergen. 1983. *Autistic Children: New Hope for a Cure*. London: Allen & Unwin.

Yates, J. 1986. "Communication and Intentionality in Autism." *Educational and Child Psychology* 3: 55–60.

II

PLAY ASSESSMENT AND RESEARCH

6

The Use of Play and Narrative Story Stems in Assessing the Mental Health Needs of Foster Children

Sheila Hudd

Finding ways of encouraging children to use their imagination to create and tell stories is what the play therapist aims for in an attempt to share the child's journey in sorting out their chaos, loss, and trauma. In addition to this primary aim, children gain a sense of pride in their creations and often develop empathy alongside.

We know that children who have experienced early deprivation, abuse, and neglect often experience difficulties in school and in their relationships with adults and peers generally. Early deprivation or abuse coupled with poor behavior and academic progress in school can lead a child to form a view of self as bad and worthless, and to experience self-blame. Children who have been removed from their birth parents and are placed in foster care will often experience considerably lower self-worth and self-esteem by perceiving themselves to blame for their behavior and the events which led to them being removed from their birth families. In addition, their disruptive behavior in school often leads teachers to use more controlling strategies, which further weakens their development of self-motivation (Cicchetti and Toth 1995a, 552–54).

In my current post I have been involved in developing a new service in Child and Adolescent Mental Health Service (CAMHS) for foster children. The focus of the service is to offer intensive support to the child's professional and foster network when the child's behavior or emotional presentation is causing significant concern to the extent that the placement is at risk of breakdown. The intervention is aimed at offering a quick response to enable the child's placement to hold or, if a move is inevitable, then for the move to take place in a planned way.

The service is one of many new projects throughout Britain which aims to reduce the number of placement moves for foster children and to improve their prospects in terms of their mental health, education, social inclusion, and later life chances.

Our service offers a period of brief but intensive support for up to twelve weeks with the child's main foster parent(s), social worker, teachers, and, where appropriate, the child. The team in CAMHS are available for consultation to the project workers and offer a specialist multidisciplinary perspective for those children with complex mental health needs. Foster children are also referred to the clinic for therapy in their own right when their network is considered to be sufficiently stable.

When it is considered appropriate for a child to be seen as part of the intensive support service, they are usually invited to meet with the caring and professional network in order that they may know we are trying to gain some understanding of the difficulties they are experiencing, what we are hoping to achieve, and to answer any of their questions.

Assessment is always based on a multimethod approach that will include obtaining details of the child's history, observations of interactions, and the content and process of sessions. Play therapy techniques can be helpful to assess the child's relationships, to gain clues to how they understand their world, and to gain some insight into how the child may function in relationships generally. When we understand more of the child's views and how they experience their world we can go on to think about how best to understand and manage their behavior with the caring and professional network. Research has shown that children who overcome early difficulties are those who have somehow managed to gain a coherent narrative and understanding of their experiences, which in turn helps to build resilience for later life events. A full evaluation of the project is currently under way, and this will be published at a later date.

This chapter sets out to describe how play therapy techniques were used to assess and assist with understanding the difficulties of three of the children referred to the project who were experiencing problems within their current placement, in school and relationships generally, to the extent that the placement was at severe risk of breakdown. Before I go on to talk about these children, I will briefly describe the role of play therapy and the theories that inform my work with foster children and their foster parents.

PLAY THERAPY

The model of play therapy from which I work is based on social construction theory; that is, play is viewed as a socially constructed process and a co-construction between therapist and child. It aims to create a space to share experiences and sort out some of the child's experiences and chaos, a space to help identify what the child's underlying worries and perceptions of themselves and their world are, and to help the child gain some mastery over the situation (Cattanach 2003).

Many children are highly anxious and cannot tolerate direct reference to their distress. Play therapy using a narrative model offers a medium whereby a child can explore his or her imagination and learn empathy. Structured play techniques are used to help the child to organize fragmented emotional experiences into meaningful narratives and provide opportunities for understanding feelings around the distress such experiences have caused. This model is particularly helpful for foster children who often experience a conflict of loyalty between birth parents and foster parents.

Play Therapy in Assessment

Play therapy using social construction theoretical ideas concerning the development of mentalization and cognitive and affective processing abilities in children are useful to explore and understand more about how children internalize their experiences and expectations.

Play therapists working in social construction theory use a range of tools for assessment and these include narrative and story techniques. The use of stories with children involves the children making up stories, the therapist telling her own stories, reading stories from books, writing stories, dictating stories, using tools to stimulate stories, such as pictures, puppets, sand tray, drawings, and story stems.

Narrative Play and Story Stems

The underlying approach to narrative is the concept of a story as a form of representation. These representations are stored not as fixed images but as "scripts" that can be understood as active sequences of behavior. People can and do construct and convey meaning through narrative (White and Epston 1990). Current work in narrative therapy considers stories as a means of gaining access to and facilitating change in basic underlying scripts. These ideas are particularly helpful when working with children who have experienced a range of difficulties and trauma in their lives. Play therapy in the safety of narrative can help to challenge family scripts and distorted beliefs and to assist with the generation of a number of alternative story lines.

Story stems are the beginnings of stories introducing characters and inviting the child to complete the story by playing and/or dramatization using a range of dolls or animal figures. Buchsbaum and Emde 1990 found that giving a child a story stem to complete is a good way of eliciting themes about their relationships and conflicts. This technique was built on and adapted to allow researchers to explore children's moral development (Buchsbaum et al. 1992). The authors' research found that children as young as three years were able to produce narrative representations of emotional themes and were able to represent moral themes in the areas of empathy, prosocial behavior, adherence to rules, reciprocity, and aspects of family relationships (Buchsbaum et al. 1992, 607). Story stems used in this way have also been found to provide an accurate way of exploring internal representations of attachment alongside experiences of being parented (Hodges 1996; Hodges 1999).

The stories they evoke provide an opportunity to capture the child's representations of his or her world. As they play out stories, which elicit themes of family relationships, conflicts, and defenses, glimpses of the child's anxieties will often appear. They are a particularly valuable way of working with any child who has difficulty verbalizing feelings, emotions, or empathy. Children often experience a conflict of loyalty and will deny bad experiences when directly asked, or deny concerns when they are feeling overwhelmed. Many abused children who have developed a story involving avoidance continue to deny abuse, even during therapy. The narrative stem technique is a valuable tool in this regard as children tend to view making up stories as a nonthreatening, enjoyable experience. They allow the child to process painful recollections without having to overtly acknowledge that they are victims of abuse.

They are particularly useful for guiding subsequent interventions with the child, their main foster parent, and the professional network.

In my work as a play therapist I tend to use story stems when time is limited. The child is allowed to choose a "family" with either animals or dolls and is then giving the beginning of a story and invited to complete it. The themes of the child's stories are then studied and will offer clues to the child's functioning and difficulties. I will actively seek out other stories that share similar themes to the ones they have told and which I believe will help the child to know that I have understood his or her feelings.

So how do children represent their internal world of relationships? Bowlby's theory of attachment (1973) elaborates the concept of early relationships and how important they are to the child's developing internal working models, mental representations, and memory structures.

The Role of Attachment Theory

Attachment theory and the research that supports it claim that an infant's attachment to its mother (or other primary caregiver) builds an internal working model of expectations and assumptions that will influence subsequent relationships and will not be easily changed (Bowlby 1973). Researchers from this perspective suggest that children's early attachment experiences have a dramatic effect on their day-to-day behavior, as well as on their social development in later life (e.g., Bretherton and Waters 1985; Main 1991; Sroufe 1983). A number of research studies have linked a disruption in attachment to a variety of childhood disorders, including attention deficit and hyperactivity disorder (ADHD), conduct disorder, borderline personality disorder, and a simple form of posttraumatic stress disorder (PTSD) (Fonagy and Steele 1997; Fonagy and Target 1998). There is also growing evidence of the link between security of attachment and the social development of cognition (see Meins 1997).

Research studies have also found that when main foster parents engage in interactions appropriate to the child's developmental level and focus of interest, this reduces the child's cognitive and emotional workload, freeing the child's cognitive resources for development and learning (McCune et al. 1994, 163).

Children who are rated as securely attached (Type B) have been found to have an internalized representation of a responsive, sensitive caregiver (Ainsworth et al. 1978; Sroufe 1989). Children rated as insecure-avoidant (Type A) have been found to internalize their experiences in a more negative way, for example by expecting rejection when in need of comfort and as adults go on to experience difficulties in expressing negative feelings (Kobak and Sceery 1988). Insecure-ambivalent children (Type C) tend to have expectations for an unavailable, ineffective parent, resulting in a dependent helpless relationship (Cummings and Cicchetti 1990). Some researchers argue that while children rated as insecure-ambivalent are able to express their negative feelings rather than manage them, they tend to be overwhelmed by such feelings and become fearful, sad, or angry (Oppenheim, Emde, and Warren 1997; Sroufe 1983). Children rated as disorganized-disoriented (Type D) are those who have been noted to show fear in the presence of their main foster parent and/or those who have experienced trauma and abuse.

There is now a wealth of research that supports the view that the majority of neglected, abused, or traumatized children often form insecure and disorganized attachments to their caregivers. These children are considered to be at high risk for:

- Dysfunctional emotion regulation as a result of not receiving appropriate parental support. As they get older, such children often have problems regulating their aggressive feelings and behaviors, and are constantly in survival mode. These are the children who often find concentrating and sitting still in class extremely difficult.
- The development of cognitive skills, for example, delay of symbolic play and a failure to imagine. These children have often been left unstimulated and their emotional and physical needs neglected. Children

with cognitive delay will experience difficulties in school, but a failure to imagine is of particular concern due to the fact that a good imagination and ability to organize experiences is linked to resilience for later life experiences.

- Negative representational skills, which includes a confused sense of self and low expectations of significant others, adults, and peers.
- Story themes associated with attachment type.

Type B: Securely Attached Children

- Internalize representations of a responsive sensitive caregiver
- Develop a sense of self as someone who is acceptable/lovable to the main foster parent
- If they are lost, upset, scared, frightened they expect to be comforted by a main foster parent or someone close

Type A: Insecure-Avoidant Attached Children

- Internalize less adaptive internal working models in an effort to organize their experiences
- Develop a sense of self as unlovable to correspond with unavailable caregiving
- Their stories have characters who expect rejection when in need of comfort

Type C: Insecure-Resistant Attached Children

- Internalize an unavailable, ineffective parent
- They also feel unlovable but a dependent, helpless relationship ensues
- They can express negative emotions in their stories, but rather than manage them they can appear overwhelmed, and become fearful, sad, or angry

Type D: Disorganized-Disoriented Attached Children

These children have often experienced neglect, abuse, or trauma and tend to

- Internalize unpredictability, possibly as a result of a nurturing/punitive foster parent
- They also lack a sense that comfort is not available when distressed, will avoid and approach a main foster parent, and in addition fear harm from them

- Develop a sense of self as unworthy of love and of being "bad" that then turns into aggression and anger
- Anger and aggression are expressed by lashing out, hitting, kicking, throwing objects, or at the more extreme end, by killing and dying

Children who are rated as having a disorganized attachment have often been found to tell overly elaborate stories where:

- Disasters and crises occur without warning
- Situations deteriorate quickly and spin out of control
- Dangerous events or people appear, go away, and return, causing increased fear and continued anxiety
- The main characters are helpless in the face of danger
- Parents fail to provide any protection and/or safety
- Anxiety distress and conflict are never resolved and expected to continue

CHILDREN IN FOSTER CARE

According to Bowlby, the child whose emotional and physical needs have not been met, who feels unsuccessful in efforts to gain access to main foster parents, or, worse, rejected, will build up a negative set of assumptions about himself and believe himself to be unworthy of love or respect and ashamed of who or what he is.

Children identified as needing social services support, and those who are placed in foster care, have often experienced a long history of early deprivation. Family support services have often been involved with parents misusing drugs and/or alcohol for long periods in the hope that things may change. Parental relationships under stress and/or alcohol or drug addiction too often result in the children witnessing or experiencing violence, emotional and physical neglect, and sexual abuse. The pattern of the mothers of these children are often those who have been depressed, have alcohol or drug dependency, or mental health problems and are often overwhelmed by their children's needs and demands, which are more difficult to manage as the children grow older (see Hudd 2002).

Children of these backgrounds are often observed to regress to baby behavior in mother's presence in an effort to gain attention, and may regress further during the initial stages of being placed in the care system. Some parents and foster parents find this behavior particularly difficult to deal with and respond by insisting that the child "acts her age." Knowing the child's early history, separations, and losses, and something of the child and foster parent's attachment style is vitally important when trying to understand and manage the child's behavior.

Many children who end up in the foster care system are rated as having disorganized attachments. Disorganized children find it very difficult to resolve attachment-related distress in whatever way it appears in their stories. It is often sad to hear the clarity and vividness of the stories the children produce, and to observe indicators of representational models that have developed as a response to specific family experiences. These include:

- Inappropriate aggression and abusive language when frustrated
- Neglect (being cold, hungry, scared, in the dark)
- Statements of self (main character) as being bad, for example, "because she is always bad"
- Pervasive lack of people coming to the aid of an injured animal or doll, for example, "it's her or his own fault"
- Extreme punitive behavior from adult characters/animals to their young
- Lack of empathy to victims, for example, "shut up," "go away," "who cares?"

NADIA (FIVE YEARS OLD)

Nadia is a child of white British and African Muslim parentage. Her mother suffered mental health problems for which she was often hospitalized, and was also dependent on alcohol. Nadia's father was thought to be an educated man who dominated the household. There was a history of domestic violence and an allegation by mother, but not substantiated, that father had tried on several occasions to kill her. Nadia and her mother escaped to a shelter when she was three years old. Professionals became involved when mother and two daughters were given independent accommodation and there were concerns about the level of mother's alcohol misuse and general lifestyle, which included many male visitors to the home. Nadia's behavior caused considerable concern in nursery and mother often failed to bring and/or collect her. Nadia and her younger sister were placed in the care system when she was four and a half years old when her mother acknowledged that she could not cope with her own illness and with Nadia's emerging demanding and difficult behavior.

Nadia's foster parents and her teachers in school described her as an active, impulsive, distractible child who was oppositional to adults/teachers generally and who continually sought to gain control over her environment. When this failed she withdrew into herself and was often observed to suck on inanimate objects, often until her mouth bled. She appeared to be unaware of her actions and/or acknowledge any pain associated with the activity.

Nadia presented as a very attractive, mature little girl with an adult-seeming confidence. She initially showed particular interest in the dolls' house and the family of teddy bears. This was her first story stem:

Once upon a time there was a mummy bear, a daddy bear, and two baby bears. One day one of the little bears went out for a walk and got lost. [Show me what happens next.]

Well . . . I don't know . . . she went into the woods . . .
She came to a park by a river.
All the baddies lived in a tree.
All the goodies wanted to take some leaves to make a nest.
But they couldn't because the baddies stopped them.
And then the mummy bear came.
But she got fed up and went back to her bed.
And the baddies didn't even see the little bear left behind.
And so she took some leaves.
And she made it really tidy and she thought, "no one will see me make this nest."
And then she got in it and went to sleep.
And then the teddy bears got out of their beds to look for her.
But they couldn't find her.
SUDDENLY . . .
She sees a little boy eaten up by a big tiger.
And then the tigers see the girl "lets eat her too."
"No, said the other one—let's be kind."
"I am not going to eat you, my darling."
But then he hurts her and pushes her to the ground.
"WHAT ARE YOU DOING IN MY HOUSE?" shouts the mummy bear.
"Well I . . ."
"Don't you DARE do that to my child again!"
The mummy bear takes the babies and goes to another bear's house.
"Can we stay with you?"
"Okay . . . I have got two beds for you to sleep in.
"You can sleep in this bed and you two can sleep in this bed," she says.
They are all safe now.
"Goodnight, sweet dreams."
"Daddy's bad but he is never going to come back again."

Nadia's story stem was quite powerful and I wondered whether this was her way of exploring early experiences, the story that had built up around mother leaving father and going into a refuge with her child, or a combination of both early and more current experiences. The fear that someone might reject you if you make too many demands creates an anxious avoidant response in relationships.

Nadia's later story stem provided more evidence of this type of attachment:

"THE BRAVE PRINCESS"

Once upon a time there lived a king and a queen and a prince and princess.

They lived in a castle far, far away.

One day the princess was in the tower and she couldn't find her family.

So she went down the stairs and . . . [Show me what happens next.]

The queen was crying . . .

"Don't leave me, my husband . . . I love you . . . you will always be my husband."

"Get away from me!" [The "king" punches, kicks, and jumps on the "queen."]

"Leave my mummy alone!" said the princess.

"You are not my child . . ." said the king and queen. [Both hit the princess and the princess is thrown across the room while the king and queen continue to fight.]

[The princess looks badly hurt—do you think she will be crying too?]

NO! SHE IS A BRAVE PRINCESS—she doesn't cry.

[She doesn't cry . . .]

NO! Well . . . she cries inside . . . lots . . . But no one can see . . .

[That is sad . . . where do you think all the tears go to?]

I don't know . . . [Shrugs.]

[Do you think anyone will come to help her?]

NO! She will just have to get on with it . . . [Returns to the couple fighting and shouting abuse at each other. The king searches for something sharp—Nadia has to be distracted from using a pair of scissors from my desk and so grabs a pencil instead to continue her play. The queen is stabbed with the pencil and the king finally runs off.]

[I wonder who will help the queen now?]

The brave princess! [The princess puppet is collected from across the room and returned to the scene to comfort the queen—she now has one leg missing.]

[She appears to have broken her leg.]

She's all right . . .

"Don't cry . . . I will look after you my darling."

[Who says that?]

The QUEEN to the PRINCESS! [Nadia looks irritated.]

[Is the queen being a nice mummy now?]

NO! She is a HORRIBLE mother . . . along comes a wizard.

"Hello . . . I will look after you and your children." [Queen and wizard kiss.]

"Go away" says the queen to the princess.

"I don't want you anymore . . . I am going to marry the wizard and get rid of you!"

[The princess is once again thrown across the room and left on the floor. Nadia returns to the dollhouse.]

[What will happen to the brave princess now?]

I don't know . . . [Shrugs.] Let's tuck the teddies up in their bunk beds . . .

Can I make some extra blankets? I will draw them and then cut them out . . .

Nadia's stories enabled her to let me know the good and bad parts of how she experienced her world and the confusion, anger, and pain this caused her. Nadia's play in story allowed her to explore her feelings of ambivalence toward the queen, extreme anger when she was rude and neglectful to her needs, and a wish to look after her when she was "asleep." The safe environment where she was cared for involved a clean bed and warm food and drink. The good mother was someone who liked to relax but always came if her children called for her.

There could be many interpretations to Nadia's play, but I considered Nadia was able to use the sessions to show me her experiences of home and being in care and to work through some of the complex and ambivalent emotions they evoked and to try and dispel any fantasies she may have that her mother had abandoned her to marry someone else. Working together, we were able to acknowledge the pain and fear of the main characters. The professional network was enabled to understand how the trauma and chaos of Nadia's experiences had impacted on her attachment style and behavior. Nadia's foster parent was given consultation on ways to help her understand and manage her behavior and an improvement was noted in both the home and school setting. Nadia was referred for therapy in her own right.

NATHAN (SEVEN YEARS OLD)

Nathan is a child of mixed black British and black Caribbean heritage. Nathan's parents separated when he was five years old due to father's use of illegal substances and domestic violence, which Nathan witnessed. Mother soon became pregnant in another relationship where alcohol and violence played a major part. Nathan's behavior deteriorated to the extent that his mother found it difficult to cope and sent him back to live with his father. Nathan was removed into the care system after he suffered a severe beating from his father.

Nathan's behavior in placement continued to be difficult and dangerous to himself and others and he experienced many placement breakdowns. He wanted to return to his mother and became extremely angry when told this was not possible. Nathan's behavior in school became increasingly chaotic and he was on the point of exclusion. His latest placement was significantly at risk of breakdown due to his aggression toward her own children and other foster children living in the family.

After several weeks working with the caring and professional network, Nathan agreed to meet with me to help sort out some of his difficulties. Nathan presented as a bright, attractive young boy who was inquisitive, and eager to explore the toys, going from one to another asking questions but not waiting or listening to my replies. He finally settled on the play farm and equipment and I offered him the following story stem:

[Once upon a time there lived a farmer and his wife and they had lots of animals to look after. One day they all went off to the shops and . . . before I could complete the story stem Nathan responded as follows:]

They . . . they posted a letter off to Africa and asked if they could have a worm: the BIGGEST worm in Africa.

[They wanted a worm because?]

Because . . . because the birds in the country where the farmer and his wife lived didn't have enough to eat. One day they got a parcel sent to them but . . . before they opened it they said, "YES . . . We hope it is a big worm or lots of worms!"

But when they opened it they were very sad because it was not a worm but a SNAKE! They telephoned Africa and shouted at them saying, "We never wanted a SNAKE, we wanted WORMS!!!"

But they decided to keep it. Because they had lots of rats in their house.

And the snake slithered around for the rats. But then the CAT got really, really angry and jealous because the snake took his place in the family . . .

So the cat ran down to the garden and started scratching the farmer and his wife. The farmer and his wife were very, very angry. "Will you be good and finish your work," they said.

The cat said, "But the snake is going to do something DANGEROUS!"

They understood why the cat was jealous but then said to the snake, "We don't want you in the house you can slither around in the garden." And so the snake went into the garden.

After that it was night time and the farmer and his wife were going to bed. And while they were still sleeping they heard a BIG BANG! They thought, "I bet that is that snake." But they saw an earthquake and they jumped out of their beds. And they felt dizzy!

And then when it was the morning they realized it was only a dream! But then they never cared about the snake and took it back to Africa. And brought back lots of worms.

The snake was happy because he was going back to his own country. And the farmer and his wife were happy together. And the birds had their worms! The End

This story clearly illustrates how Nathan perceives his experiences of living in foster care with different families and how difficult it is for him to negotiate all the complex levels of relationships existent in any one family. When he finally gains some role in the family and begins to be accepted by them this causes jealousies between the other children in the family, so once again he is rejected and eventually has to move. His main wish is to return to his birth family then everyone will be happy. Of course the painful reality is that Nathan is not wanted or accepted by his birth family either, because of his difficult behavior and jealousy toward his younger half siblings.

After this session I selected a story called "The Frog Who Longed for the Moon: A Story to Help Children Who Yearn for Someone They Love." It aims to help the child acknowledge the pain of yearning and the terrible emptiness and lonely feelings such yearning produces. The story ends by giving hope in that when Frog looks around he can see he was facing the place of very little and had his back to the place of plenty.

Nathan accepted this story and it became one of his favorites, and often provided a positive end to the sessions.

The majority of Nathan's stories continued to involved a main character who was mistrusting, bitter, retaliatory, violent, and very, very, bad, especially for loving yet hating his mother and siblings. Nathan blames himself and so he becomes the villain, but this too is painful and difficult to acknowledge, and so he displaces his anger onto all grown-ups and people in authority.

Nathan's stories provided evidence that close relationships were experienced as unsafe and frightening. His professional network was helped in understanding his behavior in terms of attachment theory. Nathan's stories enabled me to identify themes to address and play out, thus assisting him in understanding emotions of happy, sad, angry and afraid and to talk about them. Nathan began to recognize that he often became aggressive when he felt vulnerable, sad, and confused and to know that his anger might trigger inappropriate behaviors that made matters worse. This work then led on to play which helped sort out his confusion between being kind and hurting

others, and his need to try to distance himself from others with acting out behaviors when he began to feel close to someone.

During Nathan's play with puppets I asked him which of the characters he
was most drawn to and he answered that he liked the wizard. Despite offering him a story stem in the third person he chose to identify with it himself
and the beginnings of empathy emerged in the following story:

[Once upon a time there lived a wizard who could change ANYTHING
in the world. Tell me what you think he would do.]
Well . . . if I was a WIZARD I would . . .
Turn my old head master into grass and would STOMP on him!
I would turn my old teacher into a tree and PICK off the leaves of her
head!
I would turn all the other teachers into FROGS, all slimy and dirty,
and squeeze them and THROW them in the dirty old pond!
BUT
Well . . . My teacher wasn't bad all the time so I would turn her into a
dragonfly . . .
[And . . .]
Well . . . the other teachers were okay sometimes . . .
[So . . .]
I would put lily pads in the pond so when they got fed up with the
dirty old water and slime. They could rest for a while on the lily pads
[And . . .]
Well . . . The headmaster could stay as grass because . . . his face was
all red and he used to shout at us for nothing . . . and SCARE us!
I would have fun stamping on him!!!!
But . . . perhaps . . . Not ALL the time!

MICHAEL (FIVE YEARS OLD)

Michael's mother is white British and his father is black Caribbean. Michael's
mother had been in the care system from an early age. Michael resulted from
a transient volatile relationship and was born when his mother was sixteen
years old. Michael had been kept close to her during her many changes of
address and subsequent partners. Michael had never attended play group,
nursery, or school and it was feared that he was kept inside the house for
long periods, especially during winter months when there was no money for
electricity or heating. Michael was removed by the police and taken into care
at age 4.

Michael's behavior in placement was causing the foster parent to seriously
consider whether he had mental health problems as a result of his early ex-

periences. She was finding it difficult to manage his extreme aggression to-ward his younger brother followed by extreme withdrawal and cowering when reprimanded. His angry behavior escalated when contact with his mother ceased abruptly and her whereabouts became unknown. Michael began urinating in secluded places in the foster home and was thought to be responsible for the death of his own pet.

Working closely with the foster mother we helped her in understanding why Michael was acting in this way. For this purpose we needed to look back at his own mother's history in that her mother had rejected her and her partners had rejected her also. She wanted a baby, something of her own to love and understand her, but the baby also had needs she could not meet. Michael was good company sometimes but other times he was naughty and did not understand how bad this made his mother feel. It seems she often hit him, shouted at him, possibly even threatened to kill him and so Michael feels he is bad—so bad that his mother had to get rid of him. Michael is con-fused by his feelings for his mother in that he loves her when she cuddles him but also hates her when she hits and/or abandons him and this is all he knows. The foster mother was advised to explain to Michael why little boys do naughty things, for example, because they are cross and feel left out, they are frightened of grown-ups, because they are angry they are not living with mum, and they are worried about mum, and to ask Michael to come to her when he was being cross, upset, or angry and that she would see what she could do about it.

When Michael attended his first session, he was difficult to engage in any one activity. We spent much time on boundaries and rules for play, as he ap-peared to have a wish to destroy everything in the room. Michael ignored the story stems offered and in an effort to encourage him to participate I resorted to offering just a beginning line with a family of dolls in the dollhouse:

[Once upon a time there was a little boy called . . .?]
  Mr. Angry Boy.
  [Mr. Angry Boy was angry because . . .?]
  He just WAS.
  [Who was he angry with?]
  THE POLICE. [Grabs a large police car from toy box.]
  [Why was Mr. Angry Boy angry with the police?]
  Because they took the girl and the man and the children away.
  [Where did they take them?]
  Out of the house and THREW them in the road and DRAGGED the girl by the neck. "Get OUT THERE," they said.
  [Michael then makes a grab for the dolls, hits them, pushes them, and throws them about the room and is reminded of our boundaries and play rules.]

[I wonder if Mr. Angry Boy saw this?]

YES HE DID!

[Continues to bash and thump the dolls and play equipment, but less harshly.]

[I wonder what Mr. Angry Boy was feeling when he saw all this?]

HE WAS SAD . . . HE CRIED. "Don't go . . . don't go," he cried. But no one took any notice and the police took them away and then they all DIED.

[They all died . . . that is a very sad story.]

Yes it is . . . Mr. Angry Boy was left in the street!

[In the street! Did he get to go in another car?]

No . . . he was left in the street . . . he died too . . . [Bashes doll figure.] AND HE WAS ANGRY. [Makes growling noises.]

[Mr. Angry Boy was sad, angry, and I wonder if he was a bit scared too.]

NO . . . JUST REALLY, REALLY ANGRY. [Gets up and leaves the mat.]

[What do you think Mr. Angry Boy will do?]

He is gonna FIGHT everyone. [Begins doing karate kicks around the room.]

[Yes he is very angry . . . and I expect he will get told off a lot if he fights everyone . . .]

Yes . . . he does . . . [Sits down again.]

"What are you doing?" [As I look at the chaos of the toys.]

[Well, I was wondering what was going on now. Perhaps we could see if we could make an end to the story?]

I don't want to do that any more.

[Okay . . . I know a really good story about another angry boy, would you like to hear it?]

M: Go on then . . .

In view of Michael's expression of not being heard when upset in the story, I considered it important to let him know I had heard and understood something of the distress he was communicating and the extent of anger he was feeling. I decided to make up a short story about a little boy who wanted so much to be grown up and help his mummy when mummy wasn't feeling well and especially when other people came and got cross with her, but he was just *too little* and this made him very, very angry and cross with everyone. He got even more cross when he had to go and live with someone who was not his mummy and he was left worrying about how she was, who was looking after her, but he was also angry with her too for making him worry. He became so angry he thought he might explode!

Michael listened intently to this story and asked if I had any pictures, so I said I didn't but we could draw some. Michael declined this idea so I introduced "Angry Arthur," a story about another angry boy whose anger caused floods and earthquakes. Michael asked lots of questions about the angry boy in the book, enabling us to talk more about how bad angry feelings can make children feel and what we can do to help. We then thought about some ways Angry Arthur and Mr. Angry Boy could get rid of some of their angry feelings without hurting or destroying things. Michael entered into the exercises offered very well while we continued to refer to aspects of both stories. In an attempt to find a solution to Mr. Angry Boy's sadness we played out a story where we went to look for an old wise owl. The wise owl was able to tell a story about how some mothers try very hard but cannot look after their children and so the wise owl helps them to find another mother and father. Michael engaged in the acting out of this story, asking lots of questions and nodding seriously to the wise owl's responses.

This session provided a space for Michael to explore his traumatic experiences through the safety of the story. Through the story he had an opportunity to recognize and name feelings, and later to reflect on the ways in which events impact on feelings and behavior. His foster parent reported that after this session he was unusually tired and did not resist bedtime routines as he usually did.

On the second occasion that we met Michael responded to the following story stem.

[Once upon a time there was a mummy pig and two baby pigs. One day one little pig went out for a walk and got lost . . . Show me what happens next . . .]

Well . . . suddenly a tiger appeared and began to chase the little pig. "I'm going to eat you all up," he said.

"Mummy, mummy," cried the baby pig. "There is a tiger here who is going to eat me." The mother came out and chased the tiger and chased after him. BUT the tiger then chased after the mummy.

Then the mummy fell asleep.

[What do you think happened to the little pig?]

Well . . . a nice penguin came to the house. BUT he turned bad and began to eat the mummy. The tiger called again and he ate the mother and the baby pigs.

The next day the elephant came and saw the three pigs lying dead. The big elephant wanted some of their blood and so drank it.

The next day the hippopotamus came. He wanted some of the blood and then ate the dead pigs all up.

Then the lions came and they ate some of the pigs' skin.

And then the MONSTER came and he ate the bones and EVERYTHING.

Until there was nothing left.

That's the end of the story.

Michael's stories provided yet more insight and understanding of his attachment style and where he was at emotionally. We don't know what he has experienced or witnessed but his play suggests lots of violence, chaos, and possibly abuse. The themes of Michael's stories enabled me to work with the professional network to help them understand and work with Michael's anger and to think together about strategies for foster parents and teachers to deal with his aggressive behavior in a consistent way. Ongoing consultation and support offered to the foster parent enabled her to commit to keeping Michael until permanent foster parents were found. Michael was offered play therapy to assist him to work through his many issues of trauma, separation, and loss. Michael often sought the wise owl's views in many of his later stories in play therapy.

CONCLUSION

Attachment theory is a theory of personality development in close relationships and helps us understand why children who have suffered adverse relationships in their early years go on to find relationships difficult in the future. It is no surprise when parents of foster children consider some to be resistant to all efforts and attempts at closeness in any relationships and/or experience their behavior as extremely difficult to manage when they demonstrate a desperate need to manipulate and control their environments. It is only when foster parents are helped to understand the child' s attachment style and the behaviors resulting from their early relationship experiences that they can go on to learn new ways of helping and assisting the child to develop new ways of relating to others.

The stories of foster children who have suffered trauma, separation, and loss tend to show insecure, avoidant, and disorganized patterns of behavior. Their stories are complex and multilayered and provide a space for the child to work through some of his or her experiences and provide clues to where further work with foster parents and professionals may be focused.

While the use of narrative and story stems is not the only tool used in assessment, story stems are a useful tool as part of assessment and during any brief intervention which aims to gain clues to a child's functioning and difficulties which will provide indications as to what type of care the child may need, and what type of support the foster parent may need. Once assessment has been completed, if the child's support systems are deemed to be secure, then play therapy can be offered. Play therapy goes on to continue to use story formats, actively help the child develop more adaptive coping strategies, challenge cognitive distortions, and rely less on negative behavior to communicate distress.

REFERENCES

Ainsworth, M. D. S., M. C. Blehar, E. Waters, and S. Wall. 1978. *Patterns of Attachment: A Psychological Study of the Strange Situation*. Hillsdale, N.J.: Lawrence Erlbaum Associates.

Bowlby, J. 1973. *Attachment and Loss*. Vol. 2, *Separation: Anxiety and Anger*. London: Hogarth.

Bretherton, I., and E. Waters, eds. 1985. *Growing Points of Attachment Theory and Research*. Monographs of the Society for Research in Child Development 50. Serial no. 209.

Buchsbaum, H. K., and R. N. Emde. 1990. "Play Narratives in 36-Month-Old Children: Early Moral Development and Family Relationships." *Psychoanalytic Study of the Child* 45: 129–55.

Buchsbaum, H. K., S. Toth, R. B. Clyman, D. Cicchetti, and R. Emde. 1992. "The Use of a Narrative Story Stem Technique with Maltreated Children: Implications for Theory And Practice." *Development and Psychopathology* 4: 603–25.

Cattanach, A. 2003. *Introduction to Play Therapy*. New York: Brunner-Routledge.

Cicchetti, D., and S. L. Toth. 1995. "A Developmental Psychopathology Perspective on Child Abuse and Neglect." *Journal of American Academy of Child and Adolescent Psychiatry* 34, no. 5: 541–65.

Cummings, E. M., and Cicchetti, D. 1990. "Attachment, Depression, and the Transmission of Depression." In M. T. Greenberg, D. Cicchetti, and E. M. Cummings, eds., *Attachment during the Preschool Years*, 339–72. Chicago: University of Chicago Press.

Fonagy, P., and M. Steele. 1997. "Morality, Disruptive Behavior, Borderline Personality Disorder, Crime and Their Relationship to the Security of Attachment." In L. Atkinson and K. Zucker, eds., *Attachment and Psychopathology*, 223–74. New York: Guilford.

Fonagy, P., and M. Target. 1998. "How 'Theory of Mind' Mediates the Attachment Problems of Individuals with Borderline Personality Disorder: Evidence and Implications for Treatment."

———. 2000. "Attachment and Borderline Personality Disorder." *Journal of the American Psychoanalytic Association* 48: 4.

Hodges, J. 1996. "The Use of Story Stems." Fourth Annual Conference Address, British Association of Play Therapy, Warwick University.

———. 1999. "Research in Child and Adolescent Psychotherapy: An Overview." In M. Lanyado and A. Horne, eds., *The Handbook of Child and Adolescent Psychotherapy*. London: Routledge.

Hudd, S. 2002. "Finding the Way Back Home." In A. Cattanach, ed., *The Story So Far*. London: Jessica Kingsley.

Kobak, R. R., and A. Sceery. 1988. "Attachment in Late Adolescence: Working Models, Affect Regulation, and Representations of Self And Others." *Child Development* 59: 135–46.

Main, M. 1991. "Metacognitive Knowledge, Metacognitive Monitoring, and Singular Coherent vs. Multiple Incoherent Model of Attachment: Findings and Directions for Future Research." In C. Murray Parks, J. Stevenson-Hinde, and P. Marris, eds., *Attachment Across the Life Cycle*. London: Routledge.

McCune, L., R. DiPane de Fireoved, and M. Fleck. 1994. "Play: a Context for Mutual Regulation within Mother–Child Interaction." In A. Slade and D. P. Wolf, eds., *Children
   at Play: Clinical and Developmental Approaches to Meaning and Representation.*
   Oxford: Oxford University Press.

Meins, E. 1997. *Security of Attachment and the Social Development of Cognition.*
   Brighton: Psychology Press.

Oppenheim, D., R. N. Emde, and S. Warren. 1997. "Children's Narrative Representations of Mothers: Their Development and Associations with Child and Mother
   Adaptation." *Child Development* 68, no. 1: 127–38.

Sroufe, L. A. 1983. "The Coherence of Individual Development: Early Care, Attachment, and Subsequent Developmental Issues." *American Psychologist* 34, no. 10:
   834–41.

White, M., and D. Epston. 1990. *Narrative Means to Therapeutic Ends.* New York:
   Norton.

7

Transcending into Fantastic Reality: Story Making with Adolescents in Crisis

Mooli Lahad

"You must be very patient," replied the fox. "First you will sit down at a little distance from me . . . I shall look at you . . . and you will say nothing . . . But you will sit close to me, every day . . ."

—de Saint-Exupéry 1982, 65

It was Gerald, my psychiatrist friend, on the phone. He was very tense. It was his third attempt to reach me in a week. "I am stuck with a very troublesome adolescent," he said. "He looks very distressed but says nothing. He stares at me, pale and anxious, but silent. I have taught him how to play bridge, and though for a little while he looked interested, as soon as he learned the rules he refused to play . . . I am at a loss. Will you take him and try to reach him through your art and drama techniques?"

Flattered by Gerald's request I agreed, and Gerald promised to take care of any psychiatric "holding" that might prove necessary.

I saw sixteen-year-old Alex for the first time less than a week after my conversation with Gerald. He was a tall, slim young man with dark hair and very dark, sharp eyes, dressed in an unusual manner for a person living on a kibbutz. In contrast to the generally casual style favored by most people who live on a kibbutz, he was spotlessly groomed. Instead of the usual T-shirt he wore a dress shirt buttoned to the collar. Instead of wearing jeans like most people his age, he wore cotton pants and his hair was neatly cut. Most of his peers would not have approved of his outfit.

Alex arrived on time and sat staring at me. In response to all my suggestions he either murmured or said, "Whatever you like," but did nothing. Fifty minutes later, on the dot, he stood up to leave.

Most of the time his black eyes seemed to look right through me and none of the creative methods that I attempted encouraged him to cooperate for more than a few minutes. After ten tormenting sessions I called Gerald to tell him that I wasn't making any progress and that I was thinking of telling Alex in our next session that as the process wasn't proving successful, we should probably stop meeting. Gerald was disappointed. He had really hoped that Alex would benefit from human contact in addition to medication, but he agreed that there didn't seem to be any point in continuing my sessions with him.

The next time that Alex was scheduled to see me he arrived five minutes late. He appeared at the door breathing heavily, his hair untidy and his face red. He looked as if he had been running for some time. His shirt had come out of his pants and he looked very different from the composed and reserved young man I knew.

I said to him, "You were running weren't you?" Alex nodded and said, "Yes." I asked if he had had trouble with his transportation and he told me that the usual driver had not arrived. "So what happened?" I asked. "I had to run all the way to the main road and then hitchhike," he told me. "Did your lift bring you directly here?" Alex, who was still desperately trying to control his breath, said, "No, he dropped me in the center of town and I was late. I was late." The center of town was about half a mile from my home.

I suggested that he sit down and slowly regulate his breathing. When he was breathing normally I said that I wanted to tell him a story. As usual, Alex answered, "Whatever you like." "Yes," I continued, "I would like to retell your story about what happened this afternoon in an imaginary way, but I need some help from you." For the first time, Alex looked interested as he made his usual reply. "You need you to listen carefully to the way I tell your story. When I'm finished be sure to tell me what you liked, what you didn't like and what you would like me to change." Looking intrigued, Alex agreed.

I set the story far away in an imaginary land. I told the story in the past tense, to distance it from Alex as much as possible. I described the frustrations of a man who wanted very much to be on time for a meeting that he had to attend. I described all the preparations he made, how he dressed with care and made great efforts to be on time, only to find that the carriage he was hoping to catch had left early, and so on. When I reached the end of the story Alex was staring at me, motionless but still engaged. I repeated my request that he tell me what he liked and what he didn't like and what he would like to change. Alex said, "It was all wrong."

Surprised, I asked, "What was the worst part of it?" and he proceeded to retell the story, correcting every detail until his original story was intact. However, every time he made a change I asked him to allow me to "correct" it in the context of my story, so that it took some thirty minutes of going back and forth until we arrived at his original tale. Then he was satisfied, and for the first time I saw a smile on his face.

It was also the first time that I heard Alex talk (or engaged in what could be described as "talk" for him). This was a breakthrough. From that day onward Alex was much more cooperative, although he was still quite guarded.

Years passed and one day I received a call from Alex, who was twenty-four years old at the time. He asked to meet me. He said he wanted to discuss some difficulties he was having at work. When we met, he suddenly asked if I remembered the day when he arrived late. I was very surprised that he mentioned this after more than eight years, and I told him that yes, I did remember. Alex smiled, one of his satisfied smiles that I had come to know, and said: "I was testing you that day . . . I was trying to drive you crazy with my thousand and one corrections. I actually liked your story, but I wanted to see if you were really interested in me." I felt embarrassed to admit to him that it was the same day that I had planned to terminate his therapy.

Alex's case marked the beginning of my exploration into fantastic reality and its effects on the psyche in difficult situations, as well as the use of the story making technique that I call The Story That You Need to Hear Now.

TRAUMA, RECOVERY, AND FANTASTIC REALITY

"If dreaming is the nocturnal functioning of the psyche that is essential for our existence, what then is day-dreaming and dissociation? Is it what some writers will describe as 'an isolated, lifeless world of private obsessions'" (Levine 1997, 33), or is it an act of survival that can be used therapeutically to help trauma patients to heal their emotional wounds?

Let me define what I mean by a "traumatic experience."

Trauma is the subjective experience of inner terror. At times it includes a personal feeling or perception of near death, physical or psychological, of oneself or of others. It makes no difference if one knows the people or has only observed them. The personal interpretation of the situation as life threatening is what is important. It is also relevant that this is often a non-verbal experience.

This horror is experienced repeatedly, each time as if it is really happening, regardless of how many years have passed. It may lead to a numbing of all emotions, as if a huge eraser has wiped out the ability to feel.

LeDoux (1996) found that the limbic system, the combination of the amygdala and the hippocampus, remembers the trauma in sensory terms: colors, scents, sounds, sensations, pictures, emotions, and tastes. Only a few words or meanings are attached to these sensations, and they may be classified as survival words: danger, alert, fear, or happy, satisfied.

The limbic system is responsible for our survival. We are born with it, unlike the neocortex, which develops over a period of months and years. This is the system that helps the baby distinguish the pleasant from the unpleasant or dangerous, such as a gentle touch and soft voice saying "sweetie, darling, honey," as opposed to signs of danger such as rough touching, falling sensations, and the frightening sounds of shouts or screams.

When we experience near-death annihilation feelings, we are using this survival system to detect the signs and react in three options known as fight, flight, freeze.

This system registers the experience, and the verbal aspects of the incident in many cases are added at a later stage. So when we want to arrive at the source of a traumatic memory we must use limbic system experience, which is very close to what I call the right hemisphere language, as described in my book (Lahad 2000). This includes images, sensations, emotions, colors, movement, and so on. It is interesting to note that for Melanie Klein the fear of death is the source of creativity (Klein and Riviere 1937, 43). It is very similar to the language of dreams.

How do we know that it is natural for the brain to use these processes in the face of danger? Shouldn't we accept that dissociation is a dangerous phenomenon, for it may lead to the development of a dissociative personality (Herman 1994)? "Winnicott makes a clear distinction between 'fantasy' and 'imagination.' Fantasy is imagination manque; it refers to the kind of daydreaming that walls the person up in his or her internal world and leads to no form of doing, of efficacy. Imagination, on the other hand, is the means by which we reach out and connect with otherness" (Levine 1997, 33).

Levine then states that "play is the operation of imagination, not of fantasy. In a certain sense, we could say that the goal of therapy is to replace fantasy with imagination, to transform psychological space from an isolated, lifeless world of private obsessions into a connected, vital field of play. Therapy then can be understood to be a re-vitalization of the imagination, a turning-back to an original connection between self and world" (Levine 1997, 33). Levine, one of the leading experts in the conceptualization of expressive therapy as a form of psychotherapy, has taken a clinical stand.

Research shows a strong connection between exposure to trauma, abuse, and severe punishment and positive hypnotic ability (Nowlis 1969; Cooper and London 1976; Hilgard 1970; Nash, Lynn, and Givens 1984). In abused children, this ability is related to skill in experiencing dissociation (Sanders, McRoberts, and Tollefson 1989). These mechanisms of dissociation were described by Putnam (1993) as coping mechanisms to deal with severe trauma.

> The dissociative mechanisms are probably sophisticated methods that survivors of trauma developed in order to cope with unbearable experiences. These mechanisms are not only restricting but are also effective coping mechanisms with impossible reality. As reality was so difficult, the only way to survive was to transcend to other realities, more pleasant and rewarding. The ability to imag-

ine, fantasize, to experience oneself in a different time and space saved these survivors from unbearable painful experiences. (Megged 2001, 23–24)

"These special abilities that survivors of trauma have developed can be used not only to escape but also in order to learn new, effective methods of coping" (Megged 2001, 24). Kluft (1991) and Spiegel (1988) suggest that hypnosis, which is closely connected to dissociative phenomena and its understanding, may be a suitable method for identifying and healing many of the posttrauma psychopathologies

> because of post traumatic victims' natural ability to use dissociative states it is possible and plausible to use these methods in their coping with their terrifying experiences. Hypnosis as well as metaphors invite the client into the dissociative state. They invite the client to imagine, fantasize, daydream, to be in a place so different from their reality. These methods are suitable for trauma survivors more than many other therapeutic methods. (Megged 2001, 24)

Alkavetz (1992) seems to take a different position from Herman (1994) about the way to deal with posttrauma, especially in children. She suggests that "children who have been severely traumatized need to forget the trauma in order to remember" (151). "Helping these children to heal therefore calls for a different processing method, a delicate and gentle way that respects their need to hide and forget" (153). "Our assumption is that it is possible to process and work-through the trauma with unconscious processes and that these approaches are better, especially when we deal with traumatized children, and more so with prolonged or recurrent trauma" (Megged 2001, 28).

In the fantastic reality one can play roles one may never have played in reality, such as the role of perpetrator or of the punishing or avenging person one may have wished to be. One may also play an opposite role to gain mastery over a situation or to "step into the other person's shoes." This space permits the acting out of wishful thinking, such as the desire to be rich, strong, loved, and cared for, as well as the chance to act out taboos such as the wish to murder or to exterminate. In this respect it is a compensating experience, providing comfort to "wounded souls." The fantastic experience actually empowers the daydreamer and may serve as a substitute for aggression.

From this perspective we can easily see the parallel between dreams, dissociation, and the fantastic reality. We can call them the "as if" space. This "as if" space is where the impossible is possible or "in the 'as if' space all the ifs are possible" (Lahad 2000, 12). What makes it possible? Perhaps the most important aspects that allow the transcendence are the rules of fantastic reality that are at 180 degrees to reality.

Whereas in reality we may only be in a certain place at a certain time and generally, only in one role, fantastic reality allows us to be in several spaces at the same time and to experiment and experience several roles.

You, the reader, are now sitting somewhere reading this chapter. You are reading it at a certain time in a day that is constantly progressing. You may find it very hard to read and do gardening at the same time. However, if you transcend into fantastic reality, you can be yourself and at the same time imagine you are a captain on a boat in the Caribbean Sea enjoying peaceful sailing and good company.

You can also remember the time you had a fight with your sibling when you were teenagers. Although the whole event only took a few minutes, you may reflect and think and imagine it for an hour and more. So we can see how fantastic reality is similar to dreams and other altered states of awareness.

Cohen (1997) studied a large group of adults for daydreaming. He reports that 50 percent said it was satisfying wishful thinking and 64 percent felt at ease daydreaming. Only 5 percent reported that they depended on daydreaming and 7 percent said it was a flight from reality. Cohen's sample reported that they were daydreaming at least 50 percent of their waking moments, while 50 percent said they imagine talking to and hearing another person.

When his sample included only people who had recently experienced a major loss (such as the loss of a spouse or the experience of hasty emigration), the widows and widowers reported daydreaming as comforting and as helping them to cope with reality. Emigrants reported a 28 percent increase in daydreaming, most of which was about memories of the place and friends they had left behind. None reported that the daydreaming disturbed their efforts to integrate into their new society, and some said it was their main comfort during this difficult period in their lives.

CAN WE REPRODUCE THIS PHENOMENON VOLUNTARILY IN THERAPY OR INTERVENTION WITH TRAUMA VICTIMS?

In over twenty years of dealing with traumatic incidents and treatment of children, adults, and families, my experience has shown that fantastic reality can be recreated in the therapeutic encounter using the expressive modalities such as dramatherapy, bibliotherapy, and metaphoric work. All of these use an imaginary space and aesthetic distancing, creating a safe and secure place for the traumatized clients to reexperience and master their pain through metaphoric milieus.

WHAT DOES IT TAKE TO MAKE THESE PHENOMENA WORK?

The answer to the above question is both simple and complex. For the client to believe that our invitation is genuine, and that we are not going to surprise her with interpretations or disclosure work, we must establish a safe, secure space and relationship where we accept any story, any pace, or the silence of our client.

We must believe in everything that is said or raised in the session. We must assume the position of participant/observer and even more so of witness, and to encourage "active forgetting" (i.e., the dissociation process) to make sure nothing is done without the full consent and collaboration of the client, and with much patience.

Paradoxical as it may sound, this distancing/dissociative process causes the client to "remember what he had 'forgotten'" and to create an alternative story or a bearable story for himself.

THERAPEUTIC METAPHORS AND THEIR EFFECTS ON THE PSYCHE: THE STORY THAT YOU NEED TO HEAR NOW

The Story That You Need to Hear Now is a therapeutic method that combines the art of storytelling, the wisdom of the metaphor, and the use of paradoxical and Ericksonian principles.

The purpose of this instrument is multifaceted:

First, this instrument enables the therapist to transfer to the client messages about his condition on various levels of consciousness, or to look into aspects of his situation while using the protective distance that the "story" provides. This distance is known as the space between the "if" and the "as if." This distance enables us to simultaneously talk "as if" (that is an agreed lie, that "it's only a story") and at the same time allows the client to explore another option "if" (could that option be possible for me?).

Second, this instrument enables the therapist to combine therapeutic suggestions both indirectly and nonthreateningly by relating them to characters in the story.

Third, the client undergoes a unique experience of unconditional acceptance. The therapist tells him a story that is made especially for him.

Fourth, the client experiences the therapist's total attention and at the same time maintains control, through the ability to "correct" the story according to her needs.

Fifth, while in the story format, the therapist can risk options that in reality are impossible, such as changing the time completely (e.g., if the story is set in summer, the therapist can ask, "What happens there during the winter?"). The therapist can check the reactions of the client to various situations, clarify positions, and weave in therapeutic assumptions that he has regarding the client and her condition.

WHAT IS "THE STORY THAT YOU NEED TO HEAR NOW"?

The Story That You Need to Hear Now is a therapeutic method in which the therapist makes up a story for the client with the client's consent and at times with some help from the client. This method can be used in different ways:

- A structured story composed of day-to-day elements, like Alex's story, can be constructed for the client.
- A story may be constructed jointly, through guided/open-ended questions asked by the therapist. This option is reminiscent of the six-piece story-making method (Lahad 1992).
- A fairy tale, fable, or tale that the therapist feels suits the client's condition may be "matched" to a particular client (Gersie 1992).
- An image created by the client may be expanded into a story, with the therapist's help. One example is the scribble method (Oaklander 1978).
- A personal story may be constructed for the client by means of the Ericksonian method, using physical clues displayed by the client to build suggestions, as in other hypnotic approaches (Rosen 1996).

SOME WORDS OF CAUTION PRIOR TO USING THIS METHOD

The most important thing to be aware of when choosing to use The Story That You Need to Hear Now is the danger of countertransference. Because the therapist tells the client a story either by filling in gaps or, often, by composing the entire story, there is a distinct possibility that the therapist will tell the client a story in which the personal materials and needs of the therapist will be its central components. In order to deal with this possibility, the therapist must be aware of his personal materials and identify them when and if they surface. Furthermore, the therapist must be fully attentive to the client and to the clues that he provides while the story is being composed.

A major safeguard rooted in this method is in posing questions: What did you like in the story? What didn't you like? What would you like me to change? The answers to these questions are an indication from the client to the therapist about which potentially "foreign" material should be removed from the story. This includes elements that disturb the client as irrelevant, unsuitable, or incongruent with his story. That is why, when using this method, we don't question why the change has been introduced but respect the client's request and respond accordingly.

Another danger lies in using the method too often. The therapist "works" very hard when using this method. He or she is attentive, produces the story, amends it, and so on. This may cause the client to assume the demanding role of a child who rejects or accepts his "food" without making any effort. This may drastically affect the client's motivation to reveal personal material or to invest in the therapeutic process.

The recommended rule is to ensure that this method is used carefully and that the therapist plan his use of it in advance of introducing it into the therapeutic encounter. It is recommended that this method be applied in the following situations:

With depressive/traumatized/introverted clients who continue to come to sessions, and whose suffering is evident, while their ability to communicate is limited due to their emotional state

With traumatized clients who have been through the "exposure work" and suddenly close down and become depressed and frightened

At the point at which we want to suggest an idea to the client

As part of open-eye hypnotic therapy

With adolescents who display passivity, constricted verbal communication, detachment, indifference, and remoteness

As part of "nurturing" a terminally ill patient

In order to bypass resistance

Another danger is the use of this method by an inexperienced therapist. Metaphoric communication, which resembles hypnotic, trance-like methods, is a powerful method with great therapeutic and metatherapeutic potential. By its very nature the metaphor penetrates defenses and communicates with the unconscious, despite the fact that it appears to be a conscious function. Thus an inexperienced therapist may find that he and his client are suddenly confronting subjects with which neither of them has the ability to cope. Therefore it is recommended that this method be used only after practicing with, being coached by, or under the close supervision of a qualified therapist who is licensed to use hypnotic and trance methods.

Which elements should we use to The Story That You Need to Hear Now? To create the story we have to first establish its "nesting place." The foundation elements, borrowed from drama, are time, space, and atmosphere. By setting the stage and creating the scenery, we begin to build the structure on which the story will reappear.

The Focusing Components

I. Time, Place, Season, Weather, Character, Object
   A. Time: daytime, dusk, evening, morning, noon, afternoon, dawn, midnight, etc.
   B. Place: far, near, inside, outside, seaside, city, lake, forest, village, mountains, etc.

C. Season: summer, winter, fall, spring
D. Weather: hot, dry, rainy, snowy, etc.
E. Character: male, female, young, old, average, tall, short, fat, thin, bent, etc.
F. Object: big, small, type of material, old, new, fragile, durable, heavy, light, etc.

II. Universal Truths

The therapist will use an aphorism to create an atmosphere of agreement, understanding, and empathy. These are words or idioms that cannot be refuted by the client when he hears them. These sayings are generally related to natural phenomena or to our general universal knowledge. For example, if the client chooses winter as the season, then a universal truth will be an expansion of the feeling of cold, damp, rain, and so on. If the chosen time is dusk, then a universal truth would say, "It will soon be dark." And if the chosen place is out in the sun, then a universal truth would be, "He will soon feel hot."

Using what is implied in a universal truth makes it possible for the storyteller to transfer to the client a feeling of understanding, mutuality, and even "mind reading," which is a condition related to hypnotic trance. In addition, it enables the therapist to anchor the client with facts, to confront him with reality, to verify the situation with him and to check options.

Sometimes the universal truth allows the therapist to guide the story to an end as, for example, in the case of a client who chooses dusk. After the story is expanded and verified the therapist can say, "Slowly, slowly the day is turning into dusk and soon it will be night. What happens then . . .?" And then he can direct the client toward the possibilities of sleep, rest, relaxation, and closure—and take a break.

III. Yes Set

The use of universal truths, intensification, and kinesthetic empathy (see IV) makes it possible to lead the client into a state of low resistance or no resistance—preconscious consent. Once he is in this state, he can be eased into a semihypnotic state in which he listens to the story and is open to suggestion. The Yes Set concept means that we ask short questions, the answers to which are always yes.

For example: Therapist: "So it is dark?" Client: "Yes." Therapist: "And it is difficult to see?" Client: "Yes." Therapist: "And there is almost no light?" Client: "No, there is some light from a nearby house." Therapist: "Oh, I see there is some light from that nearby house but otherwise it is dark." Client: "Yes."

The general belief is that a continuous yes response leads the client to further agreement with the therapist's suggestions and thus leads to the possible development of the client's commitment to "the story."

IV. Kinesthetic Empathy

This is a state in which the therapist uses the client's physical clues (posture, breathing rate, etc.) and weaves them into the text or incorporates them into the story by intensifying these kinesthetic elements. For example, the description is of a young man in bed. The therapist will supply details, describing the feel of the mattress, the softness of the pillow, the pillow cover, the texture of the blanket, the youth's weight on the bed, and so on.

Yes Set is effective because universal truths or physiological imprints are set as generalities in our consciousness and force the listener to say to himself, "Yes, yes indeed, this is true." According to Erickson, this process is related to prehypnotic preparation and to positioning a person into a state of agreement and trance. The Yes Set process enables the client to be psychologically relaxed, as the story is progressing in a desired and known direction that has his approval.

V. Connecting Two Disconnected Elements

Milton Erickson maintains that when a situation is created in which the client "consents," then it is possible to connect two elements that are essentially not connected. This may help the therapist lead the client to a desired destination, relax him, or decrease symptoms. For instance, "The more your hand shakes, the more you feel freed from tension" or "Imagine yourself holding the object (that was mentioned in the story), feel how smooth and nice it is, its weight, its size. As you feel this object in your imagination, remember that each time this happens it will be easier for you to do . . ."

VI. Confirmation

The story describes precise sensations and experiences that heighten sensitivity to details, atmosphere, and situation and afford the client an opportunity to confirm to himself that indeed he had the experience. These allow him to examine whether it was actually so or whether he needs to correct the therapist's words so that they will concur with the experience that he had.

VII. Reflection

Returning the story to the client often clarifies for her things that she was not previously aware of or that she had chosen to ignore, as in the following example. After the therapist precisely repeated the story of "this morning," the client became angry with the therapist because she omitted a very important section of the story. A reexamination showed that section was never told and it was the client who had omitted it. This was explored and the renarrating of the story included the omitted part.

In another case the story questions lead the client to inadvertently describe a behavior of the main character. When the therapist retold the story (as the method requires), the reflection of the story clarified for the client a type of behavior that she usually tried to ignore—and forced her to face the "truth" that she told without being aware that she had done so.

VIII. Intensification

Often, during the transformation of the realistic, simple story (see page 146) into an imaginative one or into a different type of story, a situation arises in which there is intensification of behavior, sensations, or thoughts.

This intensification results in a focusing on and an expansion of content or material that the client had not noticed or had preferred to hide. Intensification, as a technique, requires the discernment of the therapist and careful usage because embedded in the semihypnotic structure it gains such power that it may halt or frighten a client. For example, the client talks about the desert in the middle of the day and the therapist intensifies the description and says, "That was a barren desert, yellow and brown forever, and so dry. The eye can see only sand and more sand. And it was almost noon, the sun was almost at the center of the sky, and it was very hot. In fact it had been hot for the past few hours. Yes, during the early hours of the morning it was a little cooler but as the day drew closer to noon it became hotter and hotter still and now it is very hot."

IX. Commitment

Since The Story That You Need to Hear Now process is usually initiated and controlled by the therapist, it is very important for the client to feel commitment to the content and to the process.

Commitment can be achieved by intensifying the attention to details supplied by the client, by supporting a process of internal investigation, by total acceptance or through the amendments to the story made by the client.

To strengthen the commitment of the client to the story, one can use the following techniques:

A. Options

Posing options at important points and giving the client a choice.

B. Conflict

The moment a conflict is detected by the therapist (for instance, the wish to stay versus the wish to leave), it is either clarified or options are presented and the client is encouraged to accept or reject the alternatives offered.

C. Ratification/control

At every possible turning point in the story the client is asked to provide a linguistic ratification and in so doing we return "control" of the story to the client. Likewise, the therapist periodically checks whether or not the present story is satisfactory or if it is possible and desirable to continue (see ending below).

D. Opposites

A 180-degree turn of the situation allows the therapist to determine whether the client is or is not committed to the story or the events. Examples: A change in the time of day—what happens in the day/night? A change in the weather—the story is about winter and the therapist asks what happens in the summer.

Overturning the pictorial image—if the story stems from a graphic image, it is possible to turn the page around and ask the client to look at the page from the opposite direction—what happens now? Do you want to return to the original perspective or stay here?

Like every manipulative action in therapy, using opposites in a story requires discretion and caution.

E. Normalization

During the story the therapist interprets what the main character defines as normal. This is done by accepting or attributing the hero's behavior to many people in a similar situation. Example: " . . . and sometimes people who walk in deserts dream of water . . ."

F. Questions

The therapist should avoid as much as possible the use of exclamations or statements and use questions instead. Questions are much easier to reject, and they give the client the opportunity to make a choice. If a statement was already made, the therapist can at least make the tone of his voice sound questioning or end with "isn't it?"

X. Ending

"And they lived happily ever after" is the traditional ending of fairy-tales. It means let's allow the events in the story to take their own course. The story ended and that in itself is the substance. However, in the "story that you need to hear now" method we can use various endings:

Solution: The suggestion of a solution to a situation is presented in Gardner (1986) in the technique of mutual storytelling, whereby the therapist suggests a new solution or insight or an alternative solution in the story that he returns to the client. For example, in the case of a shy teenager who decides not to go to a party because he is too shy to talk to people and convinced that he will therefore have a terrible time, the therapist ends the story with a new solution. In the therapist's story, the boy may realize that if he chooses to stay at home he has no chance of enjoying himself at the party, whereas if he goes, he at least has a chance of having a good time.

A. Reconstruction

The very act of retelling the story to the client from beginning to end at the conclusion of the process grants a sense of coherence and of structure. The use of the aesthetic structure of a story gives the client a sense of structure, beauty, and acceptance. As part of this process, when the therapist wishes to intensify the hypnotic effect and the focus of the client on the metaphor, he reiterates all the details of the story and he may intensify sensations or add reflections.

B. Reflections

As an ending to a story the storyteller/therapist will insert a section in which the hero reflects on the journey, its outcomes or beginnings. His thoughts will be either focused or general. This can assume the form of conclusions, plans, contemplation, and so on.

XI. The "Returning Control" Questions at the Conclusion of Therapy

A. Is this is a good place to stop?

B. What did you like in the story?

C. What didn't you like in the story?

D. What would you like to change?

E. What surprised you in the story?

F. Which scene would you like to work on?

USE OF SCRIBBLING TO LOCATE A METAPHOR AND TRANSFORM IT INTO A METAPHORIC STORY

Raja, a sixteen-year-old girl, came to see me because of trouble at school. Her parents had divorced about a year earlier and she constantly fought with her mother. She played truant from school, took up with juvenile delinquents, and talked about life as a dark option. Raja was very passive but came to my office almost on time, and almost every time she had an appointment. She was very upset but didn't really want to open up. I knew that she did not write much in her notebook in class, but rather filled page after page with scribbles and squiggles, and so I asked her to scribble without looking at the page. When she had finished scribbling, I asked Raja to look at the doodles and see if she could identify anything. I could see that she saw many things, but was trying to find a "neutral" object, so I didn't comment. At last Raja found a jug in her scribbles.

I used Raja's description as a tool to assess her BASIC Ph (Lahad 1992), based on the BASIC Ph model for coping with acutely stressful situations. BASIC Ph is an acronym for the six main channels through which people approach the world in an attempt to make sense of and cope with life. The acronym stands for the six channels: B = belief, A = affect, S = social, I = imaginative, C = cognitive, and Ph = physiology (action or relaxation). Lahad (1992) suggests that the psycholinguistic structure of the story a person tells is a reflection of the way that person perceives the world and thus is a manifestation of his coping mechanisms. By identifying these channels, the therapist can direct his intervention (in this case, story making) to the actively operating channels of the client and thus bypass some aspects of resistance. Only in later stages are nonoperative channels used. For example, if a person uses concrete, accurate descriptions, the story will start with reality elements and emotional or imaginative elements will be introduced later on.

The Story

Raja chose a neutral object in her scribbles and began to describe it.

Raja: A bottle (jug), half full of oil standing in a corner on a straw stand. [C]. The bottom is round, hard to put on the table. [C, Ph] Opaque, thin glass, if opened not possible to close and the oil will spill. [Ph]

Therapist: Where do you see the bottle with the oil in it, the oil vessel with a stopper? [C, Ph]

Raja: The jug with the oil is in Haifa, in a house. [C]

Therapist: Is it pure oil? [C]

Raja: Yes. Because of this nobody opens it. They don't want to waste the original bottle, which is eighty to ninety years old. [C]

Therapist: What's its size? [Ph]

Raja: It's a bottle bigger than a wine bottle. [C, Ph]

Therapist: What color is the glass? [C, Ph]

Raja: The glass is a little bit light green and very thin and very transparent.

Therapist: Full to the brim with oil?

Raja: No, less than half. [C]

Therapist: What kind of oil? [C]

Raja: Very thick and dark, [cold press] first.

Therapist: What kind of oil?

Raja: Olive oil: can't smell that it stinks because it's closed; you can use it for massage.

Therapist: Which room in the house is it in?

Raja: It's on a small porch in a small corner.

Therapist: Oh, so it is on a small porch, and it is half full of oil standing in a corner on a straw stand. It is a little bit light green and very thin and very transparent. It is olive oil from the first press, and it can be used for massage too, can't it?

Raja: Yes.

Therapist: You said that it is at least eighty years old. How was it kept? Is it protected in any way?

Raja: It is on a straw stand (basket) that protects it, and it is a ragged, crumbling stand [The therapist receives approval that he can continue with the story and there is a clue about "protected and protects."]

[Note: Up to this point the central language is Ph, C, trying to hint at S, I.]

Therapist: The house in the story, the owners, have they owned the house for many years? [S enters belonging]

Raja: Many years. [Still returning to C]

Therapist: Is there a lot of light on the porch? [Returning to C]

Raja: A bit.

Therapist: Are there any other things on that porch? [An attempt to talk about S through C]

Raja: It's a porch where things are kept that one wants to hide or just forgotten items or rejects. [S is revealed]

Therapist: Let's go back a bit. The jug is about eighty years old; has it ever left this porch?

Raja: No. It arrived because somebody from the family of that house bought it because he thought it was a bargain. Maybe he wanted to get rid of it and so it came to be that there wasn't anything to do with it and it arrived here. It's been on the porch for fifty years. [Clear S = family, etc.]

Therapist: That's also . . . a long time.

Raja: Yes, exactly.

Therapist: There is something interesting about this bottle.

Raja: Something nonfunctional, very beautiful.

Therapist: Someone wanted it terribly and what does one do with it? [S and a clue to check A]

Raja: Because if it didn't have oil in it, it would be wonderful as a decoration, if it didn't have oil in it. It's not a vessel anymore.

Therapist: I have a funny feeling that I'd like to check with you. If we look at the bottle and its special color, I have the feeling that it was hand blown. What's the feeling, was it made by an artist?

Raja: [Not stopping as if the story is there for her.] First there was oil, and whoever made it looked for ways to store it. He heard about the glassblower, who makes bottles for wine, went to him, and found a vessel and it's the bottle. And thus this was the solution for how to store his oil.

[A conflict of internal uncertainty, some internal doubts—where to put the oil?— emerge here, also more movement.]

Therapist: How old was the man who made the bottle?

Raja: Middle-age. The bottle maker is old and this is the only thing he knows how to do.

Therapist: He had more bottles.

Raja: But not exactly suitable for oil.

Therapist: Was the bottle that was taken for oil disappointed that oil was put in it and not wine? Was the dream that it would be filled with oil? Myrrh oil or vinegar? [Raises another conflict; A, B]

Raja: Oil is okay. It was interesting for it because perhaps the bottle was made for wine and oil was put in it. [Answers in C]

Therapist: And the man who takes it did he also cork it? Then what happens to it, why does it suddenly leave the oil man? [Acutely raises S]

Raja: Because it was a green bottle of neither here nor there. In the bottle shop it had oil in it. In the shop they preferred to buy oil in conventional packaging. It came to that family via a vendor and it was in the straw stand. The vendor has lots of things and also the bottle.

Therapist: Let's try to see that picture. There is the vendor who has lots of things and also the bottle.

Raja: The vendor came to one woman in Hadera who collected unnecessary things that are surely good for something. She didn't consider how to seal it. [Finally a clear S reaction]

Therapist: And the bottle, what happened to it when it was chosen? [An attempt to develop A]

Raja: I think that the bottle was used to being moved around, it didn't get excited about being moved. [Answers also in A]

Therapist: "And so the woman from Hadera took it home and then . . ."

Raja: After some years she died and her relatives came to clear out her home. One took the bottle and soon after left it on the porch for years. It was forgotten there.

Therapist: Does anyone ever see it?

Raja: Only on rare occasions when an old broom is thrown onto the balcony it notices the bottle. But, because it is not a useful tool anymore either, it doesn't care about the bottle in the basket.

Therapist: You mentioned that it has a round bottom. Did it ever happen that it didn't stand securely?

Raja: Yes. You could see signs that it was left on its sides and it took time until it was transparent again. [Raja is becoming more and more committed and her voice turns very soft and hoarse.]

Therapist: What happens that flows in the direction of the neck? [An attempt through the bottle to create kinesthetic empathy]

Raja: There is a flow in all directions. It gets to the narrow place, it feels like pressing to open up and then retreat, and there is more thickness.

Therapist: What happens in the middle section of the bottle?

Raja: In the middle. There the oil flows and it's not so thick.

Therapist: How does it feel in the bottle?

Raja: Two reactions, one regarding the oil, one the bottle. The oil is happy when it is moved. There is heaviness and denseness, it gets aired. The bottle itself: happiness, excitement that more of its corners feel the oil and it bursts and gets to the top. [Clear A]

Therapist: You can shut your eyes and feel both of the sensations, the bottle and the flowing oil reaching every spot in the bottle, and the moving oil that isn't so heavy.

Raja: The movements are very harmonious, round, covering, releasing and returning. The straw hides a major part of the oil and it has to be taken out of it.

Therapist: Where in the entire bottle is there more weight and pressure and the oil doesn't reach it?

Raja: The bottleneck is where there is pressure; there it is pushed and it is stuck. But in the other parts that are heavy there is denseness; in the area that is thicker that it returns to from the trip, of being aired, it goes back into density. (The idea of feeling pressure and the ability to relax was transferred and absorbed.)

Therapist: Moves from one kind of density to another?

Raja: Yes.

Therapist: I would like again to go over the journey from density in one place and the other and to the place where the sides get the oil. Check if in your body there is a spot that contains heaviness or pressure. When it reaches the nozzle, all of the heaviness gathers there and returns to the sides. [Use of I and Ph to practice relaxation; calm and control of the feeling of pressure]

Raja: The only place and the significant one, when it reaches the neck I suffocate, and everywhere else that connects to the higher neck.

Therapist: I want you to try and imagine something now. Bring the oil so it will also reach there, breathe in a lot of air when the oil reaches a spot that presses.

[Silence. Raja organized in a comfortable sitting position, extends her legs, moves, breathes.]

Therapist: Tell me what is going on.

Raja: When I exercised with it and "moved" it forward and in a place that feels pressure, it moves more, gets stuck less, but there is still pressure.

Therapist: Remember that if you put it back in the basket you know that the oil will sink and the bottle neck area will be free. [Using her story and a universal truth to anchor the ability to have control over the sensation of pressure.]

Raja: Now I understand why he is always stuck in the straw basket.

Therapist: The lady from Hadera had a fantasy to use the bottle for something else. [Distancing to allow observation]

Raja: She thought of selling it for a lot of money.

Therapist: But as she did not, I have a feeling that until something is done with this oil the bottle will remain stuck on this porch.

Raja: Yes, if someone found it he would take it, break the seal, and use it and anything is possible and the bottle would be in great demand.

Therapist: So the seal should be broken and the oil used. Or the oil should be poured out and the bottle used. [Use of a seemingly logical saying to enhance confusion]

Raja: Yes.

Therapist: For fifty years the straw basket prevented suffocation and the solution was good. I wonder if after fifty years the straw that saw summers and winters is still solid.

[Raja stares and nods yes]

Therapist: Perhaps the stand is crumbling a little. Perhaps the solution is no longer viable. Is it possible to thank the cork and the basket? Now that you sense how the oil wants to get out, is it appropriate? Should the oil be thrown away, or is it possible to accept all, to accept that sometimes there is a bottle, and sometimes there is oil; therefore, there is a basket and a cork? They were vital. [Using confusion and primary language]

[Raja nods yes]

Therapist: Close your eyes. Is it possible to say good-bye to the basket, or is it possible for the cork to open? Is there someone who is willing to use the oil, to allow it to be sold, to enjoy it? [Grave sadness is reflected on R's face, and she is shedding tears.]

Therapist: Close your eyes. The color of the bottle is light; at its bottom there is thick oil that has in it all of the good components of oil. It is in the straw basket that protects it, and it has a cork like it had in the beginning that guards the opening. Here and there the straw basket has grown old, ragged, and shabby. Because the basket doesn't hold [it securely] anymore, there is more movement in the bottle, a pleasant movement, but it's always good that there is a basket and a cork that make sure it doesn't escape.

Check in your mind's eye if it is possible to give up the basket and the cork: but it is not necessary. You can keep everything. You need to think of fixing the basket so that the bottle won't break and the oil won't spill.

Raja: Some of the straw is crumbling; it's necessary to make a different stand for it and then maybe something will happen there.

Therapist: But it's still an option. Where do you see it now, still on the porch?

Raja: No. Now I see it in my garden.

Therapist: Is it a safe place?

Raja: No, among rocks.

Therapist: Is protection possible?

Raja: In the case of an earthquake. Now it is positioned half lying.

Therapist: Is there oil on the sides?

Raja: Yes.

Therapist: Is it actually in the light or in the shade?

Raja: A bit more in the shade.

Therapist: A bit better lit than the porch?

Raja: More visible. I think this is a better place for me today. A good place, another, additional. Good, not good . . . This is an intimate place. I am preserving the oil, the bottle, the basket and the cork. If I open all, I will be detached. I will be where my brothers are who don't remember and don't know anything. The bottle and the oil are things like . . . there were such relationships.

Therapist: What became possible for you at this stage?

Raja: I could move the basket elsewhere, the words being stuck, the mere fact that I changed its location and position: there is progress in the movement that began to be here [Points at body and neck], all that is related to alternative space. Now this is a new chapter in the story. It no longer sees junk, it's in a well-lit place. It's because of my relating to the oil in me, and it's the feeling like the jug. I can see it positioned on its side, it can rest.

THE STORY THAT RAJA NEEDS TO HEAR NOW

Many years ago, somewhere, there was a big guy, who was busy manufacturing oil. However, the story begins in a closed porch in Haifa, where things are thrown, so that all will remain okay. [Here the confusion structure is maintained.]

On this porch there is a jug that once belonged to this guy who manufactured oil some eighty years ago. One day he decided to sell the oil or maybe he wished to store it and he went to a glassblower, who was an older man. The place where the glassblower made bottles looked special as he was blowing bottles of various sizes and shapes. Most of the bottles had straight bottoms, but some were "born" with a round bottom for an unknown reason.

The bottle maker was very happy making these wine bottles. Some of the bottles he made stood on the floor and some were scattered around. The young man arrived and looked for a bottle for oil. He believed that he had lots of oil. But in reality it seems that he had not produced as much oil as he thought he had. The old man took a bottle made of beautiful glass and, although made for wine, he said it would be good for oil, too. He also gave him a straw basket that was made by a woman elsewhere, but it was somehow suitable for the bottle, it's not clear in what way. The young man took the basket with the bottle and went home. Only the bottle knows this story. [Intensification of the suggestion]

And then it becomes apparent that there is a problem; there is less oil. This was very unsuitable for whoever wished to buy oil from him. He takes the bottle, and this is the first time the bottle feels that the movement of the oil feels good when it touches all of its parts. Sometimes when the oil reaches the nozzle, it gives a sensation of pressure, but then it goes back and strokes the sides. As there is no buyer for the oil, the bottle ends up with the vendor who bought it and he puts it with the many other items he has. And then the bottle in the straw basket with the oil moves from place to place with this vendor. Each time the peddler offers it to someone he asks: "What are you going to do with it?" And the bottle isn't bought. Once it was almost bought: but then it wasn't.

One day the vendor reaches a woman in Hadera. He sells her all kinds of things, including the bottle. But what happens to the bottle is that for the first time in a long period it is left lying; the oil doesn't move from side to side, it is at rest for a long time. Sometimes it thinks about the workshop of the man who made it, it misses traveling with the peddler. But not long after there is complete silence around it. Soon after the house is cleared out and it is taken elsewhere. It is taken to Haifa and again it feels the movement of the oil. It is excited, maybe this time . . . When it is brought into the house, it is the first, and actually the only, time that it sees the entire house. Now this is really surprising: it is a very neat house and the bottle thinks that perhaps it will finally be put on display, but very quickly it finds itself on the porch. In the beginning it was almost alone on the porch, and when they went out they noticed it and it noticed them. Over the years undesirable objects—junk—were moved onto the porch. The door is shut, and all that goes on in the house comes through in sounds and odors. With the passage of time the straw basket begins to crumble. It has never heard anybody explain anything about the meaning of this. It absorbs odors and sensations. Fifty years go by; it is already eighty years old. A light green glass jug, standing on a dark porch. It is corked and has straw around it that is slowly crumbling. In recent years the sounds and odors have changed. It is stuck in the porch that is used for storing disregarded objects. It feels the passage of time through the disintegrating basket.

If the basket disintegrates the bottle will fall and the oil will flow, but it is possible that someone will decide to take the basket and have the straw repaired and this jug will be found, a kind of feeling that a lot of things can happen.

When sometimes there is a slow movement of the disintegrating basket, there is the sensation that the straw around it and the oil aren't completely stable, and the bottle moves and produces a good feeling. It yearns for the movement up toward the neck and slowly down back to the middle along the sides and than the restful calm feeling once it arrives back at the bottom.

And now, taken completely by surprise, it is in the garden on its side and the oil is touching the sides. It is in a lighter place. It can see clear skies and green all around. It is well protected and it is open so that it can breathe easily. And it knows that whatever happens the oil is used, the cork removed and fresh air can come in. And then again whenever someone spots it in the garden the owner of the garden can tell the story of this special light green glass jug with a round bottom.

And this is the story of the straw basket that had in it a light green glass jug containing oil that was sealed with a cork.

Therapist: What was your favorite part of the story?

Raja: Favorite [Thinking] that because the basket couldn't survive, the oil began to move. It excited me, this motion.

Therapist: Was there a part that made you feel that something was becoming focused to you, clearer?

Raja: Whatever was focused caused me to feel heaviness and excitement. This is a story that I didn't think about at all when I saw a jug in the scribble. But now it is clear to me.

Therapist: I observed that you became excited when I said that the odors and voices in the house changed.

Raja: True, it was the changes in the house, in my life, you know. And the scents and sounds that are no longer, since we left, my father and my two bigger brothers. I suddenly remembered the old balcony we had in my home, where I lived until six years ago. I felt that something is stuck, the porch, the jug. I believe that the basket can be renewed but there is something that doesn't move there. But the fact that I moved it to the new place gives me the feeling that there is a possibility that something can happen and move.

[After a few weeks Raja reported that the jug story was becoming more and more significant in her life and that through it she was finding more and more meaning that was helping her in various ways.]

TRANSCENDING INTO FANTASTIC REALITY AND BACK

In impossible situations, even when the client feels depleted and worthless she is able to contain a story. She is able to remove herself from the unbearable pain of her reality by listening to her own story as the therapist/storyteller takes good care of it and allows the listener to enjoy therapeutic distancing, rest, and an opportunity to recharge. At times the therapist may feel the need to take the lead for a while, however the reins remain with the client as it is always up to him to accept or reject the parts or the whole story.

In Ericksonian terms we can explain the therapeutic process as using a metaphoric space (fantastic reality), which is a "right hemisphere space," in order to suggest a solution to the insoluble. At the same time paradoxical control is maintained by inviting the critical aspect of the brain (left hemisphere) to check whether this "fantastic solution" is accepted by the person as a whole. If, as Erickson and Rossi (1979) suggested, "symptoms are expressions in the language of the right hemisphere, our use of 'mythopoetic' language may thus be a means of communicating directly with the right hemisphere, allowing the use of the metaphors in its own language" (144), then we can attribute to The Story That You Need to Hear Now method the qualities of healing in impossible situations. This is accomplished by translating symptoms into sensation, or into visual, artistic, or poetic language, and by weaving them into a fantastic story where resolutions/solutions, or merely proffered acceptance, can relieve the pain and suggest hope.

As Erickson and Rossi continue to suggest (1979), "This (use of metaphorical language to communicate directly with the right hemisphere) is in contrast to the conventional psychoanalytic approach of first translating the right hemisphere's body language into abstract patterns of cognition of the left hemisphere, which must then somehow operate back upon the right hemisphere to change the symptoms" (144).

"Metaphor, on the other hand goes straight for the target area: the right brain process and that, in Mills and Crowley (1986)" explains why metaphorical approaches to therapy were less time consuming than psychoanalytically oriented approaches (18).

The effectiveness of The Story That You Need to Hear Now method can be further understood through Erickson's and Rossi's (1980, 430–51) explanation of the dual level process described above as transcendence into fantastic reality while maintaining control. "While the conscious mind is listening to the literal aspects of the story, the carefully designed, interspersed suggestions are activating unconscious associations and shifting meanings which accumulate and finally 'spill over' into consciousness" (448).

Another way to understand the therapeutic effect of the method is by looking at Bandler and Grinder's (1975) theoretical understanding of the Ericksonian method. They propose that the metaphor operates on a kind of triadic principle by which its meaning moves through three different levels:

1. The metaphor presents a surface structure of meaning in the actual words of the story (in our case understanding and using Raja's BASIC Ph),
2. which activates an associated deep structure of meaning that is indirectly relevant to the listener (in our case getting involved in the story of the bottle),
3. which activates a recovered deep structure of meaning that is directly relevant to the listener (Raja's connectedness to the physiology of being choked and the story of herself versus her brothers and the feeling of not being taken care of).

"Thus by a process of derivational search, the client generates the meaning which is maximally relevant for his ongoing experience" (Bandler and Grinder (1975, 22). Or as Lewis Carroll (1991) put it in *Alice in Wonderland*:

> "Cheshire Puss," she began, rather timidly, as she did not at all know whether it would like the name: however, it only grinned a little wider. "Come, it's pleased so far," thought Alice, and she went on. "Would you tell me, please, which way I ought to go from here?"
>
> "That depends a good deal on where you want to get to," said the Cat.
>
> "I don't much care where—" said Alice.
>
> "Then it doesn't matter which way you go," said the Cat. "—so long as I get SOMEWHERE," Alice added as an explanation.
>
> "Oh, you're sure to do that," said the Cat, "if you only walk long enough." (26).

REFERENCES

Alkavetz, A. 1992. *Live Company*. London: Routledge.

Bandler, R., and J. Grinder. 1975. *The Patterns of the Hypnotic Techniques of Milton H. Erickson, M.D.* Vol. 1. Palo Alto, Calif.: Behavioral & Science Books.

Carroll, L. 1991 [1865]. *Alice in Wonderland*. Millennium Fulcrum Edition 2.7. Duncan Research.

Cooper, L. M., and P. London. 1976. "Children in Hypnotic Susceptibility. Personality and EEG Patterns." *International Journal of Clinical and Experimental Hypnosis* 25:147–66.

de Saint-Exupéry, A. 198 [1943]. *The Little Prince*. London: Pan.

Erickson, M., and E. Rossi. 1979. *Hypnotherapy: An Exploratory Casebook*. New York: Irvington.

———. [1976] 1980. *Two-Level Communication and the Microdynamics of Trance and Suggestion*. In E. Rossi, ed., *The Collected Papers of Milton H. Erickson on Hypnosis*. Vol. 1, *The Nature of Hypnosis and Suggestion*. New York: Irvington.

Ericksonian Methods: The Essence of the Story. 1994. Edited by J. Zeig. Contains the edited proceedings of the Fifth International Erickson Congress.

Gardner, R. G. 1986. *Therapeutic Communication with Children: The Mutual Story-telling Technique*. Northvale, N.J.: Jason Aronson.

Herman, J. L. 1994. *Trauma and Recovery*. Tel Aviv: Am Oved.

Hilgard, J. R. 1970. *Personality and Hypnosis: A Study of Imaginative Involvement*. Chicago: University of Chicago Press.

Klein, M., and J. Riviere, eds. 1937. *Love, Hate, and Reparation*. London: Hogarth.

Kluft, R. P. 1991. *Hypnosis in Childhood Trauma, in Clinical Hypnosis with Children*. Edited by W. W. Wester II and D. J. O'Grady. New York: Bruner/Mazel.

Lahad, M. 1992. *Story-Making in Assessment Method for Coping with Stress: Six-Piece Story Making and Basic Ph*. In S. Jennings, ed., *Dramatherapy Theory and Practice 2*. London: Routledge.

———. 2000. *Creative Supervision*. London: Jessica Kingsley.

LeDoux, J. E. 1996. *The Emotional Brain*. New York: Simon & Schuster.

Levine, S. K. 1997. *Poises: The Language of Psychology and the Speech of the Soul*. London: Jessica Kingsley.

Megged, A. 2001. *Fairies and Witches: Metaphoric Stories in Treatment for Children at Risk*. Haifa: Nord.

Mills, C. J., and J. R. Crowley. 1986. *Therapeutic Metaphors for Children and the Child Within*. New York: Brunner Mazel.

Nash, M. R., S. J. Lynn, and D. L. Givens. 1984. "Adult Hypnotic Susceptibility, Childhood Punishment, and Abuse: A Brief Communication." *International Journal of Clinical and Experimental Hypnosis* 32: 6–11.

Nowlis, D. P. 1969. "The Child-Rearing Antecedents of Hypnotic Susceptibility and Naturally Occurring Hypnotic-Like Experiences." *International Journal of Clinical and Experimental Hypnosis* 17: 109–20.

Oaklander, V. 1978. *Windows to Our Children: A Gestalt Therapy with Children and Adolescents*. Moab, Utah: Real People.

Putnam, F. W. 1993. "Dissociative Disorders in Children: Profiles and Problems." *Child Abuse and Neglect* 17: 39–45.

Rosen, S. 1996. *My Voice Will Go with You: The Stories of Milton Erickson*. Haifa: Nord.

Sanders, B., G. McRoberts, and C. Tollefson. 1989. "Childhood Stress and Dissociation in College Population." *Dissociation* 2: 17–23.

Sanders, S., ed. 1986. Special Issues of *American Journal of Hypnosis* 29, no. 2.

Spiegel, D. 1988. "Dissociation and Hypnosis in Posttraumatic Stress Disorder." *Journal of Traumatic Stress* 1: 17–33.

8

Assessment of Sibling Relationships Using Play, Art, and Stories

Kate Kirk

I work as an independent play therapist assessing sibling relationships for court and welfare agencies. (The names, ages, and sex of the children in this group have been changed to preserve confidentiality.) I chose to write up a case study of an assessment I carried out some time ago. The children had been separated from each other and their parents for several months when I was appointed by the court to carry out an assessment of their relationship.

THE CHILDREN IN THE GROUP

The children were removed from their family of origin because of severe and chronic neglect that years of intervention from the statutory agencies could not change. In addition, all four children had witnessed long-standing domestic violence and two of them had been sexually abused.

Gloria, 12, was placed with a single foster parent who had grandchildren, some her age. This worked well because it provided Gloria with friends of her own age and helped her to adapt to the placement.

Pat, 9, received a specialist foster placement with the family's own grown children. At the beginning of the assessment it looked as though this placement would not last. Pat looked older than his years. He was very slim and had a thick mop of curly hair. He wanted to live with his dad and his younger siblings but not with Gloria because she was too bossy for him.

Helena, 6, was a skinny child with thin, wavy hair. Robert, 4, was a robust little boy who never sat still for a minute. Robert had severe speech delay with no underlying organic cause. They were placed an hour's drive away from their older siblings and were not in contact with them as regularly as

they should have been. Robert's behavior was difficult to manage because
he would bite and hit the other children and he had temper tantrums when
he was told no. Helena wanted to live with Gloria and she did not mind if
Robert came or not.

THE REFERRAL FOR ASSESSMENT

It is now standard practice to assess the relationship between brothers and
sisters when they have to leave their family of origin and are placed in long-
term foster care, in adoptive homes, and in some cases within their extended
families. Social workers often have difficulty finding families for large sibling
groups and therefore their referrals might be based around which of the siblings could be placed together and which of them could not. Lord and
Borthwick (2001) state even at this early point it is wise to clarify who are the
siblings, who do the children believe are their siblings, and who could safely
be placed together. All brothers and sisters need the opportunity to consider
who is important to them and with whom they would wish to live. Dunn
(1991) and colleagues suggest the term "sibling" should be interpreted quite
widely to include half siblings, stepchildren, or children raised together who
may not be physically related.

Referral for assessment could come from the courts via the Children's
Guardian or it could come directly from any Social Services office. The referrer in this case asked me to assess the level of attachment between a sibling group of four, two of whom were already placed together and the two
older children who were in separate placements. The referrer also wanted
me to comment on their therapeutic needs and how these might be addressed in their future placement. The above information could apply to almost any referral received through my office.

When undertaking this work, I ask the referrer, What is it that you need to
know about the relationship, which bit of it do you wish me to assess? Attachment is only one dynamic of the relationship. According to Dunn and
Kendrick (1982), trying to describe the sibling relationship implies something more ambitious than to say that we are trying to describe the interaction between them. Siblings fight with one another, they provoke each other
and irritate one another with devastating lack of inhibition. They amuse and
excite one another and engage in uproarious games. They comfort and care
for one another and no psychologist is needed to point out the passion, fury,
and jealousy that can quickly swing to gentle sympathy when one of them is
punished or unwell. I think this could adequately describe the children I see
in practice. Over the years I have tried out many different ways of assessing
siblings and the methods listed below work well in creating a picture from
which a story can be created about the sibling relationship.

I normally use a video recorder to record the sessions, and written consent is needed prior to the sessions. However, a parent has the right to withdraw consent during the recording or after it is made. Parents also need to know who will see the recording and what will happen to the tapes when the assessment is completed.

THE ASSESSMENT METHODOLOGY

It is wise to gather information on each individual child as well as on how the children function together as a sibling group. I use the checklists and questionnaires listed below to gather data from all the adults who are involved with the children. To complement what I observe, I use a number of different measures to assess the children. This ensures the spectrum of the relationship is noted and evaluated. In addition it gives a picture of their overall functioning and will often provide an insight into their former and current family situations. I use the following:

- The play therapy observational instrument
- Sibling relationship checklists (SRC)
- Family relations test (children's version)
- Questionnaire for teachers (unpublished)
- Questionnaire for foster parents (unpublished)
- The draw-a-person inquiry
- The family kinetic drawing
- Attachment story completions task

The Play Therapy Observational Instrument

The play therapy observational instrument (POTI) was devised by Howe and Silvern (1981) and revised and adapted by Perry and Landreth (1990). Observing the play behavior of the siblings both separately and together is invaluable and if the sessions are video recorded this allows me to review the tapes over time and it is an asset to have them available during supervision. A great deal of information will be gathered in this way and it highlights vulnerabilities, developmental delay, and any social skill deficits that the children have. Conversely, it also highlights their strengths and competencies.

The PTOI was constructed after an extensive review of the play therapy literature in which Howe and Silvern (1981) identified behaviors described as important indicators of important clinical concepts. Perry's research supports the use of the PTOI and she identified twenty-three of the thirty children tested as adjusted or maladjusted. Maladjusted children's play expressed significantly more dysphoric feelings, conflictual themes, play disruptions, and negative self-disclosing statements than were expressed by the play of well-adjusted children. I find this instrument useful as a checklist to note the frequency or absence of all the listed behaviors.

Sibling Relationship Checklists (SRC)

I first saw this checklist in patterns and outcome in child placement research produced by the Department of Health and published by HMSO in 1991. As the PTOI allows for observation of the child's play, the SRC enables the therapist to observe different aspects of the sibling relationship to be considered. According to Lord and Borthwick (2001), it is based on the research of the Bridge Child Care Consultancy Service. Furman and Buhrmester (1985) outlined the key factors that need to be addressed in sibling relationships:

1. The degree of warmth
2. The degree of conflict
3. The degree of rivalry
4. The degree to which one sibling dominates the other

It has proved to be a useful tool in assessing the relationship of this sibling group. I ask parents to complete the checklist from how they remembered the children to be when they were living in their family. I ask foster parents to complete two checklists on each child. The first one might be done retrospectively from their diaries about the relationships of the children on arrival at the foster home and the second would be completed in the third week of my assessment. I use the checklist as an observational tool during the joint sibling sessions to look at the key areas outlined in Lord and Borthwick (2001).

Family Relations Test

Although this is a very old test, it is very useful in helping to make sense of how children see family relationships and in particular their relations with siblings. Differences found between the child's idea of her family and her de facto family should be regarded as additional data about her emotional life at home and this was borne out in Dunn and Kendrick's (1982) research. The good thing about this test is the playfulness of posting little cards into boxes, which appeals to younger children in particular. According to the authors the emotional attitudes that play the main role in the interpersonal relationship of a child include strong feelings of love and hate and milder feelings of like and dislike.

The version for older children is designed to explore the following attitude areas:

- Two kinds of positive attitude, ranging from mild to strong, the milder items having to do with feelings of friendly approval and the stronger ones with the more sensualized feeling associated with close physical contact and manipulation
- Two kinds of negative attitude also ranging from mild to strong, the milder items relating to unfriendliness and disapproval and the stronger ones expressing hate and hostility

The form for younger children consists of the following areas:

- Positive feelings, coming from the child and experienced by the child as coming from others
- Negative feelings, coming from the child and experienced by the child as coming from others
- Feelings of dependency on others

Questionnaire for Teachers

This questionnaire was useful because it give a rounded picture of the child's ability to make and sustain relationships with peers as well as a picture of his or her social behavior and ability to concentrate and learn outside of the home setting.

Questionnaire for Foster Parents

This questionnaire added valuable information on the child's behavior on arrival in the home, eating and sleeping patterns, likes and dislikes, strengths and vulnerabilities. Comparisons could be made with the before and after behavior and could be seen as measuring progress or the lack of it since their admission to the care system.

The Draw-a-Person Inquiry

In the individual sessions with the children I use a number of projective expressive techniques.

According to Kaufman and Wohl (1992) drawings have been involved in child psychological assessment since 1926, when Goodenough developed an intelligence test based solely on the scorings of drawings. Machover (1949) was the first to analyze human figure drawings (HFDs). Pearce and Pezzot-Pearce (1997) advised caution about over interpreting the figure's graphic representation especially about relying on the symbolism of the drawings. Supplementing the drawing with an inquiry may serve as a catalyst to elicit more direct material. The inquiry was added at a later stage by Robertson.

Children are asked to draw a person and are then asked a set of questions around feeling states and asked how they would look if they showed the feelings for each emotion in the inquiry.

The Kinetic Family Drawing

According to Burns and Kaufman (1972) in the kinetic family drawing (KFD) the unconscious speaks through symbols and like the above measure the author advises against over interpretation. The KFD is described as a method of asking children to draw their family doing something. It was hoped that adding an action to the drawing would mobilize the child's feelings not only in relation to themselves but also in the area of interpersonal relations. This particular measure proved useful with the older child in this group and highlighted the older child's parenting role in the family.

Attachment Story Completions Task

Story stems have been widely researched by Bretherton (1986) and Hodges, Steele, Hillman, Henderson, and Kaniuk (2003) as a means of finding out what mental representations of family life children are left with when they have experienced severe abuse and neglect. Children develop defenses and organize their behavior to cope with abuse, and often these defenses reduce their capacity to experience something new and different in a new family situation.

I used story completion stems in sibling assessment to explore the effects of children's early parenting experiences of neglect and abuse and how these experiences might impact on their relationship with each other and in their current fostering situation.

The story completion stems consist of six story beginnings that are to be acted out with small figures and other simple props. The idea is that the child will project his or her experience of family life on to each situation. Each story is designed to elicit responses regarding a particular attachment issue. The issues addressed in the story beginnings are:

- The birthday party: a warm-up story
- The spilled juice story: the issue is the attachment figure in authority role
- The hurt knee story: the issue is pain as an elicitor of attachment and protective behavior from the parents
- The monster in the bedroom: the issue is fear as an elicitor of attachment and protective behavior from the parents
- The departure story: the issue is separation, anxiety, and coping ability
- The reunion story: the issue is welcoming responses to the parent's return or avoidance, resistant, or disorganized reunion behavior

THE SIBLING ASSESSMENT SESSIONS

First Sibling Session

Participant Observation Based on the SRC as an Observational Tool

- The degree of warmth, help, and comfort
- Initiates play and responds to overtures to play
- The degree of overt affection; the degree of conflict and the resolution through age-appropriate reasoning
- The degree of rivalry, hostility, and blame
- The degree to which one sibling dominates the other

On arrival Gloria and Helena were quiet and watchful. The two boys did not show any anxiety about meeting new people. Gloria nursed Helena and Helena responded by laying her head on Gloria's shoulder. I asked the children if they knew why they had come to see me. Gloria answered for all of them and said she had been told that I would be asking them lots of questions. I tried to reassure them that there would be few questions and lots of playful activities. I explained that I would be looking at how they all got on with each other and I wanted to find out what they liked doing together.

I engaged the children in a balloon game without difficulty. They had drinks and biscuits, which showed their ability to share and notice the distress of others when there were insufficient drinks and biscuits to go around. Pat decided that they would all dress up and create a story of their own. The other children put up no resistance to this plan and the story duly unfolded.

Pat played a warrior who wanted to kill the other members in the story. The noise was deafening as Pat bellowed out instructions to his siblings. When they did not comply exactly with his wishes, he physically pulled them into whatever position he wanted them to be in. Gloria played on the periphery of the group humoring or ignoring Pat as and when it suited her. Helena was the least verbal. Nevertheless, she made choices about the roles she wanted to play but she was thwarted by Pat's insistence that she did as he told her. Pat found a wooden sword and he waved this about without concern for the safety of the other siblings. Pat passed a death sentence on all of them. They would be tied up and hung on a stake to die. I wondered if there could be another ending to his story but he was adamant that was the one he wanted. He had difficulty ending the play. Gloria suggested a stereotypical ending where everyone lived happily ever after. Robert and Helena were ignoring Pat by this time and were practicing their own story lines. Robert played at being an angry bird. He pecked and squawked at Helena who veered between being an old witch and a helpful doctor.

Analysis and Interpretation of Session 1

The children certainly enjoyed being together and their play was imaginative and creative if a little on the dark side. Pat surprised me by sharing his sweets, biscuits, and drink with Gloria without hesitation when he found that there wasn't enough. Robert took the biggest portion of everything. This action of taking too much is usually indicative of deprivation when it appears in this context and it was one that Robert was to repeat in every session.

Interestingly, Gloria behaved like a parent. She waited until the others had their drinks and biscuits and did not complain when there was none left for her. Gloria's behavior toward Helena was like that of a mother hen looking out for her special chick. Helena was the least verbal child and Gloria anticipated her needs, which might have negated her need to verbalize them.

She made no effort to see that Robert had anything, even though he was the youngest of the group. Despite his speech delay he made his needs known by taking what he wanted or screaming loudly. There was evidence of a reciprocal attachment bond between Helena and Gloria and only time would tell if this bond met the needs of both children appropriately.

Robert and Pat were outsiders. Robert played alongside the others, and Robert's play behavior, like Pat's, could be described as aggressive albeit in the role of a fierce bird. In this session there was no display of intimacy between Robert and the others or between Pat and the others. Even though Robert did not say much, he liked to know exactly where his sister Helena was. In terms of their relationship this showed a bond that had meaning for him and perhaps added to his security.

Pat's play behavior was worrying in that he appeared to be preoccupied with punishment and death. Pat was very controlling and he took charge of the session and Gloria allowed him to. He dominated the younger children both physically and verbally. His dominance took the form of verbal denigration. For example, he shouted "stupid idiot" and handled them roughly.

Second Session

Observation

The aim of the session was to look at the siblings' ability to share, protect, and comfort. I also wanted them to do the KFD.

Pat and Gloria arrived first and Robert and Helena arrived shortly afterward. This provided an opportunity to observe their reunion. Initially both youngsters ran toward Pat and kissed and hugged him and Pat responded. Helena then went straight to Gloria and cuddled her but Robert ignored her and started to remove his coat. Pat was unwell with a stomach bug but he told me he did not want to miss the session. He looked pale and he was noticeably quieter. Gloria was very caring toward him and kept patting his arm in sympathy.

The children baked cakes to take back to their respective foster homes. The younger children were short on some ingredients while older children had far more than they needed. Neither Gloria nor Pat offered to share with Helena and Robert. Gloria helped both Helena and Robert with their cooking later in the session, but this was after she had got her own cakes in the oven. Pat decided he wanted to dress up and left the room and went next door to the playroom. He returned later dressed up as a holy man.

When the baking was finished, I asked the children to do a drawing game where they could all move around the room and all draw on the same piece of paper. This proved to be an enjoyable game for all of them except Gloria, who was not impressed by having to change places every few minutes. I then asked them to draw their family doing something and to make sure they put themselves in the picture.

Analysis and Interpretation of Session 2

There was evidence of comforting. Gloria was caring and nurturing of Pat and was able to give him comfort and he accepted it, or at least he did not reject it. The reunion behavior between them was moving. However tenuous their relationships might be on this occasion, they showed pleasure in seeing each other with the exception of Robert. After greeting Pat, he ignored Gloria and she made no attempt to engage him during the session.

The two older children did not share with the younger children. I considered this was understandable and in context with their neediness. Pat's play behavior continued on the theme of punishment and death. When it was time for the session to end, he could not find a way of ending and he sulked because he had to leave. In part this was in keeping with his need to keep control and it seemed to be connected to his internal chaos and helplessness.

Robert and Helena became absorbed in the cooking and the drawing. Both of them managed to take turns and wait for help when they needed it. They mostly responded to the therapists' requests. They ate the uncooked mixture in handfuls and could not wait until the cakes were finished. I considered that this behavior might be tied in to their level of emotional satiety inasmuch if they don't eat it now it would not be there later.

Pat's KFD drawing contained himself, mum, and dad and no other family member. The mum was on the periphery of the page, which fit in with his view of his closeness to her. The focus was Pat and his dad playing football with both of them facing each other and the ball. He told me dad was the saddest in the picture because Pat was not living with him and mum was the maddest because she was mad and the two that got along best were Pat and his dad. The figures were immature and rather an odd shape and there was no differentiation between the adults and the child in size.

Gloria's drawing showed the family at home. Mother was hovering and the family was placed in a straight line. There was no differentiation between the children and the adults. The family floated in the middle of the page and no one paid any attention to anyone else. The only one in the picture with hands was the mother. Gloria thought her stepdad might be the saddest in the family while her mum was the maddest because she was always loud. She got on best with her stepdad and her sister and they got on best with her. She thought they all liked each other and they would probably be together when they were older.

Third Session

An Observation of Unstructured Play to Observe Evidence of Reciprocity

This took place in the foster parent's home during a contact session when all the children were present. Pat took charge of the younger children's play and suggested that they perform a number of plays, songs, and dances. The children dressed up in the kitchen and Pat led them into the lounge. The foster parent was the musician and she banged on the drums to give Pat his cue to start. Gloria stayed on the periphery and Helena engaged in parallel play while Robert was thrown about by Pat. I asked the foster parent to leave us with the children because she was monitoring Pat's responses and had she stayed I might have had a very different picture. Much of Pat's play centered on domination and verbal denigration of the two younger siblings. He handcuffed all of them in turn and pulled Robert's wrist until he hurt him. He also handcuffed Gloria to the wall and pretended to set her alight. Robert joined Pat in rough play and showed signs of pain, especially when Pat twisted his wrist. He followed Pat and he also showed he was able to initiate play. Pat in the role of a soldier commented about his own evil nature. When the play session finished, the foster mother joined us.

Analysis and Interpretation of Session 3

The themes of the play explored dominance, destruction, and death. There was very little evidence of reciprocity in this session. Pat's behavior swung between elation and overt aggression albeit as part of the play. Pat spent most of the time in the fantasy of the play, and it was evident again in this session that he was unable to make any kind of satisfactory endings to his stories. There was a continuous theme of disintegration, and the descriptive language was often violent and abusive. This type of angry story and the inability to reach a healthy resolution is usually seen in children who are depicted as controlling and disorganized. "Disorganised/controlling children not only create stories in which they are helpless to control the events round them but they also reveal themselves to be helpless to control their own narratives" (George and Solomon 1999).

Pat's intrusive play behavior ensured that he stayed the center of attention. His tendency to shout the other children down meant that he automatically interfered with and sabotaged their ability to get their needs met consistently. From what I observed his normal interactional style is aggressive and coercive, and this was evident in all of the sessions. There was a worryingly primitive and bizarre quality to his play and he continually demonstrated a range of coercive responses.

Pat's style contrasts with Gloria's more inhibited and avoidant pattern where her own feelings appear to be buried and it is more acceptable and safer to care for others than it is to care for herself. Gloria can take on a number of roles. The one she was most comfortable with was the caretaking role. Of course this is one role that brings her to the attention of her mother as "mother's little helper," which was how she saw herself. Helena might also fall into the avoidant pattern of attachment but she was harder to assess than Gloria was. Helena lacked Gloria's resilience and even temperament. There was excellent evidence of Robert's ability to use pretend play. Robert took on several roles and like his brother he appeared to get lost in the fantasy of the role. Despite her parenting role Gloria did not intervene to protect Robert from Pat's rough play and this was left to me.

Session 4: An Individual Focused Session with Pat

In this session I used the story completion stems to elicit how Pat might project his ideas on how parenting figures might react in a number of different situations. The birthday story had a fairly predicable ending. I introduced the story and I asked Pat to show me with small figures what happened next. He seemed oblivious to the birthday party theme and wanted to concentrate on the father figure's sexual activities. He told me the father had just dumped the mother figure because he loved someone else. Then he made the figures fight and hurt each other. Mother threw dad out of the window and then the children started to fight. One child figure was thrown out of the window and the other one fell out. The whole family died in an explosively angry manner.

The Spilled Juice Story

The spilled juice did not elicit a nurturing or understanding response from the parent. Pat got caught up in the father figure's relationship and the theme of the story was forgotten while Pat imposed his own story. He told me the father figure had a new girlfriend, and he demonstrated how they kissed and cuddled. He told me that dad sat next to the new girlfriend at the table. They kissed and cuddled and wanted to make babies and they wanted to do the things that mums and dads do. I interrupted him and asked him to think about the story line. Pat showed the boy figure spilling the juice and the dad shouting at him. The table was thrown over, the crockery was broken, and the boy died by falling out of the window.

There Is a Monster in the Bedroom

In the monster story Pat showed me what had happened. The parents come to the rescue of the boy but they are too late; the monster had already killed the boy and thrown him out of the window. The parents tried to get an ambulance but it was too late.

The Hurt Knee Story

In the hurt knee story Pat demonstrated what had happened at the park. The toy figures ignored their parents' advice and climbed up a large rock and fell off and both of them died. The mum buried the girl and then the dad buried the boy figure near their house.

The Separation Story

Pat ignored the story line and imposed his story line. The mum and dad figures go out in the car. The granny and the children stay in the house. A monster appears and eats the children. The family return home and tell granny off. Then they all come alive again and mum and dad take them out in the car.

Analysis and Interpretation of the Story Stems

The outcomes of Pat's story completion stems were disorganized and fearful. In situations where intimacy is expected of him, he feels anxious and the chaos of the past floods him with fear and disorganized behavior. Sadly the story endings were almost predictable and bore out what the foster parents described as his uninhibited behavior in social situations and supported my earlier observations in other sessions.

In my view the story stems give a clear picture of Pat's disorganized and controlling attachment pattern. All the stories ended with a catastrophic fantasy. Physical aggression and punishment formed a part of his story and ruled out the possibility of help being offered or being able to receive help from an adult figure.

Session 4: An Individual Focused Session with Gloria

Gloria's story stems were stereotypical and everyone lived happy every after. Gloria's overall presentation in this assessment suggests that she is a child who has an avoidant attachment pattern. She described herself as her mother's little helper and she also acted as a parent figure to her siblings when her stepfather left home. She has demonstrated a level of parental behavior toward Helena and to a lesser extent toward Pat. She did not display the same level of feeling or concern for Robert.

As a growing child, she was not encouraged to show her feelings or it might not have been safe to have any. Research informs us that many children who present in this way learn to act happy when they might be frightened and angry or as a way of staying close to the attachment figure without making any demands. Crittenden (2000) suggests that these children find caregiving strategies to cope with their situation, and these strategies increase their safety in their family but compromise their ability to maintain satisfactory relationship in adulthood and often recreate the same pattern with their partners.

Session 4: An Individual Focused Session with Helena

Helena clearly found the story stems difficult. She engaged with the birthday story, and the cake fell over before they could eat it and then she disengaged. Similarly with the spilled juice, she engaged briefly to say that the dad would make another drink and then she disengaged. Helena avoided becoming engaged in the subsequent stories. Instead she chose to play in the sand tray. The play behavior in the sand centered on being lost and found. Family members in the form of small dolls were buried and retrieved.

Throughout the sessions Helena was the hardest child to assess because she was so quiet it was easy to overlook her. I had to make a conscious effort to note what she did because Pat overshadowed everyone else. When I observed her in her foster home, she was more gregarious and played appropriately with their daughter. Occasionly she needed to know where Robert was and from time to time she went to see if he was still playing. When Robert got told off for being naughty, she went to see what was going on. She did not do or say anything to him but the fact that she was alert to the fact he was in trouble in my view showed a measure of care. It was hard to say what pattern she fell into. Initially I was tempted to identify an avoidant pattern but I did not see enough of her behavior to highlight a particular pattern.

Session 4: An Individual Focused Session with Robert

Robert's play behavior was chaotic in the individual sessions. I did not attempt to do stories stems with him. Robert's play was always comprehensible but aggressive. There was no outward show of aggression toward me but the destruction of toys (four in all) and level of violence in the play theme was striking. He bashed toys together in the sand. His mood vacillated between happy and dysphoric and the violence of play action albeit symbolic suggested he was releasing predominantly unpleasant feelings. Robert's attachment pattern appears to be disorganized, and he will need help to make healthy adjustments and develop the capacity to attach in a permanent placement.

Session 5: An Individual Focused Session with Gloria

As part of my overall assessment with Gloria I used the Children's Version of the Bene-Anthony family relations test with Gloria. This involved presenting Gloria with a series of cutout figures that she identified as members of her family. With each figure there is an associated posting box. A series of messages was read to Gloria, who then indicated by posting which of her family members or other significant people are relevant. This allows for an evaluation of positive and negative outgoing and incoming feelings.

The majority of Gloria's incoming positive messages were from her stepfather and her sister Helena. For example, she believes that her stepfather thinks she is clever and he listens to what she has to say. He is good to her and he is always there for her. Her positive outgoing feeling were very much toward her stepfather, her sister, and her current foster parent. Some of her outgoing feelings were in the direction of nurturing of her mother. However, some of her negative incoming feelings were from her mother. There were mild negative feelings from her brother Pat. Gloria also had negative outgoing feelings about her mother as untrustworthy and unreliable about attending the contact visits. Gloria did not want to go home and preferred to remain where she was. She wanted Helena to live with her but not Robert.

Other themes that emerged during this assessment included the children's exposure to violence and a recurring theme of the lack of nurturing.

Summary of the Sibling Relationships

Pat's overall presentation is a child who has no attachment strategies other than coercion; he demonstrated this in all the interactions I observed, with the exception of one session when he was unwell. He presents as a restless little boy who cannot sit still for long. He requires a high level of care and attention from his foster parents, and it is unlikely that he could be safely placed with any of his siblings.

This child has few internal controls or rules of behavior from his experience to guide him. His disturbed behavior patterns are long-standing and are possibly the outcome of his experiences in his early years. The representations of domestic life and his interactions with the adults in his life suggest Pat has never experienced a nurturing relationship in his family. The discourse in the stories suggests he has been exposed to adult sexuality and a high level of domestic violence. His younger siblings are likely at risk from his controlling aggressive advances. This cannot be brushed aside but must be acknowledged wherever he is placed, as any younger children in the placement would be vulnerable.

It is hard to say whether or not Pat has an attachment to his siblings. He seemed genuinely pleased to see them but almost as soon as they arrived he went into control mode and bullied and coerced them into doing what he wanted them to do. The younger children will always be vulnerable to Pat's uncontrolled impulses. The foster parents' observations are noteworthy: Pat does not miss any of the siblings and he cannot empathize with them. He is violent to Robert if Robert does not conform to his requirements and he will attempt to blame Robert for things he has done himself. These traits featured strongly in the checklist completed by the foster parents and was also supported by my observations. The only important relationship Pat claims to have is with his father and he wishes to continue to see him. He did not request contact with his siblings, and he would like to see his mother occasionally.

Gloria nurtured Helena and she sees Helena as being very close to her. There is a clear gender bias acknowledged ("She is my only sister"), and she hopes to see her grow up. Pat is less loved by her but she still wishes to stay in touch with him. At the moment Pat is less of a risk to her than he is to the younger children. Robert was the only sibling she did not acknowledge, and she did not have a view about seeing him in the future.

Helena clearly has an attachment with Gloria. She also has an attachment with Robert. Although she was pleased to see Pat, I believe she is frightened of him. When Pat is around she is more quiet and much more wary and in my view this might be a strategy for survival. The foster parents noted that Pat always had to have the biggest share of attention. In my view it would be very hard for any child to get attention with Pat around. The foster parents also noted that Pat's presence in Helena's life was detrimental to her overall growth and development.

In my view Robert's closest attachment is with Helena. This is borne out by the foster parents' observations. They commented that he was like Helena's shadow but sometimes was hostile and aggressive to her for no obvious reason. I observed Robert's relationship with Pat, and although Robert might benefit from a play partner I considered that it was often at a cost to his overall development in terms of picking up undesirable habits and a lesson in how to disregard the wishes and feelings of others.

Robert and Helena need to remain together. Their need for a permanent family is closely linked to their therapeutic needs. If these children were placed in an adoptive home, I believe it would break down because of their attachment difficulties. It would be pointless putting in play therapy or any other help at this stage as their greatest need is to belong to a family. When a family is identified they should be referred to an attachment project so that the family and the children can have every chance of developing together and attachments can be made with the family from the outset and not with the therapist.

Contact is an ongoing development need for all the children in the future regardless of where they are placed or the type of placement there are in to see each other regularly in order to maintain the family link.

REFERENCES

Bene, E., and J. Anthony. 1978. *Family Relationship Test Children's Version*. London: Nelson.

Burns, R., and S. H. Kaufman. 1972. *Actions Styles and Symbols in Kinetic Family Drawings. K-F-D*. New York: Brunner/Mazel.

Dunn, J. 1991. "The Developmental Importance of Siblings' Experiences within the Family." In K. McCartney and K. Pillemer, eds., *Parent-Child Relationships through the Lifespan*, 113–24. Hillsdale, N.J.: Erlbaum.

Dunn, J., J. Bruner, M. Cole, and B. Lloyd. 1985. *Sisters and Brothers*. Cambridge: Harvard University Press.

Dunn, J., and C. Kendrick. 1982. *Siblings*. Cambridge: Harvard University Press.

Dunn, J., and R. Plomin. 1939. *Separate Lives: Why Siblings Are So Different*. New York: Basic.

Furman, W., and D. Buhrmester. 1985. "Children's Perceptions of the Personal Relationships in Their Social Networks." *Developmental Psychology* 21: 1016–24.

George, C., and J. Solomon. 1999. *Attachment Disorganization*. New York: Guilford.

Greenberg, M., D. Cicchetti, and M. Cummings. 1990. *Attachment in the Preschool Years: Theory, Research, and Intervention*. Chicago: University of Chicago Press.

Hodges J., M. Steele, S. Hillman, K. Henderson, and J. Kaniuk. 2003. "Changes in Attachment Representations over the First Year of Adoptive Placement: Narratives of Maltreated Children." *Clinical Child Psychology and Psychiatry* 8(3): 351–67.

Howe, P., and L. Silvern. 1981. "An Observational System for Rating Play Therapy Behavior." *Journal of Personality Assessment* 45: 168-83.

James, B. 1996. *Treating Traumatized Children*. New York: Free Press.

Jennings, S. 1993. *Playtherapy with Children*. London: Blackwell Scientific Publications.

Kaufman, B., and A. Wohl. 1992. *Casualties of Childhood: A Developmental Perceptive on Sexual Abuse Using Projective Drawings*. New York: Brunner/Mazel.

Klepsch, M., and L. Logie. 1982. *Children Draw and Tell: An Introduction to the Uses of Children's Human Figure Drawings*. New York: Brunner/Mazel.

Lord, J., and S. Borthwick. 2001. *Together or Apart*. London: British Agencies for Adoption and Fostering.

Machover, K. 1949. *Personality Projection in the Drawing of the Human Figure*. Springfield, Ill.: C. C. Thomas.

McKinsey-Crittenden, P., and A. Hartl-Claussen. 2000. *The Organization of Attachment Relationships*. Cambridge: Cambridge University Press.

Mullender, A., ed. 1999. *We Are Family: Sibling Relationships in Placement and Beyond*. British Agencies for Adoption and Fostering.

Pearce, J. W., and T. D. Pezzòt-Pearce. 1997. *Psychotherapy of Abused and Neglected Children*. New York: Guilford.

Perry, L., and G. Landreth. 1990. *Manual for the Play Therapy Observational Instrument*. Denton: University Press of North Texas.

Ruston, A., C. Dance, D. Quinton, and D. Maynes. 2001. *Siblings in Late Placements*. British Agencies for Adoption and Fostering.

Schaefer, C. E., K. Gitland, and A. Sandgrund, eds. 1991. *Play Diagnosis and Assessment*. New York: Wiley.

Thoburn, J. 1991. *Patterns and Outcomes in Child Placement*. London: HMSO.

9

The Erica Method of
Sand Tray Assessment

Jytte Mielcke

PROJECTIVE METHOD AND THERAPY

In clinical child psychology, the Erica Method, uniquely, originates from two classical traditions, as an assessment tool or a projective technique and as therapy. Thus the Erica Method provides both a theoretical and a practical starting point for both assessment and therapy. However, in literature, play as used in diagnosis has been accorded far less attention than its perceived importance in psychotherapy.[1]

Projective Imagery Testing

Within the clinical child psychology field of research, the projective technique implies that the child is placed in a standardized but relatively unstructured situation, contrary to quantitative psychometric assessment, which avails itself of more objective, measurable methods. The theoretical basis for the projective methodology is that the subject will structure situations in keeping with previous experience, emotions, and needs as well as particular areas of conflict.

Psychodynamic tests began to be developed as a direct result of Freud's theory of psychosexual development and formulation of instinct between 1900 and 1920. The first and least structured test was the Rorschach test from 1921. It reflects several need-driven responses and is particularly useful for dealing with several areas of conflict while gaining an insight into the child's attempts at mastering these conflicts. The Thematic Apperception Test (TAT)[2] and the Children's Apperception Test (CAT)[3] represent a higher degree of structure because both reflect a variety of social situations and unconscious fantasies.[4] The more structured the test situation, the more the perception of features is predetermined by the received impressions. The more unstructured the situation, the more the personality-related functional factors come into play.[5] Through use of projective tests of a varying degree of structure it is possible to gain an insight into different levels of the personality. Those methods, which imply hands-on use of toys and play material, are particularly adaptable to children.

Projective Play Assessment

The varying degree of structure is also reflected in the different play assessment methodologies. Charlotte Bühler also established standardized play material intended for diagnostic use. Bühler applied a more quantitative perspective, scoring the child's playing and creations. The play material was inspired by Lowenfeld's "World Test."

Similarly to Rorschach's picture material, the Erica Method is vaguely structured. The Rorschach test and the Erica Method enable, to a greater extent, the application of layers of interpretation with respect to the child's personality, whereas CAT and other tests are more suitable for the thematic definition of current life and conflict areas in the life of the child.

THE TWO CLASSICAL ANALYTIC TRADITIONS

In the early nineteenth century the Western world became increasingly aware of children's special needs and their means of self-expression. Psychoanalysis, the emergent child psychology and pedagogy, gained ground. With Freud's theoretical contribution and analysis of "Little Hans" around 1909, as well as Hermine von Hug-Hellmuth's description of a case concerning a boy in therapy, the foundation was laid for psychoanalytic child therapy.[6]

Along with Anna Freud and Melanie Klein, Margaret Lowenfeld belongs to the group of pioneers who focused their work on "discovering childhood" and developing the understanding of children's thinking and emotions. Whereas A. Freud and M. Klein, alongside S. Freud and Hug-Hellmuth, achieved historic significance through pioneering psychoanalytic child therapy in the light of the child's play and language, Margaret Lowenfeld's achievement is her development of play material and methodology.

Like Hug-Hellmuth, Klein used the symbolic play interpretation method, working more intensively with the child's spontaneous play activity and these symbolic expressions as the direct link to the unconscious. Anna Freud thought it more important to exploit the child's ability to verbal self-expression and its conscious volition, aversions, and delusions.[7] She therefore also deemed it crucial to combine psychoanalysis with "pedagogy, or the science of upbringing." "The analyst accordingly combines in his own person two difficult and diametrically opposed functions: he has to analyse and educate, that is to say in the same breath he must allow and forbid, loosen and bind again."[8] Thus two camps evolved within classical child therapy—the English Kleinian school and the Viennese school.

The Kleinian tradition included infancy analyses on the assumption that all children go through phases of serious abnormalities, including psychotic and depressive conditions. The Viennese school limited child analysis to the most serious cases of preschool child neuroses, as its proponents believed the use of analytical expertise in pedagogical therapy would normally suffice.

Ever since Sigmund Freud's times, transference has been viewed as the most important tool in psychoanalytic therapy. Sigmund Freud noted that patients working with a therapist relived impressions and emotions from their past. Reliving these incidents led to the comprehension of previous conflicts and the possibility for changes in the patient's life. The main differences between the two schools of thought were (1) the age at which action should be taken and (2) the importance of language in transference as a technical aid to child analysis. Anna Freud believed that the prerequisite for every child analysis was to establish, right at the outset of any analysis, the necessary transference paths between child and therapist. The premise for this is the child's ability to prepare for and comprehend the purpose of therapy. Thus language and dialogue are fundamental communication tools in the methods of the Viennese school.

The Kleinian school also considers communication essential but places equal emphasis on a wider use of symbolic interpretation of the child's play and behavior, as play and enterprise are here put on an equal footing with the adult's free associations in classical adult analysis. Melanie Klein on her technique in child analysis: "As soon as the young patients have helped me gain some insight into the nature of the complexes—either by playing, drawings, fantasies, or the child's behaviour in general—can and should the interpretation be initiated. When dealing with children, the transference exists right from the beginning, and the precept saying that not until the transference has started, should the analyst commence his interpretation, is therefore not broken."[9]

Klein emphasizes the importance of on-time, in-depth analysis, reaching beyond the material's symbolic representation to the emotions associated with the material. Only then can the therapist establish the analytic situation and contribute to reducing the child's fear.[10]

Lowenfeld and "the World"

Margaret Lowenfeld was born in London and educated as a physician. Like Anna Freud and Melanie Klein, Lowenfeld gained influence as a leading historic figure within the field of treatment of emotionally damaged children both before and after World War II. Lowenfeld's work is part of the history of psychoanalysis, the child guidance movement, and developmental psychology. Contrary to her contemporaries, Lowenfeld was particularly concerned with the inadequacy of words when expressing those aspects of childhood thoughts and emotions, which interested her the most. Lowenfeld's observations of the preverbal phases of mental development are compared to Kleinian psychoanalysts' attempts at understanding the origin and function of thought and symbol development. Inspired by Erik Erikson, Anna Freud, Arnold Gesell, Melanie Klein, and Jean Piaget[11] and psychometric testing, she combined physical observation of children's disorders with the clinical assessment of development levels with regard to chronological age, family background, and social conditions.[12] Lowenfeld's principal interest was the observation of children's action as a means of gaining insight into their emotions and fantasies. The purpose was to observe, accompany, and try to understand but wherever possible avoid forcing the therapist's own thoughts and ideas on the child and to be as nonintervening as possible. Concurrent with Lowenfeld's work with a more rational system of age-related changes and different kinds of play, the use of transference was toned down. It was decided not directly to interpret children's use of material or what they said in the playroom. This loose structure was tantamount to the perception of play, not exclusively as a means to releasing energy and reducing tension, but rather as a medium through which children could express themselves or think. The prime objective of therapy was to enable children to express ideas and fantasies and, on their terms, clarify aspects of their personality, which were causing difficulties and conflicts.

Lowenfeld was particularly interested in how to prove that transference took place, away from the relationship and apart from what was brought into the conscious domain by child and therapist. Klein criticized Lowenfeld for attaching insufficient importance to transference in a child–therapist relationship. Her focus was on the dynamic, the paramount factor in transference, which is expressed in the way inanimate objects are arranged in the world rather than through the relationship between child and therapist.[13] When the therapist refrained from intervening or making suggestions to the child, something new and excitingly creative grew from the child's constructions. In this way, the World technique was created by the children themselves.[14] "The World technique apparatus should appeal to the heart of the Jungian, seeing that the 'World' cabinet is richly furnished with already completed archetype symbols."[15]

With the intention of reducing the problem of interpreting the direct relationship between child and therapist, where distinguishing between the mental material of the child and that of the therapist might prove difficult,

Lowenfeld tried to create a more objective benchmark. In order to enable a direct study of the structure of transference, Lowenfeld found it necessary to establish a method that allowed detailed study and comparisons even when the subject was not physically present. She therefore developed a technique that is equally applicable to child and adult therapy and facilitates the simultaneous emphasis on several personality traits, even when those traits conflict.

In 1928 she started a Clinic for Nervous and Difficult Children in London and in 1929 introduced the play material she called the World: a combination of a sand tray and around four hundred toys divided into adult and child dolls, humans of various races, soldiers, tame and wild animals, material for roads, houses and transport. Added to this were building blocks, crayons, paint, and paper.[16]

Compared to Klein's material, the "World" was advanced for greater detail in application. The material could be used for diagnostic purposes, but Lowenfeld did not regard the material a test and therefore had no wish to standardize it. However, in practice it turned out that children's mental condition could be inferred by evaluating the things they build, their handling of the material, and their presence in the playroom with the therapist. The toys were kept in a small cabinet with drawers. When children were playing with the toys, they were deliberately encouraged to create realistic depictions in the sand of scenes from their everyday life. Lowenfeld was especially interested in the individuality of the child's use of symbols and the suitability of the material for reflecting and differentiating between the prime system (emotions, fantasy, and imagery) and the secondary system (rationality, logic, and language) in the child's expression.[17] "Sometimes they act, sometimes they play, sometimes they recount dreams or paint, write stories or recount fantasies that come into their heads. The 'World' takes its place among other pieces of apparatus and forms of expression as a clinical instrument used in the process of treatment and study of the child, but upon which the whole burden of treatment does not rest."[18]

The Evolution of the Erica Method

As mentioned earlier, Lowenfeld's "World" material came to serve as a model for and exert a more direct influence on the development of play material and method in child assessment and therapy within the European tradition. On a study tour in 1933 the Swedish teacher Hanna Bratt visited the Institute of Child Psychology in London, where she met Margaret Lowenfeld. Hanna Bratt had just retired from her job as head teacher of Fernanderska Skolan in Örebro, Sweden. Inspired by Lowenfeld's work, she returned home and founded a small experimental enterprise in a room on the

Anna Sandströms Skolen in Stockholm. In 1934 she succeeded in gathering a group of doctors, teachers, and social workers who agreed on founding an institution, which on Hanna Bratt's recommendation was named the Erica Foundation after her favorite flower, bell heather *(Erica cinerea)*. The symbolic meaning of the name was its combination of the qualities strength and suppleness, seen as the two essential characteristics of clinical practice: the structured situation and the schooled intuition. Hanna Bratt introduced both toys and sand tray from the outset in 1934. The first academically trained child therapist of the Erica Foundation, Gudrun Seitz, started using the sand tray in child psychotherapy in 1942. At the same time the playroom was furnished as a one-way screen room. Allis Danielson, who was employed as a child psychotherapist with the Erica Foundation from 1946, wrote the following about Gudrun: "She said you must let 'the material live,' meaning that the therapist must accept having to be, at all times, one step behind the child in its play."[19] Her attitude was that the therapist had to avoid inventing and instead let the process be guided by the child's ideas and listen to its secret—be "attentive to" the constitution of inner alertness. You should hence let the material live and evolve from inner alertness, beware of premature interpretation, and avoid unnecessarily exacerbating the fear.[20] Gudrun Seitz was an eclectic who used neither Klein's analytically active attitude nor Lowenfeld's passive observation stringently. She considered the therapist's attitude important. The therapist was a partner on the symbolic level of the monologue the child carried out in its play. The therapist's role was actively receiving rather than, as emphasized by Lowenfeld, passively accepting.

Gösta Harding, a consultant at the Erica Foundation, became particularly interested in the possibilities of the sand tray material in psycho-diagnostics. His main concern was how to draw conclusions concerning children's development, personality type, possible emotional conflicts, neuroses, or psychoses from their play and creative use of toys. Harding also saw an opportunity for a more methodical use of the material in child diagnostics. Under Harding's leadership, in 1947 Allis Danielson and a group of the Erica Foundation's clinical staff compiled an observation method, named the Erica Method. Through the Erica Method it became possible to carry out a structured play diagnostic test with sand tray observations as a starting point. Over the following years, Allis Danielson headed most of the observations at the Erica Foundation, while work continued on varying the compositions of the material, its divisions into categories, and positioning. At the same time, experiments were carried out on observation and registration procedures intended for evaluation. The material was enhanced as it was found to be inadequate for the purpose. In 1949 a material with 360 toys was introduced, which is still in use today.[21]

THE ERICA METHOD AND THE MATERIALS

The Erica Method can be characterized as a "performance-projective" and "constructive-projective" technique. The child's motor function, language, and creative talent can be observed in a wider context than by using other test methods. However, observation and analysis of the child's play encounters the same difficulties as with any other projective method.

The Erica Method is a standardized method, which means that it attempts to encourage free creativity in the child while simultaneously keeping certain factors under constant observation. In this way the attitude during observation is kept as unbiased as possible by eliminating the risk of extraneous influences and stimuli, from anything other than the toys, the sand, and the actual situation, including the adult presence and a specific room layout. A more active observation method risks forcing the child into a therapeutic relationship and provokes transference to the assessor.

The material consists of 360 miniature objects, a cabinet with 12 shelves, and 2 sand trays in a wide wooden frame containing dry and wet sand respectively. Cabinet and sand tray have specific, fixed objectives. The play material is comprised of soldiers, cowboys, Indians, and various other human figures, including neutral, mythical, and specific professional figures such as doctor and nurse. In addition there are tame and wild animals and their young. Furthermore the material includes means of transport—trains, cars and lorries, handcarts, and auxiliary vehicles such as an ambulance, a fire engine, and a crane, as well as a hearse. Transport vehicles also include planes, military and commercial vehicles as well as sailing and rowing boats. The Erica material also includes military equipment, cannon, explosions, and fire. The buildings in the material comprise churches, houses, and mansions. Fixtures include a limited amount of dollhouse furniture and bedding, telephones, and potted plants. Fencing and traffic auxiliary materials comprise trees, railings, railway, road barriers, traffic signs, and petrol pumps. Apart from the toy objects, the Erica material contains a lump of brown moldable clay that was originally included so that the child could create anything not already specifically included among the toys.

The toys are positioned on specific shelves relative to other toys, but should, apart from this restriction, be placed there randomly. Within individual shelves, toys should not be placed in a particular order or grouped with related items. This reduces the risk of outside factors influencing the child's choice of toys.[22] For the same reason, the psychologist is placed in a specific part of the room, close to one of the longer sides of the sand tray near the corner so that the child has room to move freely around the entire sand tray.

Instructions and the Role of the Observer

Given an initial brief instruction, the child builds up its world in the sand tray. Contextual and formal aspects of this world are subsequently evaluated and so provide an image of the child's frame of mind. Using the Erica Method means the complete exclusion of commentary and evaluation in the course of the observation and thus avoids releasing instincts or raising unconscious desires and conflicts into the conscious mind. It is the task of the diagnostician to pinpoint the child's developmental and emotional position in life as well as the cause of the child's difficulties. The therapist's task is to help the child move toward change.

The Erica Method is used for children between three and twelve, although it is considered most suitable for children between five and ten. The observation process covers three sessions with the child, for a maximum of forty-five minutes per session. During the three sessions the psychologist continuously takes process notes. Anything the child touches, positions, makes, or plays with is written down in therapist's notes; as well as the first object the child places in the sand, and its position in the sand. The child's appearance, body language, and facial expressions are described. Speed of construction and playing as well as latency period are noted.[23] Furthermore the child's commentary and any questions posed by it are recorded. A record protocol with instructions on which formal aspects should be recorded during the observation process is also a part of the Erica material.

During observations, the psychologist's attitude is "nondirective," passive, and neutral in that she does not actively participate in the child's play or creativity but listens attentively and actively and supports the child in its efforts to solve or find a way around any problems experienced while playing with the toys. The nondirective technique also implies a higher degree of encouraging the child as opposed to the therapist acting the oracle to answer all the child's questions. It is important that the psychologist does not come to appear to give the child the cold shoulder but instead expresses her interest and sympathy through tone of voice and provides the child with the feeling of security he or she needs.

Once the observation session is completed, the psychologist attempts to get the child to explain, as spontaneously and freely as possible, what he or she has created in the sand tray. The dialogue must not seem strained or interrogative or guide the child's attention in a certain direction but needs to be tailored to the individual child. The psychologist refrains from praising the child but maintains an interested, accepting atmosphere.

Although it aims primarily at establishing a diagnostic situation and obtaining comprehensive information, the Erica Method does not exclude work on the evaluation of the child's interpersonal and social skills.

Recording Formal Aspects

The standard recording protocol covers four pages. Part of the first page lists a summary of the course of observation during the three sessions. Items recorded are the child's treatment of the sand, type of game, changes and corrections in displays, indication of time. On the same page, the circumstances of the three final displays are recorded. This record includes the degree to which the sand tray was incorporated, compositions in ascending order of development, and any notable compositions and arrangements.

On pages 3–4 there is room to insert pictures of the three final sand tray scenes. Page 4 contains an index of all the objects. The objects used by the child in the sand tray and the scope of usage are recorded here.

The formal variables make up the objective data on which the various observers agree. The outcome of the three observations is noted in the fields under "description." Hypotheses on how to interpret the behavior are recorded under the heading "hypotheses." Changes occurring during the observation process are observed under each variable and make up the sequence analysis, which is considered of paramount importance. The formal aspects comprise:

- The child's use of sand, recorded in the following categories: scoops and spreads, smoothes and strokes, digs and hollows out, shapes, marks, makes impressions and creates patterns, hides objects in the sand, adds water, other sand, or similar.
- The child's play type is recorded in one of three categories:

  Explorative play, primarily of an investigative or experimental nature
  Functional play in which the child exploits the toys' functions
  Role and fictitious play in which the child demonstrates its empathic ability and the play has a fixed aim

- Timing is noted by

  The latency period—the amount of time from when the psychologist gives her initial instructions and until the child places the first toy in the sand tray
  Construction time—the period from the point at which the child places the first toy until the child completes its activities in the sandpit
  The child's activity and passivity levels during observation are recorded here

- The final arrangement is recorded both in relation to the degree of use of and presentation in the two sand trays, as well as the degree of composition in the child's display

- The degree of composition is recorded in the following categories, along a developmental scale from the lowest to the highest level:

Indifferent arrangements, in which the toys are spread out incoherently

Sorting, in which the toys are placed in groups by size, color, or other common characteristics without any meaningful connection

Configuration, where the toys are arranged in a geometric pattern, for example, in a row, in a circle, and so on

The toys are combined on a simple, primitive level: chair by table, and so on

The toys are juxtaposed: those that are coherently related to each other are placed together, albeit without being intelligibly organized relative to each other

Conventional grouping describes a display in which things are grouped meaningfully, but without the group(s) relating to the tray overall

Complete coherence describes displays in which everything is meaningfully connected in relation to the rest

- Special compositions and arrangements comprise three types:

Chaotic arrangements characterize displays in which objects have been successively spread out across the whole without interrelating. Often this involves an overfilled sand tray in which the child was unable to limit himself

Bizarre grouping describes exceptionally peculiar combinations of toys where the combination gives a bizarre impression, for instance a crocodile on top of a church

Enclosed world where the display is framed or enclosed in an incomprehensible and severely exaggerated way

Analysis and Evolution of the Formal Aspects

A record form has been compiled for the Erica material, for use during analysis and evaluation of the formal aspects and variables. The Erica Method's authors are aware that there is no definitive "key" to evaluating psychodynamic methods. It is therefore imperative here, as it was in the Rorschach test, that the psychologist ensures that the individual detail and sequence analyses are made en route, prior to proceeding to the final statement and preparation of an overall evaluation. In this way it becomes feasible to estimate how a hypothesis is strengthened and weighed up or rejected by others. Another essential condition for the reliability of the Erica Method is that it must be undertaken by psychologists with significant clinical experience and insights into psychoanalytic techniques and symbolic imagery as well as long-term experience with this method as used for different age groups.

Choice of Sand and Treatment of Sand

Dry sand is often experienced as beautiful, delightful, fine, white, and warm. Touching the dry sand is seen symbolically as an expression of feelings concerning the oral period's symbiotic phase and the deep fulfilment of infant needs. The playing may, for instance, represent disturbances in the gratification of oral needs or express regression with regards to compensation for unbearable, conflict-filled experiences at a later development stage.

Wet sand is associated with something hard, cold, and dark, something divisible that can be experienced as an isolate material. In psychosexual terms the wet sand represents the anal-aggressive phase. Work with the wet sand expresses vitality, strength, and aggression. The handling of the sand (leveling, digging, marking, etc.) is noted meticulously and worked through methodically for the formation of hypotheses.

As mentioned earlier there are many detailed variables and observations, which have a bearing on, the evaluation of the symbolic meaning of the work with sand and which between them form the basis for the final formulation of hypotheses. The most important parts are the descriptions of the assorted variables within individual observations, followed by determining the links between the three observations in the process.

At this point, features such as changes in the handling of sand, the number of objects, and categories that are increased or decreased during the course of the process allow insights into impulses, activities, and involvement with regard to control and inhibitions. Improvements and deterioration of the compositional level are given equal importance. Observation of repetition in building method and reinforced or weakened play types also has a bearing on the evaluation of how serious a developmental disorder could be. For example, it would be regarded as a minor disturbance if the structure and handling of sand in the displays show successive improvements and become more constructive throughout the observation process. By the same token, the sequence analyses throughout the observation process offer hints on whether resolving the issues appears to be a viable option. Hence the Erica Method offers systematic assessment of the child's play and enables the sand play to be used as a diagnostic springboard. Through detailed evaluation of the child's choice of material, types of play, positioning in the sandpit, building style, and use of time, and so on, the method offers the skilled therapist an accurate impression of the child's problems.

Content Analysis

The content is what the displays or sand scenes represent. The psychologist takes notes throughout the process, from the first object the child chooses to the final tableau. The content analysis elaborates on the formal analysis and with it constitutes the overall assessment of the child. Through his projective expression and specific symbol language, the child communicates, verbally and nonverbally, emotions, self-awareness, and inner conflicts as well as relations with relation objects and the outside world. Apart from analysis of the child's choice and use of material, the psychologist avails herself of other sources of information such as proximity and distance, ambivalence and emotional outbursts, in order to appreciate areas of conflict and fixations as well as the various forms of defense.

The Erica material evolved from a basis of psychoanalytic theory and child psychotherapeutic experience as well as a common denominator for symbolic content in objects and situations that have been shaped through culture, history, religion, language, traditions, and environment. Within the psychoanalytic tradition, symbols are biologically based while in Jungian psychology symbols relate to archetypes based on the assumption that a common human unconscious exists. In diagnostic methods the selection of toys is governed by the assumption of a certain symbolic world.[24]

The Toys and Their Symbolic Value

When Harding commenced work with the Erica Foundation, the therapy room was equipped with material similar to that of Margaret Lowenfeld in London. Freudian and Kleinian thought formed the premise of this development. One fundamental principle was that it ought to be possible to create both a peaceful and an aggressive-hostile world. The main categories for the most important types of material were deemed to be:

- Scenery display: buildings, trees, animals, boats, and trains
- Military scenes: explosions, soldiers, planes, and warships
- Town scenes: buildings, cars, road signs, people, and trees
- Pastoral scenes: houses, domesticated animals, fencing, and trees
- Zoo and open countryside scenes: wild animals, fencing, and trees
- Domestic scenes: table, chair, beds and bedding, stove, toilet, telephones, flowers, and people

The Erica Method, based on a wealth of material gained from experience, enables the therapist to interpret the child's use of living creatures, in particular the animals, and of transport and stationary objects. The many objects each have their very own symbolic loading and their use allows the therapist to gain insight into the child's personality development and any problems therein.

The Erica Method's Status and Relevance

Today the Erica Method is still an important observation method in connection with diagnostic and aptitude assessment for psychotherapy in Sweden. The method is today used pragmatically, in both Sweden and Denmark, in the observation of children, in that a less directive brief in connection with the introduction to the playroom and the purpose of the child's stay here with the psychologist is used. In this way the child is most frequently invited to choose what it feels like doing, with no particular demands being made on displays or the creation of a scene/a world. It is therefore up to the child to decide whether to create arrangements, play or just be in the room without carrying out any particular activity. On this basis the psychologist makes her observations of the child's activities or absence thereof, its contact and presence in the room.

The Erica material remains the fundamental material for play observation and therapy in many places in Scandinavia. In Sweden and Denmark, today's playroom layout also shows signs of a pragmatic attitude to the application of the method and material. For example, today's material is typically supplemented with other material, which has proven especially relevant in a therapeutic situation. There is often a dollhouse, a fort, larger toy telephones as well as the tiny miniature telephones, coffee service, sand objects as well as a large selection of Play-Doh, crayons, paint brushes, and papers. The more gentle approach to observation is also reflected in the fact that the psychologist does not sit in a specific and fixed place, but frequently moves around, depending on what is appropriate in relation to the child and in deference to the child's activities and boundaries.

The temporal framework remains valid with regard to the forty-five minutes per observation and the expediency of a continuous process covering three sessions. Based on these descriptions of observations of the child's behavior, contact with the psychologist, handling of sand and toys as well as its verbalization; the psychologist documents her hypotheses and analysis in a report containing proposals for further action.

The Erica Method's Future: The Need for
Theoretical and Methodological Advancement

In 1934 when the Erica Method was established, Harding originally intended it to form a meaningful basis for research by standardizing testing and assessment. However, the method has also proved meaningful in clinical usage. By contrast to other projective techniques, its peculiar strength was its applicability to work with infants and children with linguistic limitations, as it did not presuppose any particular linguistic competencies. At the same time the method contributed to reflecting distinct sides of the child's personality, competency, and functional facets. With psychotic clients, the method proved cathartic as it enabled them to communicate at an earlier stage through the play material than they could have done through words.[25] It may therefore also be assumed that the method would be particularly appropriate for the assessment and diagnosis of children within the autistic spectrum, for example, for assessing the ability to generate mutual interest, and so on.

During the assessment of fifty Iranian children who fled to Sweden in traumatic circumstances, the method proved well suited for young children and children with limited proficiency in Swedish. In some of the children a variety of posttraumatic play was reflected in their sand trays, this being a conspicuous characteristic of children suffering from posttraumatic stress syndrome (PTSS).[26] The Erica Method thus distinguishes itself by its value in differential diagnostic, and it is also used as a test tool in connection with neuropsychological problems.[27]

The versatility of the assessment is secured through the analysis of formal aspects that are objectively observable, combined with more subjective aspects on the content level. Through the symbol interpretation work on the content level, the psychologist obtains information about the child's need and urge-driven development and the structure of the ego with its strengths and weaknesses.

The Erica Method was developed in accordance with Melanie Klein's model in London, on a theoretical foundation that not only encompassed the classical psychoanalytic method but also builds on a more holistic theoretical establishment, influenced by Jungian thought. This theoretical background constituted the premise for eclectic depth psychology which here evolved into a fundamental psychodynamic theoretical outlook.[28] On the other hand, the method's observational and analytic mechanisms are strongly influenced by psychoanalytic theory and its symbols and concepts. It is, however, also important to take communicative aspects and the role of interaction in the test situation into consideration.

Since the Erica Method was developed, theoretical reform has swept the field of clinical child psychology. Behind the assumption that children's endeavors in the sand tray and playroom have provided such riches of information stands the theory that the child's play and creative activity reflect its psyche, experience, and stages in its relational and personality development. Going forward it is imperative that Harding's and other scientists' work and research into classical psychoanalytic theory, and the experience and knowledge of symbol imagery, psychosexual and defensive theory be evolved further, incorporating theories that have evolved in the latter half of the century. The recurrent question must therefore be whether relations between theory and practice are balanced or whether a displacement exists so that one area is more evolved than the other.

Considering the theoretical shift that has taken place it would be relevant to ask whether there is a need for defining new concepts or for reorganizing old, pertinent aspects of any theoretical advance.[29] It is therefore essential for the Erica Method to evolve further, its conceptual and theoretical framework, which relies on the motivational concept of psychoanalysis, which is dominated by psychosexual theory. Urges spring from physiological processes and in the tension-filled state they imply, gratification is sought through object encounters. In the encounter with the surrounding world's prohibitions and regulations, these tensions are internalized and live on as conflicts on the intrapsychical plan. It is these "motivational power centers" we encounter and treat in our clinical work. With the rise of ego psychology in the 1940s and 1950s, with Anna Freud as one of the key figures, the main focus was shifted to the functions and defense mechanisms of the ego emphasizing competencies and limitations in actions and behavior, with the emergence and impact of object relation theory and ego theory in clinical psychology, and throughout the 1970s and 1980s, led by Winnicott and Stern, Kohut, and Wolf, psychosexual theory's monopoly has been broken. Other significant theoretical progress has been made in infancy research, with Lichtenberg (1981) as one of its foremost representatives.[30] In addition to urges as a driving force, these theorists also include people's social needs as a vital psychodevelopmental source of stimulation. Through the weighting of social relations we obtain the option to combine the intrapsychic perspective with the interpsychic level and ideal, toward a wider dynamic psychodevelopmental theory. Focusing on transference patterns, mirroring, and idealization in connection with ego development, Killingmo undertakes crucial bridge building with respect to ongoing theory development in dynamic psychology while linking to Rogers and the entire humanistic psychological tradition. Despite the need for a concept of self, it is important that we are not tempted into attributing qualities to the omnipotent and so allowing it to replace the psychoanalytic personality model's three instantiations, which Killingmo considers unsurpassed as a conceptualization of intrapsychic conflicts. If we scupper the conflictual concept we therefore lose something central to psychodynamic theory.[31] While psychoanalytic theory perceives misdevelopment as a consequence of intrapsychical conflicts and defensive regression, the object relation and egotherapist perceives it, to a greater extent, as the result of insufficient affirmation and reflection of self-esteem and being. Killingmo argues the case for integrating classical and later theories and refraining from underestimating the weighting, in psychoanalysis, of the importance of aggression and the deep archaic sources in understanding psychical phenomena and human relations.[32] From the psychoanalytical focus on "the threatened child" and moral condemnation and threats of punishment, interest in later relational theories has been focused more on "the wounded child" and its experience of failed care at various developmental stages in childhood.

For these theoretical considerations it is important to stress the need for the Erica Method to be revived for diagnostic and therapeutic purposes. Restructuring of the theoretical and conceptual framework with respect to interpretation and evaluation on the intrapsychical conflict, self, and relational level should also carried out. Such adjustment and progress would also imply changes to the composition of the material.

THE ERICA METHOD'S FUTURE, THE NEED FOR ADAPTATIONS TO THE MATERIAL, AND THE EVOLUTION OF THE METHOD

Through many years of clinical experience of applying the Erica material, and despite the domineering role of high-tech toys (Gameboy, computer games, etc.) in children's everyday play, the cultural and archetypical play material has proven so appealing that the majority of children are quickly caught up in expressing their self and their experience of the world through their creations in the sand tray in the playroom. The child usually adapts quickly to the fact that playing and contact in the playroom have a special meaning, confirmed by the introduction and the framework within which they take place. In research carried out in 2000 by 250 psychologists in child psychological and child psychiatric employment in Sweden, the application of the Erica Method was investigated. This investigation encompassed the application of the Erica Method in diagnostic situations and therapy. The research findings demonstrate that just over half the participants used the protocol as a record, that almost all took photos during the observation process or at its conclusion, and that only a third made use of both features. Furthermore, that the Erica Method was the most frequently employed investigative method.[33]

The Erica Method's advantages demonstrate that the permissive and word-free atmosphere with no performance expectations or demands allows a place for catharsis. In addition, the unstructured situation opens up many possibilities for the child and for much information to be gained by the psychologist. In the participants' experience, the Erica Method facilitated a variety of observations of play development and symbolization skills, motor function, cognitive and tactile expression, and competencies, as well as imagination and creativity. Alongside the Rorschach test, the Erica Method was described as the most in-depth psychological assessment method in which urges and inner conflicts including fear and defense as well as object relations and self-image are expressed. Add to this the fact that the Erica Method is easy to use and the examiner need not be as controlling as is the case for other investigative methods.[34]

The Erica Method's drawbacks were indicated in the results, for example, that the method is time-consuming and that the free and unstructured situation might cause frustration and fear. Another drawback was highlighted, namely, that the interpretations are difficult and may easily become subjective, something that clearly impacts on the method's reliability and validity. A further criticism was that the method and material was outdated, and the psychosexual perspective too domineering.[35]

For purposes of research, there is a need to gather and document experience with the Erica Method in clinical practice, not only with regard to theory and concept development; but with a view to integrating four major psychological theories: psychoanalytic theory, ego psychology, object relations, and self theory. Development of the material could then be reviewed in light of the theoretical shift. For example, through this writer's own experience in practice with the Erica Method, back in the early 1980s before being acquainted with Winnicott's containment concept, it was deemed that a container lorry might carry a particular symbolic value. The container lorry is not included in the standardized Erica material but was listed alongside tractor and JCB as a sample supplementing material for therapy during my employment at the Child Psychiatric Ward in the University Hospital, Århus.

Apart from the development of the play material, it is also important to be aware of another significant development area. With electronic and digital advances, new opportunities for a more objective assessment and documentation have become available for observation of play patterns, contact, facial expression, and language. Today video recording and surveillance, as well as photographic techniques, often deliver additional observational techniques. In the past there would often be a one-way mirror that gave others the opportunity to supervise the sessions undisturbed, but they could not be reviewed as with the technology of today.

NOTES

1. Schaefer in C. E. Schaefer, K. Gitlin, and A. Sandgrund, *Play Diagnosis and Assessment* (New York: Wiley, 1991). Here quoted after M. Ryman, *Ericametoden* (Stockholm: Stockholms Universitet Psykologiska Institutionen, 2000), 8.
2. TAT was developed by H. Murray in 1943.
3. CAT was developed by L. Bellak and S. S. Bellak in 1950.
4. Schaefer, Gitlin, and Sandgrund, *Play Diagnosis*, 229.
5. Schaefer, Gitlin, and Sandgrund, *Play Diagnosis*, 229.
6. Schaefer, Gitlin, and Sandgrund, *Play Diagnosis*, 37.
7. Anna Freud, *The Psycho-analytical Treatment of Children* (New York: International Universities Press, 1946), 70–71.
8. Freud, *The Psycho-analytical Treatment of Children,* 49.

9. M. Klein, _Psykoanalyse af børn_ (København: Rhodos, 1973), 76.
10. Klein, _Psykoanalyse af børn,_ 81.
11. M. Mead in M. Lowenfeld, _Understanding Children's Sandplay_ (U.K.: Antony Rowe, 1999), vii.
12. C. Urwin and J. Hood-Williams, eds., _Selected Papers of Margaret Lowenfeld_ (London: Free Association Books, 1988), 51.
13. Urwin and Hood-Williams, _Selected Papers,_ 349.
14. Urwin and Hood-Williams, _Selected Papers,_ 56.
15. Lowenfeld, _Understanding Children's Sandplay,_ 7.
16. Lowenfeld, _Understanding Children's Sandplay,_ 4.
17. U. Löfgren, "Barnpsykodiagnostik," _Nordisk Psykologi_ 4 (1965): 235.
18. Lowenfeld, _Understanding Children's Sandplay,_ 5.
19. B. Blomberg and A. Dahlgren, _Utbildningen till barnpsykoterapeut vid Ericastiftelsen 1948–1955,_ Report no. 3 (Stockholm: Ericastiftelsen, 1992), 64.
20. Blomberg and Dahlgren, _Utbildningen till barnpsykoterapeut,_ 65.
21. M. Ryman, _Ericametoden_ (Stockholm: Psykologiska Institutionen, Stockholms Universitet, 2000), 10.
22. A. Danielson, _Att bygga sin värld_ (Stockholm: Psykologifölaget, 1986), 38.
23. The latency period is the time lapse between the psychologist's instructions to the child and the child positioning the first object in the sand pit.
24. Bühler, Lowenfeld, Kamp, and Kessler; Harding according to A. Danielson, _Att bygga sin värld_ (Stockholm: Psykologiförlaget, 1986), 90.
25. Danielson, _Att bygga sin värld,_ 156.
26. K. Almqvist, 1997, in Ryman, _Ericametoden,_ 17.
27. Ryman, _Ericametoden,_ 23.
28. H. Egidius, "Psykoanalysen i Skandinavien," _Nordisk Psykologi_ 4 (1976): 237.
29. B. Killingmo, "Teoriutvikling innen klinisk dynamisk psykologi," _Nordisk Psykologi_ 4 (1986): 243.
30. Killingmo, "Teoriutvikling innen klinisk dynamisk psykologi," 245.
31. Killingmo, "Teoriutvikling innen klinisk dynamisk psykologi," 248.
32. Killingmo, "Teoriutvikling innen klinisk dynamisk psykologi," 247–51.
33. Ryman, _Ericametoden,_ 25.
34. Ryman, _Ericametoden,_ 28.
35. Ryman, _Ericametoden,_ 28.

REFERENCES

Blomberg, B., and A. Dahlgren. 1992. "Utbildningen till barnpsykoterapeut vid Ericastiftelsen 1948–1955." _Ericastiftelsen_ Rapport 3:1–112.
Danielson, A. 1986. _Att bygga sin värld._ Stockholm: Psykologiförlaget.
Egidius, H. 1976. "Psykoanalysen i Skandinavien." _Nordisk Psykologi_ 4: 237–41.
Freud, Anna. 1948. _Psykoanalytisk behandling af børn._ København: Ejnar Munksgaard.
Killingmo, B. 1986. "Teoriutvikling innen klinisk dynamisk psykologi." _Nordisk Psykologi_ 4: 243–52.
Klein, M. 1973. _Psykoanalyse af børn._ København: Rhodos.

Löfgren, U. 1965. "Barnpsykodiagnostik." *Nordisk Psykologi* 4: 177–284.

Lowenfeld, M. 1999. *Understanding Children's Sandplay.* U.K.: Antony Rowe.

Ryman, M. 2000. *Ericametoden.* Stockholm: Psykologiska Institutionen, Stockholms Universitet.

Urwin, C., and J. Hood-Williams, eds. 1988. *Selected Papers of Margaret Lowenfeld.* London: Free Association Books.

10

Children Talk about Play Therapy

Jo Carroll

Play therapy is between a rock and a hard place. The growing emphasis on research-based practice (Shaw and Shaw 1997) leads to efforts to undertake rigorous projects that study therapeutic efficacy and relief of symptoms. At the same time, clinicians know that the unique relationship that develops between child and therapist cannot be quantified, and thus a vital variable is excluded from quantitative studies.

This study grew from my need, as a play therapist, to develop my understanding of therapeutic processes in order to guide the development of my clinical practice. The context of this project lies in an ongoing dialogue between the rigors of academic research and my needs, ideas, and beliefs as a practitioner. Although combining roles of practitioner and researcher is challenging (Fuller and Petch 1995), both have been enriched by the research process described in this chapter.

A review of the literature reveals the obstacles that limit the undertaking of research into therapeutic efficacy, and the paucity of children's contributions to such studies (Carroll 2000). Current political thinking, as enshrined in the United Nations Convention on the Rights of the Child (1983), insists that children's opinions and feelings should be considered in matters of direct relevance to them. Researchers in allied fields (e.g., Fitton 1994; Bain and Saunders 1990; Rose 1997; Begley 2000; Costley 2000) have begun to develop effective methodologies to address issues of concern to children and young people. The study undertaken by Armstrong and Galloway (1996) is particularly relevant. They asked children whose views had been sought as part of an educational review for their reflections on the process; these children acknowledged that adults had made efforts to talk with them, but did not feel that their views had been heard or adequately reflected in decision-making processes. Children's disempowerment can be brought about by adults' assumptions about what is best for them (Armstrong and Galloway 1996, 113).

My need to develop my own clinical understanding, alongside an awareness of the silence of children's voices in play therapy research studies, led directly to this project. I set out to find a way to allow children to talk about their experiences in play therapy and to express their opinions and feelings.

METHODOLOGY

It is apparent that this is a qualitative study (Mason 1996; Padgett 1998). My interest lay in the minutiae of individual experience, which may be lost in the quantitative emphasis on statistical relevance. I wanted each child to feel that I had given him or her a voice.

Ethics and Research with Children

Ethical issues are raised by every research study; however, there are specific issues when children are directly involved. Alderson (1995) provides guidance to ensure that children's voices can be heard safely, giving due attention to issues of consent, confidentiality, and protection.

Ethical issues in research with children are underpinned by the inevitable power imbalance between child and researcher. Some have addressed this by seeking to involve children in the research design and interviewing (Ireland and Holloway 1996; Hill 1997; Alderson 2000; O'Kane 2000; Warren 2000); others have worked with children in groups (Costley 2000). Geographical considerations made it impossible for me to gather a group of children together for this study; in addition, my sample included abused and nonabused children. I did not feel it appropriate for children to be exposed to the trauma experienced by their peers. Addressing issues of power therefore fell to me, and lay in the interactions between individual children and myself.

In the past, researchers have questioned children's ability to decide for themselves whether to join such a project (Ireland and Holloway 1996). Gatekeepers—social workers, foster parents, birth parents—rightly seek to protect children from distress, but may also reinforce the power of adults by preventing children joining a study (Alderson 1995). I agree with Weithorn and Scherer (1994): children who are able to express an opinion are also able to decide for themselves if they wish to do so in the context of research, provided they are given appropriate information about it.

Children, like all research participants, are assured that discussions are confidential and they will not be identified. The children in my study found this difficult to understand; however, I invited them to select pseudonyms—some of which were idiosyncratic but were nevertheless retained and appear in the findings. In addition, researchers share the obligation of all professionals to share information about abuse of children (Mahon et al. 1996); we cannot guarantee complete confidentiality.

The Sample

I began to understand why so few researchers undertake studies such as mine when faced with the challenge of collecting a sample. I needed play therapists to identify children; to reach play therapists I approached training courses and the British Association of Play Therapists; once children were identified social workers and children's foster parents provided a secondary gatekeeping function.

Given such a tortuous method it is clear that the final sample of twelve therapists and eighteen children cannot be representative. I cannot know if a different group of children would have comparable stories to tell. There are several factors that may distinguish these children from others brought to therapy. First, I was not surprised when therapists selected children whose therapy was deemed successful, and who evidently felt warmly toward them. Finding children whose views were likely to be less complementary involved specific requests to colleagues to reconsider children on their caseloads. Second, all these children were in stable placements when they were interviewed; six had moved during the course of their therapy and therapists had continued working provided stability in children's changing worlds. Third, in spite of strenuous efforts, all these children are white. Gatekeepers effectively challenged my efforts to reach children from different ethnic groups.

Children range from six to fourteen years old. They include ten girls and eight boys; nine lived in birth families, four were in foster care, and two adopted; two brothers lived with their grandparents, and one girl was in residential care. Ten had been abused or neglected; nonabused children presented with symptoms of aggression, anxiety, depression, or conduct disorder; two had complex medical conditions.

The Interviews

My first meeting was with therapists; I felt it important that I was given sensitive information before meeting the children. In addition, therapists provided an adult view of therapeutic processes that gave an interesting alternative to children's perceptions. While narratives were largely comparable, differences are interesting and some are explored below.

I had considered inviting children to complete questionnaires, but discarded this as I felt that face-to-face discussion would help them develop their ideas and express feelings. My primary interest lay in the rich, personal data that may emerge in interviews. I developed a semistructured interview schedule, which provided flexibility to respond to children at different developmental stages. In addition, I took a range of materials: pens for children who enjoyed drawing, small figures to illustrate the playroom, and a hat for children who enjoyed role play; these materials reflect the EPR paradigm of play development proposed by Jennings (1993).

The children were interviewed at home. I hoped they would be able to decide for themselves if they needed adult support; one anxious foster parent was unable to leave and four elected to undertake tasks elsewhere. I made efforts to ensure that the feelings expressed belonged to the child and were not reflected from an adult.

These children greatly enjoyed the interview process, and so did I. I was concerned that their eagerness to describe their positive memories of play therapy—possibly seeing me as a link to a loved therapist—may have impeded those children whose views were less rosy. Nevertheless, two children were able to express negative feelings.

Data Analysis

Interviews were audio recorded and transcribed as soon as possible. The principles of grounded theory (Glaser and Strauss 1967; Pidgeon and Henwood 1997; Strauss and Corbin 1997) underpinned the development of categories and subsequent theory. The analysis was complicated by the age range of children included in the study; comparisons of children's views according to age may have been interesting, but my focus lay mainly in ensuring that each child's voice was heard. The voice of the least articulate is as important as his or her most loquacious peers (Carroll 2002).

THE FINDINGS

In the following excerpts from transcripts, therapists are referred to as T. The interviewer (myself) is I.

The findings are discussed in the following categories:

- Introduction to play therapy, which includes children's expectations, and practical arrangements for children and their families

- The therapeutic relationship
- Therapeutic processes: focused and free play, and the role of talking
- Separations: at the end of each session and when therapy comes to an end

Introduction to Play Therapy

Play therapists described carefully worded introductions to the play therapy process, before children came to the playroom. However, all these children had inaccurate expectations of play therapy:

Allan: I thought it was going to be a little room with either a really old man or a really old woman, that asked you questions that you really, really didn't want to answer, and you did a bit of coloring and drawing and that was it. So it was a big change! (age 14)

Interviewer: When you went to see her, do you remember what you thought might happen?

Britney: That we'd just talk; I didn't know we were going to play.

Interviewer: And were you worried about that?

Britney: I was worried about being bored really; it was like, I'm going to be bored just talking. Didn't know there was going to be toys.

Jamie's recollections are interesting; he had had several placements before meeting his therapist, and he saw therapy as integral to his experiences in the Care system:

Interviewer: Before you started play therapy, do you remember what you thought would happen?

Jamie: We would keep moving to different people. I've had nearly eleven foster parents so far, in my whole life.

Interviewer: Oh dear. What did you think it would be like when you went to see T?

Jamie: I'd think it was going to be good, cos she can listen to what we think, she can sort it out, and she can decide and tell the social services if we can go to someone permanently.

Interviewer: And you thought that was a good thing?

Jamie: Yeah, help us not move around loads. (age 12)

Although expectations were distorted, eight children have accurate reasons for their referral for play therapy; for instance, James's insight, given his therapist's description of him as chaotic, surprised me:

James: Cos I can't get on well, with other people, something like that. (age 9)

Tiffany's explanation is particularly interesting; having told me that her lengthy attendance followed a disclosure of sexual abuse, she described the original referral:

Tiffany: I actually know that it was because I was, I'd stopped eating, cos my nan died and I used to eat her meals—her meals on wheels—and that's why I thought she'd died, so I stopped eating. (age 13)

Tiffany's physical decline prompted the referral for play therapy, but her therapist did not mention her eating her grandmother's food. The disclosure of sexual abuse and consequent separation from her birth family became the focus of Tiffany's therapy.

However, six children, including Lee and Jack (two brothers who did not enjoy play therapy), were unable to explain why they had attended, even with gentle probing from me. Stephanie tried to be helpful:

Interviewer: Do you know whose idea it was?

Stephanie: No. I think it was my social worker's, or something like that. Or it might have been T cos she might have wanted to help children, help with education, because it makes, makes the children happy, and it lets them, lets T know how they feel, and how they feel in foster care, or something like that.

Interviewer: Right. So do you know why they thought it was a good idea for you, in particular?

Stephanie: No, I haven't got a clue. (age 9)

Perhaps most worrying is Jack, who, when invited to question me, replied:

Jack: Um . . . why did I have play therapy? (age 9)

Play therapists alone are not responsible for answering such questions. Families provide the context in which children are enabled to utilize play therapy; they are also responsible for the practical arrangements that make it possible. The willingness of some foster parents to facilitate attendance, occasionally at considerable cost to themselves, demonstrates their commitment to their children's therapy:

Interviewer: How did you get to play therapy?

Christina: Once it was a bus, before L. [previous foster parent] started to call the taxis, and the very first time it was a social worker, taking L. to see her son, who was in hospital, cos he had an accident; then the social worker took me to play therapy; and he picked me up, and then L. started getting the bus. And when I got adopted my Mum used to take the afternoon off work, I used to get the afternoon off school every Tuesday, to go to play therapy. (age 11)

Such commitment was not lost on therapists, who valued supportive foster parents and recognize their pivotal role in providing both transport and emotional support for children throughout therapy:

> His mum brought him every time, and it was extremely regularly; I think it was only one time when she had to cancel at the last minute and that was because her car broke down. But they were extremely frequent, basically they were very reliable, and I think that's part of the success of it really, that mum was very engaged, in her own right in her own therapy, but also in terms of bringing Simon and wanting them to sort their difficulties out. (Therapist for Simon)

Children knew that therapists talked with caregivers, and were undaunted by it. It seemed that children were so accustomed to adults talking about them that they did not question the need for such communication. Kerrie-Anne even welcomed the therapist's greeting her younger siblings; when asked what she liked about play therapy she told me:

> *Kerrie-Anne:* When T come to get me, in reception, she didn't just come and get me straight away. She always stopped and asked how Mum was and things, and like played with these two [indicating her sisters] for a bit. (age 13)

However, not all foster parents were able to support the play therapy so effectively. The difficulties faced by the grandparents of Jack and Lee are noticeably different from other children in this sample; they are an older, pragmatic couple, bringing up four grandchildren who had been neglected by their own daughter. They rarely talked about feelings, but regarded "just getting on with it" as a virtue. In addition, there was little evidence of play when I visited: no toys in the living room or sounds of laughter from other rooms. The boys described my play materials as "babyish." The play therapist for Jack and Lee described her contact with them:

> They were supportive of me, I had a long session with V. [the boys' grandmother] explaining something about therapy before I started seeing the boys. But later issues came up that highlighted that perhaps there was a lack of clarity. I mean she always appreciated the efforts that were being made to help the boys, but I remember a couple of things. One was when Lee had been using the clay, and I would allow him to make whatever he chose, and he made a, I think there was a gun and a dagger, and he took them home, and subsequently I discovered that V. had discouraged him from making weapons because of her own feelings, and told Lee that he shouldn't be doing that; but I thought she'd grasped that it was alright for him to do whatever he chose within the boundaries of the playroom. And there was a time when one of them, Jack I think, came and obviously had quite negative feelings about having had to come, and I discovered that it was because they'd been at another child's birthday party, and V. had picked them up early to come to play therapy. And I feel that if

they'd negotiated that with me I would have said, let them stay at the party this week. So maybe sometimes there was a bit of a problem with communication. (Therapist for Lee and Jack)

The Therapeutic Relationship

The children were highly observant of therapists' physical appearance. Descriptions were prompted by an invitation to draw the therapist; they were largely accurate with attention to details which therapists might consider unimportant:

Susie: She had long fingernails. And she always wore little plimsolls. And dungarees—with buttons. (age 14)

Lewis tried to provide an accurate description, and be generous to his therapist:

Lewis: She usually wears trousers. She usually wears [whispers] old stuff.

Interviewer: Why do you think she usually wore [whispers] old stuff?

Lewis: Well, I don't like to say; it's a bit naughty, rude; sorry, well, I'll say it, she's a bit old.

Interviewer: So do you mean old-fashioned stuff or old . . .

Lewis: Sixties style. She's really funky. She wears really funky stuff, like leopard skin trousers.

Interviewer: What did you think of those?

Lewis: Well, I don't think it was real leopard skin; but I don't really like stuff that's fake, like that, cos I really love animals. (age 11)

In addition, older children identified qualities that they admired: Legoman was in constant trouble at school; the therapist clearly provided a different experience:

Legoman: She's nice. She's really kind and everything, and she don't really get annoyed. Well, she didn't get knotted, she was really relaxed sort of thing. (age 12)

Allan admitted that he found interventions introduced by his therapist difficult; nevertheless, he valued the relationship he developed with her:

Allan: She was easy to talk to, because she was a nice lady, and she's easy to get along with. (age 14)

Jacey, at 14 one of the oldest children in the sample, was able to include a negative quality, but still maintain positive feelings for her therapist:

Interviewer: Do you know what you like about her?

Jacey: I dunno, she's just a nice person to talk to, but she can be a bit bossy sometimes.

Interviewer: What does she do that's bossy?

Jacey: I dunno, it's like, she's just a bit bossy, but I like her anyway. (age 14)

All except the youngest children extended such general descriptions, telling me of specific efforts made by therapists on their behalf. In the playroom, children perceive therapists as going out of their way to make them welcome; externally therapists intervened in the system on the child's behalf.

Kerrie-Anne: She always made sure that I was okay; if the room was too hot she'd open the window, if it was too cold she'd shut the door and close the window. (age 13)

Susie: It [the playroom] had an unusual smell to it; it's like it's just been built, and not very many people have been in it. Yeah, it smelled like I was the first one to go in there, actually walk into the room, and T's room is really clean, and not a bit of dust on it; and it felt like I was the first one there, the privilege of going in there. Yeah, cos at the start I was the very first person in there. (age 14)

Susie was mistaken; the building was aging and the playroom well established; however, her therapist evidently made her feel very special.

The provision of food was important for some children:

Christina: We used to get a cup of tea or coffee each. Whenever she got a cup of tea, I got a cup of tea; and whenever she got a cup of coffee I got a cup of coffee. Well, she never had biscuits, but I did. (age 11)

Some children were given a small present, for Christmas or birthdays, or when therapy came to an end. Although Lee was disparaging about play therapy, he valued efforts made by his therapist:

Lee: She was nice as a person.

Interviewer: Do you know what you liked about her?

Lee: She sent us Christmas cards and stuff, she was friendly. (age 13)

In interviews, therapists acknowledged the importance of surroundings providing a welcoming and safe environment for children. They also stressed the importance of giving children time and space for themselves. Seven children identified the importance of private, personal space:

Stephanie: I couldn't tell my Mum [about my feelings], cos she was like, don't know, I just feel . . . Cos I thought if I told her my Mum might get a bit upset, and I'd get all upset and so I didn't tell any of my friends, cos they might just laugh at me, I didn't tell any of my teachers or anything like that. (age 14)

Stephanie identified her therapist's attunement to her feelings:

Interviewer: Did you tell her how you felt or did she just notice?

Stephanie: She just noticed. She's quite good at predicting things, like when I went out she said, "I think you feel very happy." And I went, "Yes, you're right."

Interviewer: So she's good at working out how people feel?

Stephanie: Yeah, yeah.

Interviewer: How do you think she does that?

Stephanie: I dunno, I think she has some kind of magic power thing.

Interviewer: And what does this magic power do?

Stephanie: Like, makes her think of everything, makes her know everything, like she's psychic. (age 9)

Some children also identified efforts made by therapists to support them in the external system. In the previous section, Jamie is noted as seeing play therapy as part of a process to find him a permanent placement. This conversation continued:

Jamie: Sometimes it [moving from one placement to another] got annoying. Cos you'd like unpack your stuff, then pack it up again, then unpacked it, then packed it up again.

Interviewer: How do you think T stopped that happening?

Jamie: Cos she told Social Services our feelings, and what sort of place we would like to go to.

Interviewer: Right, and that was part of the play therapy, do you reckon? That was part of her job? Or was it something extra that she did?

Jamie: I think it was just a little bit extra, I think it was a bit extra and part of her job. (age 12)

Children's feelings for their therapist emerged most clearly in response to the "sweets question." (Children were shown a picture of a large box of sweets, a medium-size box, a small box, and no sweets at all, and asked which they would give their therapist.) Sixteen children wanted to give their therapist a large box of sweets; when asked why they commented on the therapist's kindness, and clearly wished to show appreciation:

Legoman: She didn't have to do that, I don't think.

Interviewer: What sort of things did she do that she didn't have to do?

Legoman: Like bring the games in and stuff, and on the last day when she gave me sweets and stuff. She didn't have to do that. Didn't have to do anything. She didn't have to give out the information.

Interviewer: What sort of information?

Legoman: Like the count to ten stuff. She didn't have to do anything. (age 12)

Lee appreciated efforts made by his therapist, but didn't know which box of sweets to give her. Jack opted for a middle-size box but could provide no reason.

Only the oldest children could think about the therapist having made mistakes. Tiffany, Susie, and Allan were uncomfortable with direct questions (see below); Allen forgave her, feeling that she may not have noticed his discomfort. Jacey described her therapist as bossy; this did not diminish her affection. No other child referred to any difficulties in their relationship with their therapists. Yet therapists have holidays and illness; they seek to be consistent but human failing implies that there were times when children felt let down. Recollections of such feelings did not emerge in the interviews.

Therapeutic Processes: Focused and Free Play and the Role of Talking

Play therapists in this sample utilized a variety of therapeutic techniques; some were committed to nondirective practice while others employed focused play to address specific issues. For the children, it was critical that they felt they had real choices:

Interviewer: What was really helpful [about play therapy]?

Kerrie-Anne: That she checked, that she didn't just like say, "You're doing this." She asked me what I wanted to do.

Interviewer: Do you know how that was helpful?

Kerrie-Anne: It didn't feel like I was stuck in one position; if I didn't want to do it I not got to do it, so she give me the choice of whether to do it or not. (age 13)

The categorization of children's play that follows begins with a fundamental division between play chosen by the child and focused interventions selected by the therapist. I begin with children's choices; for most children, play therapy was fun; however, older children were able to identify therapeutic components to their free play. This is followed by children's views on activities introduced by the therapist, their feelings about it and understanding of its purpose. Finally, I shall discuss children's use of talking in the playroom.

Having fun was pivotal for most children. James could not identify therapeutic components, but his delight in the play was evident:

James: Brilliant is where you can play, take toys and all sorts upstairs and like you play in the sand, I really liked playing in the sand and it's brilliant, really brilliant. (age 9)

Gemma's activities reflected difficult feelings within her family; on occasions she made clear connections between her family circumstances and her play; however, she could not always acknowledge (to me at least) helpful aspects of her play:

Interviewer: Can you tell me a bit about the sand pit?

Gemma: I used to put our house in the middle of it, and then make a gateway and trees around it and everything, I used to make our house, and my dad's house, and I used to make an airfield and stuff.

Interviewer: Did that help you?

Gemma: No, it wasn't helpful, but it was—I enjoyed it. (age 12)

Tiffany could distinguish play that was helpful, and that which was purely pleasurable:

Interviewer: What was your favorite?

Tiffany: The dolls, and the shampoos, and creams and the face paints.

Interviewer: And what did you do with them?

Tiffany: Put them on the doll. Sometimes I put them on my face as well.

Interviewer: Was that helpful? Do you think that was helping you or was that just . . .

Tiffany: That was just mucking about.

Interviewer: So what was just playing?

Tiffany: Washing doll's hair. (age 13)

Lewis enjoyed the selection of board games provided by his therapist:

Interviewer: What did you like playing with best?

Lewis: Ah, this Aladdin game where you had to roll the dice to see how much you could get without falling down a hole. Yeah, and you could be Aladdin, the lady—I don't know what her name is, or the carpet or the monkey or the genie.

Interviewer: What did you like being best?

Lewis: The carpet. Cos he flies and he's magic. (age 11)

Although therapists sought meaning in children's play, they were not blind to its pleasurable qualities:

> She would encourage games in the sand of hiding things; she'd want me to close my eyes and not look, or something—turn my head away, so I could then find the hidden things; it felt very—wanted to have fun, wanted things that were unpredictable but were safe and contained. So a lot of playfulness, that she'd want me to engage in. (Therapist for Britney)

Few children saw play as having a purpose beyond pure enjoyment. However, five older children were able to examine possible meanings in play, and their observations show considerable insight.

Christina linked play, memories, and feelings:

> *Christina*: The first time I went she used to ask me what my favorite colors were, and at that moment they were red and black. Remembering what my mother did to me, they're the colors that I could describe it in, red and black. She used to hurt me all the time. And when I used to think of her I used to just get the red and black and just make scribbles all over and say "I hate my Mum" and write "I hate my Mum" on the piece of paper. And then I used to start crying, and then T used to cuddle me. (age 11)

Tiffany used play to connect to memories:

> *Interviewer*: What was your favorite book?
>
> *Tiffany*: *Little Bear*, and *I'll Always Love You*. It was about this girl she had a dog, and it was getting really old and fat and it couldn't get up the stairs so she had to carry it up, then eventually it couldn't walk and so every night she used to tell it she'd always love it, and then she had to pull it along in the trailer when she took it for walks, and then it died eventually. And then when they buried it she went I'll always love you, when she was on her own, over the, where they'd buried it.
>
> *Interviewer*: And how did that make you feel?
>
> *Tiffany*: It reminded me of my nan really. (age 13)

On another occasion, she brought her father directly into the play:

> *Tiffany*: I made a potion to kill off my dad. [Made of] beads, soap, bleach, washing-up liquid, and paint and water and sand.
>
> *Interviewer*: How did you feel when you made this potion?
>
> *Tiffany*: I don't know, I can't remember.
>
> *Interviewer*: Do you think it helped you to do something like that?
>
> *Tiffany*: Yeah.

Interviewer: Do you know how it helped you to do something like that?

Tiffany: No. (age 13)

In the previous section I drew attention to Gemma's play that she described as simply fun. On this occasion she made unambiguous links between her play and difficulties in her family:

Interviewer: What sort of things did you paint and draw?

G. Me, my mum and my sister and my dad, like, my mum and my dad getting back together again. I used to paint that, and at a party, all of us at a party, and that sort of stuff, like art of my family, like my grandma and my granddad.

Interviewer: Do you think it helped you to do paintings like that?

G. Yep.

Interviewer: How it did help you?

G. Cos it made me, made me feel better because I could tell someone, and it's all coming out from inside of me, I'm bringing it out, and I feel much better because—I don't know why actually, but it's just that I'm bringing it all out and telling someone. So they understand and they know. We used to talk about my grandma, cos she doesn't really like me; and we used to talk about my dad.

Gemma, 12

The delight expressed, and demonstrated by most children, when talking about their play contrasts with Jack and Lee, who told me that they were bored in play therapy; however they could recall activities they had chosen for themselves:

Interviewer: What did you like?

J. Cards and ping-pong balls.

Interviewer: Right. Do you remember what you played with the cards?

J. Snap.

Interviewer: Did you win?

J. Mm (Jack, 9)

Interviewer: What did you like doing best?

L. Playing dominoes.

Interviewer: You liked playing the dominoes. Did you win a lot?

L. Yea. (Lee, 12)

"Boring" has complex meanings for children; it may genuinely mean tedium and inability to select something interesting to do. It may also imply flight from demands in both external and internal worlds: it may feel more comfortable to complain about doing nothing than face difficult feelings or tasks. In interview I asked if their therapist could have made changes that would have led to therapy being less "boring":

Interviewer. What would have made it not boring?

L. Having more older, toys for more older—maybe older people. Maybe a board game or something would have been better, something like Monopoly or something, would have been better, cos there's only cars and stuff like that, down there [pointing to my materials]. And dolls, and stuff like that. (Lee, 12)

Interviewer. So what didn't you like?

J. She took um . . girl's dolls and stuff. It was boring.

Interviewer. What could have been done to make it not boring?

J. Playing with my bike, playing football. (Jack, 9)

Their therapist employed nondirective play therapy methods; one could speculate whether focused play would have been more meaningful to Jack and Lee. Three therapists specified focused techniques, aimed to relieve specific symptoms or promote the expression of difficult feelings. Kelly faced invasive medical procedures, and her therapist explored ways to help her feel more control over the process:

K. I always get nervous about going in hospital. And T was just trying to help me calm down. She taught me a relaxation thing, to calm me down. I had to clench all my muscles one at a time in my body and had to take a deep breath then loosen my muscles up and let the breath out. Near to the beginning I had to, no, at first before I went it was, the doctors were trying to get me on to a catheter. And I would—the moment they came round and done it I wouldn't do it so after I started play therapy I had to go up to C [Ward] and I just had it done.

Interviewer. You weren't so frightened?

K. No. Well I was frightened but I just went through it.

Interviewer. What was it about play therapy that made it different?

K. Er, don't know, probably just cos I got loads of confidence. (Kelly, 11)

One therapist's practice is to introduce focused work in the early part of each session, moving to nondirected play once this activity is completed (or,

in Allan's case, often rejected). She helped Susie explore her feelings following sexual abuse:

> S. She used to like say, the dolly is you, and this is the other dolly, and it was
> just like happening with the dollies; the dollies are saying this is the bad person
> and you're the good person and you haven't done nothing wrong; but the bad
> person has done something wrong, and you shouldn't blame yourself for it. And
> then the dollies helped me; cos I used to think that it was my fault but the dol-
> lies made me think that it wasn't my fault and in the end I knew that it wasn't
> my fault. (Susie, 14)

The clarity with which children talked about these interventions, and their
understanding of their nature, suggests that therapists introduced them
clearly. However, this cannot inform us about interventions introduced by
therapists that children ignored or failed to understand; children made no
mention of such incidents and they may not be stored in accessible memory.
The study of such incidents would require a separate project, with direct observation of play therapy sessions.

Although the emphasis of play therapy is on play, thirteen children talked
about talking in the playroom. Children expressed mixed views about questions asked by the therapist: Susie clearly found talking about past abuse
very painful:

> *Interviewer:* Was there anything you didn't like?
>
> S. When T always used to talk about him [her abuser], cos it really upset me,
> when T used to ask me to explain my story again. She used to say "Well, what
> exactly happened?" and then she used to say "What did he look like?" and I
> didn't like explaining what he looked like, cos it just made me upset. (Susie, 14)

In contrast, Tiffany recognised the value of talking about her abuse, even
though it distressed her:

> *Interviewer:* When you look back, can you think of any not-so-good things?
>
> T. Making me talk about my Dad.
>
> *Interviewer:* Do you think that was ever helpful?
>
> T. It was, but it wasn't in some ways, cos it just made me bad tempered. And
> upset.
>
> *Interviewer:* Do you think that in the end talking about your Dad was a good
> thing?
>
> T. Yea.
>
> *Interviewer:* Do you have any idea why it was a good thing?
>
> T. Cos it got things, it cleared my head and I didn't have to worry. (Tiffany, 13)

Christina's perceptions are interesting. Her experience appears to mirror Tiffany's; however, her therapist employs clear nondirective play therapy methods that exclude the asking of questions:

> *C.* I saw the paints ready on the table, and the paper, and I was playing with the dolls; and she started asking me questions. When we used to talk about my Mum I used to get upset, and that night I couldn't stop thinking about her, and I wouldn't eat that night if we had ever had talked about my Mum, and I used to get stomach ache, and I used to be sick and I couldn't go to school the next day. And I love going to school.
>
> *Interviewer.* Do you think, when you look back, that it was a good thing that you talked about your Mum?
>
> *C.* Now I do. Yea.
>
> *Interviewer.* Now you do. But at the time it didn't feel like that?
>
> *C.* No, cos I was young. (Christina, 11)

Given the nondirective stance of her therapist, one must speculate about Christina's perception that she was asked questions. Her therapist may be more inquisitive than she believes; or Christina may have rigid internal working models of adults who ask questions and thus no other way of experiencing her therapist. Children may not always see us as we see ourselves.

Children were significantly more comfortable with discussions that do not, from information given to me, appear to have developed in response to direct questioning by the therapist.

> We just sit down and talk. We usually do the same sort of thing, we usually just talk, me and T. I've seen psychiatrists before and all they do is ask you nosy questions; but T don't do that. You know, like psychiatrists ask you questions that are nosy. They ask you really personal questions, so I don't like them; but T doesn't do that; T listens if I tell her something, but she don't ask nosy questions.
>
> *Interviewer.* Do you tell her more things, different things, not as much, as the psychiatrists?
>
> *J.* Yea, I tell her a lot of stuff. (Jacey, 14)

When allowed to talk freely, talking could provoke catharsis. Jamie told me that play therapy was brilliant:

> *J.* Because it helps you express your feelings.
>
> *Interviewer.* And that's what's brilliant about it?
>
> *J.* Yea, and it's just, so you don't have to keep everything in yourself and moan about different things, you can express your feelings about yourself, and what you feel about other people. (Jamie, 12)

Three children valued the clear provision of information. Prior to difficult surgery, Kelly's therapist brought medical equipment into the playroom and enabled her to play with it, thus demystifying her condition:

K. [She helped me] realize what it was going to be like.

Interviewer: So how did she do that?

K. She tried to get hold of button caecostomy set from the theatre. She just tried to let me know what things were going to be like. (Kelly, 11)

Stephanie needed to know why she was in foster care:

S. T told me what it would be like if we still was living with mum. And that made be feel happy because I didn't know actually what happened. (Stephanie, 9)

Legoman's challenging behaviour in school led directly to his referral for play therapy; his therapist made clear efforts to address this issue. Legoman seemed unsure of their effectiveness:

L. She'd talk to you about, like, if you get annoyed and stuff, and you're ready just to lash out.

Interviewer: What sort of things did she suggest you do?

L. Well, she suggested to do stuff like count to ten, walk away, count to ten, and come back; if you're still angry walk away, count to twenty and come back; keep on doing that until you can't do it any more. It was a good idea but it didn't really work. I did try it a few times but it didn't work.

Interviewer: Do you think it was helpful?

L. I can't really say. I don't fight much; I used to get into fights every day, coming home with holes in my trousers, but I don't now. The only holes I get is in my knees.

Interviewer: How did you stop fighting so much? Did you decide to do that on your own, or did play therapy help with that?

L. Oh, I haven't punched anyone for ages, cos the last time I punched someone I really hurt them and I thought "Better not punch anyone again cos . . ." That was when I was really young, and that was before she started teaching me, and I hit someone and I haven't hit anyone since. Cos I hit them really hard; it was like I cut the side of their jaw. And it got clicked out of place. I can click mine out of place.

Interviewer: So that was something you decided or did you decide that with T?

L. I decided it on my own.

Interviewer. So do you think the fact that you don't fight with people now, has that got anything to do with play therapy, or is that something you did for yourself?

L. It was both. (Legoman, 12)

Such interventions generally fall within the remit of anger management; however, alongside such direct approaches to his behavioural difficulties his therapist engaged Legoman in entertaining board games, designed to help promote social skills. He regarded games as "just fun," and behavioural techniques as of questionable value; nevertheless he was able to demonstrate his gratitude to his therapist for her efforts to help him.

After contributing a perception of play therapy as "boring" there has been little mention of Lee or Jack. Neither boy was able to engage in discussion of helpful aspects of therapy, nor consider its relevance in their lives.

The opinions of other children were universally positive; underpinned by sustaining relationships with their therapists, the children were able to make full use of materials and experience the full joy of playing. Some were also able to consciously use play to explore problems and express feelings. Focused work, introduced by some therapists, helped children address specific issues. In addition, the value of direct, verbal communication was seen as essential for some children, providing valuable information as well as facilitating emotional expression.

Given the depth of the therapeutic relationships described by these children, sensitive management of the endings of therapy, at the close of sessions and when the relationship is finally severed, is essential. I turn to the issue of endings in the following section.

Separations: At the End of Each Session and When Therapy Comes to an End

Given the central role given to the therapeutic relationship in children's testimonies; their experience of breaks in that relationship warrant particular attention. Separations occur at the end of each session and when play therapy ends.

Children and therapists also separate at holiday times; therapists help children prepare for these holidays and anticipate the expression of strong feelings. My clinical experience includes children who interpret such breaks as abandonment. However, none of the children in this sample made any mention of holiday breaks.

Evidence from therapists demonstrates the care with which they approach the ends of sessions. All the children were told, a few minutes before it was time to leave, that the end was approaching. Allan's therapist acknowledged his difficulty and occasionally allowed him to take a puppet home, returning it the following week.

Nevertheless, six children talked about finding the ends of sessions difficult. For some the problem lay in leaving the playroom:

Interviewer. Was there anything you really didn't like?

B. Going home. I wanted to stay there.

Interviewer. What did you do, when it was time to go home, if you didn't want to go?

B. The way I started to act, like [grumpily] "Bye." I didn't like going home, cos I wanted to stay there some more. Britney, 11

Interviewer. How did it feel at the end of sessions, when T. said it was time to go?

C. I was disappointed, I was in the middle of a game, but . . .

Interviewer. Did you sometimes work it to make sure you were in the middle of a game?

C. I didn't know what time it finished. Yea, cos it was always, really early to leave.

Interviewer. And you always felt you were in the middle of a game? You wanted to stay and finish it?

C. Mm, for at least another hour. (Christina, 11)

Jacey identified a difficulty regulating emotions outside the playroom after exploring difficult feelings or memories:

Interviewer. Was there anything you didn't like?

J. It only lasts for an hour.

Interviewer: How long would you want it to be?

J. Dunno, two hours, and hour and a half, something like that. So you can do the sort of like hour of really talking, and then sort of talk about something else. So, you're not feeling like all, a bit upset, cos of the stuff you've been talking about. (Jacey, 14)

When therapy finally came to a close at least sixteen of these children needed to find ways to cope with the loss of a significant relationship, and to give meaning to the process of ending. Thoughtful management of termination processes should help children express feelings of sadness and explore the possibility of hope for the future (Carroll 1998).

Testimony from children and therapists did not always agree when they talked about ending therapy; Gemma told me (accurately) that her mother had made the decision:

Interviewer: Who decided when it was time for therapy to stop?

Gemma: My mum.

Interviewer: Do you want to tell me a bit about how that worked out?

Gemma: I stopped like cos my mum couldn't afford it cos it was £25.00 an hour. (age 12)

Children who decided for themselves were very clear:

Kerrie-Anne: When we sat down and talked about it she said, "Do I want to leave it for a while?" So she asked if I wanted to go back every now and then, just in case problems started again.

Interviewer: So it was your decision to stop and your decision to, well if you wanted to go back?

Kerrie-Anne: Yeah. (age 13)

The data is more confusing if therapist and child made the decision together, or caregivers were consulted. Kelly and Lewis told me that it was a joint decision; therapists told me that they had also invited comments from teachers and caregivers to ensure that termination was agreed and understood by all; the children seem unaware of these consultations:

Interviewer: Can you remember who decided it was time for your play therapy to stop?

Kelly: I think it was T and me.

Interviewer: You decided together. How did you do that?

Kelly: Well, T just thought that I've had enough, and she asked me if I was okay to go without. (age 11)

Five children told me that their therapists made the decision; yet two therapists recounted consulting caregivers.

Jack's therapist disagreed that he had taken the decision to end his therapy. Narratives from Lee and Jack are interesting; both told me that they took the decision for themselves, and Lee took matters into his own hands by refusing to attend. However, Jack's therapy lasted for twenty sessions; his therapist agreed a final date with him, and he was able to keep this agreement and tolerate a thoughtful ending:

I was aware with Jack that he was very bad at beginnings and endings. He would never say hello and he would never say good-bye. And I really wanted to make sure that we had a good ending, and for it not to be such a sudden disappearance as it had been with Lee. To do it in a planned way, and have a good ending, and then I would follow up with a home visit, toward the end of the summer or September, and check how things were going, and there was always the option of further sessions if need be in the future. (Therapist for Jack and Lee)

Therapists planned endings carefully, talking with children and discussing the final session over several weeks. Rosy's therapist's planning for closing her therapy was mirrored by other therapists:

> It was a good six sessions, thinking about endings, looking at what she would like to do, at the end. Just exploring it really. And I always use a wall chart with how many sessions we've got, so we could work out how many we had to go; and then as the sessions went on we started to look more into what she would like to do at the end. (Therapist for Rosy)

Allan's recall is close to that of his therapist. Allan does not recall weeks of planning, but was aware of gentle preparations:

Interviewer: Do you know how long it was between you deciding, and when you actually stopped?

Allan: A couple of sessions.

Interviewer: And what did you use that time for, do you remember?

Allan: Packing up, and sorting out, getting through the rest in a bit of a hurry, the stuff that she thought I really needed to speak about, she tried in the last couple of sessions. (age 14)

However, six children had no memory of preparing an ending:

Interviewer: How long between deciding it was time to stop and stopping? Was it quick or . . .

Lewis: It was in between them all. Quick and really slow.

Interviewer: You don't know roughly how long?

Lewis: I'd say, tell T on a Tuesday and we'd stop doing it on Thursday. (age 11)

Christina's therapist was painstaking in the preparations she made; yet Christina told me:

Interviewer: Did you know, a few weeks beforehand, that it was going to stop?

Christina: Um, no. (age 11)

Final sessions are significant; they mark an official ending of the relationship, an opportunity for child and therapist to say good-bye. Eight children told me of special arrangements made for last session. For Rosy, this was the highlight of her play therapy:

Rosy: I know the best thing that I did. At the end, where we had that little tea party.

Interviewer: Before you had your tea party, do you remember thinking about that, or was that tea party a surprise?

Rosy: T asked what I can choose. And I chose that [a tea party].

Interviewer: I wonder why you chose that?

Rosy: Cos I like chocolate. And I like Pringles. And I like oranges. And a large drink, and chocolate cake. (age 6)

Not all endings were this lavish, but efforts made to celebrate the day were acknowledged:

Susie: She said to me, "Oh, I won't ever be seeing you again now, will I Susie?" And I just said no. And she gave me this little set thing, it said "Be Safe—The Never Never Club" it was; I had a little badge with a little red cross on it, and I had a little card and a little badge and a little bookmark; it was really good. (age 14)

Understanding the reason for therapy to end helped children make sense of the loss of their therapist. Only Stephanie and Jamie could not provide an accurate reason why therapy came to an end. It had been agreed that the therapist would engage the children in life story work after play therapy had ended; regrettably, that did not happen. Both children sought to justify the conclusion of therapy:

Interviewer: When it came to time to stop altogether, who decided that you didn't have to go any more?

Jamie: I think it was either the social worker or T.

Interviewer: Why do you think they decided it was time to stop?

Jamie: Cos we was getting, I think we was getting a bit too old. (age 12)

Stephanie: Cos I think they thought that um, it would be better if we had like, um, a . . um . . time on our own, like, no—I dunno, actually. (Stephanie, 9)

Other children provided realistic explanations for therapy coming to an end. Some recognized that their social lives began to override their therapeutic needs:

Tiffany: It was alright, cos I wanted to do my riding anyway, and I only got half the session (at riding) that everyone else got. Cos I only got half an hour and then I had to go to get back to school for the taxi to pick me up to take me. T saw me until about four o'clock, which was when they'd finished riding then. (age 13)

Five children told me that they were managing their situations better when play therapy came to a close:

Lewis: I felt I can stand on my own two legs, I can sort of like say things that I never knew I had the guts to say. I can stand on my own two feet, I can sort problems out myself. (age 11)

Lee, unable to connect with the therapeutic process, terminated his therapy by simply failing to attend; he told me:

Lee: It got boring and I, there wasn't anything, wasn't doing much, doing stuff what I could have been doing at home.

Interviewer: So you could have done the same things here?

Lee: Yeah. With my brothers and friends and stuff. (age 12)

Many children acknowledged complex feelings when therapy came to an end. Jack and Lee could not talk directly about such feelings. However, by ending his therapy himself Lee communicated a preference for living without it. Jack's feelings are more complex; he was unable to talk about them with me.

Some children struggled to admit to difficult feelings when therapy ended.

Interviewer: So how did that feel when she stopped coming?

Jamie: I just felt a bit sad, because we weren't having fun before school.

Interviewer: Right. How do you feel about it now?

Jamie: I'm getting used to it, cos I've just got to get on with my life, and not worry about things like that. (age 12)

Jacey's play therapy was provided automatically in her residential home; she was interviewed shortly before moving away. Her feelings, knowing therapy would end when she left, are particularly poignant:

Jacey: You just get to know someone, and then you have to leave them. You just start talking about things that hurt you, or things that you like, and sharing the secrets, and then you have to leave them. And you feel like, she sees loads of people so, so it don't really make much difference what I tell her, cos she sees loads of people. (age 14)

Other children who felt positive when therapy ended talked about other aspects of their lives that were facilitated by leaving therapy:

Tiffany: It was all right, cos I wanted to do my riding anyway, which meant that I could actually join in with competitions that they have now. (age 13)

Kelly was delighted with the change she observed in herself:

Kelly: Before play therapy I used to be really scared of fireworks. And balloons, but now I'm playing with balloons and one firework night I actually uncovered my ears and counted a load of fireworks. (age 11)

Five children expressed mixed feelings; Kerrie-Anne recognized she no longer needed therapy but expressed her feelings about the loss of the therapeutic relationship:

Interviewer: How did you feel, when play therapy stopped?

Kerrie-Anne: I felt upset, not because I was stopping it but because I wanted to go and see T again. (Kerrie-Anne, 13)

Allan's comments are interesting; he had asked to end his therapy, finding discussing his feelings painful and insisting that outside interests were paramount. His therapist agreed reluctantly, believing he had issues that continued to trouble him.

Allan: I felt okay, actually, cos I'd got most of the stuff off my chest, but I did sometimes miss going back there and playing, but normally I had, I was going out with my friends so I didn't really think about it.

Interviewer: How do you feel about it now?

Allan: Sometimes I think I should have stayed for a bit longer. (age 14)

Allan was one of the oldest children interviewed and most reflective about his time in therapy.

DISCUSSION

I set out to provide a forum for children's voices to be heard undiluted by adult interventions. These findings provide such a forum. The focus of this discussion lies in my reflections, as a therapist, on the children's narratives; readers who skip the findings and hope to find solutions in a discussion will have missed the point of this chapter. However, it is my responsibility as a researcher to highlight themes which have emerged in the data.

Play therapy interacts with children's internal and external worlds (Preston-Shoot and Agass 1990). Both micro- and macrosystems (Bronfenbrenner 1992) need to be supportive of children if they are to make full use the therapeutic experience. The lack of such supports for Jack and Lee, when contrasted with the efforts made on behalf of other children, is striking.

However, these systems also have a responsibility to provide accurate information for children prior to engaging in therapy; for these children this was clearly inadequate. I agree with Paul and colleagues (2000) that this matters. In a political climate in which both children and adults are invited to consent before engaging in any therapeutic procedure, understanding that procedure is essential. Given their limited cognitive capacity young children cannot be expected to weigh advantages and disadvantages of alternative approaches. However, these children did not commit to memory any information regarding the nature of the intervention, and not all understood its purpose. Further research is needed to find ways to prepare children for play therapy effectively.

Play therapy also interacts with children's internal worlds. Psychodynamic and attachment theories propose that therapeutic relationships may be an agent of repair for damaged internal working models and object relations (Bowlby 1980; Crittenden 1995; Glickauf-Hughes and Wells 1997; Summers 1999). Sixteen of these children talked with great warmth and overt affection for their therapists; even Lee and Jack conceded that she had tried to help. They had internalized a supportive therapist, one who will listen without judging, and who believes in the child's ability to sustain him or herself. Alvarez (1992) suggests that, for some children, such a relationship performs a vital function in bringing positive experiences into their inner world, providing a foundation on which more difficult feelings may be processed.

In addition to the expression of such feelings toward their therapists, children highlighted the fun of playing. Therapists looked for meaning, while for many children the experience of pleasure, with a trusted adult, was the therapeutic experience. From a phenomenological standpoint (Moustakas 1994), the child's intentionality was to have fun.

Slade (1994) argues that, for younger children, play may be sufficient to prompt a relief of distress, and interpretation may interfere with internal curative processes: "The change [takes place] not in the realm of understanding, but in the realm of playing" (Slade 1994, 101–2).

However, older children, capable of more complex thinking (Piaget 1952), may be able to observe therapeutic agents in their play. In my small sample, it was the older children who were able to make connection between their play and events in their lives or difficult feelings; nevertheless they continued to stress its pleasurable component.

I was surprised at the inclusion of talking as a therapeutic factor by these children. It may have been the verbal nature of our interaction that led to such comments. Nevertheless, they include useful observations. It was clear that children found discussion easier if they introduced the topic; for some the provision of information was invaluable while others utilized conversation to express their feelings. However, questions from therapists could lead to discomfort—although it was accepted that talking about feelings was eventually helpful.

Given the intensity of the therapeutic attachments described by these children, it is unsurprising if they struggled to talk about its ending. Such a discussion could involve the recall of difficult feelings and memories. The inaccuracy of some of these recollections is interesting. It may be that internal cohesion is briefly disturbed during the termination phase, leaving memories incomplete; alternatively accurate recall may be too painful. Children who felt they had some control over the process had greater understanding of reasons for ending, and appeared more honest with themselves about their feelings. The testimony of these children confirms the importance therapists attach to helping children manage the end of therapy comfortably.

Jack and Lee have also contributed to this study, yet have made only a brief appearance in this discussion. It is clear that the system containing them did not provide the support they needed to engage with therapy. By leaving therapy precipitately Lee confirmed that the process had no meaning for him. However, Jack's position is more complex: he was able to attend for twenty sessions and manage a reflective ending. His disparagement may be genuine; alternatively he may have felt unable to disagree with his brother yet still able to gain enough from the therapeutic process to complete his therapy, leaving him in the difficult position described by Gabel and colleagues (1988) when commitment to therapy challenges existing loyalties.

CONCLUSION

All research ends with a plea for further study, and this is no exception. This project took place in the United Kingdom, with a very small group of children. Their stories are exciting, and provide a perspective that we have not known before. It would be helpful to extend this study to different cultures, and to explore further the connection between children's opinions and the nature of therapeutic interventions.

Notwithstanding the shortcomings of this study, it has had a profound impact on my role as a practitioner. To hear children talk of the therapists with such affection and respect is humbling. Their feelings are precious and I must contain them gently. Their understanding of the roles of play appears to develop as cognitions become more complex, highlighting the importance of adjusting interventions to meet the developmental potential of each child. And enabling children to leave the relationship with their internal worlds intact and a positive view of themselves remains a therapeutic challenge.

ACKNOWLEDGEMENTS

I am indebted to Linnet McMahon, who supervised this project with wisdom, patience, and humor. This chapter was submitted for consideration for a Ph.D. at the University of Reading, England.

REFERENCES

Alderson, P. 1995. *Listening to Children, Ethics and Social Research*. London: Barnardos.

———. 2000. "Children as Researchers: The Effects of Participation Rights on Research Methodology." In P. Christensen and A. James, eds., *Research with Children: Perspectives and Practices*, 241–57. London: Falmer.

Alvarez, A. 1992. *Live Company*. London: Tavistock/Routledge.

Armstrong, D., and D. Galloway. 1996. "How Children with Emotional and Behavioural Difficulties View Professionals." In R. Davie and D. Galloway, eds., *Listening to Children in Education*, 109–20. London: David Fulton.

Bain, O., and M. Saunders. 1990. *Out in the Open*. London: Virago.

Begley, A. 2000. "The Educational Self-Perceptions of Children Who Have Down Syndrome." In A. L. Lewis and G. Lindsay, eds., *Researching Children's Perspectives*. Buckingham, U.K.: Open University Press.

Bowlby, J. 1980. *Secure Base: Clinical Applications of Attachment Theory*. London: Routledge.

Bronfenbrenner, U. 1992. "Ecological Systems Theory." In *Six Theories of Child Development*, 187–550. London: Jessica Kingsley.

Carroll, J. 1998. *Introduction to Therapeutic Play*. Oxford: Blackwell Scientific.

———. 2000. "Evaluation of Therapeutic Play: A Challenge for Research." *Child and Family Social Work* 51: 11–22.

———. 2002. "Play Therapy: The Children's Views." *Child and Family Social Work* 73: 177–87.

Costley, D. 2000. "Collecting the Views of Young People with Moderate Learning Difficulties." In A. L. Lewis and G. Lindsay, eds., *Researching Children's Perspectives*. Buckingham, U.K.: Open University Press.

Crittenden, P. M 1995. "Attachment and Psychopathology." In S. Goldberg, R. Muir, and J. Kerr, eds., *Attachment Theory: Social, Developmental, and Clinical Perspectives*. Hillsdale, N.J.: Analytic.

Fitton, P. 1994. *Listen to Me: Communicating the Needs of People with Profound Intellectual and Multiple Disabilities*. London: Jessica Kingsley.

Fuller, R., and A. Petch. 1995. *Practitioner Research: The Reflexive Social Worker*. Buckingham, U.K.: Open University Press.

Gabel, S., G. Oster, and G. Pfeffer. 1988. *Difficult Moments in Child Psychotherapy.* London: Plenum Medical Book Company.

Glaser, B. G., and A. L. Strauss. 1967. *The Discovery of Grounded Theory: Strategies for Qualitative Research.* New York, Aldine de Gruyter.

Glickauf-Hughes, C., and M. Wells. 1997. *Object Relations Psychotherapy: An Individualized and Interactive Approach to Diagnosis and Treatment.* Northvale, N.J.: Aronson.

Hill, M. 1997. "Participatory Research with Children." *Child and Family Social Work* 23: 171–83.

Ireland, L., and I. Holloway. 1996. "Qualitative Health Research with Children." *Children and Society* 102: 155–64.

Jennings, S. 1993. *Playtherapy with Children: A Practitioner's Guide.* London: Blackwell Scientific.

Mahon, A., C. Glendenning, C. Clarke, and G. Craig. 1996. "Researching Children: Methods and Ethics." *Children and Society* 102: 145–54.

Mason, J. 1996. *Qualitative Researching.* London: Sage.

Moustakas, C. 1994. *Phenomenological Research Methods.* Thousand Oaks, Calif.: Sage.

O'Kane, C. 2000. "The Development of Participatory Techniques: Facilitating Children's Views about Decisions That Affect Them." In P. Christensen and A. James, eds., *Research with Children: Perspectives and Practices,* 136–60. London: Falmer.

Padgett, D. K. 1998. *Qualitative Methods in Social Work Research.* Thousand Oaks, Calif.: Sage.

Paul, M., D. M. Foreman, and L. Kent. 2000. "Out-Patient Clinic Attendance Consent from Children and Young People: Ethical Aspects and Practical Considerations." *Clinical Child Psychology and Psychiatry* 52: 203–11.

Piaget, J. [1936] 1952. *The Origins of Intelligence in Children.* New York: Norton.

Pidgeon, N., and K. Henwood. 1997. "Using Grounded Theory in Psychological Research." In N. Hayes, ed., *Doing Qualitative Analysis in Psychology,* 245–73. East Sussex, U.K.: Psychology Press.

Preston-Shoot, M., and D. Agass. 1990. *Making Sense of Social Work: Psychodynamic, Systems, and Practice.* London: Macmillan.

Rose, M. 1997. *Transforming Hate to Love: An Outcome Study of the Peper Harrow Process for Adolescents.* London: Routledge.

Saunders, E. J., and J. A. Saunders. 2000. "Evaluating the Effectiveness of Art Therapy through Quantative Outcome-Focused Study." *Arts in Psychotherapy* 27, no. 2: 99–106.

Shaw, I., and A. Shaw. 1997. "Keeping Social Work Honest: Evaluating as Profession and Practice." *British Journal of Social Work* 2, no. 7: 847–69.

Slade, A. 1994. "Making Meaning and Making Believe: Their Role in the Clinical Process." In A. Slade and D. P. Wolf, eds., *Children at Play: Clinical Developmental Approaches to Meaning and Representation,* 81–107. Oxford: Oxford University Press.

Strauss, A., and J. Corbin. 1997. *Grounded Theory in Practice.* London: Sage.

Summers, F. L. 1999. *Transcending the Self: An Object Relations Model of Psychoanalytic Therapy.* Hillsdale, N.J.: Analytic.

UN Convention on the Rights of the Child. 1983.

Warren, S. 2000. "Let's Do It Properly: Inviting Children to Be Researchers." In A. L. Lewis and G. Lindsay, eds., *Researching Children's Perspectives*, 112–34. Buckingham, U.K.: Open University Press.

Weithorn, L. A., and D. G. Scherer. 1994. "Children's Involvement in Research; Participation Decisions: Psychological Considerations." In M. A. Gridin and L. H. Glantz, eds., *Children as Research Subjects: Science, Ethics, and Law*. Oxford: Oxford University Press.

11

Building an Empirical Foundation for the Use of Pretend Play in Therapy

Sandra W. Russ

The use of play in child therapy has been a major way of helping children since the 1930s. Child therapists have learned to use play as a form of communication with the child and as a vehicle for change with many types of emotional and behavioral problems. Much of the knowledge base about how to use play effectively has emerged from the clinical literature (both from theory and case presentations), from supervision by experienced child therapists, and from clinical experience that the therapist gains over time from working with children.

Recently the field of child therapy has increasingly emphasized the need for empirically supported treatments. It is crucial that play interventions are investigated with rigorous methodology and that systematic research programs be carried out.

There are existing research literatures that are relevant to the use of play in child therapy. One is the research on pretend play and child development. Some of the findings from the child development research support basic principles of play therapy. A second literature is on the use of play interventions with children in stressful situations. These bodies of research need to be integrated with one another and with the clinical literature, so that more refined play interventions can evolve.

This chapter will review the research literature, discuss what we know and implications for clinical practice, and present suggestions for next steps for empirical work.

PRETEND PLAY AND CHILD DEVELOPMENT

Pretend play is important both in child development and in child psychotherapy. When the word "play" is used throughout this chapter, the specific type of play referred to is pretend play. Pretend play involves pretending, the use of fantasy and make-believe, and the use of symbolism. Fein (1987) stated that pretend play is a symbolic behavior in which "one thing is playfully treated as if it were something else" (282). Fein also stated that pretense is charged with feelings and emotional intensity, so that affect is intertwined with pretend play. Fein viewed play as a natural form of creativity.

Many of the cognitive, affective, and interpersonal processes in play are related to and facilitate important adaptive abilities in child development such as creative problem solving, coping ability, and social behavior. These adaptive abilities are important in the general adjustment of the child (for a full review of this literature, see Russ 2003).

CREATIVITY

Many of the processes that occur in play are involved in creativity. Much of the research on play and child development has investigated creativity because of the theoretical link between pretending and the creative imagination. Sawyer (1997) conceptualized pretend play in young children as improvisational. Improvisation is an important feature of adult creativity. Sawyer stated that play is unscripted yet has loose outlines to be followed.

Two major categories of cognitive processes important in creativity are divergent thinking and transformation abilities. Both of these processes were identified by Guilford (1968) as being important in and unique to creative problem solving. Divergent thinking is thinking that goes off in different directions. For example, a typical item on a divergent thinking test would be "how many uses for a brick can you think of?" Guilford thought the key concept underlying divergent production abilities was variety. Wallach (1970) stated that divergent thinking is dependent on the flow of ideas and the "fluidity in generating cognitive units" (1240). Divergent thinking involves free association, broad scanning ability, and fluidity of thinking. Divergent thinking has been found to be relatively independent of intelligence (Runco 1991). Transformation abilities enable the individual to reorganize information and break out of old ways of thinking. They enable the individual to transform or revise what one knows into new patterns or configurations. Transformation abilities involve the ability to break out of an old set and see a new way to solve a problem.

Other cognitive processes important in, but not unique to, creative problem solving are sensitivity to problems and problem finding (Getzels and Csikzentmihalyi 1976); task persistence and trying alternative problem-solving approaches (Weisberg 1988); breadth of knowledge and wide range of interests (Barron and Harrington 1981); insight and synthesizing abilities (Sternberg 1988); and evaluative ability (Guilford 1950; Runco 1991).

Research has supported a relationship between play and a number of these creative cognitive processes (Dansky 1980; Fein 1981). Although most of the studies are correlational in design, well-designed experimental studies and longitudinal research suggest that causal inferences can be made. Saltz, Dixon, and Johnson (1977) found that fantasy play facilitated cognitive functioning on a variety of measures. They theorized that fantasy play is related to cognitive development because of the involvement of representational skills and concept formation. Singer and Singer (1976) concluded that the capacity for imaginative play is positively related to divergent thinking, verbal fluency, and cognitive functioning in general. Sherrod and Singer (1979) proposed that fantasy play and cognition is a transactional system—each facilitates the other.

Early research on play and creative problem solving investigated play and insight ability. Sylva, Bruner, and Genova (1976) concluded that play in children between three and five facilitated insight in a problem-solving task. In one study they had three groups of children. One group played with the objects which were later used in the problem-solving task. A second group observed the experimenter solve the problem. A third control group was exposed to the materials. Significantly more children in the play and observation groups solved the problem than in the control group. The play group was more goal oriented in their efforts on the task and was more likely to piece together the solution than the other groups.

Vandenberg (1980), in a review of the insight and play studies, concluded that all of these studies had the consistent finding that play facilitated insightful tool use and enhanced motivated task activity. Variables of task type and difficulty and age were mediating factors. Vandenberg pointed up the similarity between play and creativity. In both play and creativity, one is creating novelty from the commonplace and has a disregard for the familiar.

There is a substantial body of studies that has found a relationship between play and divergent thinking. Singer and Singer (1990) viewed play as a way of practicing divergent thinking ability. In several important experimental studies, play facilitated divergent thinking in preschool children (Dansky and Silverman 1973; Dansky 1980). In particular, Dansky and Silverman found that children who played with objects during a play period gave significantly more uses for those objects than did control subjects. In the later study, Dansky (1980) found that make-believe play was the mediator of the relationship between play and divergent thinking. Free play facilitated divergent thinking, but only for children engaged in make-believe play. Also, in this second study, play had a generalizing effect in that the objects in the play period were different from those in the test period. These two studies are important because they are experimental studies that show a direct effect of play on divergent thinking.

Fisher (1992) conducted a meta-analysis of forty-six studies in the play and child development area up to 1987. He investigated the impact of play on cognitive, affective-social, and linguistic processes. Both correlational and experimental studies were included. In general, he found a modest effect size (ES) of .347. The largest effect size was for divergent thinking and perspective-taking criteria (ES = .387 and .392 respectively). He concluded that play does result in improvement in children's development. The strongest effect size was for cognitive abilities important in creative thinking. Fisher also found that play impacted basic language acquisition.

Until recently, the research on play and creativity has focused on cognitive variables as the explanatory mechanism underlying the relationship. Explanations have included practice with divergent thinking, the recombination of objects and ideas, symbolic transformations, breadth-of-attention deployment. And the loosening of old cognitive sets or cognitive flexibility. Affective processes could also account for the relationship between play and creativity (Russ 1993). The involvement of affect could broaden the associative process (Isen, Daubman, and Nowicki 1987). Russ (1987, 1993) developed the Affect in Play Scale (APS) to meet the need for a standardized measure of affect in pretend play. Play sessions are five-minute standardized puppet play sessions that are individually administered. The play task utilizes two neutral-looking puppets, one boy and one girl, and three small blocks that are laid out on a table. The instructions direct the child to play with the puppets any way they like for five minutes. The play session can be considered to be a free-play period. The play task and instructions are unstructured enough that individual differences in the use of affect in pretend play can emerge. The APS is appropriate for children from six to ten years of age. The play sessions are videotaped so that coding can occur at a later time.

The APS measures the amount and types of affect expression in children's pretend play. The major affect scores are frequency of affect units expressed and variety of affect categories expressed. There are eleven possible categories, such as happiness and sadness. The APS also measures cognitive dimensions of the play, such as quality of fantasy and imagination.

In a series of studies using the APS, affect in play did relate to divergent thinking (Russ and Grossman-McKee 1990; Russ, Robins, and Christiano 1999). These relationships were independent of IQ. The Russ, Robins, and Christiano (1999) study followed up children who had received the APS in the first and second grades. Thirty-one children in the fifth and sixth grades participated in the follow-up. The major finding of the study was that quality of fantasy and imagination in early play was predictive of divergent thinking over a four-year period. Interestingly, although the affect in play was related to divergent thinking in the original sample, only the more cognitive play scores were predictive over time.

PLAY, COPING, AND ADJUSTMENT

Creative problem solvers should be better copers because they bring their problem-solving skills to everyday problems. Good divergent thinkers should be able to think of alternative solutions to everyday problems. There is some empirical support for this concept. Russ (1988) found a relationship between divergent thinking and teacher's ratings of coping in fifth grade boys. Similarly, Carsen and colleagues (1994) found a significant relationship between figural divergent thinking and teacher ratings of coping.

Looking specifically at play and coping ability, Christiano and Russ (1996) found a positive relationship between play and coping and a negative relationship between play and distress in seven- to nine-year-olds. Children who had more affect and imagination on the APS implemented a greater number and variety of cognitive coping strategies during an invasive dental procedure. There are a number of other studies that found that play ability is related to coping and to adjustment . For example, Singer and Singer (1990) concluded that imaginative play ability is related to academic adjustment and flexibility of thought.

Pretend play has also been related to measures of empathy and social functioning. Fisher (1992), in his meta-analysis of play studies, found a modest effect size of .392 for the impact of play on perspective taking. In the studies that he reviewed, perspective-taking was defined as empathic role assumption that is related to cooperative behavior, sociability, and popularity.

IMPLICATIONS FOR USE OF PLAY IN THERAPY

Research findings on children's play, creativity, emotion, coping, social functioning, and adjustment have not yet had a direct impact on the use of play in child therapy (Russ 2003). Many of these adaptive abilities are probably being worked with and affected in play therapy, but not in a direct, systematic way. One can conclude from the empirical literature that pretend play relates to or facilitates (Russ 2003):

- Problem solving that requires insight ability
- Flexibility in problem solving
- Divergent thinking
- The ability to think of alternative coping strategies in dealing with everyday problems and the ability to cope

- The experience of positive emotion
- The ability to think about and express both positive and negative affect themes
- The ability to understand the emotions of others and to take the perspective of the other
- Some aspects of general adjustment

When a therapist is working with a child in play therapy, many of these processes are being influenced. We need to develop and investigate techniques that affect the play processes that are involved in these adaptive abilities. It would be useful for the child therapist to be aware of how the individual child could benefit from strengthening specific processes and then to develop play therapy techniques that focus on them.

It is important that the research in child development has supported the role of play in the development of problem-solving ability. Child therapy helps the child deal with problems of daily living. We need to close the gap between these two arenas and learn how to integrate specific techniques that target specific processes into child therapy.

PLAY INTERVENTION STUDIES

In a review of the current state of play therapy research, I made a distinction between psychotherapy outcome research in general and play intervention research (Russ 1995). Play intervention studies investigate the effect of play on specific types of problems and in specific populations. These studies are a good bridge between empirical laboratory studies of the effect of play on specific processes (like creativity) and more global clinical practice outcome studies. Usually they involve only a few sessions with no emphasis on forming a "relationship" with a therapist. On the other hand, these studies differ from specific process research in child development in that they are problem focused and are not as fine-tuned as they would be in laboratory research. They fall in the middle of the continuum with laboratory play research on one end and global therapy outcome research on the other.

Phillips (1985) reviewed two studies that would fall into this play intervention research category. Both involved the use of puppet play to reduce anxiety in children facing surgery. Johnson and Stockdale (1975) measured Palmer Sweat Index level before and after surgery. Puppet play in this study involved playing out the surgery. Johnson and Stockdale found less anxiety for the puppet-play group before and after surgery. The one exception was immediately before surgery, when the increased information may have elevated their anxiety. Cassell (1965) used puppets with children undergoing cardiac catheterization and found that anxiety was reduced before surgery for the puppet-play group compared with the no treatment group. There were no differences after surgery. The treatment group was less disturbed during the cardiac catheterization and expressed more willingness to return to the hospital for further treatment. Rae and colleagues (1989) investigated the effects of play on the adjustment of forty-six children hospitalized for acute illness. Children were randomly assigned to one of four experimental groups:

- A therapeutic play condition in which the child was encouraged to play with medical and nonmedical materials. Verbal support, reflection, and interpretation of feelings were expressed by the research assistant.
- A diversionary play condition in which children were allowed to play with toys but fantasy play was discouraged. The toys provided did not facilitate fantasy, nor did the research assistant.
- A verbally oriented support condition in which children were encouraged to talk about feelings and anxieties. The research assistant was directive in bringing up related topics and would ask about procedures.
- A control condition in which the research assistant had no contact with the child.

All treatment conditions consisted of two 30-minute sessions. The main result of this study was that children in the therapeutic play group showed significantly more reduction in self-reported hospital-related fears than children in the other three groups. There were no differences among the groups for parent ratings. Because this study controlled for verbal expression, one can conclude that the fantasy activity itself resulted in fear reduction.

Another specific problem area that lends itself to focused play intervention research is that of separation anxiety. In an excellent example of a well-designed play intervention study, Milos and Reiss (1982) used play therapy for preschoolers who were dealing with separation anxiety. They identified sixty-four children who were rated as high-separation-anxious children by their teachers. The children were randomly assigned to one of four groups. Three play groups were theme related: the free-play group had appropriate toys; the directed-play group had the scene set with a mother doll bringing the child to school; the modeling group had the experimenter playing out a separation scene. A control group also used play with toys irrelevant to separation themes (blocks, puzzles, crayons). All children received three individual ten-minute play sessions on different days. Quality of play was rated. The results showed that all three thematic play conditions were effective in reducing anxiety around separation themes when compared to the control group. An interesting finding was that, when the free-play and directed-play groups were combined, the quality of play ratings were significantly negatively related ($r = -.37$) to a post-test anxiety measure. High-quality play was defined as play that showed more separation themes and attempts to resolve conflicts. One might speculate the children who were already good players used the intervention to master their separation anxiety. Milos and Reiss concluded that their results support the underlying assumption of play therapy, that play can reduce anxiety associated with psychological problems. The finding that quality of play was related to effectiveness of the intervention is consistent with the finding of Dansky (1980) that free play facilitated creativity only for those children who used make-believe well.

A well-designed study by Barnett (1984) also looked at separation anxiety and expanded on work by Barnett and Storm (1981) in which free play was found to reduce distress in children following a conflict situation. In the 1984 study, a natural stressor, the first day of school, was used. Seventy-four preschool children were observed separating from their mothers and were rated anxious or nonanxious. These two groups were further divided into play or no-play conditions. The play condition was a free-play condition. The no-play condition was a story-listening condition. For half of the play condition, play was solitary. For the other half, peers were present. The story condition was also split into solitary and peers present segments. Play was rated by observers and categorized in terms of types of play. Play significantly reduced anxiety in the high-anxious group. Anxiety was measured by the Palmer Sweat Index. There was no effect for low-anxious children. For the anxious children, solitary play was best in reducing anxiety. High-anxious children spent more time in fantasy play than did low-anxious children, who showed more functional and manipulative play. They engaged more in fantasy play when no other children were present. Barnett interpreted these results to mean that play was used to cope with a distressing situation. The findings supported her idea that it is not social play that is essential to conflict resolution, but rather imaginative play qualities that the child introduces into playful behavior. Actually, the presence of peers increased anxiety in the high-anxious group.

CONCLUSIONS AND IMPLICATIONS FOR CLINICAL PRACTICE

When play intervention studies are focused and well-controlled, play has been found to reduce fears and anxiety. Fears have been reduced around medical procedures and around separation anxiety.

Several studies suggest that the imagination and fantasy components of the play are key factors in reducing anxiety. Finally, play is more effective for children who already have good fantasy play skills.

These research find lin   t e b s sterit wit t   p chodynamic theoretical and clinical literature tha   t izi s b ay to help w   ll ernal conflict-resolution and mastery of develop (ital i s es, as w l   h external traumas and stressful life even s. s   s lt of the conflic e llll n and problem solving, anxiety is reduced. Psychodynamic approaches also suggest the use of insight, conflict-resolution approaches for children whose fantasy skills are normally developed and who can use play in therapy.

These research findings are also consistent with cognitive behavioral uses of play where playing out fears and anxieties would result in gradual exposure and extinction of inappropriate anxiety. Children who could use fantasy better would be more able to imagine various scenes, and extinction of fears would be more likely to occur than for children with poor fantasy skills.

Investigating how fantasy play helps reduce anxiety is an important research question. Developing conceptualizations of how play helps children process and regulate emotions should provide a theoretical framework for this research area.

These play intervention studies do support the use of play to reduce fear or anxiety. Although the research has focused on medical situations and separation anxiety, other populations struggling with anxiety, such as post-traumatic stress disorders, should also be appropriate for play therapy. However, research also suggests that children should have good play skills to begin with for play therapy to be effective.

What about the use of play for problems other than anxiety? The clinical literature supports the use of play with depression (Altschul 1988) and post-traumatic stress disorders (Terr 1991). To date, no research studies have investigated the use of play interventions with these populations and types of problems. These kind of studies need to be carried out. However, the research findings from a variety of studies in the child and adult area suggest that other types of negative affect, like sadness or extreme anxiety and fear, should be helped by play intervention.

PLAY TRAINING AND PREVENTION PROGRAMS

Can children be taught to improve their play skills? If play is an adaptive resource for children, then we should try to develop techniques that help children play better.

Dansky (1999) reviewed the play tutoring literature and found that "more than a dozen studies have shown that play tutoring can increase not just the quantity of play displayed but also the richness and imaginativeness of children's pretense" (404). These play tutoring studies usually involved eight to twelve small group sessions with an adult who models and encourages participation in social interactive pretense. Usually the sessions are spread out over three to six weeks. The pretend activities usually involve everyday activities or fairy tales. Freyberg (1973) was one of the first to demonstrate that training sessions improved imagination in play, which generalized to everyday free play over a two-month period.

Dansky (1980) carried out a study with preschoolers that involved three groups: a sociodramatic play tutoring group, exploration tutoring, and free play group. Both tutoring groups received equal amounts of verbal stimulation and attention from an adult. After a three-week intervention, the play tutoring group had a greater amount of, complexity of, and imaginativeness of pretense in daily free play. In addition, the play group had more imaginativeness on other measures of imagination. Udwin (1983) also found that a play-tutored group had more imaginative play, positive affect, and cooperation with peers during free play. Dansky (1999), after reviewing the literature, concluded that there were consistently positive results in studies with adequate control groups. He concluded that play tutoring, over a period of time, did result in increased imaginativeness in play and increased creativity on other measures.

Singer and Singer (1999) have developed a video-based program for parents and other caregivers of preschool children. The video and accompanying manual uses play and learning games to strengthen social readiness skills in children from three to five. The tape and manual provide clear examples and instructions for parents and caregivers that model how to use play to help children use imagination and learn through play. Singer and Singer (2000) also have a book for parents and teachers that reviews games and activities for imaginative play.

In my research lab, my students and I have carried out a study with first and second graders that is "trying out" different play instructions, prompts, and scenarios to determine if we can improve play skills and increase performance on a variety of outcome measures. We are trying to develop manuals for parents, teachers, or therapists to improve children's play skills over a short period of time. If we can develop play intervention scripts that work, then they can be used as a foundation for a play therapy manual. Manual-based treatment could be applied to the use of play in therapy.

GUIDELINES FOR FUTURE RESEARCH

A systematic program of research needs to be carried out in the play intervention and play therapy are, at both the micro and macro level, with continuing interaction between laboratory research and research in clinical settings (Russ 1995, 2003). It is important to:

- Investigate play interventions with situations and populations that have anxiety as a focus. Investigating the effectiveness of play with other types of anxiety disorders and posttraumatic stress disorders are next logical steps. Also, investigating the use of play with specific types of anxiety producing situations (in addition to medical procedures) and after specific traumas, such as accidents, natural disasters, and loss of a parent is warranted. Carrying out studies of children who experienced trauma will also investigate the use of play with some types of depression that involves mourning and loss. The field needs to develop an empirical base for the use of play in these areas. Carrying out treatment efficacy studies under controlled conditions that involves random assignment and control groups is essential.

- Refine specific play techniques and develop play therapy manuals. Research needs to investigate the effectiveness of specific techniques in facilitating specific play processes. When is modeling most effective— for which processes and populations? How do we help children better regulate their emotions? Would having children make up stories in their play that included emotion help them regulate affect? There are a myriad of interesting questions to investigate in this area that lend themselves to focused research in the lab. Results could then be tested in clinical treatment groups. The question of refining play intervention techniques bridges the research laboratory and the clinical treatment setting. Research groups could go back and forth between the laboratory and clinical setting. Play therapy manuals need to be developed based on this work. For example, Fein (1995) reported on studies that found that when four-year-olds were given problem props (toys in which one figure was incompatible with the others), they told better stories than did children with compatible toys. Fein concluded that props facilitate storytelling when they tap children's affective knowledge. Implications for clinical practice is that the therapist can set the stage by providing the right mix of toys.
- Carry out psychotherapy process research with play as a focus. Following the individual cases, with repeated measures of play (either in the session or separately), will contribute to our knowledge of how play changes in therapy, what therapeutic interventions effect play, and what changes in the child's functioning play effects.
- Investigate specific mechanisms of change. How does fantasy play reduce anxiety? What exactly is the working-through process in play? Can we break down the working-through process into components, measure it, assess its effectiveness, and teach other children to do it? This is a challenging task, but, in my opinion, is one of the most important tasks in terms of potential benefits to children.
- Carry out comparative studies of play therapy and other forms of therapy to determine optimal forms of intervention with specific problems and populations. Play therapy studies should follow the generally accepted criteria in the field using random assignment to conditions, specific child populations, treatment manuals, and multiple outcome measures with "blind" raters (Kazdin 2000). One of the challenges for play

therapy will be to demonstrate greater effectiveness than cognitive-behavioral approaches in treating childhood disorders. Having a wide variety of outcome measures will be important in contrasting the benefits of different treatment approaches.

• Investigate the use of play intervention modules with specific problems and populations. These modules could develop from the studies that are refining play intervention techniques. Different kinds of play intervention modules could be used with different kinds of problems. For example, there could be one set of play interventions for separation anxiety and another for posttraumatic stress. These modules could be used with other types of treatment techniques.

As of 1992, play in some form was used in child therapy by a majority of clinicians (Koocher and D'Angelo 1992). Although I am not aware of a current survey, I would assume that play is still used by a majority of clinicians. Play is a natural way to communicate with children. And play lends itself to a variety of therapeutic approaches. Research findings in the child development area supports play as being a major resource for children. Play intervention studies found that play reduces anxiety in children. These are encouraging findings and point the way for future empirical work to refine play techniques for use in therapy and prevention programs.

REFERENCES

Altschul, S. 1988. *Childhood Bereavement and Its Aftermath*. Madison, Wis.: International University Press.

Barnett, I., and B. Storn. 1981. "Play, Pleasure, and Pain: The Reduction of Anxiety through Play." *Leisure Science* 4: 161–75.

Barron, F., and D. Harrington. 1981. "Creativity, Intelligence, and Personality." In M. Rosenzweig and L. Porter, eds., *Annual Review of Psychology* 32: 439–76. Palo Alto, Calif.: Annual Reviews.

Carson, D., M. Bittner, B. Cameron, D. Brown, and S. Meyer. 1994. "Creative Thinking as a Predictor of School-Aged Children's Stress Responses and Coping Abilities." *Creativity Research Journal* 7: 145–58.

Cassell, S. 1965. "Effect of Brief Puppet Therapy upon the Emotional Response of Children Undergoing Cardiac Catheterization." *Journal of Consulting Psychology* 29: 1–8.

Christiano, B., and S. Russ. 1996. "Play as a Predictor of Coping and Distress in Children during an Invasive Dental Procedure." *Journal of Clinical Child Psychology* 25: 130–3 .

Dansky, J. 1980. "Make-Believe: A Mediator of the Relationship between Play and Associative Fluency." *Child Development* 51: 576–79.

———. 1999. "Play." In M. Runco and S. Pritzker, eds., *Encyclopedia of Creativity*, 393–408. San Diego: Academic.

Dansky, J., and F. Silverman. 1973. "Effects of Play on Associative Fluency in Preschool-Aged Children." *Developmental Psychology* 9: 38–43.

Fein, G. 1981. "Pretend Play in Childhood: An Integrative Review." *Child Development* 52: 1095–1118.

———. 1987. "Pretend Play: Creativity and Consciousness." In P. Gorlitz and J. Wohlwill, eds., *Curiosity, Imagination, and Play*, 281–304. Hillsdale, N.J.: Erlbaum.

———. 1995. "Toys and Stories." In A. Pellegrini, ed., *The Future of Play Theory*, 151–64. Albany: State University of New York Press.

Fisher, E. 1992. "The Impact of Play on Development: A Meta-analysis." *Play and Culture* 5: 159–81.

Freyberg, J. F. 1973. "Increasing the Imaginative Play of Urban Disadvantaged Kindergarten Children through Systematic Training." In J. L. Singer, *The Child's World of Make-Believe*. New York: Academic.

Getzels, S., and M. Csikszentmihalyi. 1976. *The Creative Vision: A Longitudinal Study of Problem Finding in Art*. New York: Wiley-Interscience.

Guilford, J. P. 1950. "Creativity." *American Psychologist* 5: 444–54.

———. 1968. *Intelligence, Creativity, and Their Educational Implications*. San Diego: Knapp.

Isen, A., K. Daubman, and G. Nowicki. 1987. "Positive Affect Facilitates Creative Problem Solving." *Journal of Personality and Social Psychology* 52: 1122–31.

Johnson, P. A., and D. E. Stockdale. 1975. "Effects of Puppet Therapy on Palmar Sweating of Hospitalized Children." *Johns Hopkins Medical Journal* 137: 1–5.

Kazdin, A. 2000. *Psychotherapy for Children and Adolescents*. New York: Oxford University Press.

Koocher, I., and E. J. D'Angelo. 1992. "Evolution of Practice in Child Psychotherapy." In D. K. Freedheim, ed., *History of Psychotherapy*, 457–92. Washington, D.C.: American Psychological Association.

Milos, M., and S. Reiss. 1982. "Effects of Three Play Conditions on Separation Anxiety in Young Children." *Journal of Consulting and Clinical Psychology* 50: 389–95.

Phillips, R. 1985. "Whistling in the Dark? A Review of Play Therapy Research." *Psychotherapy* 22: 752–60.

Rae, W., R. Worchel, J. Upchurch, J. Sanner, and C. Dainel. 1989. "The Psychosocial Impact of Play on Hospitalized Children." *Journal of Pediatric Psychology* 14: 617–27.

Runco, M. A. 1991. *Divergent Thinking*. Norwood, N.J.: Ablex.

Russ, S. 1987. "Assessment of Cognitive Affective Interaction in Children: Creativity, Fantasy, and Play Research." In J. Butcher and C. Spielberger, eds., *Advances in Personality Assessment* 6: 141–55. Hillsdale, N.J.: Erlbaum.

———. 1988. "Primary Process Thinking on the Rorschach, Divergent Thinking, and Coping in Children." *Journal of Personality Assessment* 52: 539–48.

———. 1993. *Affect and Creativity: The Role of Affect and Play in the Creative Process*. Hillsdale, N.J.: Erlbaum.

———. 1995. "Play Psychotherapy Research: State of the Science." In T. Ollendick and R. Prinz, eds., *Advances in Clinical Child Psychology*, 365–91. New York: Plenum.

———. 2003. *Play in Child Development and Psychotherapy: Toward Empirically Supported Practice*. Mahwah, N.J.: Erlbaum.

Russ, S., and A. Grossman-McKee. 1990. "Affective Expression in Children's Fantasy Play, Primary Process Thinking on the Rorschach, and Divergent Thinking." *Journal of Personality Assessment* 54: 756–71.

Russ, S., D. Robins, and B. Christiano. 1999. "Pretend Play: Longitudinal Prediction of Creativity and Affect in Fantasy in Children." *Creativity Research Journal* 12: 129–39.

Saltz, E., D. Dixon, and J. Johnson. 1977. "Training Disadvantaged Preschoolers on Various Fantasy Activities: Effects on Cognitive Functioning and Impulse Control." *Child Development* 48: 367–80.

Sawyer, P. K. 1997. *Pretend Play as Improvisation*. Mahwah, N.J.: Erlbaum.

Sherrod, L., and J. Singer. 1979. "The Development of Make-Believe Play." In J. Goldstein, ed., *Sports, Games, and Play*, 1–28. Hillsdale, N.J.: Erlbaum.

Singer, D. G., and J. L. Singer. 1990. *The House of Make-Believe: Children's Play and the Developing Imagination*. Washington, D.C.: APA Books.

Singer, J. L., and D. G. Singer. 1976. "Imaginative Play and Pretending in Early Childhood: Some Experimental Approaches." In A. Davids, ed., *Child Personality and Psychopathology*, 3: 69–112. New York: Wiley.

———. 1999. *Learning through Play*. Videotape. Instructional Media Institute.

Sternberg. R. 1988. "A Three-Facet Model of Creativity." In R. Sternberg, ed., *The Nature of Creativity*, 125–47. Cambridge: Cambridge University Press.

Sylva, K., J. Bruner, and P. Genova. 1976. "The Role of Play in the Problem Solving of Children 3–5 Years Old." In J. Bruner, A. Jolly, and K. Sylva, eds., *Play*. New York: Basic.

Terr, L. 1991. *Too Scared to Cry: Psychic Trauma in Childhood*. New York: Harper & Row.

Udwin, O. 1983. "Imaginative Play Training as an Intervention Method with Institutionalized Preschool Children." *British Journal of Educational Psychology* 53: 32–39.

Vandenberg, B. 1980. "Play, Problem-Solving, and Creativity." *New Directions for Child Development* 9: 49–68.

Wallach, M. 1970. "Creativity." In P. Mussed, ed., *Carmichael's Manual of Child Psychology*, 1: 1211–72. New York: Wiley.

Weisberg, R. 1988. "Problem Solving and Creativity." In R. Sternberg, ed., *The Nature of Creativity*, 148–76. Cambridge: Cambridge University Press.

III

PLAY THERAPY APPLICATIONS

12

"Little Monsters"? Play Therapy for Children with Sexually Problematic Behavior

David LeVay

> He who fights against monsters should see to it that he does not become a monster in the process. And when you stare persistently into the abyss, the abyss also stares into you.
>
> —Friedrich Nietzsche

Childhood sexuality is a challenging area for parents, foster parents, and professionals and is an issue that for many can provoke great anxiety and uncertainty. The idea of sexuality as a natural, healthy, and integral part of a child's development can for some be difficult to accept, perhaps because of the particular resonance it holds for each of us, and so becomes laced with feelings of caution and unease. A source of further anxiety is the notion of children and young people as potential sexual abusers. Although over the past decade there has been a growing understanding and acceptance among professionals working in this area of the levels of sexual abuse carried out by young people, it is an area that evokes powerful and complex emotional responses. It is easy enough for adult sexual offenders to be publicly labeled and demonized as dangerous, evil pedophiles, but not so easy for society to view children through this same social lens. We live in a society that seeks monsters, identifiable vessels that can contain the collective projective fears and horrors that inhabit each and every one of us, fueled by an alarmist media that thrives on public anxiety and insecurity.

This unease can seep into aspects of our daily lives, into our increasingly scrutinized and complex roles as parents and professionals, clouding our judgments around what is right or wrong, good or bad. The notion of children as sexual beings, and their developing expressions of sexuality, is particularly complex as we strive to find appropriate responses within a culture where the lines of what is and is not appropriate are being continually redrawn. Little wonder, then, that this is a territory marked by confusion, where the very elements of the media that orchestrate public witch-hunts for pedophiles at the same time seek to eroticize our children, blurring the lines between child and adult through a process of sexual objectification that can only serve to gratify the desires of the very people they demonize. And so parents, foster parents, and professionals may struggle to respond appropriately to children engaged in mutually explorative and age-appropriate sexual play, perhaps overreacting and causing unnecessary alarm and confusion. Alternatively, there is a danger that coercive and abusive sexual behavior between children may be ignored or minimized, which can have damaging long-term consequences for both victim and victimizer.

I will aim to explore in this chapter some of the processes that cause young children to display problematic sexual behavior and the connections this behavior has with their own experiences of trauma and abuse. I will then look at how play therapy can provide an effective treatment intervention in enabling children to begin to manage the very complex emotional and psychological processes that underpin this behavior and that could, without early therapeutic support, develop into the entrenched, compulsive behavioral patterns and dominant internal narratives that may ultimately provide a pathway into adult sexual offending. The question of terminology and of how to describe this group of children has been much debated. They have variously been described as young abusers, children who molest or who are sexually aggressive. While the sexual behavior in question is clearly abusive and in turn is damaging and traumatic for the victims of such behavior, I feel it is important to make a distinction between the sexualized behavior of young children and that of older adolescents. Clearly similarities exist, and in a sense we are looking at behavior that exists at different stages of a developmental continuum. However, the problematic sexualized behavior of younger children is more related to their chaotic expressions of anger and helplessness and driven by their own experiences of trauma, disorganized attachments, and disruptive family experiences. It is less entrenched than the behavior of adolescents and perhaps less defined by the more conscious desires for sexual gratification sought through premeditated and coercive patterns of behavior. Certainly, I am wary of an early process of labeling that can prove unhelpful for the ongoing needs of these children and have serious consequences for the remainder of their lives. For these reasons, I will generally be using the term "sexually problematic" to describe the behavior of these children, while not wanting to minimize in any way the impact and consequences of this behavior on others. Indeed, we are dealing here with a continuum between victim and victimizer, abused and abuser, and notions of responsibility are complex and not always helpful.

I will, throughout this chapter, be presenting examples of case material from children and young people that I have worked with. In all cases names and circumstantial details have been changed in order to prevent identification.

Government criminal statistics (1997) suggest that, for all those cautioned for a sexual offence in England and Wales, 47 percent are children and young people between the ages of ten and twenty-one. Other studies (Horne et al. 1991; N. Ireland Research Team 1991) have estimated that between 25 percent and 33 percent of all cases of sexual abuse are carried out by a child or young person. Further studies have indicated that young people might account for up to as much as 50 percent of sexual abuse perpetrated against children. At ACT (assessment, consultation, and therapy) we work with children and young people across the whole age range, many of whom are below the age of criminal responsibility and do not feature in the majority of the statistics and research that has sought to ascertain the prevalence of sexual abuse carried out by young people. However, these children are the potential statistics of the future and the importance of early, appropriate therapeutic intervention is clear.

Historically, much of the work done with young people with sexual behavioral problems has been informed by work undertaken with adult sex offenders. The nature of this work has drawn heavily on a cognitive behavioral methodology that seeks to identify and modify the cognitive distortions, or thinking errors, that can lead people into fixed, repetitive patterns of sexual offending behavior. Professional understanding of these behavior processes has been defined to a great extent by the behavioral models developed by Lane (1991), Finkelhor (1984), and others. However, the value of a structured cognitive and behavioral approach to working with young children with problematic sexual behavior is questionable.

ORIGIN OF INAPPROPRIATE SEXUAL BEHAVIOR IN CHILDHOOD

The great majority of the children referred to our service have experienced early childhood trauma and sexual abuse, and their narrative identity, their way of making sense of these experiences, involves personal constructs of shame, guilt, rage, and the very confusing physical feelings around stimulation and sexual arousal. These are children with primarily "sexually reactive" behavior, in the sense that their behavior is a physical, emotional, and psychological response to their own abuse experiences and is being acted out, often chaotically, in their social relationships. One way for children to manage these confusing, intolerable, and unbearable feelings they carry with them is to push them outward and project them onto other children, through acts of harmful and inappropriate sexual behavior. In this sense then, the identification with the role of sexual aggressor, the internalization of the abuser role, may enable the child to gain some sense of power and control and achieve temporary relief from the feelings of helplessness and confusion that they are fighting so hard to contain. The abused, victimized self is not allowed to become conscious and is instead pushed and projected into other children as a way of protecting their fragile psyche from traumatic feelings that cannot be internally processed.

A helpful model for understanding this process of trauma and abuse is Bentovim's cyclical dynamic/systemic model. At the top of the cycle, an abusive act creates an overwhelming, affective response that in turn leads to intolerable levels of anxiety and helplessness. These feeling responses become unbearable to the point where there is no room for them to become accommodated or integrated into lived experience. Consequently they are deleted and so create what Bentovim and Kinston (1991) described as a "hole in the mind," where thought is unable to take place and is instead replaced by a range of defensive processes. These processes may take a variety of forms and can lead to compulsive repetitive actions and behaviors which in turn lead to further acts of abuse either as a victim or through the abuse of others. Bentovim states that "the compulsion to act rather than experience and digest, is a characteristic of both abusers and the abused. Traumatic patterns of dissociation and addictive repetition of abuse is a characteristic phenomenon which occurs in the face of unbearable levels of anxiety and helplessness" (Bentovim 1993).

The traumagenic model developed by Finkelhor and Brown (1986) has also been helpful in providing an understanding of how and why some children who have experienced abuse will go on to abuse others. This model looks at how the experience of sexual abuse can be viewed in terms of four traumagenic dynamics—traumatic sexualization, powerlessness, betrayal, and stigmatization. Through these processes, a child's problematic sexual behavior is seen as a learned response to the trauma of being sexually abused. The abuse experience has had to become psychologically accommodated in order to cope, with the result that the child's cognitions are distorted through a process of traumagenic sexualization. This then develops into patterns of inappropriate sexual behavior as the child seeks to alleviate feelings of helplessness through abusive and controlling behavior.

So while cognitive behavioral therapy can clearly be a valuable treatment methodology for adults and some adolescents in helping them understand and modify aspects of their abusive behavior, the majority of younger children are unable, as a result of trauma, to think about their behavior on such a conscious level. Indeed, young children may not have sufficient cognitive capabilities to make use of this approach, and the extreme levels of anxiety and fear around their own victimization that they carry with them often means that attempts to talk directly about their behavior can evoke powerful psychological defense mechanisms, for example, denial, projection, dissociation, and repression. Certainly, the majority of young children with whom I have worked are either unable or unwilling to sit and talk about the behavior that is causing the people around them so much concern and anxiety, and to do so can feel unnecessarily punitive and potentially abusive in itself. Therapy and treatment that involves repeatedly talking about and working through offending behavior on a conscious level carries the danger of reinforcing the young person's need to split off those unwanted, dangerous aspects of themselves. The more emotionally defended a child becomes, the greater the potential for further episodes of sexually harmful acting out.

This area of work carries its own dominant narratives, one of which is the notion that sexual offenders need take responsibility for their abusive behavior, to express a sense of victim empathy and experience feelings of guilt or remorse. Again, these are clearly important process within work with adults and some young people and can provide valuable markers in the assessment of risk. However, application of these kinds of cognitive frameworks to work with the majority of younger children with sexual behavioral problems, and likewise adolescents with learning disabilities, can be inappropriate and of limited value.

Research undertaken by Hodges, Lanyado, and Andreou (1994), which looked at young male sexual offenders from a psychotherapeutic context, concluded that these boys were unable to empathize with their victims' feelings until their own feelings as victims had been acknowledged and contained. Interestingly, this research also led to the hypothesis that guilt was not absent in boys who were sexually abusive but was in fact experienced so intensely, along with feelings of self-hate and intrusive suicidal thoughts, that it became too unbearable to be in touch with. In this sense, the feelings of guilt were too intense to be felt or tolerated and therefore were not able to influence behavior or counteract the impulse to abuse. Their experience during the course of this research also highlighted the extreme rejection and abandonment from primary attachment figures that the boys had each experienced. In this sense, then, children's sexual behavior does not exist in isolation but is part of a wider picture of complex needs, for example, attachment disorders, trauma, learning disability, ADHD, and related conduct disorders. Therapy with these children needs to acknowledge and work with the "wholeness" of their experience, to find the space between the words, rather than focusing on specific aspects of their sexual behavior.

PLAY THERAPY INTERVENTION

My central premise, then, is that play therapy, along with other creative arts therapies, allows these children to engage in a process of expressive communication that does not threaten to overwhelm their fragile emotional and psychological states of being. The play therapy space is a transitional space, both real and imagined, in which unconscious feelings are projected onto the play objects, contained within narrative structures and creative imagery, and held through the relationship with the therapist and the safe space of the playroom. The process of symbolic play facilitates the aesthetic distance that is so critical in allowing these children to find a different space in which to explore the relationship between their internal and external worlds.

Play therapy is a process of externalization that can begin to make visible the "hole in the mind," the frightening place that holds the fears, desires, conflicts, and compulsions that drive both victim and abusing behavior. Instead of being projected onto other children, these feelings are projected onto the objects, roles, stories, and images contained within the child's play and into the relationship with the therapist whose role it is to hold and contain these feelings. Child psychotherapist Anne Alvarez (1992) talks of the need for children to be able to forget their experiences of trauma in order to be able to find a space where they can safely begin to remember. In this sense, children need to be enabled to find a space where fragments of memory, experience, feeling, and behavior can be conjured with, becoming both seen and unseen, in a process of gradual coalescence and integration. An object in sand play, holding powerful symbolic projections, will be repeatedly buried and uncovered as a child plays and has control over the parts of themselves that can be tolerated and made visible and the parts that need to remain hidden. Through dramatic enactment, monsters and burglars appear and disappear in fleeting stories about victims and abusers. The play therapy room, the objects, the roles, and the therapeutic relationship becomes a creative, transitional "third" space, which both is and is not real and where transformation and change can begin to take place.

The needs of children who are both victims and victimizers are complex. These parts of themselves cannot be addressed separately. They are both part of the same story, narrative threads that become tangled and enmeshed so that it is hard to know which end leads to which. This is the journey that the therapist and child make together, to find a way through the labyrinth, fight battles together, and gently begin to untangle some of the complex stories that are told on the way.

James was a fifteen-year-old boy with moderate learning disabilities, assessed as having an intellectual/emotional age of around seven or eight. He was referred because of the sexual abuse of his eight-year-old sister as well as allegations that he had attempted to have penetrative sex with an eleven-year-old daughter of a family friend while she was asleep. James had been sexually abused, possibly raped, while attending a school for emotionally disturbed boys, and his own offending behavior had begun shortly after this abuse took place. As a result of the family's concerns about the risk presented by James, he was placed in local authority care in a residential placement that was acknowledged as not being appropriate to his specific needs. James had refused, or felt unable, to talk about his sexual behavior and his own victimization to either his parents or professionals involved with him. There was a considerable level of anxiety around the issue of risk and how his complex needs could best be managed. While it was acknowledged that James would not engage in a formal, structured risk assessment process, it was agreed that he attend a period of play therapy, a process both less anxiety-inducing and more developmentally appropriate to his needs.

The following exchange took place after about six months of weekly play therapy sessions dominated by James's use of sand and puppet play in which he had enacted symbolic stories about himself and his relationships, and follows an earlier session in which he had first begun to talk about his abuse of his sister. While James knew why he was coming for play therapy, I placed no expectations on him to talk about his sexual behavior and trusted that the play therapy process would allow his story to be told.

James: I want to watch *The Bill* [TV program] tonight. To find out about that girl that went missing.

Therapist: I haven't seen it. What do you think might have happened to the girl?

James: Don't know. She might have been raped or something.

Therapist: Oh right. We talked about that a bit last week, didn't we?

James: Stop, stop. No more talking.

Therapist: I know. You don't like me to talk about the sexy stuff.

James: I don't want my girlfriend to know.

Therapist: What don't you want your girlfriend to know?

James: What I did to my sister.

Therapist: Right. What would your girlfriend think if she knew what you did to your sister?

James: She would think I am horrible . . . and worthless.

Therapist: I see. I wonder if sometimes you feel horrible and worthless because of what you did to your sister? [No response.] And because of what happened at [previous school where J was sexually abused].

James: No no no no no. No more. Stop talking . . . 'cos I used to have a girlfriend there, but she was taken away from me by another boy.

Therapist: You must have felt upset and cross about that. And because of what else happened there.

James: Yeah, bloody [boy's name]. He tried to touch my penis. I hate him. I want to kick him in the bollocks. I want to punch him in the chest so he can't breathe and smash him in the face. I want to get a staple gun and fire it into him. I want to kill him.

Therapist: I know. You are so angry about what he did to you that you want to hurt him and kill him. It's good that you can talk about how angry he makes you feel. [James begins to play with clay, cutting it and rolling it.]

James: It's like poo. It's poo.

Therapist: Yes, it is all like poo.

James: I'm going to make a penis.

Therapist: Whose penis are you going to make?

James: Mine.

Therapist: You are thinking a lot about your penis.

James: No [very exaggerated].

James proceeded to transform his clay penis into a racing car, with wheels, steering wheel, and driver and he inscribed upon the side of the car/penis the name of a girl pop group that he had previously talked and fantasized about. He then made a further, similar-shaped object that was a set of traffic lights. Using the models he had made, James then acted out a fleeting enactment in which the car/penis briefly slowed down and then sped through the traffic lights. I made no comment on this at the time and the significance of this momentary enactment only really struck me as I was writing up my notes and thinking afterwards about James's session. On reflection, James seemed to be depicting the overwhelming, compulsive nature of his feelings around sexuality and identity that had been driving his abusive behavior. The traffic lights, a symbol perhaps of regulation and control, were unable to contain the powerful nature of these feelings.

It was clear also that James's narrative identity was dominated by feelings of disgust and shame, and that these feelings were being projected onto his own genitalia. His penis was a bad object, made of shit, and I wondered about his need to rid himself of the overpowering feelings of badness that he was experiencing and how this connected with rape fantasies that James had expressed. The psychotherapist Donald Campbell reflected upon this process when he stated that:

> Relief is sought by resorting to actions which project the confusion, passivity and disgust onto others. The victim may try to protect himself by splitting off the disgust for himself and projecting that disgust onto the organs exposed by the abuse. Furthermore, the abused child may project his self-disgust via an abusive act onto another's body which is treated with contempt. In this way, the abused child becomes the abuser. (Campbell 1994)

The above exchange with James illustrates how children and young people struggle to verbalize the very complex feelings around their victim/victimizer experiences as a result of the overwhelming nature of the anxiety, guilt, and shame that they carry within them. James, through the gradual development of a trusting relationship and a symbolic process of play therapy, had been able to externalize his fears, to visualize, describe, name, and control them through the emotional distance of symbolic play. Eventually the words had come, and James was able to begin to acknowledge his own sexually harmful behavior and feelings around his own abuse and begin to make connections between the two.

Of course, James's story is far more complex than a simple causal relationship between abuse and abuser, just as a young person's problematic sexual behavior is simply one part of their overall behavior. He was distressed and angry about the separation of his parents and the subsequent loss of his mother when it was decided that he should live with his father. His eight-year-old sister, with whom he was developmentally close, had remained with his mother and was so a source of envy. James's abuse of his sister was as much about intimacy, anger, envy, and of a desire to find a way back into his family as it was about sex, themes of which had all been very present in his sand and puppet play. As a result of James's ability to engage in a process of play therapy, it was possible to provide a therapeutic assessment of both his needs and the level of risk that he presented to children and vulnerable young people. Placement issues were integral to the planning of James's needs and a placement was identified that could manage both issues of risk and provide James with an environment which was appropriate to his own social, educational, and developmental needs.

As with all children who are referred for therapy, it is important to be clear, open, and honest about the behavior that is causing people around them to feel concerned, and creating distress for the child. For children with problematic sexual behavior it is important during the initial agreement meeting stage to be explicit in naming the behavior for which they are coming for therapy. This can sometimes be hard, for the child, for foster parents, and for the professionals, and it is often difficult to find the right words for behavior that has perhaps not been openly named and spoken about before. Children can experience intense feelings of shame and guilt and their behavior needs to be addressed in a noncritical, nonjudgmental way that does not reinforce their overall sense of badness. Equally important is the notion of open confidentiality, a process that maintains the essence of confidentiality that is integral to the therapeutic relationship while also ensuring that relevant information is shared within the network, so that the key adults involved in the child's life are able to act in an informed and protective capacity.

Sexual abuse thrives in a culture of secrecy and silence, and within a context of anxious, disorganized family attachments, and the damaging splits, alliances, and projections that occur within abusing families can become all too easily enacted within professional systems. A child in therapy will project unbearable distress, anger, and anxiety onto the therapist, as will the professional network that carries the responsibility for making critical decisions and judgments around issues of risk and support. This process can leave the therapist feeling overwhelmed, helpless, and often isolated, somewhat like the child in an abusive family. Tony Morrison (1997) in his work around "emotionally competent organizations" talked about anxiety in organizations:

> Child abuse represents a crisis not only for the family, but also for the professional network . . . A social defence system develops over time as a result of collusive interaction and agreement between members of the organisation in order to avoid the experience of anxiety, guilt, doubt and uncertainty which are felt to be too deep and dangerous for confrontation.

And so the need for reflective, cohesive networks and open systems of communication is clear. Just as the therapist has to safely contain the anxieties of the child, organizations and professional networks need to hold and contain the powerful emotional responses that this work can engender, so that there can be clarity around the needs of these children. The need for reflective practice is vital, to create a context in which feelings of self-doubt and uncertainty can be safely expressed and acknowledged and so prevent the development of professional resistance and defensiveness.

During the process of play therapy itself it may be weeks, months (sometimes never) before a child may feel able to think and talk consciously about his sexual behavior because to do so also means having to emotionally engage with his own traumatic experiences. In this sense, then, a child knows why he is coming for play therapy but has no expressed expectations placed on him to have to talk about this during his sessions. The child's stories will begin to emerge through the unconscious, perhaps semiconscious process of his symbolic play. While this is often for both child and therapist a difficult place to be, a place of unknowing, doubt, and uncertainty, it can also be a place of magical creativity and transformation. I often recall the words of the drama therapist Alida Gersie, who said that one needs to "stay with the chaos" in order for meaning to begin to emerge. Countless times I have sat with children, helpless in the face of their intense experiences of desolation, rage, and loneliness and wondered what it is I am supposed to do or say that might make any sense. At other times I am in awe of the resourcefulness, creativity, and resilience of these children, who can find within them the strength to confront the monsters that inhabit the murky waters of their complex, tangled lives. To stay in a place of "unknowing" is difficult, for the temptation is to become more structured and directive as a way of managing both one's own anxiety and that of the professional network. However, my experience is that if you are able to "stay with the chaos" and have faith in the play therapy process and in the ability of children to find their own solutions, then meaning will and does begin to emerge.

Alec was a ten-year-old boy diagnosed with severe ADHD and referred for therapy because of his attempts to have penetrative sex with his seven-year-old sister. Alec himself had been sexually abused around the age of five by an older boy, who had coerced Alec into sucking his penis. Alec's mother had a history of childhood sexual abuse and acknowledged that her son's behavior raised many difficult feelings for her that led her at times to become angry and punitive toward him.

Alec knew why he was coming to play therapy but did not like to talk about his sexual behavior so it became known euphemistically as "it" or "the thing." He had said he came to therapy because he was bad and he had told his mother that he was scared that he had made his sister pregnant. Alec's sessions were difficult and often chaotic, marked by his flights of thought, restlessness, and general hyperactive behavior. However, we had periods of calm during the storm and in our first session we made a family play genogram (Burrma 1999) together. Alec, the eldest of three children, was able to show me how angry he felt in his family. His father was not his natural father, who had left when he was very young, and so he felt different and envious of his brother and sister. In Alec's early sessions he made sand worlds, dynamic, complex energetic, and transient worlds, the stories of which he narrated as he played and I wrote down. This was Alec's first story.

> There was a lizard, alien, and a lot of other creatures. The lizard found an egg which he thought was his although it really belonged to the alien because it had the alien's body inside. The alien had accidentally got the lizard's egg with the baby lizard inside. There was lots of chaos because they got their eggs mixed up. There were also four evil dinosaurs who lived in the desert world. The snake was curled around its own nest full of eggs and went to fight the evil dinosaurs but was teleported to the sea world. This was another mix-up because the snake had been teleported to the sea world and the shark had ended up, in the sand world. One of the aliens stole an egg from the snake's nest and took it away to study it but when the snake saw his egg he swallowed it to keep it safe. The alien shrunk himself to a shell and flew in the spaceship back to the sand world. The alien hid in the sand while the evil creatures searched the desert. The lizard and the evil dinosaur had a great fight and the lizard was transported back to the sea world and woke up the other two aliens. He told them to find the lizard and to find out where the teleporting stone was. The shark was also searching for the teleporting

stone. The boss of the aliens still had not managed to find his body which was inside one of the eggs. They eventually found the teleporting stone and the lizard and the dolphin eggs were all transported back to the sand world. The baby sharks began to hatch out.

Through sand play, Alec was starting to make visible the anxieties and fears that dominated his internal world. Powerful, organic stories about bodies, swallowing, eggs, babies, and the confusion around time, place, and where things belonged. By being able to locate these feelings outside of him and project them onto the objects in the sand play, they became something physical that he could manipulate and become tangibly engaged with. No longer were they simply the intolerable, bad parts of Alec chaotically acted out through his social relationships. He was beginning to make stories about abuse that were sufficiently emotionally distanced for him to engage with, and my role as listener, witness, and cocreator was not to interpret or impose solutions but to maintain a sense of genuine interest and curiosity, to generate a space and relationship where these stories and narratives could grow. So again we have the notion of play therapy as a process of externalization, a process that relates closely to the ideas of narrative family therapy. Indeed, parallels between narrative therapy and the creative arts therapies were made by Epston, Freeman, and Lobovits (1997), when they said that "the very process of drawing, sculpting, or dramatizing the relationship with a problem naturally evokes a visceral sense of the problem as located for reflection outside of the self . . . it can be a relief for children to literally express the externalised problem in a symbolic yet physically experienced way. This allows them to 'see' the problem and ponder it more easily."

Within a narrative model of play therapy (LeVay 2002) children construct stories about themselves and their relationships within the social context of the therapeutic relationship. It is possible, then, to reframe these stories and reconstruct ongoing narratives for the child that are less driven by their internalized feelings of guilt and shame. Play therapy in this sense is about the facilitation of the child's narrative identity so that they are enabled to explore relationships, both positive and abusive, through the symbolic and metaphorical imagery that is coconstructed during the process of their play. Play is also a healing process, and the healing narratives become embedded within the relationship between child and therapist and allow both to begin to sequence, order, and make sense of the complex, dualistic feelings that are such a feature of the victim/victimizer dichotomy.

In a later session Alec chose to use clay to make "demons," which he gave names like Lickaton and Ratso. He spent a considerable amount of time and care creating these creatures and again I wondered with Alec whether there was a story he could tell about them. This was the story he told.

Lickaton and Drake were bad demons. Ratso was a good demon, but a snake was put on him by the bad demons. The snake makes you bad, which meant that Lickaton and Drake could make Ratso do bad things even though he did not want to. Ratso had managed to break off the snake that was put on him by the bad demons and there was a large scar and hole where the snake had been. Ratacondo was another demon. He used to be like Ratso but was now all bad. He was like Ratso's evil brother. Ratso was flying around when the demons put the snake on him but another creature attacked Ratso and broke the snake off.

Alec's story presents a graphic account of the effects, transmission, and emotional scars of sexual abuse and is a clear metaphorical narrative of Alec's own abuse and subsequent abusive behavior. The inner demons that have formed such a strong part of his own narrative identity have been externalized and made visible and he can engage with them in a tangible, physical way that is removed from his own sense of badness. The internal conflict between the abused and abusive parts of the self are clear to see within the projective imagery of Ratso and his evil brother Ratacondo and these characters, expressions of Alec's narrative identity, became a key theme within his therapy. Several weeks later, amid the hyperactive chaos that often marked his sessions, Alec used a playhouse and family figures to enact a number of scenes. As he played, he announced with importance that "this is about the thing . . . you know . . . it." He said little but enacted the family scenario that provided the context for the sexual abuse of his sister. Alec was watching television in the sitting room, feeling angry after having argued with his mother who was in the kitchen. His sister was in the bath upstairs. There was a girl on the television that made him feel sexy and he went upstairs where "it" happened with his sister. It was a fleeting enactment, but Alec had reached a point where he felt able to show me something important.

Alec's problematic sexual behavior ceased, although he continued to have difficulty with other aspects of his behavior. I met with Alec's mother periodically throughout his therapy, providing her with the opportunity to reflect on the emotional responses that his behavior had evoked in her and the connections it had with her own abuse. We talked about Alec's father and his need to make sense of his family story and how she could help him with this. And we talked about her need to be vigilant and aware of her children's behavior and to supervise them closely to prevent further opportunities for abuse to arise.

One of the anxieties often expressed by foster parents is around making distinctions between natural and healthy sexual behavior and behavior that is abusive—behavior that is defined by dynamics of coercion, inequality, threat, and lack of consent. These difficulties are compounded by the secrecy that can surround childhood sexuality and parental fears that any expressions of sexuality might somehow be "deviant" and can consequently provoke a whole range of fears and fantasies arising from the social stigmas, perceptions, and myths that exist around sexuality and sexual abuse and that have become an entrenched part of our culture. As Gail Ryan (1991) stated, this sense of secrecy around childhood sexuality "not only protects the perpetrators of child sexual abuse, but also prohibits both normative and corrective learning for children." Ryan reminds us that childhood sexuality is not a pathological condition but part of an innate capacity for sexual arousal, and that the way children behave sexually is shaped through their environment and social experience.

It is important, then, that foster parents are provided with the information that can help them to differentiate between natural and abusive sexual behaviors and supported in their management of children who are displaying problematic sexualized behavior. Adults need to be able to respond to this behavior in a way that does not reinforce any feelings of shame or guilt that the child may be already experiencing. These behaviors do not exist in isolation but take place within a social and family context. In this sense it is unrealistic to expect a child to change problematic behavior without change occurring also on a social and familial level. Family therapy is often an integral part of a therapeutic intervention, providing an important parallel process to individual play therapy. Equally, consultation with social workers, schools, and foster parents is integral in enabling people both to reflect on their emotional responses to children's sexualized behavior and to think about strategies through which this behavior can be managed.

As stated earlier, children with problematic sexual behavior provoke intense anxiety in the networks that are responsible for providing and managing resources around their care. Social workers, teachers, parents and foster parents search for definitive, immediate answers about levels of risk, and the uncertainty and anxiety that drives the decision-making processes for these children can lead to extreme responses that can either leave children in positions of great vulnerability or become overly punitive and controlling through the overestimation of risk. And so once again we find ourselves traversing the continuum between poor victims and little monsters. As therapists we need to manage this paradox of working both with the abused and abusive parts of the self, both for the child and for the system within which they are held, and during the process of therapy itself it is important to hold in mind the duality of the child as both victim and victimizer. While Alvarez is right that children sometimes need to be allowed to forget in order to remember, the therapist cannot be allowed to forget that some of these children can pose very significant risks. In this sense, a great part of the therapist role is to contribute toward a sense of clarity and balance that can help the professional network in both the management of risk and the provision of support, care, and appropriate longer-term planning.

Laura was a seven-year-old girl who was referred for therapy because of concerns about incidents in which she had instigated inappropriate and abusive sexual activity with other young children, for example, attempting to suck penises, taking boys' clothes off, and lying on top of them in an enactment of penetrative sex. There had been a degree of secrecy and coercion about this behavior. Laura had been made subject of a care order, along with two younger brothers, after an investigation which revealed that her parents had been hosting and attending sex parties that included convicted adult sex offenders. It became clear that Laura had been sexualized from a very early age, witnessing and participating in a variety of sexual activities, including animals, and most likely ritually sexually abused by being passed among adults for sex. Laura was placed with foster parents with a view to a permanent fostering or adoptive placement. Her foster parents were a religious family, as was her natural family, and she attended church on a regular basis.

Laura was a controlled, self-contained girl who had become emotionally defended and unable to verbalize any of her feelings or experiences around either her own abuse or inappropriate sexual behavior. Her early sessions were dominated by safe games that I felt were about the development of trust in our relationship and she would instigate the compiling of endless lists of names, colors, feelings, and sometimes parts of the body. This would continue for weeks, and although repetitive it felt like it was part of an important process of developing some kind of emotional vocabulary together.

One day Laura arrived for her session and signaled that she was not going to speak and that she was only able to use sign language. So we made up signs, mimed and wrote things down together and Laura asked, by writing, whether she could play in the sand. We sat in silence with the sand for some time and Laura began to play by sifting it, moving it around and exploring its physical qualities. The silence was palpable and I made a reflection that it was sometimes hard to find words to talk about difficult or scary things that happen. Laura then began to construct an elaborate sand world using water and a variety of objects and animals and became silently absorbed in the process. Taking great care, she created in the center of the sand tray what was clearly a phallic object, a tower of a penis rising out of the sand. She then placed a number of baby animals in her world, marching in a long procession to the tower with some sitting on top, and in the corner a man watched the proceedings. When she finished, Laura wrote again on paper, asking me if she could now talk. I asked her about the story of her sand world and she told me that it was the "tower that reached up to heaven." The animals had to march up to the tower, just the baby ones, while the grown-up animals watched in the background. I asked about the man in the corner and Laura said that he was the man that could make the baby animals do things that they did not want to do. After her session Laura wanted to tell her foster mother about the sand world she had created and we realized together that this was the story of the Tower of Babel, the biblical tale about an attempt to build a tower that would reach heaven. God's response was to punish all the people of earth by giving them different languages so that they would become confused and unable to communicate with one another.

Something very powerful had happened in this session in the sense that a process had taken place that enabled Laura to communicate something that was very important. Laura had brought a verbal silence into the therapy room from the start of her session and constructed her sand world in response to a reflection I made about the difficulty in finding words to talk about certain things. Laura had also brought with her the story of the Tower of Babel, a story about human sin and the confusion of language and reconstructed this story within the context of her play therapy as a metaphor for the sexual abuse she had experienced, something that was too unbearable for words to convey. My feeling was that this session could not have happened without everything that had gone before, that after many weeks of establishing therapy as a safe space certain factors, events, and processes had come together which enabled her to tell a story about her abuse. Sometimes there can be a magical sense of synchronicity around the play therapy process, fragments coming together to create moments of great power and energy. The Tower of Babel became something of a motif within Laura's play therapy, appearing now and again in her sessions in different forms.

Sand is in my experience one of the central ingredients of the play therapy space. The evocative and transformational quality of sand is such that it becomes a very powerful medium for facilitating symbolic play with children and has the capacity to reach directly into the unconscious mind in a profound and often dramatic way. Weinrib (1983) defined sand play as a "non-verbal, non-rational form of therapy that reaches a profound preverbal level of the psyche" and it is this quality that makes sand play such a valuable method for engaging with children who are so emotionally defended that they are unable to explore issues of abuse on a conscious level. Sand play is a rich medium, incorporating all the elements of embodied, projective, and role play and has a deep primal energy as well as often carrying personal associations for children around early family experiences. For children like Laura and Alec, who are unable to verbalize the traumatic nature of their experiences, sand play provides an invaluable way of creating stories and images about themselves safely distanced through the symbolic process of their play. Sometimes I will invite children to construct a sand world (Lowenfeld 1979) although more often than not children will choose themselves to use the sand, creating spontaneous, dynamic, and transient sequences of play.

Children will act as their own narrators, a part of the natural human inclination to story experience, and sand play has a self-absorbing magic about it that facilitates this process.

Sarah was a girl whose experiences of sexual abuse had begun so early and become such an entrenched part of her childhood that all her relationships, with children and adults, tended to become sexualized. Sexual interaction became her way of managing the traumatic anxiety she carried with her, a process of dissociation that provided some relief from intolerable fear, confusion, and anxiety. The closeness and intimacy of the play therapy space felt at times so fearful for Sarah that she would unconsciously eroticize the therapeutic relationship through the unconscious enactment of seductive patterns of interaction. Children like Sarah have learned that they can only feel safe or special when they have become a sexual object to be abused by an adult, and so the specialness of the therapeutic relationship can be overwhelming and lead children to elicit abusive responses from the therapist. During my own work with children these moments have left me feeling anxious and uncomfortable and create a sense of caution around my own responses and potential unconscious communications. Ann Cattanach (1996) has talked about how the process of therapy can for some children mirror the dynamics of their own abuse experiences, and it is important to always be aware of the potential associations that a therapeutic intervention might have for any child. And so clear, explicit boundaries need to be in place to create a safe, nonabusive space for both child and therapist. Sometimes, also, it can be important to name for the child what is happening, to say that it feels like she may be frightened that you might hurt her or do "sexy stuff" with her as other grown-ups have done in the past, and to reaffirm therapy as a safe place and yourself as a nonabusive adult.

In her play therapy, Sarah enacted powerful dramatic scenes about a scary old man, "like a grandfather," snatching children from school playgrounds and abusing them. Sarah acted as director in these role plays and it was important that she had a sense of control over the scenes being portrayed. However, it is also important that she felt contained and so we used props and fictional names to provide a sense of emotional distance and I would frequently check out with Sarah what was happening in the scenarios, using the dramatic form to create structure around the process. Physical enactment can be a powerful process and so we would derole before ending, trying to spend some time thinking together about what it was like to play these characters, and "reality checking" by talking about what might be happening later on after the session. One has to make fine judgments about sessions like these, about what feels safe and what doesn't, and sometimes we get it wrong. As a therapist you need to take your cue from the children and they will let you know about what can be tolerated within their therapy.

Within her residential placement Sarah began disclosing abuse through traumatic flashbacks triggered by social activities that mirrored the grooming behavior of her grandfather, and the adults around her had to work hard to enable Sarah to feel emotionally contained and held. She needed support to manage her sexualized behavior, in conjunction with her play therapy, so that both she and the other young people she lived with could be kept safe. The staff group in the residential home were also offered consultation to help them reflect on their own emotional responses to Sarah's behavior.

It is important to acknowledge the significant emotional impact of working with this client group. The unconscious processes of projection, transference, and countertransference can be very powerful as children use play and the therapeutic relationship to rid themselves of overwhelming feelings of disgust, anger, and violation, feelings that might otherwise be acted out through the sexual abuse of other children. This sometimes feels like containing the uncontainable, and can leave the therapist holding the desperate emotions carried by the child. Eliana Gil has talked about the range of children's transference responses to the therapist, for example, the therapist as parent, sexual object, persecutor, or rescuer and the countertransference responses that can lead to the therapist feeling incompetent, aroused, angry, victimized, or overly punitive and controlling. Gil reinforces the fact that it is "imperative that therapists working with children in general, and abused and abusing children specifically, maintain a constant vigil on the children's transference issues, as well as their own countertransference responses" (Gil 1993). Nick Bankes has also written at length about the powerful unconscious processes that this work can evoke in the therapist and emphasizes how an awareness of these processes is "crucial in order to prevent them from being acted out in the therapy in unhelpful, anti-therapeutic or dysfunctional ways" (Bankes 2002). These therapeutic interactions leave one changed, as indeed they should, but at the same time it is necessary to maintain a sense of emotional health and professional objectivity. For these reasons, consultation, supervision, and personal therapy are integral to the therapist's ability to explore and understand the responses engendered through this work and to maintain a healthy therapeutic space for the child.

My aim throughout the course of this chapter has been to illustrate how play therapy can provide a different space for children with problematic sexual behavior. Play therapy is about a way of being with children, about the establishment of a relationship that accepts, absolutely unconditionally, the child as a whole person who is valued and held in high esteem by the therapist. This is a powerful intervention for children who experience themselves, and are often experienced by those around them, as bad and of little worth. Children presenting problematic sexual behavior are communicating a degree of developmental confusion and anxiety that will often elicit responses from those around them that are defined by feelings of fear, un-ease, rejection, and even disgust. For the therapist to accept a child and all the anger and distress that he is experiencing is the most important part of the therapeutic relationship and provides the grounding for everything that follows.

For me as a child-centered play therapist, the process of working with chil-dren like those I have spoken about in this chapter is essentially no different to the way that I would work with any child. Play therapy addresses the wholeness of a child's experiences, rather than a collection of presenting symptoms, and in this sense one cannot separate out the problematic sexu-alized behavior of young children without also addressing their own experi-ences of abuse, trauma, and chaotic social relationships. However, the con-text of this work is unique in relation to the degree of complexity and intensity it presents on an individual, family, and wider organizational level.

As stated above, the figures for sexual abuse carried out by children and young people are high, and early intervention is vital in preventing the es-tablishment of fixed patterns of offending behavior in later life. It is also sig-nificant that younger children with problematic sexual behavior have to an extent been something of an invisible client group, in the sense that there has been a historical reticence on the part of professionals to refer children who have difficulties around their sexual behavior. This reluctance has per-haps partly been about a lack of appropriate resources, but has also been about a fear of labeling and a reflection perhaps of the difficulty in accept-ing that children have the capacity to be sexually abusive. This situation is clearly changing for the better with the increasing awareness and under-standing of this issue, although there is still much to be done in the estab-lishment of professional resources and responses that can provide appropri-ate assessment and therapy for these children. And so play therapy can play a valuable role in providing early therapeutic intervention for these children, not as an alternative to other treatment approaches but as a complimentary process for children who have difficulty reflecting upon their experiences and behavior on a verbal, conscious level.

REFERENCES

Alvarez, A. 1992. *Live Company: Psychoanalytic Psychotherapy with Autistic, Bor-derline, Deprived, and Abused Children,* 151. London: Routledge.

Bankes, N. 2002. "I'm Sorry I Haven't a Clue: Unconscious Processes in Practitioners Who Work with Young People Who Sexually Abuse." In M. Calder, ed., *Young Peo-ple Who Sexually Abuse*, 68. Lyme Regis, UK: Russell House.

Bentovim, A. 1993. "Children and Young People as Abusers." In A. Hollows and H. Armstrong, eds., *Children and Young People as Abusers: An Agenda for Action*, 15. London: National Children's Bureau.

Bentovim, A., and W. Kinston. 1991. "Focal Family Therapy." In A. Gurman and D. Kniskern, eds., *Handbook of Family Therapy*. Basic.

Burrma, D. 1999. *The Family Play Genogram: A Guide Book*. Family Play Therapy Press.

Campbell, D. 1994. "Breaching the Shame Shield: Thoughts on the Assessment of Adolescent Child Sexual Abusers." *Journal of Child Psychotherapy* 20, no. 3: 16.

Cattanach, A. 1996. Play Therapy Lecture. University of Surrey, Roehampton.

Finkelhor, D. 1984. *Child Sexual Abuse: New Theory and Research*. Free Press.

Finkelhor, D., and A. Brown. 1986. "Sexual Abuse: Initial and Long-Term Effects: A Conceptual Framework." In D. Finkelhor, ed., *A Sourcebook on Child Sexual Abuse*, 180–98. Sage.

Freeman, J., D. Epston, and D. Lobovits. 1997. *Playful Approaches to Serious Problems: Narrative Therapy with Children and Their Families*, 147. Norton.

Gersie, A. 1992. Dramatherapy Lecture. St. Albans College of Art and Design, Hertfordshire University.

Gil, E., and T. Cavanagh Johnson. 1983. "Transference and Countertransference." In *Sexualised Children: Assessment and Treatment of Sexualised Children and Children Who Molest*, 325. Launch.

Hodges, J., M. Lanyado, and C. Andreou. 1994. "Sexuality and Violence: Preliminary Clinical Hypotheses from Psychotherapeutic Assessments in a Research Programme on Young Sexual Offenders." *Journal of Child Psychotherapy* 20, no. 3: 289.

Home Office. 1998. *Criminal Statistics for England and Wales* 1997, Cmd 4162. Home Office.

Horne, L., D. Glasgow, A. Cox, and R. Calam. 1991. "Sexual Abuse of Children by Children." *Journal of Child Law* 34: 147–51.

Lane, S. 1991. "The Sexual Abuse Cycle." In G. Ryan and S. Lane, *Juvenile Sexual Offending: Causes, Consequences, and Correction*. Lexington.

LeVay, D. 2002. "The Self Is a Telling: A Child's Tale of Alien Abduction." In A. Cattanach, ed., *The Story So Far: Play Therapy Narratives*. J. Kingsley.

Lowenfeld, M. 1979. *The World Technique*. London: George Allen & Unwin.

Morrison, T. 1997. "Emotionally Competent Child Protection Organisations: Fallacy, Fiction or Necessity?" In J. Bates, R. Pugh, and N. Thompson, eds., *Protecting Children: Challenges and Changes*, 65. Aldershot.

Nietzsche, F. 1886. "Maxims and Interludes." In G. Colli, M. Montinari, and B. Gruyter, eds., *Beyond Good and Evil*, sec. 146. 1980.

Northern Ireland Research Team. 1991. *Child Sexual Abuse in Northern Ireland*. Greystone.

Ryan, G. 1991. "Perpetration Prevention: Primary and Secondary." In G. Ryan and S. Lane, eds., *Juvenile Sexual Offending: Causes, Consequences, and Correction*. Lexington.

Weinrib, E. L. 1983. *Images of Self*. Sigo.

13

Creative Interventions to Engage Resistant Children in Therapy

Liana Lowenstein

Many children in counseling have difficulty verbalizing their presenting issues because they are reluctant to self-disclose and they are anxious about the therapeutic process. Activities that are creative and play based can engage otherwise resistant children and help them to express their thoughts and feelings. This chapter presents a number of play therapy interventions that can be used to break through the resistive barrier and help children embrace therapy.

DEFINITION AND CAUSES OF RESISTANCE

Resistance can be defined as "some attitude, belief, or behavior, often on the part of the client, that interferes with the progress of therapy" (Van Fleet 2000, 35). Resistance can result from a number of factors:

1. The child's characteristics and behaviors (i.e., a child who has experienced multiple losses may have difficulty trusting the therapist and engaging in treatment)
2. The family's characteristics and behaviors (i.e., secrecy or a closed communication style within the family may influence the child's readiness to be open and honest in therapy)
3. The therapist's characteristics and behaviors (i.e., a therapist's negative feelings toward a particular child may interfere with the treatment process)

4. The relationship between the therapist and the child (i.e., the therapeutic rapport between the therapist and child may not be firmly established)
5. Cultural influences (i.e., the therapist's lack of cultural awareness or
   sensitivity may block the client's willingness to embrace therapy, or the
   client may not feel comfortable with a therapist who is ethnically or
   racially different)

Since resistance is an interplay of a number of dynamics, therapists need
to explore and address all possible contributing factors, in order to facilitate
a successful therapeutic outcome. This chapter focuses primarily on children's resistance to therapy, and presents play therapy interventions to break
through the resistive barrier.

There are many reasons why children are resistant in therapy. Children
usually express their resistance through their behavior. Children who are
withdrawn, noncompliant, disruptive, or unmotivated are communicating an
underlying message, for instance, "I don't trust you," "I don't need to be
here," "I don't want to be here," "I'm nervous," "I need to feel in control,"
"I'm not ready to deal with this," or "this is boring." Therapists need to deci-
pher the message behind the child's behavior, so that the child's needs can
be better addressed.

Resistance can occur at the outset of therapy, and/or it can surface later in
treatment. For instance, the child may be initially guarded and unmotivated,
but over time may become more open and responsive. The child may shut
down again in later stages of treatment if he becomes threatened or disinterested. Not only do therapists need to engage children initially in therapy, but
they need to sustain children's interest and motivation throughout the various stages of therapy.

REFRAMING RESISTANCE

Therapists typically have a negative perception of client resistance, and view
it as something that needs to be conquered. However, resistance should be
seen as a normal, predictable aspect of the therapeutic process. As Van Fleet
(2000) highlights, "When therapists view resistance as something that needs
to be eradicated, they may unintentionally be setting up antagonistic relationships that are inconsistent with the changes they are trying to facilitate.
Instead, it can be helpful for therapists to alter their expectations: They
should instead think of resistance as a natural part of the change process"
(39). Reframing resistance in this manner is more likely to facilitate a positive
therapeutic process.

GUIDELINES

The interventions outlined in this chapter are aimed at providing play thera-pists with techniques to engage children in counseling and help them ex-press their internal conflicts. In using these interventions however, the fol-lowing guidelines should be considered:

Be Well Grounded in Theory and Practice

Mental health professionals using the activities in this chapter should have clinical training and a sound knowledge base in the following areas: child development, psychopathology, child management, and play therapy. Be-ginning therapists should use the activities under the guidance of a skilled clinical supervisor.

Have a Strong Theoretical Foundation

Practitioners should be well grounded in their theoretical orientation be-fore using any activities in this chapter. The activities outlined below can be integrated into any theoretical orientation that uses a directive play therapy approach. This author adheres to a prescriptive play therapy approach that "challenges the clinician to weave together a variety of play interventions into one comprehensive, tailor-made treatment program for a particular client" (Schaefer 2001). Prescriptive play therapists need to be well trained in a number of theoretical approaches, so they can match appropriate theories and techniques to children's particular treatment needs.

Build and Maintain a Positive Therapeutic Rapport

All children need relationships that provide them with a feeling of security, acceptance, and self-worth. For children who enter therapy, this is even more significant because these children typically have a damaged sense of self and many have few social supports. In order to form a therapeutic relationship, the therapist must be nonjudgmental and convey a sense of empathy and re-spect for the child. The interventions in this chapter will not be effective un-less a positive therapeutic rapport is established. The rapport that develops between therapist and child forms the foundation for therapeutic success.

Involve the Child's Caregivers

Whenever possible, the child's primary caregiver should be involved in the treatment. The caregiver may be a parent, stepparent, foster parent, grandparent, childcare worker, or some other adult responsible for the care of the child. Parental resistance or lack of follow-through with treatment is less likely if the caregiver is part of the process.

The caregiver can play a critical role in helping the child work through treatment issues. Moreover, caregiver involvement can help reduce the child's feelings that he is the "damaged" one. The extent to which the caregiver becomes involved in the child's treatment should be based on the abilities of the caregiver, the caregiver's motivation, and the child's needs.

Select Activities That Fit the Child's Needs

There are a variety of interventions to choose from in this chapter. The child's age, interests, and abilities should be considered to ensure that the selected activity is appropriate. It is also important to be aware of cultural issues. The therapist should become competent in multicultural counseling and utilize interventions that are culturally sensitive.

Be Well Prepared in Advance of Sessions

Before using any interventions in this chapter, the therapist should prepare for activity implementation by reviewing the intervention, gathering materials, and if necessary, constructing the activity. If the therapist lacks confidence, then practicing and rehearsing the activity with a colleague before the session may be helpful. As children are often unpredictable, the therapist should plan for various ways the child may respond to the activity. However, no matter how well prepared the therapist is for the session, the unforeseen can happen and flexibility is therefore essential.

Never Force a Child to Participate in an Activity

Coercing a child to participate in a therapeutic activity will increase his level of tension and resistance. It is important to proceed at the child's pace and to engage him in treatment by creating and adapting activities that fit with his interests, abilities, and emotional readiness. If a child is exhibiting strong resistance to a particular activity, respond by exploring his feelings. If, after a thorough exploration of the child's emotional state, the child continues to show resistance, then this may be a cue that the activity is inappropriate for the child. The activity should then be adapted or changed. If the child remains resistant beyond one particular activity, this may signal difficulties in other areas. If this is the case, the therapist should explore and address other underlying causes of the resistance, such as a lack of therapeutic alliance with the child or possible countertransference issues.

Be Process Focused

The play-based activities in this chapter make it is easy for both therapists and children to enjoy the sessions and forget about the process and therapeutic objectives. Therefore, therapists must remember that these activities are tools for intervening therapeutically with troubled children. So, by all means create a playful atmosphere, but implement the activities carefully, thoroughly, and sensitively, always keeping in mind the child's treatment objectives.

The therapist should consider how to introduce, process, and bring closure to each activity. When introducing an activity, the therapist should be enthusiastic in order to engage the client. The purpose of the activity should be outlined and the instructions clearly explained. As the child moves to a more engaged and ready state, deeper issues can be skillfully explored and processed. When the activity has been completed and sufficiently processed, the therapist brings closure to the activity.

Listen to the Child

Children often feel ignored and unheard. An important role of the therapist is to listen and make the child feel that what he has to say is important. During the activity, focus on the child's verbal and nonverbal cues. Ensure that the focus of the session remains on the child, not the therapist. The therapist should refrain from talking too much, even during silences. The use of reflective listening will not only be helpful to the therapeutic process, but it will also model important listening skills for the child.

Set Firm But Fair Limits

Lack of boundaries and controls during a treatment activity can overwhelm the child and lead to feelings of heightened anxiety. As such, there is a need to provide the child with limits and structure. The nature and intensity of the limits will depend on the child's existing capacity for self-control, as well as his responsiveness and ability to handle such limits.

Be Aware of Transference and Countertransference

Transference occurs when a child displaces patterns of feelings and behavior originally experienced with other significant figures onto the therapist. When transference is maladaptive, inappropriate, or prevents a child from healthy growth and development, the therapist must focus on helping a child to establish new interactional patterns.

Countertransference is the unconscious influence a therapist's past needs and conflicts have on his or her understanding, actions, or reactions within the treatment situation. Therapists need to have insight into their own personality dynamics so that their unconscious issues do not become a hindrance to the therapeutic process.

Transference/countertransference issues are often difficult for the therapist to deal with. The therapist may find it useful to obtain guidance from a skilled supervisor, consultant, or coworker.

Be Creative

The creative use of structured games and expressive arts techniques can be a source of enjoyment for children. The interventions in this chapter are designed to appeal to children so they will embrace therapy and have a positive counseling experience. Therapists are encouraged to be creative and modify the activities to meet the distinct needs of their clients.

INTERVENTIONS

The "I Don't Know, I Don't Care, I Don't Want to Talk about It" Game

Explain the game as follows: "We're going to play a game that's going to help us get to know each other. It's called the I Don't Know, I Don't Care, I Don't Want to Talk about It game. I'm going to begin by asking you a question that will help me get to know you better. If you answer it, you get a potato chip, but if you say I don't know or I don't care or if you don't answer the question, I get your potato chip. Then you get to ask me a question. If I answer the question, I get a potato chip. But if I say I don't know or I don't care or if I don't answer the question, you get my potato chip. The game continues until we've asked each other ten questions."

The therapist should order and pace the questions appropriately. Begin with neutral questions such as, "What do you like to do when you are not in school?" and "What is your favorite color?" Feelings questions can come next, such as, "What is something that makes you feel happy?" and "How do you feel about being here today?" As the child begins to feel more at ease, questions that involve greater risk taking can be asked, such as, "What's something you wish you could change about your family?" and "Why do you think you're here today? (Since this is an engagement activity, the therapist should be in tune with the client's readiness to answer questions that may feel threatening.) End the game on a positive note with a question such as, "What's your happiest memory?"

The therapist should handle the child's questions with discretion. Some self-disclosure is required, but only information that is appropriate and helpful to the child should be shared. If the child chooses not to answer a question, the therapist can respond, "You must know yourself really well; you know what you feel comfortable talking about and what you want to keep private for now." This is an empowering message for the child.

Top Ten Worries about Therapy

Prepare the activity by copying the top ten worries kids have about therapy (below) and placing it in a sealed envelope:

1. I'll have to talk about stuff that I don't want to talk about
2. I'll have to come here even if I don't want to
3. Other people will find out I'm coming here
4. Coming here means I'm crazy
5. You'll tell my parents about what I say to you
6. Coming here will be boring
7. You'll think I'm weird if I tell you about what happened to me
8. I'll miss out on other things I'd rather be doing when I come here
9. You'll hurt me
10. You won't like me

Explain the activity by stating: "I have worked with lots of kids over the years and have come to realize that most kids feel nervous about therapy. So I decided to ask some clients what their biggest worry was when they first met me. The list of top ten worries kids have about therapy is in this envelope. Let's see if you can guess any of the worries on the list. You get a prize if you guess any of the worries."

The child's guesses are written down. The therapist opens the envelope and reads aloud the worries on the list. The child's list is compared to the top ten list, and the child is awarded a prize for any similarities. The therapist normalizes the child's feelings by making statements such as, "I see other kids feel the same as you." This activity helps children understand that their fears and concerns about therapy are normal. This sense of validation helps children feel more at ease talking about their initial concerns and it helps to establish a therapeutic rapport.

About Me Puzzle

Prepare the activity by photocopying the puzzle from the book *More Creative Interventions for Troubled Children and Youth* (Lowenstein

2002). Glue the puzzle onto a piece of cardboard or heavy colored paper. Glue a magazine picture appropriate to the child's interests onto the other side. For example, a picture from a sports magazine might appeal to a child who enjoys sports, while another child might enjoy a picture of animals. Cut the puzzle along the dotted lines and place the eight pieces in an envelope.

The child completes the puzzle by writing a response to the first question and progressing to question number eight. (If this activity is used with younger children, the therapist can transcribe the child's answers.) Once a response has been written for all eight questions, the child can assemble the puzzle and tape it together. The child can then turn the puzzle over to uncover the picture.

This activity offers a simple yet engaging way to get to know the child. It is a good starting point in therapy and sets the tone for creative strategies to elicit information from clients. Therapists can be innovative in their selections for the puzzle, individualizing them to meet each child's unique needs. Use pictures from magazines such as *Sports Illustrated, Teen People, National Geographic,* or perhaps the comics from the newspaper or a page from a joke book.

Picture This

The client is provided with a disposable camera to take home and asked to take pictures of people, places, and things that are important to him. The pictures are then developed and discussed in subsequent sessions. If desired, the client can make a collage with the pictures. Phototherapy can be a particularly effective strategy to engage resistant teens in meaningful dialogue. The drawback of the activity is obviously the expense of the camera and film development.

All Tied Up in Knots

Introduce the activity by pointing out that everyone has problems and worries. Outline the different ways the body reacts to stress; for example, when a person is scared, his heart might pound faster, or when a person is sad and about to cry, he might feel like he has a lump in his throat. Ask the client if he has ever heard of the expression "All tied up in knots." If the client is unfamiliar with the expression, offer an explanation, such as, "When you are worried or nervous about something, your stomach might feel funny or tight, as if you are all tied up in knots. You don't *really* have knots in your stomach, it just feels like you do."

Provide the client with a piece of string and have the client identify personal concerns or worries, and tie a knot for each problem identified. Big ger knots can be tied for bigger worries. The client may need verbal prompting to identify problems. If so, the therapist can ask, "What's a problem or worry you have about school? What's a problem or worry you have about your family? What's a problem or worry you have about other kids? What's a problem or worry you have about the world?" As the client identifies each worry, facilitate further discussion by asking open-ended questions, such as, "Tell me more about this worry." Discuss how it feels to be "all tied up in knots."

Next, explain, "Each time you come here, we'll talk about a problem on your string of knots. When all your feelings about the problem have been explored, and you don't feel so worried, then we will untie a knot. Life will never be perfect because everyone has worries, but you will feel better as we deal with your worries and untie your knots." (To add appeal to the activity, shoestring licorice can be used instead of string, and the client can eat a knot each time a problem is addressed.)

Color the Circle (Adapted from Lowenstein 2002)

Cut out ten three-inch paper circles and use a black marker to write one of the statements below inside each circle:

It is hard for me to talk about my problems.
I pretend that everything is okay even when I feel upset.
I feel loved and cared for.
I get along well with my family.
I get along well with other kids.
I am worried I will not do well in school.
I often feel afraid.
I feel I am a good person.
There are things that I do well.
I am glad I am getting help now.

Provide the client with a pencil and explain the activity as follows: "Read the statements in each circle and fill in each circle to show how you feel. If you totally agree with the statement, color in the whole circle. If you agree a bit, color in part of the circle. If you do not agree at all, leave the circle blank."

The client's responses can be explored and used as a foundation to assess treatment needs. This is a particularly useful activity with clients who have difficulty articulating their feelings because the client can communicate salient information without having to verbalize. The activity can be modified depending on the client's age and the assessment information to be gathered.

Coloring Book

Have the child draw pictures to illustrate the items below. Explain that the items must be drawn, not written.

An activity I enjoy doing
An activity I hate doing
Outline of a hand
Drawing of the therapist
Drawing of myself
Drawing of me and my family doing something together
Facial expression to show how I feel about my family
Something that makes me happy
Something that makes me scared
A problem I need help with
A worry
A wish

The pictures are processed by exploring likes/dislikes, feelings, and so on. The pictures are compiled into a booklet and the child can title and decorate the cover.

This activity facilitates communication from nonverbal or resistant children. It enables clients to reveal information about themselves and identify treatment goals. Information gathered through the activity will provide the therapist with direction for future treatment.

Balloon Bash

The therapist and child are each provided with three three-by-three-inch-square pieces of paper, three balloons, and a pencil. The activity is explained by stating: "We will both write three questions, each on a separate piece of paper. They should be questions to get to know each other better, such as, What is something you enjoy doing? Each piece of paper with the question written on it is then folded into a small clump and inserted into a balloon. The balloons are blown up and tied. We will then throw the balloons into the air and bounce them in the air as long as we can. Once the balloons drop to the floor, we will take turns picking up the balloons, bursting them, and answering the question on the paper that was inside each balloon."

This activity provides a fun and active way to engage the child. The activity can be used in subsequent sessions with different questions.

Guess Which Cup (Adapted from Lowenstein 2002)

Prepare the activity as follows: Choose three questions from the list below and copy them onto separate slips of paper: (The questions can be modified to suit the age and treatment needs of the client.)

What three words best describe you?
What animal would you choose to be and why?
What's something you would like to change about your life?
What's the best thing that ever happened to you?
Tell about a problem you had this week.
What are three things you like about yourself?
Describe a memory you have from when you were very young.
What's something you worry about a lot?
What helps you to feel better when you are upset?

Fold each strip of paper several times to form small paper squares. On a separate slip of paper, write "extra prize." Place four paper cups on a table (open end down) and place one paper clump under each cup.

Introduce the activity by stating: "We're going to play a question game. Under each cup is a folded piece of paper. We're going to take turns moving the cups around (without lifting them up) and when the cups stop moving, one player chooses a cup, turns it over, unfolds the paper clump, reads aloud the question, and answers the question. If the player answers the question, he gets a chip. One of the cups is special and the player who picks it gets an extra prize. The game continues until all the questions have been answered. The chips are traded in at the end of the game for a prize."

Open discussion of thoughts and feelings is encouraged through this game. Focusing skills are also encouraged. This activity can be used again in later sessions with different questions, and the child can be encouraged to make up questions for the game.

(Note: The therapist may wish to place a discreet mark on the extra chips cup so the therapist knows not to pick that cup and the child then gets the extra chips.)

Feelings Mish-Mosh (Adapted from Crisci, Lay, and Lowenstein 1997)

Introduce the activity by stating, "Everyone has feelings—comfortable feelings like happy and excited, and uncomfortable feelings like sad and scared. It is normal and okay to have all kinds of feelings. Sometimes we feel confused or mixed up because we have so many different feelings. Today, we are going to make a mish-mosh of mixed-up feelings."

Fill a freezer bag with about a half cup of water, then add several drops of yellow food coloring to the bag of water. As the yellow food coloring is dropped into the bag, say: "Let's pretend this yellow food coloring is for the happy feelings we have inside. What are some reasons children may feel happy?" Give the child an opportunity to respond. Proceed in the same manner with the other food coloring (e.g., blue for sad, red for mad, green for scared). After several drops of each color food coloring have been added to the bag, zip the bag so it is tightly sealed. Be careful at this point not to shake the bag, so the mixture maintains its "rainbow" appearance. Next, explain: "These colors show different feelings we have. If we shake the bag, the feelings get all mixed up and look kind of yucky. (The therapist shakes the bag.) When we have lots of different feelings, it can be very confusing and we might feel like we have a mish-mosh of mixed-up feelings. That's why it is important to talk about the mixed-up feelings so we can let the feelings out and start to feel better."

The therapist and child take turns talking about times when they felt happy, sad, mad, and scared. As the feelings are shared, the therapist opens the bag and slowly pours the liquid out into a sink or a cup, thus metaphor-ically letting out the feelings. At the end, exclaim, "We let out our feelings and now we don't feel filled with a mish-mosh of mixed-up feelings!"

The mish-mosh bag is fun to make and excites and fascinates young chil-dren. It can be used to help children express a range of emotions.

Feelings Tic-Tac-Toe (Adapted from Lowenstein 1999)

The therapist and child are each provided with ten three-by-three-inch squares of paper and markers.

The activity is explained by stating: "We are going to make our own spe-cial version of the tic-tac-toe game. We are going to each think of ten feel-ings, then draw a feeling face or small picture to illustrate each feeling. Each feeling face or picture is drawn on a separate paper square."

Once the twenty feeling faces have been drawn, the child selects nine to use for the game. The nine squares are laid out in three rows of three to form the tic-tac-toe game board. Candy is used instead of Xs and Os (two differ-ent kinds of small wrapped candy can be used). The child selects from the two kinds of candy that he will use and will be used by the therapist. The child and therapist alternately place their candy pieces on one of the feelings faces in an attempt to get either an uninterrupted horizontal, vertical, or di-agonal line of three. As the candy is placed on a feeling square, the player must describe a time when he experienced that particular feeling. Players can eat one candy each time they win a round. The game is played until each player has won a round.

Most children are familiar with tic-tac-toe and will enjoy this version of the game. As the child talks about feelings, the therapist can reflect, validate, normalize, or ask the child to elaborate. When it is the therapist's turn to share, the therapist can tailor his own responses in a way that would be therapeutically beneficial to the child (i.e., I feel scared when I meet someone for the first time). Children enjoy playing games and "even the most resistant youth will usually participate in game therapy" (Schaefer and Reid 1986).

Basketball (Lowenstein 1999)

Prepare the game by cutting out ten three-by-three-inch pieces of yellow cardboard and ten three-by-three-inch pieces of blue cardboard (yellow and blue index cards can be used). Draw a happy face on one side of each of the ten yellow cardboard squares, and write a question on each reverse side. Each question should be about a happy feeling or experience (i.e., tell about the happiest moment of your life; describe a good dream you had; tell about a time you were able to solve a problem you had). Draw a sad face on one side of each of the ten blue cardboard squares, and write a question on each reverse side. Each question should be about a sad or upsetting feeling or experience (i.e., tell about a sad moment in your life; describe a scary dream you had; tell about a problem you experienced this week).

To play this special version of basketball, the therapist and child take turns shooting a basket. If a player successfully throws the ball through the basketball hoop, he picks a card from the yellow "happy face" question card pile. These questions relate to happy experiences in a person's life. If a player misses the basket, he picks a card from the blue "sad face" question card pile. These questions relate to unhappy experiences in a person's life. The game continues until all the questions have been answered, or until each player has had a prechosen number of turns. If all of the question cards have been answered before the game is over, the pile of cards can be shuffled and reused.

To motivate the child, tokens can be awarded as players answer questions, and traded in at the end of the game for a prize.

Modifying the traditional game of basketball can help otherwise resistant clients openly identify and express their feelings. The therapist can use this game to assess the child's feelings, attitudes, and style of interaction, and to intervene therapeutically when the child is being emotionally guarded, oppositional, or socially inappropriate. The "happy" and "sad" question cards can be used to enable the child to become aware of and express both positive and negative feelings and experiences.

The Envelope Game (Adapted from Lowenstein 2002)

Prepare the activity as follows: Tape six envelopes to the wall. Write "prize" on one piece of paper, fold it, and place it in one of the six envelopes on the wall. Write five questions, each on a separate piece of paper. The questions can be geared to specific issues. For example, if the session is focused on expressing feelings, then the following are sample questions: Show with your face and body what someone looks like when they are excited; How would you feel if someone said something mean to you? Tell about a time when you felt upset. If the session is focused on self-esteem building, then the following are sample questions: What is something you do better than others? What is something you have accomplished? Tell about a time you were helpful. Fold the question sheets and place each in one of the remaining five envelopes. Fill a bag with small prizes, such as stickers, inexpensive toys, or candy.

To play the Envelope Game, the therapist and child take turns pulling a card from one of the six envelopes. When a player selects a question card, that player reads the question aloud and answers it. If a player gets a prize card, that player gets a prize. The game continues until all the envelopes are empty. Players who actively participated in the game can select an item from the prize bag at the end of the game.

This activity facilitates verbalization, using the game format as an engaging tool. The therapist's participation in the game helps to engage the child. As Schaefer and Reid (1986) indicate, "By self-disclosing in response to game cards, the therapist becomes more human to the child. The child is able to know the therapist better and the therapist, through empathic responding, communicates understanding to the child. By serving as a model for self-disclosure, the therapist can also encourage the child to become more expressive."

Paper Dolls (Adapted from Crisci, Lay, and Lowenstein 1997)

The child makes a string of eight paper dolls (for instructions, refer to Crisci, Lay, and Lowenstein 1997, 29).

The child uses the paper dolls to complete the activity as follows: "Label each doll by writing the names of the people who are important to you. Include yourself, your family, and other people who are important to you either because you like them a lot or because you are upset with them. For example, you may want to include certain relatives, your teacher, someone who hurt you, a best friend, baby-sitter, foster parent, therapist, or pet. Next, you are going to use stickers to show how you feel about these people. Put a happy face sticker on the people who feel happy, and explain why they feel happy. Put a bee sticker on the people who feel mad and explain who they are mad at and why they feel mad. Put a spider sticker on the people who feel afraid and explain why they feel afraid. Put a pretty heart sticker on the people who help you and explain what they do to help you." As a closing activity, the child can make a sticker book to take home.

The paper dolls and stickers are used to engage children and to help them express thoughts and feelings regarding family and community relationships. This expressive arts technique is particularly effective with children who have difficulty articulating their feelings, as they can convey salient information without having to talk.

Pin the Tail on the Donkey (Adapted from Lowenstein 1999)

A Pin the Tail on the Donkey game will be needed for this activity, as well as a blindfold and inexpensive prizes. The game can be purchased at party supply stores or some toy stores. Remove any reference to "Happy Birthday" on the Pin the Tail on the Donkey game (i.e., cover it with a sign that reads Pin the Tail on the Donkey). Write questions on various parts of the donkey. For example, if the activity is being used in an initial group session to help members get to know one another, then the following are some suggested questions: What is your favorite toy? What is something you do well? If you had three wishes, what would they be? (The questions can be modified to suit the age of the children and the purpose of the group session.) Tape the game to a smooth wall or door at a height that all the children in the group can reach.

Begin by asking the children if they have ever played Pin the Tail on the Donkey. For those who are unfamiliar with the game, quickly go over the rules and for those who do know it, tell them that the group is going to play a different version, described as follows: "One person is chosen to go first. This player is given a cardboard tail with a piece of tape attached to it (the game should come with these tails). The leader blindfolds the player, spins the player around twice, and faces the player toward the donkey game. The player walks up to the game and sticks the tail onto the picture. The tail must be taped to the first place it touches. The player must answer the question that corresponds with where the tail landed on the donkey. If the player misses the donkey, then all the group members must hop on one foot five times. If the player gets the tail on the donkey, then instead of answering a question, that player gets to hand out prizes from the prize bag to all the players. The game continues until all the group members have had a turn."

Since children typically find Pin the Tail on the Donkey enjoyable, they should easily engage in this version. The prizes add excitement to the game. Hopping on one foot channels the children's energy into a positive outlet and maintains the interest of all group members even when it is not their turn. During the activity, there is ample opportunity to gather information, observe group dynamics, and enhance peer interaction skills.

CONCLUSION

There are a number of factors that create resistance within the therapeutic process. This chapter has focused on client resistance, and ways to engage children in therapy. Children will more readily embrace therapy if it is engaging, innovative, and immersed in play. Therapists can select from the activities presented in this chapter, modify the activities, or create their own. Regardless of the technique used, the therapist must keep in mind that the activity is not the therapy, it is merely the tool to facilitate the therapeutic process.

The emphasis is therefore not on the activity itself, but on how the activity is used to engage the child and help the child work through treatment issues.

The activities in this chapter are designed to appeal to children so that a positive counseling experience results. Therapists *can* break through the resistive barrier, engage children in treatment, and have successful therapeutic outcomes.

REFERENCES

Crisci, G., M. Lay, and L. Lowenstein. 1997. *Paper Dolls and Paper Airplanes: Therapeutic Exercises for Sexually Traumatized Children*. Indianapolis: Kidsrights.

Lowenstein, L. 1999. *Creative Interventions for Troubled Children and Youth*. Toronto: Champion.

———. 2002. *More Creative Interventions for Troubled Children and Youth*. Toronto: Champion.

Schaefer, C. E. 2001. "Prescriptive Play Therapy." *International Journal of Play Therapy* 10, no. 2: 57–73.

Schaefer, C. E., and S. E. Reid. 1986. *Game Play: Therapeutic Use of Childhood Games*. New York: Wiley.

Van Fleet, R. 2000. "Understanding and Overcoming Parent Resistance to Play Therapy." *International Journal of Play Therapy* 9, no. 1: 35–46.

14

Play Therapy for Disruptive Behavior Disorders

David J. Hudak

The disruptive behavior disorders in children (attention deficit hyperactivity disorder, ADHD; oppositional defiant disorder, ODD; and conduct disorder, CD) tend to dominate referrals to child mental health practices. Because of the insidiousness of core behaviors such as impulsiveness and intrusiveness in rule-governed situations, reactive anger and argumentativeness, or the violation of the basic rights of others, the disruptive behavior disorders can have deleterious impact in the family, in the classroom, on the playground, or to a child's self-concept. Children diagnosed with one or more disruptive behavior disorders (DBD) are often not very popular among peers and have social/relational skill deficits that make life difficult wherever or whenever they are unable to control their symptoms.

The purpose of this chapter is, first, to explore the characteristics of the play of children diagnosed with disruptive behavior disorders, including a discussion of some key developmental aspects. Second, a clinical description of each disruptive behavior disorder will be provided along with new research. Third, play therapy techniques will be illustrated that can address core symptoms of the disruptive behavior disorders using case examples.

The play of children with disruptive behavior disorders is often fraught with chaos, conflict, disorganization, and difficulty with game rules, unfair play, and lack of reciprocity. Children diagnosed with a disruptive behavior disorder can vary from being bossy and controlling, to argumentative, to being disconnected and difficult to engage in play. For example, children with ADHD tend to become easily distracted and often have poor organizational skills, can bounce from one play activity to the next leaving toys disordered or getting too bored to complete a game. Siblings and peers of children with ADHD get angry when the child with ADHD cannot wait his or her turn, needs to be the boss, or just cannot seem to play fairly. Similarly, children diagnosed with ODD are often negative in their attitude, refuse often, and blow up in anger easily if things do not go their way. Children with ODD can be loud and argumentative during play with others, sometimes becoming verbally aggressive. Children diagnosed with conduct disorder, nonaggressive type, can have trouble with affective underarousal and show little care or concern for others. Engaging these children in play can be difficult, and they commonly cheat in games. They typically experience little sense of joy or playfulness in the play process. On the other hand, children diagnosed with conduct disorder, aggressive type, can be forceful, coercive, and physically aggressive in their play.

Understandably, due to the core symptoms of the disruptive behavior disorders, children who carry these diagnoses often exhibit disturbed play that can be evidence of both their core symptoms and the pathological development of coping with these symptoms. For example, if a child with ADHD is inattentive (core symptom) during a game of checkers, his playmate may easily capitalize on this inattention by making a three-step jump. Instead of accepting this lapse in attention and failed strategy by responding to his playmate with the acknowledgment, "Oh, nice move, I really wasn't paying attention to that one," the more troubled child with ADHD might react angrily shouting, "Hey, no fair, you can't do that!" (poor coping with core symptom). Another example might be a child with ODD heatedly argues (core symptom) about a game rule and his playmate tries to compromise by suggesting taking turns playing by two different rules. Instead of accepting this compromise, the child with ODD still defensively refuses his playmate's attempt to compromise (poor coping with core symptom). Or a child with a conduct disorder pushes a playmate down (core symptom) on the playground that is winning in a kickball game and injures him. When he is made to apologize as part of his consequence for this act, the conduct-disordered child defensively isolates his affect and does not exhibit any possible feeling of remorse (poor coping with core symptom). Arlow (1987) noted, "When play takes on a compelling, obsessive quality, it is no longer play. It becomes a symptom."[1] It can be helpful to explore the fundamentals of play, including what some of the early theorists noted as *developmental stages of play*, to more fully understand how children with disruptive behavior disorders fit in.

Lewis (1993) notes from Neubauer (1987) that research on the definition of play describes three primary characteristics of play:

> First, play involves a mental act that includes conscious and unconscious fantasies and wishes. Second, it involves a physical act through which mental acts are carried into an observable behavior. Third, it includes an awareness that what is being enacted is not real; thus, an act that is accomplished on a level of symbolic meaning, a characteristic that differentiates play from work.[2]

This third characteristic presumes that play must include pretending. Piaget (1951) believed that children could cognitively develop the ability to pretend at about two years of age, though in clinical practice, it is apparent that children vary in their willingness or ability to pretend.[3] My experience with children with disruptive behavior disorders is that they tend, as a group, to be less willing or able to pretend in play. Perhaps this is due to the overwhelming nature of their core symptoms, which can cause their play to be more frenetic, fragmented, coercive, or reactionary often lacking a story line. These children frequently prefer action-oriented games, which involve the structure of rules, thus limiting creativity, fantasy, and pretend.

After reviewing work by many theorists (Piaget, Anna Freud, Waelder, Peller, Winnicott), Lewis (1993) distills the following stages of play:

> The development of play may be projected along an integrated line that begins with impulse (in infancy); moves through a phase of practice or mastery play; draws upon the maturation of cognitive abilities to permit symbolic play; then builds upon these cognitive capacities, as well as on the development of new and more sublimated ego abilities (including self and object constancy) to allow the emergence of fantasy-based playacting; to the point where sublimation permits the child to engage in daydreams, hobbies, and games. Finally, the developmental line extends into work, in which the reality principle prevails.[4]

Many professionals assume that the disruptive behavior disorders are largely constitutionally based (a part of an infant's neurological makeup, temperamental traits, or genetic predisposition); therefore, symptoms of these disorders can appear in infancy and affect normal play development. Children who show early signs of a DBD are less likely to glide easily through the stages as previously described by Lewis. It can be difficult for an infant with ADHD, who may be inordinately restless, to settle enough for himself or mother to fully learn the pleasure of playing with mom's body parts—the first evidence of play. If a child is particularly impulsive and inattentive, practicing and imitative play prior to age 2 can be fragmented and disorganized, which may postpone the development of symbolic play. A three-year-old exhibiting early signs of ODD because of many refusals, negativity, and blowing up in anger easily may have a difficult journey developing mastery of certain aspects of play, and may be immature in the development of cognitive capacities to permit fantasy-based play or playacting. Similarly, an aggressive eight-year-old boy with CD, because of the lack of empathy for others, may have an impaired sense of what the rules should be for a certain game, and will have no trouble breaking or changing theses rules to suit his needs; thus making the mature development of game play, hobbies, and sports far reaching. Lewis (1993) notes, "Play also reveals elements of the child's object-relatedness. The degree and style of involvement of the clinician and whether the child's play may be described as solitary, parallel, or interactional are all useful indices of the child's capacity for human relatedness."[5] Children with a DBD often have an impaired ability to relate to others appropriately due to poor social skills and behaviors that others find offensive. This impairment may be due to a combination of how core symptoms compel children with a DBD to respond to themselves and others, and how others respond reciprocally to disruptive behavior. For example, all children at age 2 have a level of impulsivity and short attention span relative to their age; however, a budding hyperactive two-year-old who is playing by herself may have an inordinate number of these traits and, unable to control herself, may get extremely frustrated trying to put a piece of clothing on her doll, scream, and throw the doll instead of asking a parent for help. Parents may react by yelling back or using coercive actions toward the child, and thus begins the setup of disturbed and negative object relations between child and parent. Repeated scenarios such as these can begin to form a self-concept of "I'm bad" in the child. Negative affect can become associated with play. The same child may project a "harsh parent" object relationship onto a day care provider who reminds the child of her parent, and repeat similar negative and habitual interactions with the day care provider. The day care provider may then begin to label the child as a "behavior problem," which the child directly or indirectly picks up on, thus reinforcing the notion of "bad self" in the child. Disturbed object relations due to a DBD and the responses of others to a DBD are particularly indicated in children with CD. If a ten-year-old with CD steals his friend's basketball after a game with friends and persistently lies about it, this can have an irreversible negative impact on the friendship and has the potential of getting the boy labeled "thief" in the community. This kind of negative self-object and disturbed object relations with family and peer relationships can be common with a DBD.

The last developmental aspect of play I'd like to discuss, before moving to a description of each of the disruptive behavior disorders, is the notion of play versus playfulness. The *American Heritage Dictionary* defines play as "to occupy oneself in amusement, sport, or other recreation, or, to pretend to be, mimic the activities of."[6] Playfulness is defined as "full of fun and good spirits; frolicsome; sportive; humorous; jesting."[7] E. A. Plaut (1979) states, "In psychoanalytic theory, play has been assumed to have a subordinate role, with the exception of early childhood play. In the past seventy years much evidence has accumulated that play is of central importance throughout life."[8] Solnit (1998) further suggests that "play evolves into playfulness, which, over developmental time, is involved in moving from parallel to interactional play and from imitative behaviors to empathic identifications."[9]

Children with ADHD have a tendency to be labeled "class clown." While they are inherently playful and good-natured and they have outgoing personalities, many times it is too much at the wrong time. Repeatedly cracking up classmates over time can wear down and anger teachers and annoy classmates. Verbal jesting can be of poor taste and hurtful. Children with ODD, depending on the etiology of their ODD, can be less playful and can carry an irritability or poutiness that comes across as repulsive rather than playful. Children with CD may have steeliness to their affect, showing very little emotional response in play situations. These children often show very little empathy for others, and thus "playfulness" can have the quality of jesting that is aimed at control, manipulation, or trickery that is hurtful.

The developmental considerations above purposely amplify some of the problematic aspects that can occur with children with DBD. This is not to say that all children with DBD run into these stumbling blocks. Therefore, prior to entering a discussion of play therapy techniques for children with DBD, it is important to have an understanding of the nature of how these children tend to relate in play.

The following overview of the disruptive behavior disorders is essential to give clarity to symptoms and current research that informs therapeutic intervention.

OVERVIEW OF ADHD

The American Psychiatric Association's *DSM-IV* describes attention deficit hyperactivity disorder as inappropriate levels, for a child's age, of (1) inattention and (2) hyperactive-impulsive behavior. The criteria of six or more symptoms persisting for a period of at least six months must be met for either inattention or hyperactivity-impulsivity.

Inattention

1. Often fails to give close attention to details
2. Often has difficulty sustaining attention in tasks or play activities
3. Often does not seem to listen when spoken to directly
4. Often does not follow through on instructions and fails to complete tasks
5. Often has difficulty organizing tasks and activities
6. Often avoids, dislikes, or is reluctant to engage in tasks requiring sustained effort
7. Often loses things necessary for tasks or activities
8. Is easily distracted by extraneous stimuli
9. Is often forgetful in daily activities

Hyperactivity

1. Often fidgets with hands or feet or squirms in seat
2. Often leaves seat in classroom or in other situations where sitting is expected
3. Often runs about or climbs excessively in situations in which it is inappropriate
4. Often has difficulty playing quietly
5. Is often "on the go" as if "driven by a motor"
6. Often talks excessively

Impulsivity

1. Often blurts out answers before questions have been completed
2. Often has difficulty awaiting turn
3. Often interrupts or intrudes on others

Other criteria include some symptoms are apparent before age 7; some symptoms are present in two or more settings; symptoms must clearly impact social, academic, or occupational functioning; and symptoms are not better accounted for by another mental disorder.[10]

Judging from my clinical experience, not all children with ADHD are alike, and core symptoms are on a continuum of severity. These children can vary in their presentation from being full of energy and playfulness, bouncing off the walls, loud and impulsive, to sluggish and "spacey," characteristic of "an absent-minded professor." The focus of this chapter is on ADHD with hyperactivity-impulsivity or combined type with inattention, and *not* the primarily inattentive type because the primarily inattentive type does not generally produce disruptive behaviors.

In recent years there has been significant research regarding ADHD. This research includes neuroscience findings, search for an ADHD gene, and the reconceptualization of what is the essence of ADHD. Russell Barkley (1997) suggests that at the core of ADHD is a problem with "response inhibition" or "behavioral inhibition," which is a cognitive and behavioral process. Barkley (1997) explains that "behavioral inhibition refers to three interrelated processes: 1) inhibiting the initial prepotent response (a response for which immediate reinforcement, positive or negative, is available) to an event; 2) stopping an ongoing response or response pattern, thereby permitting a delay in the decision to respond or continue to responding; and 3) protecting this period of delay and the self-directed responses that occur within it from disruption by competing events and responses (interference control)."[11] Barkley (1997) argues that children with ADHD have deficiencies with the process of behavioral inhibition. Furthermore citing research in neuropsychology,

Barkley (1997) elegantly explains the connection between behavioral inhibition and the cognitive processes of the "executive function" of the brain.

Barkley (1997) defines executive functions as "those self-directed actions of the individual that are used to self-regulate."[12] Neuro-imaging and neuropsychological research has located the executive functions in the prefrontal lobes of the brain. Barkley (1997) writes,

> Behavioral inhibition provides the foundation for the other four executive functions: 1) nonverbal working memory; 2) verbal working memory; 3) the self-regulation of affect/motivation/arousal; 4) reconstitution. In behavioral terms these functions are: 1) convert, self-directed sensing (nonverbal working memory); 2) covert, self-directed speech (verbal working memory); 3) covert, self-directed affect/motivation/arousal, or emoting to oneself; and 4) covert, self-directed behavioral manipulation, experimentation, and play (reconstitution).[13]

In simpler terms, it is very difficult for children with ADHD to inhibit responses, stop or continue a behavior required, and filter distractions adequately to carry out a behavior. Additionally, the cognitive processes of taking information into the working memory, such as a simple task, holding on to that information in the working memory, referencing the past for strategies that have helped to complete the task, using internal speech to problem solve, controlling affect to keep frustration down and motivation up, and finally putting all the above together into a planned action to complete the task, is at the heart of what is deficient in people with ADHD. Barkley (1997) also emphasized that "time is the ultimate yet nearly invisible disability afflicting those with ADHD."[14] Paule and colleagues (2000) suggest that "accurate perception of time is an important determinant of behavior: it facilitates the ability to predict and anticipate events, to organize and plan sequences of action, and prepare fast responses."[15] Simply stated, managing time—staying focused to perform a task or play activity and planning, strategizing, and following through in a timely manner—is very difficult for people with ADHD. Additionally, "clinical descriptions indicate that individuals with ADHD have marked difficulties in conforming to directions containing time parameters, meeting deadlines for work assignments, and in adjusting the timing of their behavior to the pacing of the immediate context (e.g., calling out in class, interrupting an ongoing conversation, difficulty waiting turn)."[16] The longer the time frame the more likely there will be deficiencies in performance. For example, this is why children with ADHD have a more difficult time being successful at a game such as baseball, in which there is a lot of wait time in between pitches and batters. Barkley's (1997) theory of ADHD brings about several implications for treatment.

Barkley suggests it is difficult for children with ADHD to manage time, remember, and internalize behavioral and cognitive strategies for such problems as organization, social skills, skills for completing tasks, or managing anger; therefore, it is important for these children to have cognitive and behavioral strategies *externalized* "at the point of performance."[17] This means, for example, instead of explaining two days prior to a friend coming over to a child with ADHD strategies on how to control frustration when their friend wants to play football outside instead of watching TV, a parent should have the child role-play and demonstrate (externalize) strategies to deal with frustration and how to compromise fifteen minutes prior (close to the point of performance) to the friend coming over to play. This increases the likelihood of strategies being followed through. Also, "externalizing sources of motivation and drive" at the point of performance can be very helpful.[18] Prompts, cues, reminders, "cheerleading," and coaching by parents are important for children with ADHD to be successful. For example, when a parent signals an ADHD child to soften his tone of voice (external prompt) while he is playing cards with his younger brother (at the point of performance), then the child complies and the parent reinforces compliance with praise (cheerleading). There is a greater chance of follow-through than if the parent reminded the child a day earlier to control frustration with his brother in play. Implications for these theories of ADHD will be woven into play techniques in the intervention section of this chapter.

OVERVIEW OF ODD

The *DSM-IV* describes oppositional defiant disorder as "a pattern of negativistic, hostile, and defiant behavior lasting at least 6 months, during which four (or more) of the following are present":[19]

1. Often loses temper
2. Often argues with adults
3. Often actively defies or refuses to comply with adults' requests or rules
4. Often deliberately annoys people
5. Often blames others for his or her mistakes of misbehavior
6. Is often touchy or easily annoyed by others
7. Is often angry and resentful
8. Is often spiteful or vindictive

Symptoms must cause clinically significant impairment in social, academic, or occupational functioning; behaviors are not exclusive to a mood or psychotic disorder; criteria are not met for conduct disorder or antisocial personality disorder.[20]

Children with ODD can vary in their presentation. Some have outgoing and friendly personalities; however, when things do not go their way they can blow up in anger and become argumentative. Others are not very friendly, display a flat, serious affect, and from the get-go are difficult to relate with and exhibit poor reciprocity in interactions. Recent research on ODD by Greene and Doyle (1999) proposes that ODD can have many different origins, often coexists with other disorders, and as a result requires heterogeneous treatment approaches.[21]

Greene and Doyle (1999) discuss the importance of viewing ODD as a disorder founded in the transaction between child and adult. ODD symptoms happen "in relationship" with another (caretaker, teacher, peer, or other family member).[22] "These behaviors are almost always present in the home and with individuals the child knows well, and often occur simultaneously with low self-esteem, mood lability, low frustration tolerance, and swearing."[23] Treatment of ODD has typically focused on correcting faulty parenting practices such as those described by Chamberlain and Patterson (1995):

Inconsistent discipline: parents who respond indiscriminately to a child's positive and negative behaviors; evidence poor or inconsistent follow-through with commands; give in when a child argues; and unpredictably change expectations and consequences for rule violations

Irritable explosive discipline: parents who issue high rates of direct commands; frequently use high-intensity, high-amplitude strategies such as hitting and yelling; threatening, which increases the likelihood the child will respond in an aggressive, defiant manner

Low supervision and involvement: parents who are unaware of their child's activities outside of their direct supervision; rarely engage in joint activities with their child; and do not provide supervision even when aware of the child's association with antisocial peers

Inflexible rigid discipline: parents who rely on a single or limited range of discipline strategies for all types of transgressions[24]

Greene and Doyle (1999) suggest that the heart of ODD lies in the reciprocal interaction between parent and child, and to be effective in helping children with ODD consideration of the specific causes of ODD in the child must be carefully assessed and understood to guide treatment interventions.[25] Further Greene and Doyle (1999) discuss the four areas of child development that can lead to children having problems with compliance and subsequently developing ODD: *poor self-regulation, poor affective modulation, language-processing disorders,* and *cognitive distortions and deficiencies.*[26]

POOR SELF-REGULATION

As described in the previous overview of ADHD, Barkley's (1997) theory of behavioral inhibition and executive functions explains why children with poor self-regulation have great difficulty with compliance and task or play performance. This problem is not volitional. Children with ADHD lack neurologically based skills to perform tasks and activities in a facile manner. Many parents and educators become frustrated with children with self-regulation problems and coerce or repeat strategies that are not working, which can create a defensive posture in the child and thus may only increase ODD behaviors. ADHD and ODD commonly coexist in children, making it necessary for clinicians to be aware of the complexity of interplay between two disorders.

POOR AFFECTIVE MODULATION

Children with ADHD often can have associated features that may include "low frustration tolerance, temper outbursts, bossiness, stubbornness, excessive and frequent insistence that requests be met, mood lability, demoralization, dysphoria, rejection by peers, and poor self-esteem."[27] Mood disorders can coexist with the disruptive behavior disorders. Mood problems such as anxiety and depression, as well as bipolar disorder, inherently can make managing the stress and frustration of tasks, play, and commands very difficult without outbursts of anger or loss of emotional control, thus setting up ODD. Children with disruptive behavior disorders can have difficulty regulating affective arousal in either direction.

As mentioned previously in the overview of ADHD, affect modulation is an executive function that can include problems arousing motivation or inhibiting excessive reactions to frustration and anger. Affect modulation is a developmental process that normally progresses from infancy on; however, due to impaired ability to regulate affective responses children with disruptive behavior disorders can have trouble with both over- or underreactivity to a wide range of affectively charged situations.[28] Greene and Doyle (1999) suggest that "children whose tendency is to overreact to affectively charged situations may find the physiological and emotional arousal associated with such situations difficult to regulate, may become cognitively debilitated in the midst of such arousal (a phenomenon referred to as "cognitive incapacitation" by Zillman [1988]), and may consequently respond to such situations with more affect (e.g., screaming, swearing) than reason (rational problem solving) and a reduced capacity to inhibit aggression."[29]

LANGUAGE-PROCESSING DISORDERS

Delays or deficits in the area of language development in children can compromise internal speech, as in the executive function of the verbal working memory, hamper verbal identification of emotions in problem situations, and impede the articulation of problem-solving strategies to effectively deal with conflict in which verbal skills would be helpful. Depending on the specific type of language-processing problem, these children may find themselves at a disadvantage. For example, if a child has an "auditory processing problem" obtaining a clear understanding of verbal commands or instructions by adults can cause frustration in the child and promote oppositional and defiant behaviors. Similarly, if a child has a problem with "word acquisition and retrieval" the ability to effectively access and utilize language in a moment of great frustration can make a strategy such as "talking through" the child's anger highly improbable.

COGNITIVE DISTORTIONS AND COGNITIVE DEFICIENCIES

Greene and Doyle (1999) cite Kendall (1993), who makes a distinction between cognitive *distortions* and cognitive *deficiencies* in the treatment of aggressive children, with the former referring to dysfunctional thinking processes and the latter to an insufficient amount of cognitive activity in situations in which greater forethought prior to action is needed.[30] It is my experience that children with disruptive behavior disorders often have trouble accurately reading social cues, misinterpret the actions of others, can be very rigid in their thinking, can have an excessive sense of unfairness, can tend to attribute negative rationale to situations of conflict, often feel persecuted or defeated, and tend to blame or "externalize the locus of control."

It is difficult to know if cognitive distortions and deficiencies are caused by, proceed, or coexist separately from the other developmental problems discussed above. For example, the misinterpretation of a social cue of a child who may jokingly roll his eyes at the comment of his friend who has ODD may cause an extremely angry response in the child with ODD. In this situation, did poor affect regulation "fuel" a defensive response and contribute to the ODD child's misinterpretation? Or, vice versa, or a combination of the two problems? Treatment focuses on teaching this child to more effectively read social cues or strategies to control frustration, or teaching both strategies, may bear differing results. Thus this also supports the importance of careful assessment, tailoring of treatment, and being able to be a flexible and creative therapist when treating the disruptive behavior disorders.

Greene and Doyle (1999) convincingly explain that due to multiple likely etiologies of ODD a "one-size-fits-all" approach to treatment will not be most effective.[31] Treatments need to be tailored to address specific problems as discussed above. For example, home-based token reward systems are touted to be effective behavioral change agents for the disruptive behavior disorders. However, some children diagnosed with ODD do not "buy into" the concept of being rewarded to comply or argue about the reinforcements making this treatment ineffective. Additionally, parents' abilities and deficiencies need to be carefully considered with regard to treatment, since ODD occurs in the reciprocal interaction between parents and children. For example, in clinical practice when trying to set up a home-based token reward system, I have experienced that some parents may have trouble with organization, consistency, motivation, and follow-through and thus cannot effectively implement such a program. These ideas will be applied to play therapy techniques in the final section of this chapter.

OVERVIEW OF CONDUCT DISORDER

Conduct disorder (CD) is described in the *DSM-IV* as a "repetitive and persistent pattern of behavior in which the basic rights of others or major age-appropriate societal norms or rules are violated." These behaviors fall into four main groupings: aggressive conduct that causes or threatens physical harm to other people or animals; nonaggressive conduct that causes property loss or damage; deceitfulness or theft; and serious violations or rules.[32] Three or more of the following criteria must be present in the past twelve months, with at least one criterion in the past six months:

Aggression to People and Animals

1. Often bullies, threatens, or intimidates others
2. Often initiates physical fights
3. Has used a weapon that can cause serious physical harm to others
4. Has been physically cruel to people
5. Has been physically cruel to animals
6. Has stolen while confronting a victim
7. Has forced someone into sexual activity

Destruction of Property

1. Has deliberately engaged in fire setting with the intention of causing serious damage
2. Has deliberately destroyed property that belongs to others

Deceitfulness or Theft

1. Has broken into someone else's house, building, or car
2. Often lies to obtain goods or favors or to avoid obligations
3. Has stolen items of nontrivial value without confronting a victim

Serious Violations of Rules

1. Often stays out at night despite parental prohibitions, beginning before age 13
3. Has run away from home at least twice
3. Is often truant from school, beginning before age 13

The disturbance in behavior needs to cause significant impairment in social, academic, or occupational settings and occur prior to age 18; antisocial personality disorder should be ruled out prior to age 18. There is generally a poorer prognosis for children who develop CD prior to adolescence.[33] However, Nagin and Tremblay (1999) indicate aggressive behavior can be common in children up to age 4, and dissipate or continue as the child develops.[34] This is why effective early intervention is important for children with conduct problems.

It goes without saying that CD is the most troubling of the disruptive behavior disorders and the most difficult to treat. There is considerable overlap between ADHD, ODD, and CD. There are particular similarities between ODD and CD. Cohen and Flory (1998), using longitudinal data from the Upper New York Study, found that the risk of the onset of CD was four times higher in ODD cases than in children without prior ODD or CD.[35] Burke, Loeber, and Birmaher (2002) suggest that as children mature there is usually a change in manifestation of CD symptoms that implies continuity rather than stability.[36] Burke and colleagues (2002) further cite Kelley, Loeber, and colleagues (1997) to suggest a developmental progression of CD:

1. An *overt pathway* progressing from minor aggression to physical fighting and then to violence
2. A *covert pathway* before age 15, from minor covert behaviors to property damage (fire setting or vandalism), and then to moderate to serious forms of delinquency
3. An *authority conflict pathway* before age 12, progressing from stubborn behavior to defiance and authority avoidance (truancy, running away, staying out late at night)[37]

It is difficult to know the percentage of children who progress from CD to antisocial behavior in adulthood, but this is an obvious risk if CD is not remedied by adolescence.

Research on the biological, genetic, and environmental aspects of the development of CD is ongoing. Of particular interest to play therapy and treating disruptive behavior disorders are factors such as temperament, parenting and attachment, social cognition, autonomic nervous system arousal, and aggression.

Sanson, Prior, and Smart (1999) concluded that early temperament (specifically negative emotionality, intense and reactive responding, and inflexibility) is predictive of externalizing behavior problems by late childhood.[38] Due to the fact that temperamental traits are constitutional, like personality, they "spread to the many fibers of the being." Consequently the therapeutic stance needs to be on managing and effectively coping and compensating for symptoms rather than curing.

As mentioned earlier, faulty parenting such as harsh and coercive, permissive, inconsistent, or abusive styles can increase externalizing behaviors. Conjoint therapy with parents, either meeting with parents separately to discuss or provide parent training, or family therapy is paramount to the overall effectiveness of treatment for children with a DBD.

While research on attachment problems for disruptive behavior disorders is not conclusive, my clinical impression is that there are often significant attachment problems between parents and children diagnosed with a DBD. DeKlyen and colleagues (1998) suggest that mothers of children with behavior problems are less warm (1971, 1980) and less positively involved (1987, 1989, 1996) than other mothers, and disruptive preschool boys are less likely to be securely attached to their mothers (1991).[39] Regarding the father's role, there is some evidence that for clinic-referred boys, low paternal involvement, lack of warmth, and unaffectionate father–son interactions are associated with serious antisocial problems (1996, 1990, 1984).[40]

It has been previously mentioned that children with a DBD fail to properly read social cues from others. Burke and colleagues (2002) report that aggressive (1993) and incarcerated delinquent boys (1999) demonstrate a bias to attribute hostile intentions to others.[41] Boys diagnosed with a DBD, compared with control group boys, focus on concrete and external qualities and adopt an egocentric bias in describing their peers (1995).[42] Regarding empathy, it is widely understood that conduct-disordered individuals tend to lack empathy for others, which likely influences their tendency to easily violate the rights of others. Cohen and Strayer (1996) suggest that boys and girls with CD are lower in empathy and lack the ability to identify interpersonal cues.[43] For therapists treating disruptive behavior disorders, peer relationship problems need to be addressed because the disturbance in social functioning can have a serious impact on self-esteem and self-concept and the perpetuation of symptoms.

There is research providing evidence that children with ODD and CD often experience a general physiological underarousal, including lowered heart rate (1999).[44] Additionally, the absence of "sufficient anxiety" may be a common problem for children with CD. Burke and colleagues (2002) suggest that anxiety is "hypothesized to inhibit children from engaging in disruptive or criminal behavior."[45] It is likely that this underarousal is connected to how children with CD have such a difficult time showing empathy and remorse for others, due to a physiologically based problem generating care or concern. This poses a considerable problem for therapists teaching empathy or remorse skills and pits the therapist against constitutional roadblocks.

Finally, aggression complicates the clinical picture of children diagnosed with a DBD. Whether the disorder is ADHD, ODD, or CD, added aggression makes symptoms more pronounced, problematic, and difficult to treat. Greene and Doyle (1999) identify two forms of aggression. "The first, *non-impulsive* aggression closely resembles proactive aggression in animals. This form of aggression is conceived as controlled, planned, and goal oriented; is thought to involve a low level of physiological arousal; and is typically not associated with affective instability. The second, *impulsive* aggression closely resembles affective aggression in animals. This form of aggression is said to be explosive and uncontrolled; is thought to involve high levels of arousal; has been found to be associated with disinhibition and affective instability (but not necessarily antisocial tendencies)."[46] While aggression is common in early childhood, when it persists through latency and adolescence more disturbed behaviors (verbal and physical violence, fighting, battles with parents and peers, more serious violations of the rights of others, and breaking the law) can occur. Play therapy, physical recreation, and sports can help dissipate or channel aggression.

INTERVENTION

Discussion

The disruptive behavior disorders respond optimally to multimodal or multisystemic treatments. For example, ADHD is commonly treated with medication, behavioral therapy for the child with ADHD, parent training to improve home management, school-based interventions, and sometimes family therapy to help siblings deal with ADHD behaviors. ODD is cared for with medication, behavioral therapy, and communication skills focused on parent–child interactions, and cognitive problem solving and skill building for the child with ODD. CD is managed with medication, parent management training (PMT), individual therapy to address relational and personality problems, family therapy to improve parent–client relationships, and the coordination of systems (i.e., school and the Department of Juvenile Justice) with therapy. Play therapy is not typically considered as effective with the disruptive behavior disorders; however, I have found that there are forms of play therapy that can be integral to treatment when combined with some of the above-mentioned therapies to form a treatment package.

Three types of play therapy will be described in the intervention section of this chapter: social skills play therapy, problem-solving play therapy, and solution-focused play therapy. Each of these therapies is behavioral in nature. They are also relational with emphasis on assisting child clients, via skill building, to conform to socially acceptable standards of behavior in the contexts of family, peer, and public (teachers, other adults) relationships/ settings. These therapies can be useful for children across the developmental spectrum through adolescence. However, case examples later in this chapter will be limited to children in the latency years.

Assessment

Assuming that a diagnosis of disruptive behavior disorder has been made, determining and specifying problematic behaviors as thoroughly as possible is critical to effective treatment. As discussed in the section on ODD, not all disruptive behavior disordered children are the same simply because they fit the same diagnostic criteria. Children with ADHD can have varying blends of impulsivity, inattention, and hyperactivity. Children with CD can have various types of conduct problems with more or less severity. As a result, psychosocial history, clinical observation, psychological testing, information from school (including teacher ratings), parent ratings, and assessments of marital, parenting, and family functioning are all important diagnostic tools for the therapist treating a child with a DBD. Widening the assessment lens can give the therapist additional insights, for example, how family members may be involved in maintaining problem behaviors.

Play assessment often elicits information about children with a DBD that is diagnostic. In the first or second session, a play assessment can be done. In this session, it is best if the therapist is as nondirective as possible, allowing the child to freely choose toys or games. If the child is inhibited, defended, or disinterested, low-key prompts inviting the child to play can be made by the therapist. However, this must be done carefully, without persuasion, or it could interfere with the spontaneity and authenticity of the client. Lewis (1987) writes, "The degree of spontaneity and freedom of the child's play may be seen as reflecting his or her degree of comfort with needs, impulses and fantasy. At one extreme are children who reveal themselves as inhibited or compulsive, with a rigid and stereotyped quality to their play. At the other extreme are children who seem unable to manage their impulses and the freedom of the play situation and become behaviorally out of control."[47] Typically children diagnosed with a DBD show symptoms of their diagnosis in play. Children diagnosed with ADHD can be loud, impulsive, aggressive, and disorganized, or they can get easily bored and make multiple shifts in play. They can be bossy and controlling, can always need to win, and can tease or brag. Children diagnosed with ODD can be negative, critical, or unwilling to play. They can show signs of poor frustration tolerance and even blow up in anger or cry if things do not go their way. Children diagnosed with CD can show very little interest or sense of enjoyment in their play, cheat in games, and show levels of aggression without remorse or empathy—in symbolic play or toward the therapist. The therapist needs to take note of behaviors that are problematic, such as those mentioned above. Play interventions, after the initial nondirective assessment session, will be targeted with corrective responses by the play therapist.

Social Skills Play Therapy

Social skills play therapy involves the teaching/coaching of prosocial behaviors during play. During the nondirective assessment session the therapist has targeted specific social skills problem areas, such as playing too loudly, being bossy, cheating, complaining, criticizing, and so on. Depending on the child's preference, social skills play therapy can be used during creative and spontaneous play, or more rule-bound play as in game play.

Steps to Conduct Social Skills Play Therapy

1. The therapist informs the child that she or he will help the child with behavior problems that are causing trouble for him or her by practicing new behaviors to help him or her get along better with others.
2. After the child spontaneously (if not with low-key, open-ended invitations by the therapist) engages in play, the therapist asks to join in the play, if not already invited by the child.
3. As the child begins to display faulty social/relational behaviors the therapist, at first in a Rogerian fashion, makes a reflective observation. For example, if a boy likes to be boss and always have control of the play, the therapist might remark, "I can tell it's important for you to decide what we play." Sometimes the child will respond with an insight to explain her behavior, which can allow the therapist to explore feelings and cognitions underlying the behavior.
4. As illustrated previously, the therapist suggests an alternative behavior: "What would happen if I got to chose the next thing we play?" This intervention could raise anxiety, anger, or agreement in the child. However, depending on the skill of the therapist, if the child got angry, the practitioner might offer a compromise. For instance, "Okay. How about if you choose the next thing we play and I'll choose the one after that?" The effort of the therapist is to challenge the child, with a DBD, to experience and practice more positive alternative social skills in the session. Support, validation, and positive verbal reinforcement of the new positive social skills, when performed by the child, are essential.
5. At the end of the session the therapist reviews the new skills learned by the child and suggests the child practice these skills between sessions.

6. Since it is a common problem for child clients to remember, practice, and "generalize" the use of skills in various settings, it is optimal to teach parents social skills play therapy. Depending on the skill of the parent, this can be accomplished by the parent observing the therapist in the session. Once the parent gets the hang of it, the therapist invites the parent to take over the play session and coach the child (as in filial play therapy).

Case Example 1

Jason is an eight-year-old boy with ADHD and ODD. He is an only child and both parents have suffered from alcoholism and marital conflict; however, at the current time parents are doing much better. Jason has difficulty in peer relationships due to being bossy and needing to win in games. This following is an excerpt from the sixth session (a total of 15 were held):

(Jason is playing with the army men in the office and is splitting the men and artillery to suit him.)

Therapist: I notice you're going to make sure you have more help on your side.

Jason: Well, you can have these (gives therapist two soldiers to his ten).

Therapist: Thanks. But I feel like I don't have a chance with so few soldiers.

Jason: (With a tone of noticeable frustration.) All right! Here (handing the therapist several more army men).

Therapist: (The therapist verbally reinforces the child's willingness to play fair.) I know you really like to win and it was hard for you to play fair, but since you gave me more men I feel like playing rather than quitting. Thank-you. (The therapist acknowledges the difficulty the child had playing fair and gives a realistic visceral response to how "playing fair" feels better to others.)

Case Example 2

The following example involves two siblings. Eleven-year-old Michael is in the sixth grade, has severe ADHD and mild CD, and attended an alternative elementary school for children with behavioral and emotional problems. Troy is his four-year-old brother who is a bit impulsive and aggressive for his age. Michael tends to rile Troy up and treat him aggressively, which causes an aggressive response back from Troy. Their mother is concerned that Troy is learning "bad habits" from Michael. She is finding staying home, "to be there more for her sons," more stressful than rewarding. The therapist has seen this family for several years and during this time there was a period of improvement and treatment was discontinued. However, recently it has been necessary to resume the sessions. This is an excerpt from the family's first session after recontinuing therapy.

Therapist: (The therapist has engaged the boys, who are both seated together on the couch, by playing a game of bounce and catch with a Koosh basketball. Mother is seated separately in another chair.) So, I've heard from Mom about how you guys fight a lot. Are there times when you get along? [Solution-focused exception to problem-behavior question]

Troy: No. (Michael grabs the ball the therapist just bounced to Troy in a rough fashion.) Get off!

Mom: Michael, leave your brother alone! (Michael laughs and pays her no mind.)

Therapist: Troy, I'd like you to switch seats with your mother. (Mom and Troy switch seats. This intervention was aimed at requiring Michael to regard personal boundaries and to model for mother how to set limits behaviorally.) Michael, what made you grab the ball from your brother?

Michael: I don't know. Just messing around.

Therapist: So, were you being playful or teasing him?

Michael (grinning): Being playful.

Therapist: Troy, was it fun and playful that your brother grabbed the ball from you?

Troy: No, I didn't like it.

Therapist: Michael, can you see how Troy felt?

Michael: Yeah.

Therapist: Can you say something to your brother that would help him feel better?

Michael: Sorry, Troy.

The above problem-solving sequence supports Troy, models for mom, and attempts to get Michael to take seriously how his behavior affects Troy.

The following sequence is in the middle of the session during a game of pickup sticks (I have a set of three-foot long giant pickup sticks that children find novel) the boys have chosen to play. The example is intended to illustrate the process of reinforcing positive social behavior.

Michael (notices that his brother is excited but overwhelmed by the colorful display of large pickup sticks covering the floor; it is Troy's turn and he seems uncertain as to which stick to go for; Michael carefully moves closer to his brother): Troy, try to pick up this one, it's not leaning on the others.

Troy (accepts his brother's help and successfully picks up the stick): Yes! (Smiling and clearly proud of himself.)

Therapist: Michael. (For inattentive children, calling their name will facilitate eye contact and will improve listening.) (Michael looks at the therapist.) Way to be helpful to Troy! That's being a great big brother to him! (Said with enthusiasm and joy by the therapist; again to model for mom and to shift the therapy to more "solution talk" versus "problem talk.")

Mom (picks up on the solution talk): Michael can be very helpful to Troy.

(While the boys are playing appropriately the therapist asks mom for more examples of Michael being helpful to Troy. Mom mentions several examples that the therapist "fleshes out" in Michael's presence to reinforce "being helpful.")

The session above continues in a positive fashion. The therapist has demonstrated for mother, using play, how to structure the play, deal with problem behavior, set limits, and reinforce positive social skills. The siblings are experiencing getting along and Michael is learning how to regard boundaries and be helpful to Troy. Troy is experiencing his brother in a positive helpful role. Mom eventually picked up on what the therapist was doing and joined in on the "coaching" of social skills. Additionally, the therapist can positively reinforce mother's interventions to build her sense of competency.

Discussion

Social skills play therapy can be used as a primary or ancillary treatment to promote positive social behavior for children with disruptive behavior disorders. This treatment can be used for short-term or long-term therapy sessions. Family members enhance the effectiveness of this form of play therapy when parents utilize this technique at home in order to generalize and internalize the acquisition of skills.

Problem-Solving Play Therapy

Problem-solving play therapy utilizes basic problem-solving strategies during play situations, in which problems occur, to find effective solutions to problems and to build skills for child clients. Another effective problem-solving format is the reenactment of behavior problems, using play or role play to discover solutions. The rehearsal of solutions to problems increases the likelihood of new skills being internalized by child clients.

Steps to Conduct Problem-Solving Play Therapy

1. The therapist freezes a problem occurring during play by halting the play and addressing the problem, or a problem is selected by the child or therapist to work on via enactment using play.
2. Therapists generally follow a basic problem-solving format to guide and teach the child:
   a. How did the problem get started?
   b. Whose problem is it?

c. What is the desirable outcome?

d. What is the best solution to solve the problem?

3. Enact the solution to the problem during the play or using role play.

Case Example 1

Robbie is a diminutive, cute nine-year-old who comes from a competitive, high-striving family. He struggles with ADHD and ODD and has an explosive temper. While very intelligent, Robbie has a language retrieval problem, and thus he has great trouble expressing anger/frustration verbally. In the past he has thrown things, broken things, and punched others when angry. The therapist has engaged Robbie in a game of tip ball—a game in which two or more players try to "tip" a soft Koosh or Nerf ball back and forth with the palms of their hands or tips of their fingers in an underhanded volleyball fashion. A running count of how many times the ball passes back and forth is kept. If the ball hits the ground, the game stops and the score is the number counted before the ball hits the ground. This is a cooperative game in which players must work together for a team score (2,000).[48] Robbie is very athletic and loves this game. Each session he tries to break our previously established record. Robbie has been in counseling for two years, first weekly, then gradually tapering off to monthly (as of this writing) for support. The following dialogue is an excerpt from session 8:

> *Therapist* (Robbie makes a great save to keep the game going as we are tipping the ball back and forth.): Nice save!
>
> (Robbie smiles. One minute later into the game Robbie misses an easy one.)
>
> *Robbie* (yells): AAAHH! (throws the ball into the couch).
>
> *Therapist*: (When Robbie ignites quickly he is very difficult to reason with and due to his language difficulties he cannot utilize "talking through" his anger easily. Thus the therapist is directive at first to prevent further escalation and help Robbie calm himself.) That was frustrating. We were doing so well. (Robbie says nothing but stomps around the room.) Robbie. (Robbie looks at the therapist.) Let's do some "cleansing breaths" to calm down. (The therapist models breathing in deeply and letting out breaths, as in a sigh, three times. Robbie complies and begins to calm down.)

Considerable new research suggests that venting anger may not be cathartic, but may actually perpetuate anger problems (1999).[49] This is likely due to the fact that venting still allows for the aggressive expression of anger rather than containing, calming, or deescalating. The cleansing breath in the above sequence is an approach to teach calming skills.

> *Therapist* (noticing Robbie is calming down and seated on the couch): Good work pulling it together (therapist reinforces Robbie calming down, a feat that is diffi-

cult for him). Let's rewind the tape here to learn about what happened and how to help you control anger in the future. Do you want to control anger better?

Robbie: Yes.

Therapist: We were playing nicely, we were focused, and our score was 320. Then what happened?

Robbie: I got mad.

Therapist: Yes. What made you mad?

Robbie: I missed an easy one.

Therapist: Okay. That was certainly disappointing, but was it so bad you needed to yell and throw the ball? (As in cognitive-behavioral or rational-emotive therapy, the therapist challenges the distorted cognition, "awfullizing" in this case, which is an extreme reaction that is a core problem for this child.)

Robbie: No.

Therapist: What could you have done differently to control anger here? (Solution-focused therapy is useful in this situation. This question assumes that clients have the solution to problems and only need some guidance to uncover them.)

Robbie: Tell myself it's not that bad?

Therapist: Yes! Excellent! (Therapist makes a big deal out of the solution Robbie has come up with.) Do you think if you practice telling yourself, "It's not that bad," when you start getting angry, it will help you control your anger better?

Robbie: Yes.

Therapist: Good. I'd like you to practice this now. Let's role-play. Pretend we are back at 320 (score) and you miss that easy one again, only this time you control anger by telling yourself, "It's not that bad." (Therapist restarts the game of tip ball and Robbie joins in; the therapist counts the score) 318, 319, 320. (Robbie pretends to miss an easy one and the therapist watches Robbie intently to witness him practice.)

Robbie (talks softly to himself, "self-talk"): It's not that bad.

Therapist: Great! How do you feel?

Robbie: Okay. Not that mad.

Therapist: Good! You know, Robbie, no one is expecting you to not get mad. Everyone gets mad sometimes. I'm just trying to help you to not get so mad that it causes problems for you (clarification and normalization). Do you think you can use this strategy you came up with when you get angry with your brother? (Robbie's brother triggers massive blowups at home.) The therapist makes a suggestion for Robbie to generalize this strategy to other situations.)

Robbie: Yes.

Following the session the therapist gets Robbie's permission to review the anger control strategy learned today with his mother, so that she can coach Robbie to practice this strategy at home and in school.

Case Example 2

Tim is an aggressive seven-year-old with ADHD, ODD, and the potential to develop conduct problems due to his combative nature. Tim's sister, Denise, is five. She can be strong-willed, antagonistic, and also aggressive. Both children get into physical confrontations, which are escalating and becoming more aggressive. Typically Tim initiates the confrontations with his sister; however, Denise is beginning to physically attack her brother when she feels slighted. Tim is also very argumentative and defiant with his mother. Mother tends to lose her patience easily and at times feels unable to get both children under control.

The family is in ongoing counseling as of this writing. The following is an excerpt from session 5. The therapist is discussing a recent incident that occurred in the family home, in which Tim defied his mom and triggered a fight with his sister.

> *Therapist*: So Tim, in your own words, tell me what happened with the fight with your sister regarding the computer.
>
> *Tim* (verbal and articulate): Well, I was playing on the computer and Denise came in and wanted to play, but I was right in the middle of a game.
>
> *Therapist*: So, what were you feeling at that point when Denise wanted to use the computer?
>
> *Tim*: I was mad, because I didn't want to stop.
>
> *Therapist*: Okay. You really wanted to keep playing, even though you knew it was time to share the computer with Denise. What did you want to see happen?
>
> *Tim*: I don't know. (Pause.) I wanted her to go away so I could finish my game.
>
> *Therapist*: So, what did you do?
>
> *Tim*: I yelled at her to go away, then she grabbed the mouse and I really got mad so I pushed her down. She started crying and Mom came in and yelled at me and then I got punished to my room.
>
> *Therapist*: Okay. Let's rewind the tape here a minute. You really wanted Denise to go away for a while so you could finish your game. How could you have tried to get her to wait until you finished your game?
>
> *Tim*: I could have asked her to wait.
>
> *Therapist*: Yes! And what if she didn't want to wait?

Tim: Um . . . I could have saved my game and let her play for a while, and then come back and play my game later.

Therapist: Fantastic idea! Let's use the puppets. (Tim loves the puppets and often asks to play with them.) Play out this solution you came up with.

Tim (enthusiastically): Okay!

(Tim goes to the toy cupboard and brings out the basket of puppets. Tim likes to take charge and can be very creative. Already he is planning the scene.)

Tim: Can we use your computer?

Therapist: Sure.

Tim: Let's see . . . Mom can be the kangaroo, I'll be the chipmunk, and Denise will be the raccoon. Can you play mom? (Speaking to the therapist.)

Therapist: I'd be happy to.

Tim: I'll play me and Denise. Okay. (Tim sits the chipmunk down in the chair at the computer and in his other hand, Denise the raccoon hovers off to the side watching as the scene begins).

Chipmunk (begins pressing the mouse button): Yes! One more and I'll get to the next level.

Raccoon (whining): I want to play now! (Grabs the mouse.)

Chipmunk (calmly and assuredly): Okay. Just let me save the game and I'll let you play now, then I'll finish my game later.

Raccoon: Okay.

Kangaroo: Nice work! Way to solve the problem, kids!

This intervention led to Tim using better problem-solving skills with his sister at home over the next several weeks. A problem in this case has been getting mother to practice social skills and problem-solving strategies at home. However, as of this writing, mother has purchased some cooperative games, and both she and father have been working with the siblings in a play format, with success.

Discussion

Problem-solving play therapy can be used separately or in conjunction with social skills play therapy. It is intended to target specific problematic behaviors for children with disruptive behavior disorders. The key aspect of this form of play therapy is for child clients to acquire new skills to solve problems, since many children with a DBD are at risk for developing very low self-esteem due to feelings of incompetence.

Solution-Focused Play Therapy

Solution-focused play therapy is way of incorporating the theory and practice of solution-focused therapy (SFT), created by Steve De Shazer and Insoo Berg, in a play format. There are many aspects that define solution-focused therapy; however, only elemental aspects will be described in this chapter. SFT takes the stance that clients have the skills to solve their problems and the therapist is a collaborator/facilitator to assist clients to find solutions. First, the therapist asks the simple question, "What is your goal in coming to counseling?" The client will then typically describe a problem. Next, the therapist asks, "What would you like to change about this problem?" Depending on the client's wish, the therapist can then ask a question called an "exception to the problem" question. For example, "Are there times when you don't fight with your sister, and if so what is happening differently?" (or, "what are you doing differently?"). This kind of question can transform the climate in a session from dismal talk about problems to hopeful, more positive talk about client competencies. In this way, the therapist explores positive skills the client is already performing; skills that normally get ignored because of "problem talk." The therapist takes great interest in and "fleshes out" these often hidden competencies of clients in the session and encourages the practice and performance of these skills to create possibilities for change (1992).[50] Solution-focused play therapy practices the solutions using enactment of these skills via play in the session.

Steps to Conduct Solution-Focused Play Therapy

1. The therapist helps the client establish goals for counseling by asking the question, "What would you like to get from coming to counseling?" Sometimes clients do not know what they want, and information about problems stated by parents at intake can be used and explored by the therapist with the child client to establish goals.
2. The therapist asks, "What would you like to change about the problem?" If changes are identified by the client, therapist asks, "Are there times when these changes already happen?" Another effective question is, "Are there times when the problem isn't happening, and if so, what is happening differently?" These types of questions often elicit thoughts and actions that keep problems from occurring.
3. The therapist encourages the child client to enact, using play or role play, their identified thought or actions (solutions) that keep problems from occurring.

Case Example 1

Mark is a ten-year-old boy with CD manifested by chronic lying to avoid responsibility and aggression in the form of physical fighting with peers. His parents separated when Mark was three years old, and he resided with his father until age 8. His father was involved in stealing, lying, and deception, and dealing and using hard drugs. When Mark's father was jailed, Mark went to reside with his mother and stepfather. This household has provided structure and stability for Mark, but even with very supportive parenting and counseling his behaviors are entrenched due to probable genetic factors and early learning from his father. The following is an excerpt from session 2. Mark was seen fifteen times.

Therapist (after discussing Mark's fighting behavior): Mark, what do you want to see happen as a result of this counseling?

Mark: I'd like to stop getting in trouble for fighting.

Therapist: Okay. Mark, can you think of any times when you had a problem with a classmate and you solved it without fighting.

Mark (nodding): Yeah.

Therapist: What happened differently?

Mark: Well, it was a situation at gym and we were playing basketball and after I shot the ball, this boy kicked my ball.

Therapist: What did you do differently?

Mark: Well, I got angry of course, but I told myself, I'm not going to let my anger get me in trouble. So I went and told the gym teacher instead.

Therapist: Great! Did that work?

Mark: Yeah. I didn't get into trouble and the teacher said something to the boy to not do it again.

Therapist: Awesome! So do you think if you could get yourself to hold your anger and tell yourself, I'm not going to let anger get me in trouble, it could help you in other situations? (Therapist reiterates to amplify the solutions the child identified.)

Mark: Yeah.

Therapist: Okay. Let's plug in this solution to the other situation you told me about when "anger got the best of you" out on the playground and you pushed that boy down.[51] Do you want to use puppets or role play?

Mark: Let's role-play. (Mark prefers role play because he feels puppets are childish.)

Therapist: Okay.

Mark: Do you want to play the boy who cheated in dodge ball?

Therapist: Sure.

Mark: I'll play me.

Therapist (the therapist and Mark are standing in a dodge ball fashion facing each other with a soft Koosh ball): So, this guy crossed the line, which is against the rules, to throw you out. Right?

Mark: Yeah.

Therapist: Okay. Let's try it. (Therapist crosses imaginary line too close to Mark and throws the ball to get him out.)

Mark (changes to a serious expression with a slight look of anger, noticeably trying to pause and hold his anger): That wasn't fair (relatively calm tone with a sigh that seemed to resemble a cleansing breath). But I'm not going to get in trouble so I'm going to go get the teacher (walks away as if going to get the teacher).

Therapist: Fantastic! How did you feel the solution worked?

Mark (laughs): Pretty good. I really started getting angry.

Therapist (with interest): I noticed. So you really had to work hard on this one to "keep anger from bossing you around?" (An intervention that acknowledges hard work, externalizes anger, and validates the client for "being the boss of anger.")

Mark was not successful in maintaining a regular school placement and needed to attend the alternative behavioral management school in his area. However, he put to use the anger control strategies he learned to decrease incidents of aggressive behavior.

Case Example 2

Steve is a seven-year-old second grader with ADHD. He attends private school where there is limited support for his condition. He began the school year without medication, but after being diagnosed with ADHD, he started on stimulant medication. While the medication has helped significantly, Steve still exhibits some residual disruptive behaviors, blurting out in class and falling on the ground to be silly. The following is an excerpt from session 4. Steve is still attending counseling and there have been eight sessions thus far.

Therapist: Steve, these two problems, blurting out in class and falling on the ground to make people laugh, seem to be really causing you trouble. Do you want to see these problems get better?

Steve: Yes!

Therapist: Great. Let's see if we can work on this. Are there times when you are able to not blurt out and not fall down in the classroom?

Steve (nodding head): Uhhh, yes.

Therapist: Can you tell me what's happening differently when you don't blurt out and don't fall down?

Steve: Well, I raise my hand.

Therapist: Good! Does that work?

Steve: Well, I don't get into trouble, but the teacher doesn't call on me.

Therapist: So, you don't get into trouble, but you really want to be called on.

Steve: Yes.

Therapist: Well, do you think if you raised your hand a lot more than blurting out, the teacher might start calling on you?

Steve: Maybe.

Therapist: Okay. Are there times when you don't fall on the ground?

(Steve nods his head in affirmation.)

Therapist: What's happening differently?

Steve: I just sort of walk without falling.

Therapist: Okay! How do you get yourself to "walk without falling?" (Using the client's language increases a sense of understanding and collaboration. Asking with interest presupposes and reinforces client competency to solve the problem.)

Steve: I just did it because I didn't want to get into trouble.

Therapist: Great! I remember you enjoyed playing with the puppets. How about you show me with the puppets how you raise your hand without blurting out and walk without falling.

Steve (taking the puppets out of the basket in the cupboard and arranging them on the sofa): Sure. All right. These are the kids in the class. Why don't you play the teacher (handing the therapist the wizard puppet)? I'll be the beaver.

Therapist: Okay.

Steve: Okay. Ask a question like, How much is 5 + 3?

Wizard: Class: How much is 5 + 3?

(Beaver eagerly raises his hand.)

(Wizard calls on the raccoon instead; Steve the beaver flashes a disappointed look but says nothing.)

Therapist: Good work, Steve. Even though the beaver did not get called on, he handled his frustration well. I bet if he kept raising his hand the wizard would eventually call on him. Do you think?

Steve: Maybe. At least I didn't get into trouble for blurting out.

Therapist: Yes! Okay. What about "walking without falling?"

Steve: That's easy. Pretend I ask to go to the bathroom and you let me.

Therapist: Okay. (Switches to the puppet characters again.)

Beaver (raises his hand and wizard calls on him): May I please go to the bathroom?

Wizard: Yes, you may.

(Beaver carefully and steadily walks from the couch toward the office door.)

Therapist: Nice work! What were you thinking at the time?

Steve: Well, I kind of wanted to fall on the ground, but I didn't want to get into trouble.

Therapist: You did it! You "walked without falling" because you told yourself you didn't want to get into trouble! Nice job! Do you think if you practiced "raising your hand and walking without falling" you would get into less trouble?

Steve (nodding in affirmation): Yeah.

Therapist: How will your teacher think of you differently if you continue to "raise your hand and walk without falling?"

Steve: She'll think I'm getting better.

Therapist: Is this what you want?

Steve: Yes!

Therapist: Great!

Discussion

Solution-focused play therapy is a positive, competency-based approach to working with child clients. Emphasis is not on talking excessively about problems but moving quickly toward identifying, reinforcing, and practicing solutions to problems. This type of therapy may require training in solution-focused therapy. A valuable resource is the book *Becoming Solution-Focused in Brief Therapy*, by John L. Walter and Jane E. Peller.[52]

Conclusion

The disruptive behavior disorders, attention deficit hyperactivity disorder, oppositional defiant disorder, and conduct disorder, as a group, tend to be the most common referrals to general child mental health practices. Core behavior problems of the disruptive behavior disorders, such as impulsivity, argumentativeness, explosive anger, or the violation of the rights of others, cause problems for children with a DBD that affect every aspect of their lives. Since the causes for the disruptive behavior disorders are multiple and tend to be related to temperament, brain function, neurochemistry, neuropsychology, and other constitutional factors, the notion of playing out conflicts, such as in client-centered play therapy, may not benefit clients with a DBD to control core behavior problems.

Research on the treatment of the disruptive behavior disorders suggests behavioral therapies such as behavior modification, parent management training, social skills training, and problem-solving skill building are key treatment approaches (aside from medication). The play therapy approaches introduced in this chapter—social skills play therapy, problem-solving play therapy, and solution-focused play therapy—are behavioral approaches that are consistent with this theory of treatment. The use of these therapies is most effective when combined with other modalities for treatment, since the disruptive behavior disorders respond best to multimodal treatments.

The ability for child clients to acquire and utilize skills learned by these play therapy approaches takes practice, repetition, rehearsal, and parent coaching. At times it is a gradual process. Therapists need to have an abundance of energy, be positive, encouraging, and supportive, and engender hope in child clients and their parents. Selecting which of these therapies (or combination of therapies) to use depends on the fit for the client/therapist situation, therapist preference, and the therapist's knowledge of the "use of self."

NOTES

1. J. A. Arlow, "Trauma, Play, and Perversion," *Psychoanalytic Study of the Child* 42 (1987): 31–45.

2. J. M. Lewis, "Childhood Play in Normality, Pathology, and Therapy," *American Journal of Orthopsychiatry* 63 (1993): 6–15; P. D. Neubauer, "The Many Meanings of Play: Introduction," *Psychoanalytic Study of the Child* 42 (1987): 3–10.

3. J. Piaget, *Play, Dreams and Imitation in Childhood* (New York: Norton, 1951).

4. J. M. Lewis, "Childhood Play in Normality, Pathology, and Therapy," *American Journal of Orthopsychiatry* 63 (1993): 6–15.

5. J. M. Lewis, "Childhood Play in Normality, Pathology, and Therapy," *American Journal of Orthopsychiatry* 63 (1993): 6–15.

6. *American Heritage Dictionary*, 2nd ed. (Boston, 1982).

7. *American Heritage Dictionary*, 2nd ed. (Boston, 1982).

8. A. J. Solnit, "Beyond Play and Playfulness," *Psychoanalytic Study of the Child* 53 (1998): 102–10; E. A. Plaut, "Play and Adaptation," *Psychoanalytic Study of the Child* 34 (1979): 217–32.

9. A. J. Solnit, "Beyond Play and Playfulness," *Psychoanalytic Study of the Child* 53 (1998): 102–10.

10. American Psychiatric Association, *Diagnostic and Statistical Mental Disorders*, 4th ed. (Washington, D.C., 1994).

11. R. A. Barkley, *ADHD and the Nature of Self-Control* (New York: Guilford, 1997).

12. Barkley, *ADHD*.

13. Barkley, *ADHD*.

14. Barkley, *ADHD*.

15. M. G. Paule, A. S. Rowland, S. A. Ferguson, J. J. Chelonis, R. Tannock, J. M. Swanson, and F. X. Castellanos, "Attention Deficit/Hyperactivity Disorder: Characteristics, Interventions, and Models," *Neurotoxicology and Teratology* 22 (2000): 631–51.

16. Paule et al., "Attention Deficit/Hyperactivity Disorder," 631–51.

17. Barkley, *ADHD*.

18. Barkley, *ADHD*.

19. American Psychiatric Association, *Diagnostic and Statistical Mental Disorders*, 4th ed. (Washington, D.C., 1994).

20. American Psychiatric Association, *Diagnostic and Statistical Mental Disorders*.

21. R. W. Greene and A. E. Doyle, "Toward a Transactional Conceptualization of Oppositional Defiant Disorder: Implications for Assessment and Treatment," *Clinical Child and Family Psychology Review* 2, no. 3 (1999): 129–48.

22. Greene and Doyle, "Toward a Transactional Conceptualization of Oppositional Defiant Disorder."

23. American Psychiatric Association, *Diagnostic and Statistical Mental Disorders*, 4th ed.

24. P. Chamberlain and G. R. Patterson, "Discipline and Child Compliance in Parenting," in *Handbook of Parenting* (Mahwah, N.J: Erlbaum, 1995), 205–25.

25. Greene and Doyle, "Toward a Transactional Conceptualization of Oppositional Defiant Disorder."

26. Greene and Doyle, "Toward a Transactional Conceptualization of Oppositional Defiant Disorder."

27. American Psychiatric Association, *Diagnostic and Statistical Mental Disorders*, 4th ed.

28. C. A. Stifter, T. L. Spinard, and J. M. Braungart-Rieker, "Toward a Developmental Model of Compliance: The Role of Emotion Regulation in Infancy," *Child Development* 70 (1999): 21–32.

29. Greene and Doyle, "Toward a Transactional Conceptualization of Oppositional Defiant Disorder"; D. Zillman, "Cognition-Excitation Interdependencies in Aggressive Behavior," *Aggressive Behavior* 14 (1988): 51–64.

30. Greene and Doyle, "Toward a Transactional Conceptualization of Oppositional Defiant Disorder"; P. C. Kendall, "Cognitive-Behavioral Therapies with Youth: Guiding Theory, Current Status, and Emerging Developments," *Journal of Consulting and Clinical Psychology* 61 (1993): 235–47.

31. Greene and Doyle, "Toward a Transactional Conceptualization of Oppositional Defiant Disorder."

32. American Psychiatric Association, *Diagnostic and Statistical Mental Disorders*, 4th ed.

33. American Psychiatric Association, *Diagnostic and Statistical Mental Disorders*, 4th ed.

34. D. Nagin and R. E. Tremblay, "Trajectories of Boy's Physical Aggression, Opposition, and Hyperactivity on the Path to Physically Violent and Nonviolent Juvenile Delinquency," *Child Development* 70 (1999): 1181–96.

35. P. Cohen and M. Flory, "Issues in the Disruptive Behavior Disorders: Attention Deficit Disorder without Hyperactivity and the Differential Validity of Oppositional Defiant Disorder," in *DSM-IV Sourcebook* (Washington, D.C.: American Psychiatric Press, 1998), 455–63.

36. J. D. Burke, R. Loeber, and B. Birmaher, "Oppositional Defiant Disorder and Conduct Disorder: A Review of the Past 10 Years, Part II," *Journal of the American Academy of Child and Adolescent Psychiatry* 41, no. 11 (2002): 1275–93.

37. B. T. Kelley, R. Loeber, K. Keenan, and M. DeLamatre, "Developmental Pathways in Boys' Disruptive and Delinquent Behavior," *OJJDP Bulletin* (1997).

38. A. Sanson, M. Prior, and D. Smart, "Reading Disabilities with and without Behavior Problems at 7–8 Years: Prediction from Longitudinal Data from Infancy to 6 years," in *Handbook of Disruptive Behavior Disorders* (New York: Kluwer Academic/ Plenum, 1999), 397–417.

39. M. DeKlyen, M. L. Speltz, and M. Greenberg, "Fathering and Early Onset Conduct Problems: Positive and Negative Parenting, Father–Son Attachments, and the Marital Context," *Clinical Child and Family Psychology Review* 1, no. 1 (1998): 3–21; L. Deron, L. O. Walder, and M. M. Lefkowitz, *Learning of Aggression in Children* (Boston: Little, Brown, 1971); D. Olweus, "Familial and Temperamental Determinants of Aggressive Behavior in Adolescent Boys: A Casual Analysis," *Developmental Psychology* 16 (1980): 644–60; F. E. M. Gardner, "Positive Interaction between Mothers and Conduct-Problem Children: Is There Training for Harmony as Well as Fighting?" *Journal of Abnormal Child Psychology* 15 (1987): 283–93; G. S. Pettit and J. E. Bates, "Family Interaction Patterns and Children's Behavior Problems from Infancy to 4 years," *Developmental Psychology* 25 (1989): 413–20; A. Russell and G. Russell, "Positive Parenting and Boys and Girls Misbehavior During a Home Observation," *International Journal of Behavioral Development* 19 (1996): 291–307; M. T. Greenberg, M. L. Speltz, M. DeKlyen, and M. C. Endriga, "Attachment Security in Preschoolers with and without Externalizing Behavior Problems: A Replication," *Development and Psychology* 3 (1991): 413–30.

40. B. L. Baker and T. L. Heller, "Preschool Children with Externalizing Behaviors: Experience of Fathers and Mothers," *Journal of Abnormal Child Psychology* 24 (1996): 513–32; R. Loeber, "Development and Risk Factors of Juvenile Antisocial Behavior and Delinquency," *Clinical Psychology Review* 10 (1990): 1–41; P. O. Peretti, D. Clark, and P. Johnson, "Parental Rejection as a Criterion Measure of Negative Attention-Seeking Classroom Behavior among Elementary School Students," *Psychology* 27 (1984): 50–54.

41. J. D. Burke, R. Loeber, and B. Birmaher, "Oppositional Defiant Disorder and Conduct Disorder: A Review of the Past 10 Years, Part II," *Journal of the American Academy of Child and Adolescent Psychiatry* 41, no. 11 (2002): 1275–93; K. A. Dodge, "Social-Cognitive Mechanism in the Development of Conduct Disorder and Depression," *Annual Review Psychology* 44 (1993): 559–84; W. Wong and D. G. Cornell, "PIQ>VIQ Discrepancy as a Correlate of Social Problem Solving and Aggression in Delinquent Adolescent Males," *Journal of Psychoeducational Assessment* 17 (1999): 104–12.

42. W. Matthys, W. Walterbos, H. VanEngeland, and W. Koops, "Conduct Disordered Boys' Perception of Their Liked Peers," *Cognitive Therapy* 19 (1995): 357–72.

43. D. Cohen and J. Strayer, "Empathy in Conduct Disordered and Comparison Youth," *Developmental Psychology* 32 (1996): 988–98.

44. S. R. Pliszka, "The Psychobiology of Oppositional Defiant Disorder and Conduct Disorder," in *Handbook of Disruptive Behavior Disorders* (New York: Kluwer/Academic Plenum, 1999), 371–95.

45. J. D. Burke, R. Loeber, and B. Birmaher, "Oppositional Defiant Disorder and Conduct Disorder: A Review of the Past 10 Years, Part II," *Journal of the American Academy of Child and Adolescent Psychiatry* 41, no. 11 (2002): 1275–93.

46. R. W. Greene and A. E. Doyle, "Toward a Transactional Conceptualization of Oppositional Defiant Disorder: Implications for Assessment and Treatment," *Clinical Child and Family Psychology Review* 2, no. 3 (1999): 129–48.

47. J. M. Lewis, "Childhood Play in Normality, Pathology, and Therapy," *American Journal of Orthopsychiatry* 63 (1993): 6–15.

48. D. J. Hudak, "The Therapeutic Use of Ball Play in Psychotherapy with Children," *International Journal of Play Therapy* 9, no. 1 (2000): 1–10.

49. B. J. Bushman, R. F. Baumeister, and A. D. Stack, "Catharsis, Aggression, and Persuasive Influence: Self-Fulfilling or Self-Defeating Prophecies?" *Journal of Personality and Social Psychology* 76, no. 3 (1999): 367–76.

50. J. L. Walker and J. E. Peller, *Becoming Solution-Focused in Brief Therapy* (New York: Brenner/Mazel, 1992).

51. M. White and D. Epston, *Narrative Means to Therapeutic Ends* (New York: Norton, 1990).

52. J. L. Walker and J. E. Peller, *Becoming Solution-Focused in Brief Therapy* (New York: Brenner/Mazel, 1992).

REFERENCES

American Psychiatric Association. *Diagnostic and Statistical Manual of Mental Disorders*. 1994. 4th ed. Washington, D.C.

Arlow, J. A. 1987. "Trauma, Play, and Perversion." *Psychoanalytic Study of the Child* 42: 31–45.

Baker, B. L., and T. L. Heller. 1996. "Preschool Children with Externalizing Behaviors: Experience of Fathers and Mothers." *Journal of Abnormal Child Psychology* 24: 513–32.

Barkley, R. A. 1997. *ADHD and the Nature of Self-Control*. New York: Guilford.

Burke, J. D., R. Loeber, and B. Birmaher. 2002. "Oppositional Defiant Disorder and Conduct Disorder: A Review of the Past 10 Years, Part II." *Journal of the American Academy of Child and Adolescent Psychiatry* 41, no. 11: 1275–93.

Bushman, B. J., R. F. Baumeister, and A. D. Stack. 1999. "Catharsis, Aggression, and Persuasive Influence: Self-Fulfilling or Self- Defeating Prophecies?" *Journal of Personality and Social Psychology* 76, no. 3: 367–76.

Chamberlain, P., and G. R. Patterson. 1995. "Discipline and Child Compliance in Parenting." In *Handbook of Parenting*. Mahwah, N.J.: Erlbaum.

Cohen, D., and J. Strayer. 1996. "Empathy in Conduct Disordered and Comparison Youth." *Developmental Psychology* 32: 988–98.

Cohen, P., and M. Flory. 1998. "Issues in the Disruptive Behavior Disorders: Attention Deficit Disorder without Hyperactivity and the Differential Validity of Oppositional Defiant Disorder." In *DSM-IV Sourcebook*. Washington, D.C.: American Psychiatric Press.

DeKlyen, M., M. L. Speltz, and M. Greenberg. 1998. "Fathering and Early Onset Conduct Problems: Positive and Negative Parenting, Father–Son Attachments, and the Marital Context." *Clinical Child and Family Psychology Review* 1, no. 1:3–21.

Deron, L., L. O. Walder, and M. M. Lefkowitz. 1971. *Learning of Aggression in Children*. Boston: Little, Brown.

Dodge, K. A. 1993. "Social-Cognitive Mechanism in the Development of Conduct Disorder and Depression." *Annual Review Psychology* 44: 559–84.

Gardner, F. E. M. 1987. "Positive Interaction Between Mothers and Conduct-Problem Children: Is There Training for Harmony as Well as Fighting?" *Journal of Abnormal Child Psychology* 15: 283–93.

Greenberg, M. T., M. L. Speltz, M. DeKlyen, and M. C. Endriga. 1991. "Attachment Security in Preschoolers with and without Externalizing Behavior Problems: A Replication." *Development and Psychology* 3: 413–30.

Greene, R. W., and A. E. Doyle. 1999. "Toward a Transactional Conceptualization of Oppositional Defiant Disorder: Implications for Assessment and Treatment." *Clinical Child and Family Psychology Review* 2, no. 3: 129–48.

Hudak, D. J. 2000. "The Therapeutic Use of Ball Play in Psychotherapy with Children." *International Journal of Play Therapy* 9, no. 1: 1–10.

Kendall, P. C. 1993. "Cognitive-Behavioral Therapies with Youth: Guiding Theory, Current Status, and Emerging Developments." *Journal of Consulting and Clinical Psychology* 61: 235–47.

Lewis, J. M. 1987. "Childhood Play in Normality, Pathology, and Therapy." *American Journal of Orthopsychiatry* 63: 6–15.

Loeber, R. 1990. "Development and Risk Factors of Juvenile Antisocial Behavior and Delinquency." *Clinical Psychology Review* 10: 1–41.

Matthys, W., W. Walterbos, H. Van Engeland, and W. Koops. 1995. "Conduct Disordered Boys' Perception of Their Liked Peers." *Cognitive Therapy* 19: 357–72.

Nagin, D., and R. E. Tremblay. 1999. "Trajectories of Boy's Physical Aggression, Opposition, and Hyperactivity on the Path to Physically Violent and Nonviolent Juvenile Delinquency." *Child Development* 70: 1181–96.

Neubauer, P. D. 1987. "The Many Meanings of Play: Introduction." *Psychoanalytic Study of the Child* 42: 3–10.

Olweus, D. 1980. "Familial and Temperamental Determinants of Aggressive Behavior in Adolescent Boys: A Casual Analysis." *Developmental Psychology* 16: 644–60.

Paule, M. G., A. S. Rowland, S. A. Ferguson, J. J. Chelonis, R. Tannock, J. M. Swanson, and F. X. Castellanos. 2000. "Attention Deficit/Hyperactivity Disorder: Characteristics, Interventions, and Models." *Neurotoxicology and Teratology* 22: 631–51.

Peretti, P. O., D. Clark, and P. Johnson. 1984. "Parental Rejection as a Criterion Measure of Negative Attention-Seeking Classroom Behavior Among Elementary School Students." *Psychology* 27: 50–54.

Pettit, G. S., and J. E. Bates. 1989. "Family Interaction Patterns and Children's Behavior Problems From Infancy to 4 Years." *Developmental Psychology* 25: 413–20.

Piaget, J. 1951. *Play, Dreams, and Imitation in Childhood*. New York: Norton.

Plaut, E. A. 1979. "Play and Adaptation." *Psychoanalytic Study of the Child* 34: 217–32.

Pliszka, S. R. 1999. "The Psychobiology of Oppositional Defiant Disorder and Conduct Disorder." In *Handbook of Disruptive Behavior Disorders*. New York: Kluwer/Academic Plenum.

Russell, A., and G. Russell. 1996. "Positive Parenting and Boys and Girls Misbehavior during a Home Observation." *International Journal of Behavioral Development* 19: 291–307.

Sanson, A., M. Prior, and D. Smart. 1999. "Reading Disabilities with and without Behavior Problems at 7–8 Years: Prediction from Longitudinal Data from Infancy to 6 years." In *Handbook of Disruptive Behavior Disorders*. New York: Kluwer Academic/Plenum.

Solnit, A. J. 1998. "Beyond Play and Playfulness." *Psychoanalytic Study of the Child* 53: 102–10.

Stifter, C. A., T. L. Spinard, and J. M. Braungart-Rieker. 1999. "Toward a Developmental Model of Compliance: The Role of Emotion Regulation in Infancy." *Child Development* 70: 21–32.

Walker, J. L., and J. E. Peller. 1992. *Becoming Solution-Focused in Brief Therapy*. New York: Brenner/Mazel.

White, M., and D. Epston. 1990. *Narrative Means to Therapeutic Ends*. New York: Norton.

Wong, W., and D. G. Cornell. 1999. "PIQ>VIQ Discrepancy as a Correlate of Social Problem Solving and Aggression in Delinquent Adolescent Males." *Journal of Psychoeducational Assessment* 17: 104–12.

Zillman, D. 1988. "Cognition-Excitation Interdependencies in Aggressive Behavior." *Aggressive Behavior* 14: 51–64.

15

The National Story and the Child's Drama in Play Therapy in Israel

Galila T. Oren

I have been working in Israel as a drama and play therapist for almost twenty years. Throughout my work as a therapist and a supervisor, I have encountered children, and their stories and play, from all sectors of Israeli society. In this chapter I would like to share my thoughts concerning the influence borne by the national realm on the child's drama, while offering my perspective as to the complexity of comprehending and intervening within it.

February 2003, a few days after the elections in Israel. More than two years had passed since the beginning of the second *intifadah* (the violent Palestinian uprising against Israel). Terrorist attacks had almost become routine. The tension surrounding the Iraqi affair and Israel's possible involvement in it escalated daily.

I met with five colleagues to discuss work. We are all women over forty, some of us daughters of Holocaust survivors. Our parents founded this country in high hopes. We all served in the army, and all of us are mothers of children who are, or will become, soldiers. We sat around a table, hoping to escape from the tensions of external reality, delving into the fascinating world of child's play.

A colleague proceeded to describe a card game she had played with a child in therapy. In this game, a deck of cards is set in the middle of the table, facedown. Each player takes a card from the deck in turn. On each card there is a picture of one ingredient of falafel, a popular Israeli snack (e.g., sesame paste, falafel balls, pita). On some of the cards there is a picture of a torn pita. A player who picks up this card loses all of his of her cards and has to begin collecting falafel ingredients all over again. The first player to obtain all the necessary ingredients wins the game.

We listened silently to her description, and as she finished we all began to speak together—about the terrorist attacks, about the peace process, which seemed to be dying out, and about the trauma experienced by our children during the first Gulf War. There seemed to be a connection between our joint personal anxieties and the card game. We felt like our "pita country" was being torn to pieces, that all of our ingredients were about to come apart, forcing us to assemble them all over again. The room was filled by "the national situation."

The presenter went on to describe the child with whom she had played. Dan, an eight-year-old boy, had been referred to play therapy due to uncontrollable aggressive outbursts toward other children. Three years earlier, when he was five years old, as his mother drove him and his baby sister in the family car, after Dan had fallen asleep barefoot in the backseat, the car suddenly went up in flames. Terrorists had thrown a Molotov cocktail into the car. Dan awoke in great pain—his arm was burning. He grabbed a blanket and put out the fire on his body. His mother grabbed his burning sister and pushed Dan out of the car. They started to run, while the mother tried to extinguish the fire burning her baby's clothes. Dan ran barefoot until they reached an Israeli military post, and an ambulance was called. The children were saved.

Dan loved the falafel card game, reacting with laughter whenever he or the therapist picked up a torn pita card. In one of the sessions he suggested that he and the therapist would eat up all of the torn pitas, so that they would not be bothered by them any longer.

After playing the card game, Dan usually turned to the sandbox, where he played with little plastic animals. In his symbolic play he assigned a pair of lions as parents, with two calves as their children. This mixed family lived in a valley, while higher up, on top of a mountain, lived a vulture. The vulture kidnapped, burned, and ate the calves. At times Dan had the lions fight the vulture. The lions were tough, managing to defeat the vulture and bury it under a pile of sand. But nonetheless, the calves did not feel safe because the vulture was a trickster: it wasn't really dead. Rather, it was just hiding under the sand, renewing its strength and preparing itself for revenge. Thus the calves were destined to confront mortal danger repeatedly.

While listening to the story, I felt a strong identification with the calves. I thought about my own fears; for me, the vulture represented the archetypal enemy, be it the Palestinian terrorist, the neo-Nazi, or Saddam Hussein. My deepest fears came to the surface: is the enemy tricking us, like the vulture, hiding under the sand, secretly renewing its strength, preparing to rise up and destroy us?

I then left my own fears and thought about Dan. He had told the story of his personal trauma to his therapist through his play with the animals. Could he ever feel safe in face of the daily news he heard about repeated terrorist attacks? I thought of the inherent difficulty in helping Dan overcome his trauma while his parents and therapist shared many of his fears.

Then I remembered how Dan lost his temper unexpectedly, with no apparent reason, and beat other children. The vulture might also be conceptualized as a representation of Dan's own aggression.

As an Israeli therapist, in such traumatic times, I recognize a child's dramatic play is often simultaneously a story of what actually happens to him in external reality, as well as a reflection of his inner world. I propose that the child's inner world is affected profoundly by the national atmosphere and external events. Furthermore, I often find it hard to determine whether the fears and conflicts I am witness to arise mainly from the inner world, or from its interface with external reality. At times I perceive these two realms as intermingled to the extent that I find the task of choosing the correct framework for comprehension to be extremely difficult and confusing.

For a play therapist this differentiation is sometimes crucial: if I grasped Dan's aggression and fears as emanating mainly from his inner world, I would work with him within the boundaries of make-believe play. I would focus on all the roles that appear in the sandbox play, while dedicating attention to the role of the vulture. I would ask the vulture about its experience, while listening to it attentively, in an attempt to deepen Dan's understanding of his own aggression and to help him abate it.

Alternatively, if I thought Dan to be suffering mainly from a posttraumatic reaction, viewing the vulture as representing the bad enemy that hurt him, I would be much less interested in the vulture's role. Within the protected structure of dramatic play I would ask the calves and lions to describe their experiences, listening carefully to their fears, their sense of helplessness, their fury toward the vulture, and to any other emotions, sensations, and experiences that may arise.

Eventually, I would try to help Dan talk about his trauma directly. I would emphasize the difference between Dan and the calves in that the calves in the story were helpless, as opposed to his mother and himself, who had legs with which to run away and the ability to put out the fire—inner resources the calves in his story did not have.

In hearing Dan's story, my colleagues and I perceived that Dan was mainly suffering from a posttraumatic reaction. Dan's therapist said she felt in a deadlock and asked for our help, but we found it difficult to help her. Like Dan, we all identified with the calves' helplessness and could not think. Dan's trauma was too close to our fears. Only a few weeks later, when we met again, could we offer her some help.

The influence of political and social violence on the human psyche has occupied researchers from various disciplines throughout the past century. While Israeli psychotherapists have been dealing with these issues since the establishment of the state, only recently have they begun conceptualizing and writing about their unique experiences. Mann has addressed wars as they appear in the therapeutic setting (Mann 2002). She describes three arenas in which wars simultaneously occur: (1) the general society arena (between and within nations), (2) the interpersonal arena (within families and groups), and (3) the intrapsychic arena (within one's psyche). She believes that these three arenas interact vividly. Miller-Florsheim (2003) says, "The analysis of collective violence cannot be reduced to a single dimension because it targets the body, the psyche, as well as the sociocultural order. Extreme violence attacks the internalized, culturally constituted webs of trust. In this context, the boundary between inner and outer reality is rudely blurred, and so is the difference between patient and therapist" (10).

The state of Israel was born following the horrors of the Holocaust, and it has been in a continual state of war ever since. "In Israel, one of the fundamental themes that comprise the national narrative is war and coping with it" (Miller-Florsheim 2003, 11). This shared destiny has many implications on children's development, as the impact of national themes bears effect on development, especially during times of tension and real threat. Laufer's (Eldar 2003) comprehensive research on the influence of the *intifadah* and continual terrorist attacks on Jewish Israeli children shows that 70 percent of these children report that those events had some influence on their lives. While only 2 percent of Jewish Israeli children were directly attacked or witnessed an actual terrorist attack, more than 40 percent of the children demonstrated some posttraumatic symptoms (PTS). Thus it is demonstrated that children internalize the atmosphere of real threat even if they, or their families, are not directly inflicted, resulting in a disturbance in the sense of "going on being" (Winnicott 1949). When children and adults come across extreme violence in external reality, they become engulfed with fear, anger, hatred, and helplessness. This can result in the dissolution of the most basic sense of good and bad, real and not real. It affects various lines of development, such as the move from omnipotence to knowledge of one's realistic strengths, the move from dependency to independence, the ability to trust oneself and others.

The atmosphere of real danger and threat also brings about the retrieval of collective and personal memories of the traumatic history. Many Israeli children carry a part of the national narrative in which their family suffered from aggression, war, and loss. Gampel (1987, 2000) articulated the concept of radioactivity in order to describe how social and political violence influence individuals in subsequent generations. Extreme violence, as experienced by Holocaust survivors, creates unbearable suffering that cannot be comprehended or contained, and that is unconsciously transmitted to future generations. These issues unfold in the play therapy situation through symbolic play, games, and artwork—or lack thereof.

The following case examples are intended to demonstrate the aforementioned theories and themes.

TOM

Tom was ten years old when first referred to play therapy by his parents. In the clinical intake his parents reported that they were concerned about his schoolwork, while in other domains they described him as a happy, well-adjusted child. His father said he was a bit "too good" and expressed his wish that therapy would toughen him up. "I am afraid of what will happen to him in the army if he is so good," the father said.

During the period I treated Tom, I learned that his mother was the daughter of Holocaust survivors. Tom's paternal grandfather had been a pilot and was killed in a war when his son was only a year old, so that Tom's father grew up without a father. Tom's father did not think this affected Tom; during one of the few sessions in which I saw him the father questioned: "It didn't matter to me while I was a child, why should Tom care about it?" Tom, however, was far from the happy, well-adjusted child his parents had described. In therapy he emerged as an extremely frightened and lonely child, suffering many social difficulties. At the beginning of our relationship almost all of his symbolic play was characterized by themes of aggression and war. An atomic disaster, constantly threatening to destroy both his enemies and himself, hovered over his stories and artwork.

During the first phase of therapy we were busy building a three-dimensional air force base made of cardboard. The base included many airstrips and dangerous nuclear weapons warehouses. Tom was very anxious to build a checkpoint with a barrier at the entrance to the base. He wanted a gate that could be opened and closed so that he could protect the base from unwanted invaders. I suggested a barrier made of wood and offered Tom some carpentry tools. Tom was terrified. He was afraid to wound himself with the tools. We then discussed his need to be safe and his wish to encounter dangers only as part of play reality, like the cardboard representation of the nuclear warehouses, but to avoid what he perceived as the representatives of danger in external reality—carpentry tools. We spent much time and effort in trying to work out a satisfactory solution for building a gate that could actually be opened and closed, while purposely avoiding the use of the "dangerous tools." When we succeeded, Tom was proud.

In the next session he asked to use the carpentry tools to build a "strong and tall" control tower. At the time I was not aware that Tom's grandfather had been a pilot. These were relatively peaceful times in our country and my associations and thoughts during the sessions had nothing to do with national themes. It was the beginning of therapy and we were still establishing our working relationship. I found it important that we build the strong control tower and barrier together: I wanted him to know that I would enter his inner "army base" only with his permission and that I would help him to make sure, from the top of his control tower, that we enter dangerous areas carefully. At the time, I still perceived Tom's preoccupation with the building of a nuclear warehouse and its potential danger as related to his aggression. But I began feeling he needed his aggression to fight some sort of enemy. I had no idea whether the enemy was inside him or whether it was within his family, or possibly a combination of both. I had a vague sense that the intensity of his feelings had to do with some kind of intrusion of parental themes in his psyche.

In order to help Tom express his aggression in a safe way, I suggested that we work with gouache paints. In my clinic I have a wooden wall covered with large paper sheets, so children can draw and play with the gouache without fear of making a mess. I gave Tom a water gun filled with gouache paints and we sprayed the paint onto the paper-covered wall. Then we used a paintbrush to draw. Tom was delighted. He created beautiful abstract paintings, which filled him with pride and satisfaction.

Gradually, the theme of war returned. He was the commander and I was the soldier, and we fought against an unseen enemy on the paper. We sprayed the paper with gouache, shooting the enemy, and then rushed to stop the dripping paint, the bleeding of our wounded soldiers, with the paintbrushes. An abusive atmosphere began creeping into our sessions. Tom became the tough commander, while I was the dim-witted soldier who often failed. Themes of fear, humiliation, and failure entered our sessions.

Eventually, Tom asked to direct a play that repeated itself several times in different variations. In this play Tom played the role of a terrorizing villain, a terrorist, a neo-Nazi, or a gangster. I was a woman who lived peacefully in an apartment building. The terrorist came at night to my house and physically abused my grandmother, my parents, and me. In his role as a terrorist, Tom shot, burned, and killed us in various ways. In my interventions I tried to understand the villain's motivation. I mirrored his anger, I gave the victims a voice, but nothing seemed to echo. The same drama went on again and again. Even though Tom was putting on "a play," we did not play together in the sense described by Winnicott (1971). There was no freedom, no a sense of deep concentration in it. The play had to go on exactly as Tom directed it. There was a strong aura of tyranny in our sessions, in which I was forced to suffer.

One day, after the terrorist cut me and my family into pieces, shot us and burned our house, Tom put on a white costume and said, "Now you are dead—I am God and you are trying to get into heaven." For a moment I thought the abuse was going to end, but Tom, in the role of God, began interrogating me: "What's your name? What're your parents' names? Your grandmother's name? Your dog's name?" For every answer I gave, Tom yelled at me: "That's wrong, you stupid woman, you don't even know your own family! Go to hell! You can't enter heaven." "Mr. God," I pleaded for understanding, "please listen to me . . . my family and I suffered so much lately

. . . A terrorist, or a Nazi, or someone else, came and beat us, shot us and burned our house down . . . I don't know what happened to my family . . . I am not stupid. I just have suffered so much that I became confused . . . my family suffered for three generations, we don't even remember our names and who we are . . . we suffered so much!" Tom listened gently and then said: "Your family did suffer for three generations, and you suffer the most, although they don't know it. It's okay, you can go to heaven."

This session appeared to be a turning point, with the next sessions being calmer. Tom told me about humiliating events at school and shared his fears of terrorists and robbers with me, fears he was afraid to discuss with his parents, as they may have perceived them as childish. He even revealed his most terrible secrets: that he had nightmares and that he was still wetting the bed. I still did not fully realize that there was an actual background to our constant dealing with three generations of suffering. When speaking of three generations of suffering, I merely referred to the fact that Tom's play included a grandmother and parents. It seemed to me that the issue at hand was that Tom's need to overcome his vulnerability was so great that he was willing to destroy his sensitivity if he could. I thought it was important to help Tom gain empathy toward his vulnerable, sensitive sides.

I always try to listen carefully to the child's text and stay as close to it as possible when intervening. Only later did I begin to conceptualize the idea that the intensity of Tom's aggression toward his inner sensitive parts was connected to his parents' unconscious wish to eliminate the vulnerability they had to deal with from early childhood, which I saw as related to the horror of the Holocaust and the pain of parental loss.

However, Tom directed us into the arena of his family's history. He returned to the theme of the army base from a different angle, creating an army base in the sandbox. While earlier in the treatment his army base was packed with dangerous weapons but no people, this time the base was a desert full of human soldiers. The scenery quickly transformed into a large graveyard. Some of the soldiers died during bombings, while others had to dig their own graves and were then shot to death; the rest were buried alive under the sand, waiting for their friends to come and rescue them. When the saviors arrived the victims jumped out of the sand as if they had awaited their restitution in a state of deep freeze.

Even though the story was extremely painful, Tom managed to remain deeply concentrated in his play. It was rich and profound play that resonated through several layers, now close to Winnicott's (1971) description of playing. When children are so absorbed in their play, I respect their private domain and avoid reducing its richness through interpretation. When play is free, a current of shared free associations surrounding it flows naturally through both child and therapist. I sat near Tom watching him play. Every now and then he would turn to me speaking about his grandfather. Tom told me his grandfather was a pilot who died in the desert. "His army base looked exactly like the one we have built together," he said. "I was there for a memorial day ceremony." Then he wondered how it had been for his father to grow up without a father. "My father says he got used to living without a father, but I don't believe him," he continued. "I got used to living without a father, but I knew my father would come back from his business trips. My father's father never came back."

I felt that Tom's sand play was some kind of personal search for meaning, both within himself and in his family's history. Playing in the sand allowed him to bring back to life parts of himself that were frozen. We didn't have to understand all of these. Searching was a healing process that enabled us to think and to connect.

The maternal grandparents' history also resonated in my thoughts. The soldiers who dug their own graves and the large anonymous graveyards triggered within me associations about the Holocaust. For some reason that remained unclear to me, I kept these thoughts to myself and didn't share them with Tom. I felt as though there were still a lot of dead parts we had yet to understand, nor could these be discussed.

This period was followed by some improvement in the outside world; his nightmares and bedwetting stopped and his schoolwork improved. Dealing with part of his family history facilitated some growth. Tom's parents abruptly terminated his therapy a year later. We still keep in touch, and today Tom is in high school achieving good grades.

RUTH

Ruth, the oldest of three children, was nine years old when referred to play therapy. Her parents sought help because of Ruth's sudden fears.

Ruth's maternal grandmother was a Holocaust survivor, and Ruth's mother grew up with deep feelings of depression and deprivation. She wanted her daughter to be free of the pain she had suffered and could not stand any signs of frustration or sadness in her daughter. The parents had their children at a very early age and both exhibited adolescent behaviors, finding it difficult to assume their roles as parents. From a very young age Ruth seemed to rule the household, while her parents treated her as though she were part goddess, part witch.

The first phase of therapy was very enjoyable. Ruth was a sensitive, creative, and talented child. She loved to play with the dollhouse, with the dolls as if they were children who grew up without parents. The dolls had a lot of fun but also had to face danger by themselves. In the first year of therapy, Ruth used a lot of symbolic play: she danced, wore costumes, and played with puppets and dolls. In each session the whole room changed while she built a unique scenery for each play. In her plays witches and monsters would sometimes attack children who did not have parents to protect them. Other times, children would turn into witches that caused trouble. She often used musical instruments to play sad music, and asked me to hide so that I would not hear her. It seemed like Ruth felt unprotected by her parents. She feared aggression within herself and from her environment, but most of all, she feared sadness.

Ruth's artwork was beautiful. When working with art materials, she often hummed Israeli songs to herself, all of which were sad and dealt with loss. Listening to her humming, I thought she was worried about losing family members. I met Ruth's parents for consultation regularly. In one of the sessions, when I mentioned that I thought Ruth might be worried about one of the family members, her mother said, "No, I don't think so. She is a child, she thinks only of herself." The mother's tone of voice sounded as though thinking about others is sinful.

Therapy seemed to be progressing well, as Ruth overcame most of her fears and as her parents learned to set some boundaries. During the second year of Ruth's therapy, the second *intifadah* broke out. I saw Ruth's parents for a consultative session a few days after the first violent outbursts, and the political events affected them both. I asked them how Ruth felt and they said, "We don't think those things bother her, we don't talk politics at home." But in the following sessions Ruth demonstrated considerable knowledge with regard to the political situation and expressed her grave concern. One day, while we were playing Monopoly, my pawn landed on Jerusalem, to which Ruth responded, "Don't buy it. Awful city, too many terrorist attacks." Whenever our pawns landed on a city, we counted the terrorist attacks that had occurred in that city. When I asked her directly about her feelings she dismissed my referral, and we continued talking about terrorist attacks on the Monopoly board.

The *intifadah* escalated. Every week there was a serious terrorist attack. Israel suffered more casualties than ever before. Parents everywhere were at a loss as to how to protect their children. Ruth went through a rough period, fighting with her parents and friends, and started to neglect her schoolwork. In our sessions she was often bored and all she wanted was to talk about things she wished to buy. Shopping was her only pleasure. She desperately tried to convey something about her feelings. I thought she was frightened to the extent that she became inhibited in her freedom to play. At the same time, I lost my ability to engage in a meaningful dialogue with her. In one of these sessions I said that I thought she was afraid of something that scared her, something we did not yet understand. I also said that she was finding it difficult to find comfort in anything, although she was eager to find it. Ruth replied, "Yes, you are right. I want to draw." She went to the gouache wall, took a large paintbrush, and started improvising with paint on the paper. She started with bright green and pink stripes, then she drew a sweet-looking heart to which she added a few drops of red color, as though the vulnerable heart was bleeding. She added a blue Star of David and impulsively drew a black grave. She stepped back and looked at her picture, saying sadly, "This is the state of our country." She was concentrated and absorbed in her work. I sat beside her and watched her draw, feeling deeply touched by her work. "It looks like the sweet, vulnerable heart is bleeding because of the state of the nation," I said. Ruth answered, "Yes, this is the grave of a child that was killed in a terrorist attack." "Do you know of any child that was killed?" I asked. "No," she answered, "but I feel as though I do." We continued talking about how she missed the days when she could go shopping without fear, and how scary it was that neither parents, the army, nor the government could protect a little child.

Normally, in a more relaxed reality, around the age ten a process of recognizing the limitations of the parents' ability to protect the child, as well as recognition of the arbitrariness of disaster, sets in. This is actually a never-ending developmental process, as we all need to live with some degree of denial of our vulnerability. For many Israeli children over the past few years, this recognition has crystallized abruptly and vigorously—creating a crisis in their sense of security and continuity.

For Ruth, this recognition was extremely painful. It coincided with a history of feeling unprotected by her parents (the drama in the dollhouse), a feeling they had all just begun overcoming. During the next session Ruth asked to work with carpentry tools. She took a hammer and nails and aggressively beat a piece of wood, and then very gently sprinkled glitter on it. She concentrated deeply on her work. I felt free to share my associations with her. "It's beautiful," I said, "it looks like fairy dust." Ruth laughed, "I saw *Back to Neverland,* it's Peter Pan II. It's about Wendy's daughter. She lived during the period of the Second World War and didn't believe in fairies . . . it is strange that Wendy believed in fairies and her daughter did not."

"That's right" I said, "I guess it is hard to believe in fairies in times of war, and besides, Wendy believed in her imagination so much that her daughter was afraid that no one will take care of reality." Ruth laughed and continued to sprinkle fairy dust on the wounded wood.

In this period Ruth oscillated between boredom, depression, and meaningful work. A few sessions later she worked with gouache paints again. This time she drew the Israeli flag, a grave, and a hanging rope. She said it was the grave of a child in the Holocaust. She talked about her grandmother being a child during the Holocaust. She knew very little about her history and wondered how her grandmother had managed, how she had felt in hiding without her parents, and fantasized that she was there with her.

After the Holocaust drawing she moved to a more "optimistic" painting. She smeared purple, green, and brown gouache paint on a large piece of paper. She mixed the paints and started a "war of colors." "This is the war of independence," she said, mixing the colors with her whole body. "You see, one can see the green color after the war . . . the grass will grow again when the war of independence is over." Israel's whole history was on that paper. But Ruth's war of independence was not over, and the green was not ready to sprout yet. At home she struggled with her parents fiercely, fighting for her right to normal dependency and protection, as well as for her independence and freedom.

Ruth was now ten years old and suddenly lost the magic of fairies. Play therapy, under the protection of the imaginary world, didn't seem to work for her anymore. Sometimes I forgot she was only ten and talked to her like an adult in verbal psychotherapy. When that happened, she withdrew. She seemed to be an adult and a child at the same time. She was both grandma in the Holocaust and a "spoiled" ten-year-old girl, who only wanted toys and candies. We had to search for new ways to communicate. Improvising with paints and other materials allowed the inner child to explore and play freely, while the more mature parts could be reached as she observed and reflected.

When I shared her concern about the "state of the nation" with her parents, they were surprised. It was the second year of therapy and only now were her parents able to say, "We forgot that she is simply a sensitive, loving, caring girl!" For her mother, a loving, sensitive little girl meant taking on the suffering of others, and as the daughter of a Holocaust survivor, this notion had been too painful to face. This insight brought her mother to tears.

Ruth's struggle for dependency and independence is not over yet, though I believe Ruth is right when she says that once the winds of war subside she will be able to see the "green sprouts grow."

On Passover, the festival of freedom, Jewish families sit at the table, read the Passover Haggadah together, and say, "In every generation a person is obligated to regard himself as if he had come out of Egypt." Each Jewish child is asked to feel as if he suffered with his forefathers—and as if he was with them when freed. In this ceremony, children sing with their parents an ancient song: "For not just one alone has risen against us to destroy us, but in every generation they rise against us to destroy us; and the Holy One, blessed be He, saves us from their hand!" It has a prophetic sense to it: the Jewish children of our day are still bound to struggle for their existence. This year the Passover Haggadah seemed to me to be harsh and militant, as the ancient text left little room for our sensitivity—as echoed by the parents and children I have described.

Dan, Tom, and Ruth were deeply affected by the national events. Dan was a victim of political aggression and had to struggle for his existence. Tom searched for his ancestors' stories, finding it difficult to separate their stories from his own. Ruth's basic fears were intensified by the reality of the terrorist attacks. Reality on the national level both fueled her experience of being un-protected and recaptured the experience of her unprotected grandmother during the Holocaust.

As a play therapist in Israel, I often find myself playing, drawing, and talk-ing with children in order to help them, and myself, bear the duty of living with this history, but at the same time to free ourselves from its trauma in or-der to live in the present lives of our own.

REFERENCES

Eldar, A. *Ha'aretz*, April 24, 2003, 36.

Gampel, Y. 1987. "Aspects of Intergenerational Transmission." *Israel Journal of Psy-chotherapy* 2, no. 1: 27–31. In Hebrew.

———. 2000. "Reflection on the Prevalence of the Uncanny in Social Violence." In M. Robbens and M. Suarez-Orozo, eds., *Cultures under Siege*. Cambridge: Cambridge University Press.

Haggadah. 1994. New exp. ed. London: Scopus Films.

Mann, G. 2002. "Why War—Between Transformation and Termination: Links in the Field of Therapeutic Play and Beyond." In *The Play,* edited by E. Perroni. Tel Aviv: Miskal-Yediot Aharonot Books.

Miller-Florsheim, D. 2003. "Beyond the Unthinkable: Patient and Therapist in a Shared Collective Trauma." *Psychotherapy Forum* 11, no. 1: 10–18.

Winnicott, D. W. 1949. "Mind and Its Relation to Psyche-Soma." In *Collected Papers through Pediatrics to Psycho-analysis*. London: Tavistock.

Index

About the Editors

Charles Schaefer, an internationally renowned child psychologist, is professor of psychology at Fairleigh Dickinson University in Teaneck, New Jersey. He is cofounder and director emeritus of the Association for Play Therapy, and codirector of the Play Therapy Training Institute in New Jersey. Schaefer has written or edited more than fifty books on parenting, child psychology, and play therapy, including *The Therapeutic Powers of Play*, *The Playing Cure*, and *101 Favorite Play Therapy Techniques*. He is the founder of an international play therapy study group that meets annually at Wroxton, U.K. He maintains a private practice in child psychotherapy in Hackensack, New Jersey.

Judy McCormick is a registered play therapist supervisor who is currently working as a play therapist for the Mid-Western Health Board in Limerick, Ireland. She is involved in the supervision and training of play therapists and others interested in play therapy. She is the former secretary of Play Therapy Ireland. Presently she is involved in research using play therapy in an early intervention program and using filial therapy with an Irish population.

Akiko J. Ohnogi is a clinical psychologist in private practice in Tokyo, Japan. She lectures on play therapy, child psychotherapy, parenting, multiculturalism, and child development at hospitals, residential treatment centers, universities, and schools throughout Japan. She is a school counselor at the Nishimachi International School in Tokyo, Japan.

About the Contributors

Shlomo Ariel is clinical psychologist and supervisor of clinical psychology and marital and family therapy in Ramat Gan, Israel.

Susan Bundy-Myrow is counseling psychologist in Getzville, New York and affiliate trainer at the Theraplay Institute in Chicago.

Jo Carroll is play therapist at Swindon and Marlborough Child and Adolescent Mental Health Service in Wiltshire, England.

Ann Cattanach is dramatherapist and play therapist in Edinburgh, Scotland.

David J. Hudak works at the Blue Ridge Behavioral Health Services in Frederick, Maryland.

Sheila Hudd is senior social worker and play therapist at the William Harvey Child, Adolescent, and Family Clinic in Putney, England.

Sue Jennings is director of the Rowan Studio and Play For Life in the United Kingdom and Romania.

Kate Kirk is play therapist in Chichester, England.

Mooli Lahad works at the Community Stress Prevention Centre in Kiryat Shmona, Israel.

David LeVay is play therapist in Surrey, England.

Shoshana Levin is play therapist in Jerusalem, Israel.

Liana Lowenstein is play therapist in Toronto, Canada.

Jytte Mielcke works in private practice in Holstebro, Denmark.

Galila T. Oren is drama and play therapist in Tel-Aviv, Israel.

Sandra W. Russ is professor in the psychology department at Case Western Reserve University in Cleveland, Ohio.